REGENCY PORTRAIT PAINTER

SIR THOMAS LAWRENCE, P.R.A.

This unfinished self-portrait was acquired by the Royal Academy in 1863 and forms part of their permanent collection at Burlington House.

REGENCY PORTRAIT PAINTER

The life of
Sir Thomas Lawrence, P.R.A.

by

DOUGLAS GOLDRING

MACDONALD : LONDON

To

THOMAS A. LLOYD

First published in 1951 by
Macdonald & Co. (Publishers), Ltd.
16 Maddox Street, W.1
Made and printed in Great Britain by
Purnell and Sons, Ltd.
Paulton (Somerset) and London

PREFACE

MY OBJECT in this book has been to present Lawrence's life story as clearly and with as much detail as possible. In a desire to keep its length within reasonable limits much has had to be excluded regarding his professional activities which, though of interest to the student of art, was not strictly relevant to my main purpose.

Lawrence's difficulties with his sitters, from which he generally extricated himself with a nice blend of dignity and diplomacy, gave rise to an extensive but rather monotonous series of business letters, to which little space has been devoted. Similarly, I have curtailed my references to the various squabbles and intrigues of the Academicians, in which he was at times involved, as it seemed to me that those interested in such matters could more profitably read about them in Farington's *Diary* and in Haydon's *Autobiography and Journals*. Little has been said here regarding Lawrence's engravers, a subject of such importance as to justify a volume to itself, and I have also made only brief references to his various pupils, assistants and imitators, of whom the most interesting was G. H. Harlow. It has not been part of my task to include in this volume a list, which would of necessity have been incomplete, of his paintings and drawings. The arduous work of compiling a new *catalogue raisonné* of Lawrence's pictures is being undertaken by Mr. Kenneth J. Garlick, assistant curator of the Barber Institute of Art, Birmingham, and will no doubt be available in due course.

My endeavour has been to concentrate the reader's attention on a fascinating, prodigiously gifted and most lovable man, who both during his lifetime and after his death has often been misrepresented and calumniated, as he revealed himself in his relations with his family, his intimate friends and the women he loved. In view of the fact that the conclusions I have arrived at about Lawrence's abortive engagement to Maria Siddons and his real feeling for her elder sister, Sally, differ widely from those which have hitherto been generally accepted, I have thought it best to let the principal actors in this tragic drama tell the story as far as possible in their own words. The letters, first published over forty years ago by Dr. Oswald Knapp and Lady Priestley, have, therefore, been extensively drawn upon, so that the reader, with the evidence before him, will be free to form his own opinion as to the justice, or otherwise, of my interpretation of it.

Although I have been greatly helped by the encouragement, advice and suggestions of numerous correspondents, very little in the way of unpublished material has come to light. This book is therefore based almost entirely on a re-examination and careful checking of the facts recorded by earlier biographers, supplemented by the invaluable Farington, the memoirs of Lawrence's contemporaries and the letters to him, from him and about him, which were included by George Somes Layard in *Sir Thomas Lawrence's Letter-Bag* and by Dr. Oswald G. Knapp in *An Artist's Love-story*.

My thanks are due to all those who have been kind enough to supply me with information and, often at some trouble to themselves, to answer my enquiries. My first acknowledgment must, however, be made to Mr. Thomas A. Lloyd, of Ryde, Isle of Wight, but for whose flattering insistence I should never have embarked on so difficult, yet so rewarding, a task as the writing of this book has proved. He had himself begun work on a new life of Lawrence, some years before we met, but had abandoned the project, owing to the pressure of other interests. When he suggested to me that I should take it up, he most generously offered to turn over to me his notebooks and all the material he had accumulated, thus laying the foundations on which I subsequently built.

To Mr. John C. Nicholson, a great-grandson of Archibald Keightley, Lawrence's sole executor, I am under a special obligation for his kindness in putting the material in his possession at my disposal, thus enabling me to transcribe the two love letters written to Lawrence by Sally Siddons.

I am also greatly obliged to Mr. Charles Lefeaux, of the Society for Theatre Research, for copying two letters in his possession, one written by Lawrence to Mrs. Siddons and the other by Fanny Kemble to her cousin, Cecilia. Mr. Morchard Bishop, whose wide reading and extensive knowledge of the Regency period have enabled him to put me on the track of much which I might otherwise have missed, has rendered me services which I cannot too gratefully acknowledge. I have also to thank Mr. Kenneth J. Garlick and Mr. Mahonri S. Young, of the Sarah Lawrence College, Bronxville, New York, for supplying me with much valuable information and for their kindness in answering the questions I put to them.

My acknowledgments would be sadly incomplete if I omitted to record how much I owe to the personal trouble taken by my publishers to secure the photographs, over a hundred in number, from which the illustrations have been selected. Both Mr. Eric Harvey and his Production Manager, Mr. W. F. Parrish, paid visits to the British Museum to search the collection of Lawrence's prints and drawings for the subjects desired, while the latter, with inexhaustible energy and patience, followed up, in many other directions, the suggestions I made to him. To Miss Dunn, of the firm's Education Department, I owe information concerning the interesting drawing of Cowper now in the possession of the Hon. John Fremantle, which is reproduced here for the first time, with the owner's kind permission. I have also to express my thanks to Mr. Christopher Norris for supplying the photograph of Lawrence's portrait of his brother, the Rev. Andrew Lawrence, which is among the treasures at Polesden Lacey.

Of the courtesy, ripe scholarship and unfailing helpfulness of the librarians of our public libraries and the officials in charge of our public collections it would be impossible for any student engaged in research work to speak too highly. Mr. James Ross, M.A., F.L.A., the City Librarian of Bristol, and Mr. Reginald W. M. Wright, Director of the Victoria Art Gallery and Municipal Libraries at Bath, both took much trouble on my behalf, and I am also indebted to the Oxford City Librarian, to

Mr. R. W. Hunt of the Bodleian Library, Mr. John Woodward, Assistant Keeper of the Ashmolean Museum, Mr. J. E. Smith, City Librarian of Liverpool, Mr. Hodge, Town Clerk of Devizes, and Mr. C. W. Pugh, Secretary of the Wiltshire Archaeological and Natural History Museum. Mr. Graham Reynolds of the Victoria and Albert Museum, Mr. A. E. Popham, Keeper of the Department of Prints and Drawings at the British Museum, Mr. Anthony R. Wagner, Richmond Herald, of the College of Arms, all responded most willingly to my requests and went out of their way to assist me. Finally, I must express my thanks to Mr. L. G. Duke, Mr. Gilbert Davies, the late Mr. A. B. Burney, Mr. C. L. Madeley, Mrs. Greenwood, Mr. John E. Barker, Miss Marjorie Bloxam, Mr. H. R. A. Bloxam and Mr. J. B. Willans and, indeed, all the correspondents who were kind enough to volunteer their aid.

Stonar House, Deal.   Douglas Goldring
26th May 1950.

ACKNOWLEDGMENTS

The Publishers wish to express their thanks to the following: Miss Naomi Royde-Smith and Messrs. Victor Gollancz Ltd., for permission to use an extract from *The Private Life of Mrs. Siddons*; Mrs. Pamela Diamond for permission to use an extract from *Reflections on British Painting* by Roger Fry; Messrs. Methuen & Co. Ltd., for permission to use an extract from *Lawrence* by Sir Walter Armstrong.

A SHORT LIST OF BOOKS CONSULTED

The Life and Correspondence of Sir Thomas Lawrence, Kt., 2 volumes, by D. E. Williams (Henry Colburn and Richard Bentley, 1831).

An Artist's Love Story, edited by Oswald G. Knapp, M.A. (George Allen, 1904).

Sir Thomas Lawrence's Letter-Bag, edited by George Somes Layard (George Allen, 1906).

Artists and Their Friends in England, 1700–1799, by William T. Whitley.

Art in England, 1800–1820, by William T. Whitley (1928).

Art in England, 1821–1837, by William T. Whitley (1930).

The Farington Diary, volumes i–viii, edited by James Grieg (Hutchinson & Co, Ltd.).

The Private Life of Mrs. Siddons, by Naomi Royde-Smith (Gollancz, 1933).

The Greville Memoirs, edited by Lytton Strachey and Roger Fulford (Macmillan, 1938).

The Diaries of Sylvester Douglas (Lord Glenbervie), edited by Francis Bickley (Constable & Co., Ltd., 1928).

The Autobiography and Journals of Benjamin Robert Haydon, edited by Malcolm Elwin (Macdonald, 1950).

Lawrence, by Sir Walter Armstrong (Methuen, 1913).

Romney and Lawrence, by Lord Ronald Gower (1882).

Sir Thomas Lawrence (From *Lives of Remarkable Youth*, volume i) Anon. (1830).

Annals of Thomas Banks. Sculptor, Royal Academician, With Some Letters from Sir Thomas Lawrence, P.R.A., to Banks's Daughter, edited by C. F. Bell (Cambridge University Press, 1938).

A SHORT LIST OF BOOKS CONSULTED

The Diary and Letters of Fanny Burney, volume i (1842).

Literary Recollections, by the Rev. Richard Warner (1830).

The Lives of the Most Eminent British Painters, volume iii, by Allan Cunningham (Bohn's Standard Library, 1880).

Reflections on British Painting, by Roger Fry (Faber and Faber, 1934).

CONTENTS

ILLUSTRATIONS

ILLUSTRATIONS

I

BIRTH AND PARENTAGE

INTEREST is legitimately taken in the ancestry, parentage and family background of eminent persons because the facts concerning them may shed light on the origin of transmitted characteristics. As one of Sir Thomas Lawrence's early biographers very rightly observed, 'the immediate parentage of every man is of importance, as it is the source whence are derived his tone of sentiments, his habits, his deportment and, to a great extent, his morals'. Of Lawrence's ancestry on the paternal side, possibly owing to the fact that he himself had no curiosity in the matter, made no enquiries and never troubled, when he received the honour of knighthood, either to secure a grant of arms or register a pedigree, nothing appears to be known. In most histories of painting he is described curtly as the 'son of an innkeeper', although at the time of his birth his father was, in point of fact, Supervisor of the Excise at Bristol and had not embarked upon his brief and unsuccessful career as an hotelier. Lawrence's close friend and contemporary, Samuel Lysons, F.S.A., in conformity with the romantic snobbery of the period, invented a pedigree which he considered in keeping with the dignity of a President of the Royal Academy, thus providing the painter with a crest and coat of arms. He appears to have made but little use of them and preferred to seal his letters with a classical intaglio. According to Lysons, Lawrence was descended from Sir Robert Lawrence, who accompanied Richard Coeur de Lion to the Holy Land and was knighted in 1191 for his valour at the siege of Acre. Unfortunately for his reputation as an antiquarian, Lysons was careless enough to supply his friend with a great-grandfather who, though authentically descended from the crusader, was proved, by a cold-hearted official of the College of Arms, to have had no offspring. Bogus pedigrees and the use of armorial bearings without the slightest authority were, as readers of Thackeray's *Vanity Fair* will recall, common form among the *nouveaux-riches* of the Regency period. As Lawrence was, throughout his life, free from the slightest taint of snobbery, we can only conclude that he was the innocent victim of Lysons's well-meant imaginings. All we know about the Rev. William Lawrence, the painter's grandfather, is that he had been 'a violent presbyterian, and all the relations were of the same sect', and that, to quote Lawrence's first biographer, D. E. Williams, 'our artist's father, Mr. Thomas Lawrence, and his younger brother Henry, with a sister named Martha (who died in her youth), were left orphans in childhood'.

The elder Lawrence was born at Newbury, Berkshire, in 1725, but enquiries made of local authorities reveal no traces of either of his parents. There was a Presbyterian congregation at Newbury in the first half of the eighteenth century and it is possible that the Rev. William may have been their minister. The name Lawrence had for several generations been greatly honoured in Nonconformist circles, and the *Dictionary of National Biography* mentions several Puritan divines named Lawrence, two of whom came from a family settled in Shropshire, near the Welsh border. The most eminent of them was the Rev. Edward Lawrence (1623–95), who was educated at Magdalene College, Cambridge, and became Vicar of Baschurch, Shropshire, from which living he was ejected, under the Act of Uniformity, in 1662. At that time he had a wife and eight children, 'and when asked how he intended to support them, his usual reply was that they must all live on Matthew vi'. (For the benefit of those not so well versed in the Bible as their predecessors, it may be as well to recall that this chapter contains the much-quoted injunction: 'Therefore take no thought, saying, What shall ye eat? or, What ye shall drink? or, Wherewithal shall ye be clothed? . . . But seek ye first the Kingdom of God and his righteousness; and all these things shall be added unto you. Take therefore no thought for the morrow; for the morrow shall take thought for the things of itself. Sufficient unto the day is the evil thereof'.

MRS. SARAH KEMBLE

*This portrait of the mother of Mrs. Siddons is one of Lawrence's earliest known
portraits in oils. In the Victoria Gallery, Bath.*

LAWRENCE'S BIRTHPLACE, REDCROSS STREET, BRISTOL

The painter was born at No. 6, the last house on the left. From an engraving in the Lawrence Collection, British Museum, published in 1830.

In 1670 Edward Lawrence was arrested for preaching, under the Conventicle Act. In the remaining twenty-five years of his life he published several volumes of sermons which achieved great success. He died very much beloved for his unworldly simplicity, generous character, and moral courage. His nephew, Samuel Lawrence (1661–1712), also a Nonconformist divine, was the son of William Lawrence, dyer, of Wem, Shropshire, and was Minister of the Presbyterian congregation of Northwick, Cheshire, from 1688 until his death. He had three sons by his first wife, one of whom, Samuel Lawrence, D.D., became Minister of Monkswell Street Chapel, in London.

If, like Lysons, we care to amuse ourselves with guesswork about the ancestry of Sir Thomas Lawrence, our guesses will at least have a foundation of probability if we assume that he was an offshoot of the family of Shropshire Presbyterians to which Edward and Samuel Lawrence belonged. We may go even further and assume that these Lawrences were of remote Welsh extraction. Eloquence, love of poetry and the drama and artistic feeling, all of them Welsh characteristics, combined with the moral sentiments natural to a man of Presbyterian upbringing and traditions, blended in Thomas Lawrence senior to produce the vain, extravagant, engaging and often preposterous personality which has come down to us, and, certainly, all his life he obeyed the injunctions set out in Matthew vi.

The orphan sons of the Rev. William Lawrence appear to have been brought up and launched in the world by a rich 'relation', possibly a connection by marriage, 'Zachary Agaz, Esq. of Sunning Hill, Berkshire'. No details about this gentleman have been recorded. Henry, the younger boy, was sent to the East Indies, as a cadet, 'and was never heard of afterwards by his relations'. Thomas, the artist's father, was articled by Mr. Agaz to a Mr. Ginger, a respectable solicitor of Hemel Hempstead, Herts. His conduct seems to have been exemplary, and he must also have displayed some ability in his profession, for at the end of his apprenticeship Mr. Ginger offered him a share of his business as a junior partner. Fortunately for the world, Fate had marked him out for higher things than the career of a provincial attorney. He

disliked the law and, as he had just received his small patrimony
from his father's executors, he formed the scheme of enjoying a
tour through England with a fellow apprentice named Price,
who afterwards entered the Church and became the headmaster
of King Edward's School, Birmingham.

The two young men first set off to Tenbury, in Worcester-
shire, where Price had some relatives. This, for Lawrence
senior, was the end of the joint excursion for, having once set
eyes on the delightful little town, beautifully situated on the River
Teme and surrounded by orchards and hop-gardens, he found it
impossible to leave it. The attractions of Tenbury were enhanced
by the charm of the society to which young Price was able to
introduce him. Williams remarks that 'he was young, handsome, enthusiastic and of a remarkably fine person', which
suggests that even in youth Lawrence senior was an imposing
figure. As he was a young man of unblemished moral character,
it is not surprising that he soon ingratiated himself with the
respectable society of the neighbourhood 'and, in particular,
became on intimate terms with the vicar and his family'. The
Vicar of Tenbury was the Rev. William Read, of the family of
Read of Brocket Hall, who was not only the incumbent but also
patron of the living of Tenbury, Rector of Rochford, a village
two miles' distant, and first portioner of the rectory of Burford in
Shropshire. This squire-parson and clerical pluralist had married
Miss Hill, of Court-de-Hill in Shropshire, whose mother's
maiden name was Powis. His children were thus related to two
important and influential families which included such figures as
Sir Thomas and Sir Ashton Powis, Sir Adam Littleton and Lord
Littleton of Munslow. Andrew Hill of Court-de-Hill was a
person of some consequence and is described as a 'beau ideal of a
country gentleman of that period, fit for a prototype of Esquire
Western—a keeper of foxhounds, and a mighty Nimrod'.

In the household of the Rev. Mr. Read, the good-looking,
well-behaved young stranger was received, apparently with open
arms, as a welcome addition to the family circle. The fact that
the Reads were 'bigoted High Church people' while young Tom
Lawrence's father and all his relations were 'violent Presbyterians'

did not at first create any ill-feeling against the newcomer. He must have had gentlemanlike manners, he was sufficiently well-educated to have qualified as a lawyer, and he loved Milton and Shakespeare and was prepared to spout long passages from them when given the opportunity. His 'principles' were exemplary, his behaviour beyond reproach, and his friend Price, who had introduced him to Tenbury, had respectable relatives living in the locality. In addition, he had a facility for conventional versifying, at that time a popular 'drawing-room' accomplishment. Some of his verses have been preserved and are worth quoting for the light they shed on his odd personality. They were addressed to his friend Price and were written in Tenbury in 1752, the year before his marriage.

> *While you, my friend, employ your age*
> *In Horace's or Virgil's page,*
> *(Bards venerably great)*
> *Or in melodious numbers tell*
> *How the lamented Daphne fell*
> *An empty prey to fate;*
> *By pensive contemplation drawn,*
> *I rove along the winding lawn,*
> *Or tread the enamell'd green;*
> *Unnumber'd objects throng my eyes—*
> *Lost in amazement and surprise*
> *I view the charming scene.*

The attractions of the 'charming scene', enhanced, we may suppose, by those of Mr. Read's younger daughter Lucy, inspire the young Presbyterian with gratitude to the Giver of them. After rebuking the 'atheist', who 'denies that God exists', he affirms:

> *No—a superior pow'r—a God*
> *Hath fix'd in Heaven his blest abode,*
> *Whose being knows no end;*
> *Through Him, the thunder rends the air,*
> *Through Him, the flashing lightnings glare,*
> *Through Him, the rains descend.*

Hail, Great Creator! Lord of all,
Beneath thy throne, I prostrate fall;
Oh deign t'inspire my breast;
Oh lead me through this maze of life,
Through busy cares and factious strife,
To thy eternal rest.

Such lofty sentiments must have been well received at the vicarage, for even bigoted High Churchmen professed as much respect for the Creator as their Nonconformist rivals. To Lucy Read, who already had tender feelings for the poet, they must have seemed genuinely inspired. In the eighteenth century, even more than in the Victorian age, the 'detrimental' who was the recipient of the rather patronising hospitality dispensed in great houses was expected to know his place. The social gulf between a wealthy clerical squire, connected with several great county families, and the penniless son of a Presbyterian minister of obscure origin, was so enormous that it was unthinkable to Lucy's parents that young Lawrence could sufficiently forget his place as to fall in love with a girl so far his superior in birth and fortune. Unfortunately they reckoned without that disturbing factor, the artistic temperament. Though Tom Lawrence was devoid of talent, as his verses indicate, he had any amount of temperament, and all the pride and good conceit of himself which make even a bad artist convinced of his superiority to ordinary mortals. When Lucy first met her future husband she was a girl of fourteen, already showing premonitions of exceptional beauty, while Tom Lawrence was only twenty-one. The girl divided her time between her father's vicarage and her uncle's house, Court-de-Hill, which was within walking distance of Tenbury. 'In her frequent walks between these two residences,' says Williams, 'she was generally if not always accompanied by Mr. Lawrence.' As the years went by and Lucy grew from being a confiding child into a beautiful young woman, of marriageable age, the inevitable romance occurred. 'The confidence reposed in this young gentleman by the lady's parents and uncle,' says an anonymous biographer of Sir Thomas, 'may prove very fully their appreciation of his moral character and decorous habits; but it is no great proof of the discretion of a parent to have thrown into perpetual contact two such young, sensitive and congenial minds. Mr. Lawrence was now in his twenty-fifth, and she in her eighteenth year. After incessant conflicts between reason and attachment, the feelings of youth, and the influence of early precepts, the anticipations of parental displeasure, and the disregard of those calculations that would most affect their future life and, what was of more consequence, that of their off-spring,—the young persons came to the usual compromise of marrying without consent, in preference to marrying against it, or to having their affections blighted. . . .'

Such was the sympathy for this young couple that a neighbouring clergyman, the Rev. Mr. Baldwin, of Corley, consented to unite them, 'regardless of the influence of the wealthy "squire" at Court-de-Hill or that of the stern and rigid Vicar of Tenbury'.

After the ceremony, which took place in Mr. Baldwin's house, the bride and bridegroom returned to their respective homes and continued to meet as usual without revealing what had happened. In a few weeks, however, they persuaded a friend to break the news to Lucy's father and uncle. The task must have required some courage for its performance, for the announcement of Lucy's secret marriage evoked rage and consternation both in Tenbury vicarage and at Court-de-Hill, and was followed by condign punishment of the guilty girl. The father and uncle not only expelled her from their houses but even tried to prevent 'all her kith and kin from holding any communication with her or her husband'. So enraged was Mr. Andrew Hill at the marriage of his favourite niece 'that he not only never saw her more, but he altered a bequest to her in his will of £5,000 to the sum of one shilling'. Later, when Mrs. Read died, Andrew Hill refused to pay over a legacy of £4,000 due to her estate under her father's will, to prevent its distribution among her children and to deprive the erring Lucy of her share. The resulting litigation in Chancery lasted, says Williams, 'only twenty years, and an issue at common law having been decided, by Lord Mansfield, in favour of the plaintiff, the money was at length paid—after some who should have received it were in their graves'. If young Tom Lawrence

had imagined that his wife's relatives would contribute to her
support, he was thus disappointed, and history does not relate
how the couple managed to exist during the first three years of
their married life. When his wife came of age, however, they
received about £900 from property possessed by Lucy indepen-
dently of her father.

Since the whole world loves a lover, Lucy's clergyman brother
and some of her other relatives were not so hard-hearted as her
father and uncle, did what they could to soften his severity and
declined to obey the parental injunction not to hold any communication with the banished pair. The Rev. William Read,
son of the Vicar of Tenbury, who afterwards became Rector of
Munslow and Aston, we are told, 'always received his sister and
her husband as guests endeared to him by the ties of nature and
of suffering'. The first practical help to the banished lovers
seems to have come from Lucy's aunt, Ann, her mother's sister,
who had married a Mr. Gataker, a surgeon to George II. The
Gatakers lived in Pall Mall when in London, but had a country
house at Thaxted in Essex where Mrs. Gataker appears to have
offered the young couple a temporary refuge. In any case it was
in Thaxted, on the other side of England, far away from Tenbury
and its associations, that they took a small house and settled down.
The legacy of £900 which Lucy Lawrence received after she had
been married for three years does not seem much by present-day
standards, but two centuries ago, at a time when, as Goldsmith
reminds us, a country clergyman could be 'passing rich on forty
pounds a year', it was a fairly substantial sum. Meanwhile, through
the influence of Mrs. Gataker, Lawrence senior secured a post as
subordinate officer of the Excise Board and, having passed through
the intermediate stations, was appointed Supervisor of the Excise
at Bristol on 6th June 1760. Of the sixteen children born to
Thomas and Lucy, of whom only five were living at their death,
three were born in Thaxted.

Although the office of Supervisor of the Excise, even in a great
seaport like Bristol, was ill-paid, it was one which, with 'dex-
terous management', as Williams puts it, could be made to yield
a considerable profit to the holder, such illicit gains being connived

at by the authorities. It is entirely in accordance with what we know of Lawrence senior's honest but hopelessly unpractical character that he declined to accept bribes from the lawless gangs of smugglers who ran the black market of the period and whose activities it was his duty to repress. On the contrary, he became a most vigilant revenue-officer. He was a very tall, athletic man; active, and of great muscular power. His mind, says an anonymous biographer of his artist son, 'was always imbued with a spirit of enterprise, and an ardour approaching to enthusiasm. His conflicts with the daring bands of smugglers at Bristol, which was then the second port in the Kingdom, and the centre of illicit trade, could be understood only by a reference to the scale and system upon which these bands of desperate outlaws then carried on their trade. . . .' Williams says that it 'required a union of skill, vigilance, and intrepidity, in any officer to compete with such an organised body of outlaws. Sir Thomas used occasionally to mention instances of his father's presence of mind, acuteness and resolution, in circumventing the boldest leaders of the different gangs. He must have raised to him a host of very dangerous enemies; and yet, in his subsequent avocation of innkeeper, no machinations could fix upon him any charge of impropriety with respect to the revenue, although the state of the revenue laws at that period, and the machinery for executing them, by no means required innkeepers to be immaculate. Nothing is recorded of him as a supervisor but his vigilance and courage in circumventing and combating smugglers, and his inability to subsist by doing "the State some service" '. If the honest and vigilant revenue-officer made enemies among the smugglers who infested the port of Bristol, he evidently rose high in the estimation of its leading citizens. Apart from his prowess as a preventive officer, his passion for literature, love of reciting passages from Shakespeare and Milton, and facility in writing doggerel verse, had made him a 'character' regarded with considerable respect. Though we are now unable to trace the financial arrangements which made it possible for him to resign the office of Supervisor of the Excise and start in business as an hotelkeeper in Bristol, it is not altogether surprising that, with his reputation for enterprise and integrity, he should have found the necessary backing. It was characteristic of his big ideas and sense of his own importance that he took over the White Lion in Broad Street, then one of Bristol's most important hotels, soon after added to it the adjoining American Coffee House, combined with it the business of supplying post-horses and also became the tenant of a small farm in the neighbourhood of the city. As neither he nor his wife had any aptitude for commerce or any experience in the management of large and complicated undertakings, it is not surprising that their speculation failed in spite of the amount of energy which was put into it. Williams says that one of Mr. Lawrence's first cares when entering on his new avocation 'was to supply his inn with a good library for the use of his customers; and the wretched coloured daubs that had disgraced the walls of his rooms gave place to the best engravings of the painting of Salvator Rosa, and the old masters'.

A good idea of the high standard which Lawrence senior set himself to achieve can be got from his initial advertisement which appeared in *Felix Farley's Bristol Journal* on 20th May 1769:

'To the Nobility, Gentry, Merchants, and Tradesmen in general,
Thomas Lawrence
Supervisor of Excise,
Having been greatly encouraged to take that large, commodious
and well-accustomed Inn, known by the name of the
White Lion
In Broad Street, Bristol,
Now in the possession of Mrs. Elizabeth Church;
Begs leave to offer, that he shall enter upon the same,
the Third Day of June next,
When he promises himself the pleasure of answering the
Expectations of his numerous Friends, and of all
others who shall honour him with their Company; and
approve himself, in every part of his Conduct,
Their sincerely grateful,
And most obliging Servant,
THOMAS LAWRENCE.

24

N.B. If any Nobleman, Lady or Gentleman, shall be pleas'd
to honour him with their Commands, he will be always ready
to bespeak convenient Apartments for them at the Hot-Wells,
where he is most intimately acquainted.
Beds carefully air'd. Chaises with Patent Springs.
Wines neat as imported.'

In a later advertisement, published in the same journal on
2nd September 1769, he added: 'Dinners drest on the shortest
Notice by an approved Man Cook'.
After the American Coffee House had been taken over the
following advertisement was inserted, on 18th April 1772, in
Felix Farley's Bristol Journal.

'City of Bristol.
The White-Lion Inn and American Coffee House being united,
Thomas Lawrence humbly solicits the Continuance of the
Favours of the Nobility, Gentry, and others, resorting to
Bristol and the Hotwells, who may be always accommodated
to Advantage, with Beds constantly air'd, genteel Dining Rooms,
Provisions of the Best, and every necessary Convenience,
till they can properly suit themselves with Lodgings;
the very best of which are constantly known to
    Their much oblig'd and grateful Servant,
                THOMAS LAWRENCE.

Neat wines, fine London Porter in Bottles or Calk, and the
best Bottle and Barrel Cyder to be had in any Quantity.
A Genteel Coach and Four, to carry Four Passengers only,
will set out from the White-Lion-Inn in above, every Friday
morning at Six o'Clock to the Swan-Inn in Exeter, and set down
there on Saturday to Dinner; return from thence every
Monday morning at Six o'Clock and will arrive at the
White-Lion, Bristol, time enough to dine on Tuesday.
Inside Passengers to pay £1. 5s. - Outsides and Children
in Lap Half Price, and so in Proportion all the Way.
—Goods carried on reasonable Terms—No Money, Plate,

Jewels, Writings, or other Things of Value will be
accounted for, unless entered and paid for as such.—
There are Carriages passing between Exeter and
Plymouth daily.

Places in the London and Bath Coaches and neat Post-
Chaises, &c—&c. to be had at the White-Lion as usual.'

This latest venture was quickly followed by the collapse of the
whole undertaking, one source of the elder Lawrence's failure
being a disease which destroyed a great number of his post-horses.

Thomas Lawrence had been admitted a freeman of Bristol on
13th December 1769 on payment of a fine of twelve guineas.
His tenancy of the White-Lion, at that time a favourite resort of
Bristolians who approved of the King's policy towards America,
must have given him many opportunities of joining in political
discussion and impressing his personality on his customers. We
know also that he indulged his passion for 'polite literature', as his
son's anonymous biographer describes it, for his recitations and
his original verses brought down upon him 'the satirical castiga-
tion of the unhappy Chatterton, who was then about sixteen'.
The writer adds, 'the humble condition of poor Chatterton was
overwhelmed by the loud voice and giant manners of the dis-
putatious innkeeper, whose ample larder and deep cellars of
course procured him the homage of critics less restive than
Chatterton'. An interesting description of the innkeeper's
appearance at this time is given by this biographer, which, as it
is the most detailed which has come down to us and bears the
stamp of authenticity, may be quoted in full. 'His large, fine
person was decorated with a well-powdered wig, and more
elaborate and bushy than even the fashion of that day warranted.
On the top of this was a diminutive three-cornered cocked hat.
The flaps of his waistcoat, and skirts of his black coat, with his
immense ruffles, and long laced cravat, carried the remarkable
costume of the period to an almost ludicrous extravagance. . . .
He had rather a large face, which combined the expression of
drollery, of an animal enjoyment, and of intellectual shrewdness.
His gait by no means corresponded with his corporeal dignity;

it was rather expressive of the unequal and rapid transitions of his mind; and its fluttering, strutting effect formed a contrast to the importance of his figure and the impression of his manner'.

Thomas Lawrence's failure at the White Lion seems neither to have damped his belief in himself nor to have discouraged his friends, admirers and financial backers. No sooner had his tenancy of the Bristol hotel been terminated than he decided to take over the Black Bear at Devizes, then one of the most fashionable and frequented coaching inns on the Bath road. At this period almost everyone of importance paid an annual visit to Bath, and the Black Bear was the nightly resting-place of wits, actors, peers, and eminent characters of every description. For this 'magnificent speculation', as Williams calls it, the two sitting members for Bristol, Mr. Cruger and Mr. Brinckdale, advanced him the funds. There could be no more conclusive proof of the respect in which he was held.

During the twelve years in which they lived at Bristol the loving Lucy regularly provided her devoted spouse with a baby a year, most of whom died in infancy. On 13th April 1769, at 6 Redcross Street in the parish of St. Philips, her fourteenth child was born. On the 4th of May following he was baptised Thomas, after his exuberant father.

II

THE BLACK BEAR AT DEVIZES

THE EARLIEST recorded tenant of the Black Bear at
Devizes was one John Sawter, who applied for his licence
in 1599. Among subsequent landlords were John Watts
and John Child, brother of Sir Francis Child, both well-known
local people. In 1754 it was occupied by John Turner, who paid,
for the whole premises, £48 10s.6d. rent, out of which £16. 10s.6d.
was paid to Henry Wyndham for the back premises, described
as 'the new building, stables and garden'. Under his successor,
George Whatley, who, according to a contemporary newspaper,
'was esteemed the most eminent publican in the West of England',
the Black Bear became known as one of the best coaching inns
on the Great West Road. Its regular clientèle included not only
'rank and fashion' but, as Williams records, 'all the wits of the
kingdom who repaired to Bath for the season. Here Garrick,
Foote, Wilkes, Sheridan, Burke, Johnson, Churchill and others
were to be found resting for the night, or for the many hours
required in those days for a change of horses'. The local gentry
also made the Bear their centre, for here was founded the Devizes
Bear Club, which assisted poor persons, gave money to charities,
and regaled its members at an annual turtle and venison dinner.
The Bear Hotel to-day, modernised and reconditioned, retains
much of its Georgian atmosphere and is substantially the same
building as the one of which Lawrence senior became the tenant.
The former supervisor of Excise, as his trial performances at
Bristol made clear, had big ideas and a well-developed sense of
his own importance. In 1773 the following advertisement appeared in a Bath newspaper:

'Thomas Lawrence most humbly begs leave to inform the nobility,
gentry and others that he is now removed from the White Lion

Inn and American Coffee House, Bristol, to the Black Bear Inn, Devizes, where he humbly entreats a continuance of their countenance and support, assuring them that no endeavours of his shall be wanting to accomodate and oblige them in a manner most becoming.

Their most dutiful, and entirely devoted servant,

T. LAWRENCE.'

Evidence of the new landlord's enterprise and public spirit is afforded by a paragraph which appeared in the *Salisbury Journal* in the same year. 'The conduct of Mr. Lawrence, of the Bear Inn, Devizes, in a very singular instance, is highly approved of and worthy of public consideration. Posts, twelve feet high, are erecting quite across the Plain from Devizes to this city, at the sole expense of the above person, at the distance of only half a mile asunder as a sure guide to the travellers in all weathers, with a large Roman D. cut deed on one side of each post, denoting Devizes, with the distance of miles and an S. denoting Salisbury on the other.'

At the time of his translation to the Black Bear only five of the innkeeper's numerous offspring had survived. The two elder boys were probably still at a school of local eminence called The Fort, in Bristol, kept by a Mr. Jones, who limited his boarders to ten. The two girls, Lucy and Anne, were partly educated by their mother, received the training of young ladies and no doubt were kept strictly segregated from the guests and customers of the inn. This was not to be the fate of the youngest child, Thomas, whose good looks and precocious talents for drawing and 'spouting' verse were exploited with unhesitating exuberance by his vain and possessive father. Apart from two years at The Fort, between the ages of six and eight, when one of his fellow-pupils was the future Earl of Shaftesbury, Thomas junior received no regular schooling, though he had some lessons in French and Latin from a dissenting clergyman named Jervis. As he had a remarkably beautiful handwriting and was from early childhood a voracious reader, it is evident that two at least of 'the three R's' had been well taught. For the rest, like many other outstanding men, he was self-educated. Of Mrs. Lawrence, whose personality was, we gather, very much overshadowed by that of her husband, we read that she 'was valued by her friends as a sensible well-informed lady. Mild, unassuming, and of correct principles, she devoted herself to the care and education of her children. Amidst the unpleasant scenes in which she was involved by her husband's pursuits, and want of success, and for which her birth and previous habits were calculated to disqualify her, she evinced a meritorious resignation. Without forsaking the most active duties of a wife and mother, she retained, throughout all her trials, a refinement of mind and the delicate manners of a woman. Sir Thomas Lawrence always spoke of both his parents with respect and affection, and he constantly regretted that circumstances had prevented his receiving from his mother the benefit which his elder brothers had derived from her early instructions'. That Lucy Lawrence had been exceptionally well brought up and had, as a girl, received an excellent education may be inferred from a panegyric published after the death of her sister, whose upbringing in Tenbury vicarage must have been similar to her own. This lady married a 'gentleman residing near the town of Tenbury' named Theophilus Knowles, and is described as 'a gentlewoman of great natural and acquired abilities, and in several branches of polite literature well conversant. Of religion and religious worship she had a just and awful sense. . . . In her person she was graceful, and her deportment was humane, gentle, affable, and courteous. . . . In every condition and relation of life she maintained the character of the good Christian, the affectionate wife, the sincere friend and the accomplished gentlewoman'. Whether Mrs. Knowles's 'awful sense' of religion was strong enough to make her disregard her father's ban and continue on affectionate terms with her younger sister is not recorded. There is little doubt, however, that Mrs. Lawrence, no less than Mrs. Knowles, was 'humane, gentle, affable and courteous' and that she transmitted these qualities, together with her personal beauty, to her two daughters and her youngest son. How young Tom's gift for drawing was first discovered is described in an article on the 'Early Life of Sir Thomas Lawrence, P.R.A.' by

a Mr. T. B. Smith, which appeared in the *Wiltshire Magazine*
in 1866. After the painter's death, Mr. Smith visited an aged aunt,
Mrs. Nalder, who in her youth had lived with the Lawrence
family at the Black Bear, and took down her reminiscences as
nearly as possible in her own words. 'I think it must have been
about the year 1765 [1769],' says Mrs. Nalder, 'that I went to
reside with Mr. and Mrs. Lawrence; at that time they kept the
White Lion Inn and the American Coffee House at Bristol. I
remained with them about two years. Some time after this Mr.
Lawrence wrote to me saying that he had taken the Black Bear
Inn at Devizes and that he would be very glad if I would come
to them at once, to superintend the bar and to assist his wife in the
domestic arrangements'. On her arrival at the Black Bear she
saw for the first time the youngest of the Lawrence children and
described him as 'then a very beautiful and engaging child about
two or three years of age. He was a boy of remarkably fascinating
manners and frequently amused himself by endeavouring to draw
little pictures on paper with a blacklead pencil. I perfectly recollect as I was one afternoon sitting in the bar, watching him
whip his top in the entrance hall, his running up to me and saying,
"Miss Lea (that was my maiden name), sit as you are and I will
draw your picture." I did as he desired, and in a few minutes he
produced what was always considered an excellent likeness of
me. He was at this time in petticoats and, I think, not more than
four years old. I shall never forget the pleasure with which his
father caressed him when shown this, his first attempt to portray
"the human face divine!" He snatched it from the table and
ran out of the house to purchase a frame for it. It hung for some
time in the bar and was much admired by persons frequenting
the inn. I subsequently gave it to one of my brothers on his
going abroad and it was lost with the rest of his property in the
French Revolution.

'The next likeness which young Lawrence executed was that of
. . . Mr. Bennett Swayne. These portraits, I think I may venture
to affirm, were the foundation upon which the painter's fame was
raised, as from this time numbers of persons became anxious to
have their portraits taken by a child in petticoats, and the reputation

which he thereby acquired was the cause of his talents being at length directed solely to that occupation which nature had pointed out for him'.

Of Lawrence senior Mrs. Nalder observed that 'he was a man of somewhat eccentric habits. Although remarkably neat in his dress and general appearance, yet he had so great an aversion to new clothes that whenever his wife noticed that any portion of his attire was getting worn or shabby she used to send to the tailor to replace it, effecting the exchange when he was asleep. He was remarkably fond of politics, theatricals and recitations, and prided himself on his readings of Milton and Shakespeare. He was a great favourite of Garrick, who frequently visited the house, staying sometimes a week or a fortnight at a time. During one of these visits he presented his host with a folio copy of *The Spectator* to which the latter, as may be imagined, attached ever afterwards great value. . . . So fond was Mr. Lawrence of books, that in almost every room in the house there was a book-case, containing a choice selection of volumes for the use both of his guests and of his personal friends'. Mrs. Nalder presented her nephew with a crayon picture done by young Lawrence when about fourteen years of age. 'It is one of the first which he executed in this style', she said, 'for which he used to charge three guineas, frame included. It is a portrait of Miss White, who afterwards married the Rev. W. Jacobs, Rector of Shillingstone, Dorsetshire. Her father at that time kept the Castle Inn, at Marlborough, and between him and Mr. Lawrence there existed a degree of intimacy which induced the young artist to bestow especial pains upon the picture. It was given me by Mrs. Jacobs herself. Many years afterwards, at an interview which I had with Sir Thomas in town, he enquired what had become of it, and expressed the hope, when he came into Wiltshire, of being able to call upon me, and look again at one of his earliest productions.

'And here I cannot help remarking on the great kindness with which I have always been received by the late President whenever I called upon him, which was as often as I visited London, and the pleasure which he took in describing to me the portraits on which I found him engaged.

PRINCESS AMELIA

Lawrence's first Royal Commission was to paint portraits of Queen Charlotte and Princess Amelia; both were exhibited at the Royal Academy in 1790. At Windsor Castle, and reproduced by gracious permission of His Majesty The King.

MRS. ELIZABETH CARTER

This early portrait of the famous Deal bluestocking, translator of Epictetus and friend of Dr. Johnson, was exhibited at the Royal Academy in 1790. In the National Portrait Gallery.

'To return to the artist's boyish days, I often remember his father saying with tears in his eyes, when looking at his early productions, that he had no doubt that I should live to see him a great man, though he himself might not. And years afterwards when Sir Thomas was lodging in Piccadilly, and his portraits were beginning to engage the attention of the fashionable world, I called upon his father in Gerrard [Greek] Street, Soho, and was reminded by him of the predictions which he had so often uttered, in the Bear Inn at Devizes, of the future greatness of his son.'

In spite of the obsequiousness of his advertisements, there is some evidence that the landlord of the Black Bear not only offended the local tradesmen by dressing above his station, but also, like some of the amateur hotel-keepers of a later day, annoyed his more snobbish patrons by treating them as social equals, intruding on their privacy and offering, when they were tired and hungry, to give readings from Shakespeare and Milton instead of presenting the bill of fare and discussing the contents of his wine cellar. Williams says, discreetly, that he had many personal acquaintances among his guests and 'in conversation with them played the scholar more than the landlord'. The equivocal social position of an innkeeper who had started life as a lawyer and married into a wealthy county family seems to have bothered the elder Lawrence children, who had received the conventional education of the class to which their mother at least belonged. When Andrew Lawrence matriculated at Hertford College, Oxford, in 1780, he gave his father's occupation as 'gentleman', not 'innkeeper'. After the death of his maternal grandfather the second son, William Read Lawrence, spent some time with his grandmother, Mrs. Read of Tenbury, whose house must have provided a contrast to the Black Bear. The one member of the family who throughout his life never betrayed the slightest trace of snobbish embarrassment regarding his father's occupation was the painter. In this connection Miss Croft tells a delightful story in her *Recollections of Sir Thomas Lawrence, P.R.A.* 'During these years (1800–15),' she writes, 'we became acquainted with all Sir Thomas's family except Mrs. Meredith, his favourite sister, who died of consumption early in my acquaintance with him. When his brother Major Lawrence returned from abroad after a very long absence, I was invited to meet him at dinner in Russell Square, Mr. Andrew Lawrence, Mrs. Bloxam [Sir Thomas's younger sister] and several of her sons and daughters, and I shall never forget the honest delight and humility with which Sir Thomas recalled many of the events of their childhood while their father kept the Inn at Devizes. Some of the party seem'd a little mortified at the recollections, but Sir Thomas persisted the more, in a sort of playful malice. His parents made quite an idol of him, and whenever any mischief was done "little Tom" was put in front of the offenders to brave or soothe the storm. His sister Anne once sent him out to collect birds' eggs for her, and he staid so late that his father was much alarmed about him. At length when it was almost dark the young gentleman arrived whistling and singing, with his hat in his hand, half full of birds' eggs. His father, forgetting his alarm, when he saw the boy safe only remembered his anger for having been frightened, and seizing the hat began beating him about the head with it till his curly poll was one mass of broken shells and yolks, and his wrath could not but subside on seeing his ridiculous condition.

'Another time they were all assembled in "the Bar" (here some of the party winced a little at the phrase) and they were all trying, by kicking off their shoes, to hit a ball of zinc [silvered glass?] which hung from the ceiling. Unluckily little Tom at length succeeded, and down came the ball in a thousand shivers. He left his brothers and sisters to gather them up, and flying into the garden laid himself down in a celery trench for concealment, where he fell asleep and was not found until he was alarmingly chilled by the cold. It appeared his father used to be pleased with watching the miniature likenesses of his children in this convex mirror; and, strange to tell, they escaped punishment from the circumstance of his never missing it, till they were old enough to confess the misdemeanour without fear.

'Sir Thomas told me that his first impression of pictures was made at the age of four or five at the Inn at Devizes by a picture of Shakespeare, taken from the statue, and that tho' very much frightened at its pale and ghastly hue he often contemplated it

for a long time together. This painting, tho' a good deal mutilated, was in existence about fifteen years ago at the Brown [Black]
Bear, and the waiter tried to persuade me it was painted by Sir
Thomas. I felt it was not worth while to undeceive him on the
subject.'

Although Lawrence senior had from an early age taught little
Tom to declaim passages from Milton, Shakespeare and Gray
and to recite 'sundry of the odes of Collins', he quickly realised
that the boy's gift for drawing could also be exploited for the
entertainment of his guests, with profit to himself. It became his
custom to introduce the child to visitors with 'Gentlemen, here's
my son—will you have him recite from the poets, or take your
portraits?' Alan Cunningham records that 'Garrick was pleased
once, during his stay at the Black Bear, to listen complacently
while the boy, urged by his father, recited a long passage from
Shakespeare: on the great actor's return, within the space of a
month, as he alighted he called out, "Landlord, has Tommy
learned any more speeches, eh?" and ordering the boy and his
tea to be taken to the summerhouse in the garden, said, "Come
now, my man, begin"; and when the tea and the spouting were
finished, he clapped his head and said, "Bravely done, Tommy:
whether will ye be, a painter or a player, eh?" '

Strangers to the Black Bear, who expected inn-keepers to stick
to business and attend to their bodily needs, were sometimes
irritated by the landlord's behaviour, which seemed to them to
verge on impudence. A story related by Williams, although
familiar through frequent repetition, ought not to be omitted,
as it indicates how advantageous to the father was his offspring's
childish charm.

'In 1775 Mr., subsequently Lord, Kenyon arrived with his lady,
late in the evening, at the Black Bear Inn at Devizes. They were
on their way to Bath, and had felt the inconveniences of the heavy
style of travelling in those "good old times"; and, as they confessed, they were not in the best possible humour, when Mr.
Lawrence senior entered their sitting-room and proposed to
show them his wonderful child. "The boy," he said, "was only
five years old, but he could take their likenesses, or repeat to

them any speech in Milton's 'Pandaemonium'." To that place the offended guests were on the eve of commending their host to go, and the lawyer's lips were just opened to pronounce the sentence, when the child rushed in ; and, as Lady Kenyon used to relate, her vexation and anger were suddenly changed into admiration. He was riding on a stick, and went round and round the room, in the height of infantile joyousness. Mrs. Kenyon, as soon as she could get him to stand, asked him if he could take the likeness of that gentleman, pointing to her husband. "That I can," said the little Lawrence, "and very like, too." A high chair was placed at the table, pencils and paper were brought, and the infant artist soon produced an astonishingly striking likeness. Mr. Kenyon now coaxed the child, who had got tired by the half-hour's labour, and asked him if he could take the likeness of the lady? "Yes, that I can," was his reply once more, "if she will turn her side to me, for her face is not straight." Our artist learnt in good time not to speak so bluntly before ladies; but his remark produced a laugh, as it happened to be true. He accordingly took a side likeness of Mrs. Kenyon. About the year 1799, an intimate friend of Lady Kenyon's saw this portrait, and could distinctly trace a very strong resemblance to what her Ladyship had been at the period when the likeness was taken'.

The recorded incidents of young Lawrence's childhood are concerned mostly with the notice taken of him by the eminent persons who were impressed by his precocious ability. On one occasion, for example, we find Sir William Chambers, the architect, praising the child's talents, and Colonel van Homrich giving him a guinea for the beautiful handwriting displayed in his copy-book. Of more practical assistance to the young artist was the interest taken in him by Mr. Weld of Lulworth Castle, who subsequently married Mrs. Fitzherbert. Mr. Weld, who had the entrée to the great houses in the district, took his young protégé to see the notable collections of old masters at Wilton House, the seat of the Earl of Pembroke, and Corsham Court, the seat of Mr. Paul Methuen. Once, when going through the rooms of Corsham Court, 'the visitants were so absorbed by their splendour, that they totally forgot that the child was with them. He was

suddenly missed, when the parents retracing their steps, found him
in one of the rooms the party had just left. His attention was
riveted to a painting by Rubens; and, upon being taken from the
spot, he murmured with a sigh, "Ah, I shall never be able to paint
like that!" ' Another influential friend of the young artist, who
not only helped to foster his artistic education but, at a later date,
advanced money to Lawrence senior to enable the family to
settle in London, was the Rev. Dr. Henry Kent, who then lived at
Whistley House, Potterne, some two miles from Devizes. This
worthy man, noted for his eccentricities, was a familiar figure in
Devizes, where he was usually seen in a shovel hat and mounted
on a veteran grey horse. His odd appearance caught the eye of
young Lawrence, who made a drawing of him. Mr. T. B. Smith,
author of the article in the Wiltshire Magazine which has already
been quoted, thus records what happened when the existence of
the sketch reached the Doctor's ears. 'One day Dr. Kent rode up
to the Bear Inn . . . and demanded in an authoritative manner to
be shown a caricature of himself and the horse, which he had
heard was in Mr. Lawrence's possession. Mr. Lawrence, suspect-
ing his son Tom had been exercising his pencil at the Doctor's
expense, called him from his play and asked him if he had ever
drawn the likeness of that gentleman and his horse? Tom said he
believed he had, and taking the enquirers to his bedroom they
there found, sketched on one of the walls thereof, a very excellent
picture of the Doctor and his favourite white charger.

'Dr. Kent was so pleased with this performance, that he immediately took young Lawrence to the shop of a bookseller,
Mr. Burrough . . . and there made him a present of the first box
of colours he ever possessed, and also a choice selection of books.
The Reverend Doctor's friendship was from this time of the
most substantial and useful kind to the young artist and his
family, and terminated only at the Doctor's death [in 1799].
Shortly after this first introduction Dr. Kent received from his
protégé a very spirited head of Our Saviour sketched in chalk.
It is in an oval frame 9 in. by 7 in. and it has written on the back
of it, by Lawrence, "Dr. Kent is requested to accept this trifle
from his grateful friend and servant, T. Lawrence, Jun." This

picture, which is one of the earliest of his productions extant, is now in the possession of Henry Kent Norris, Esq., of Devizes, a relative of the Doctor's, and would prove a very valuable addition to any collection of the works of the late Sir Thomas.'

The drawing was reproduced by photo-lithography and accompanies Mr. Smith's article. It is an astonishing performance, resembling and little inferior to the drawings in red chalk by Guercino, which at that period enjoyed a vogue among collectors and of which the artist may have seen specimens at Wilton House and Corsham Court. Apart from its merit, it is interesting as showing at how early a stage Lawrence was influenced by the old master drawings of which, when he was able to indulge his hobby, he made a world-famous collection.

'Dr. Kent,' Mr. Smith continues, 'took pains to urge on Lawrence senior the necessity for fostering his son's talent by means of a sensible course of instruction in the principles of his art, and the books which he gave or lent to young Tom, among them Rogers's *Lives of Foreign Painters*, no doubt had this end in view. Lawrence senior, however, had ideas of his own about the value of education. He was averse to his son's reading on the subject of painting, and assumed as a principle, that genius must be its own instructor, and that any study of rules and principles would only cramp the faculty and reduce it to the mould and order already established. All that he would permit was that the boy should be allowed to see whatever collections of the ancient masters he could procure admission to in the mansions of the gentry in the neighbourhood, and that he might catch what notions he could from such rapid and transitory glances." Censorship, by parents, of their children's reading, as many of us know from experience, is usually impossible to enforce. It is thus extremely unlikely that Lawrence senior was able to prevent his son from devouring any books on painting which he found in the library at Whistley House, where he was a frequent visitor, or acquired from other sources. Preposterous as old Lawrence's attitude may seem, it is worth while recording that when, as a man of twenty-two, Lawrence came under the formative influence of an established painter who knew all the tricks of his trade, not to mention its 'rules and principles', the result was the reverse of beneficial. G. S. Layard, in his book *Sir Thomas Lawrence's Letter-Bag*, quotes a word of advice given to Lawrence by his friend, William Hamilton, R.A.

'In your portrait of the queen I hope you will be careful of individual likeness; *in the princess you have more scope for taste, as the features will soon change from what they are at present.*'

Layard's appropriate comment is: 'What poisonous counsel from an artist, who had already arrived, to one on the threshold of his career! And it is painfully evident from his subsequent work that Lawrence all too eagerly adopted this easy standard of artistic morality. Hamilton's own work has almost died of insincerity; Lawrence's, though more robust, is largely infected with the same insidious disease.' Very different from this advice was that of Sir Joshua Reynolds, on whom Lawrence called when he first arrived in London. Sir Joshua, after criticising one of Lawrence's earliest paintings, said: 'It is clear you have been looking at the old masters; but my advice to you is to study nature; apply your talents to nature.' It may therefore be said, in Lawrence senior's favour, that no instruction of a professional or academic kind is at least preferable to bad instruction.

If we are to believe the landscape painter, Thomas Barker of Bath, Sir Joshua had been shown some of Lawrence's drawings, done when he was a child at Devizes, and would no doubt have remembered the incident when, some years later, he was shown an example of his maturing talent. According to Barker, 'While Lawrence's father kept an inn at Devizes, Sir Joshua Reynolds happened to stop at his house; and the publican, understanding who his illustrious guest was, ventured to introduce himself into the traveller's apartment, with a parcel of his son's drawings in his hands; requesting his inspection and his opinion of them. Sir Joshua was surprised at their excellence; and highly gratified the anxious parent, by immediately exclaiming "this young man has begun where thousands leave off".'

From what we know of Lawrence senior's talent for publicity and showmanship we can be certain that this incident, and many others like it, was frequently referred to by the vain and possessive parent of the infant prodigy. Indeed, his activities as an 'impresario of genius' were far more successful than any of his other attempts to earn a living. By the time he reached the age of ten young Tom was already something of a celebrity and his parent's chief means of support. In his *Miscellanies*, published in 1781, the Hon. Daines Barrington wrote: 'As I have mentioned so many other proofs of early success in children, I here cannot pass unnoticed a Master Lawrence, son of an innkeeper at Devizes in Wiltshire. This boy is now [February 1780] nearly ten years and a half old; but, at the age of nine, without the most distant instruction from anyone, he was capable of copying historical pictures in a masterly style, and also succeeded amazingly in compositions of his own, particularly that of "Peter denying Christ". In about seven minutes, he scarcely ever failed of drawing a strong likeness of any person present, which had generally much freedom and grace if the subject permitted. He is likewise an excellent reader of blank verse, and will immediately convince anyone that he understands and feels the striking passages of Milton and Shakespeare.'

What was to prove the most momentous of the painter's contacts with his father's guests at the Black Bear was his meeting with a young, as yet unsuccessful, comparatively unknown but commandingly beautiful actress who was on her way to take up an engagement at Bath. The day when Mrs. Siddons walked through the graceful portico of the Black Bear and first saw Tom Lawrence—a boy with large, melting eyes, auburn hair which hung down to his shoulders in ringlets and a singularly beautiful voice—was never forgotten by either of them as long as they lived. Soon after her arrival little Tommy was, we may be sure, commanded to do his tricks by his doting father. No doubt, as the lady was an actress, Tommy was first of all put on to recite and it is recorded that the future 'Tragick Muse' pronounced that 'his voice in recitation was harmonious and his action just'. Certain it is that during her stay at Devizes, when she was a girl of twenty and he a child of six, he made the first portrait sketch of a face which he was destined to draw and paint over and over again in later years. When he reached adolescence a sublimated form of love must, we may suppose, have been awakened between the young mother and the beautiful boy who was too old to be her son but not yet old enough to cause her emotional disturbance.

The last glimpse we have of the Lawrence family during their residence at the Black Bear comes down to us in the *Diary of Fanny Burney*, afterwards Madame D'Arblay, who stayed at the inn with Mrs. Thrale in April 1780, shortly after she had admitted the authorship of *Evelina*. The two ladies were on their way to Bath from Tunbridge Wells. Although the passage has been made familiar by frequent quotation, it deserves to be given in full for the light it throws on Mrs. Lawrence, her daughters and their home life. It is interesting to note that no mention is made of the father of the family, with his enormous periwig, his ruffles and his 'giant manners,' a fact which suggests that Lawrence senior, who was already on the point of handing over the inn to his successor and retiring from business, may have been away from home at the time of her visit. Had he been present, her sharp eye for character and her satirical pen would surely have combined to give us a memorable portrait of him. The account of the Lawrence *ménage* in Fanny's Journal is dated 'Bath, April 7 (1780).

'The second day we slept at Speen Hill, and the third day we reached Devizes.

And here, Mrs. Thrale and I were much pleased with our hostess, Mrs. Lawrence, who seemed something above her station in her inn. While we were at cards before supper we were much surprised by the sound of a piano-forte. I jumped up, and ran to listen whence it proceeded. I found it came from the next room, where the overture to the "Buona Figliuola" was performing. The playing was very decent, but as the music was not quite new to me, my curiosity was not whole ages in satisfying, and therefore I returned to finish the rubber.

Don't begin to talk in an old-cattish manner of cards? Well, another deal was hardly played, ere we heard the sound of a voice, and out I ran again. The singing, however, detained me not long, and so back I whisked: but the performance, however indifferent in itself, yet surprised us at the Bear at Devizes and, therefore, Mrs. Thrale determined to know from whom it came. Accordingly, she tapped at the door. A very handsome girl, about thirteen years old, with fine dark hair upon a finely-formed forehead, opened it. Mrs. Thrale made an apology for her intrusion, but the poor girl blushed and retreated into a corner of the room: another girl, however, advanced, and obligingly and gracefully, invited us in, and gave us all chairs. She was just sixteen, extremely pretty, and with a countenance better than her features, though those were also very good. Mrs. Thrale made her many compliments, which she received with a mingled modesty and pleasure, both becoming and interesting. She was, indeed, a sweetly-pleasing girl.

We found they were both daughters of our hostess, and born and bred at Devizes. [They were born in Bristol.] We were extremely pleased with them, and made them a long visit which I wished to have been longer. But though those pretty girls struck us so much, the wonder of the family was yet to be produced. This was their brother, a most lovely boy of ten years of age, who seems to be not merely the wonder of the family, but of the times, for his astonishing skill in drawing. They protest he has never had any instruction, yet showed us some of his productions that were really beautiful. Those that were copies were delightful—those of his own composition amazing, though far inferior. I was equally struck with the boy and his works.

We found that he had been taken to town, and that the painters had been very kind to him, and Sir Joshua Reynolds had pronounced him, the mother said, the most promising genius he had ever met with. Mr. Hoare [W. Hoare, R.A., then the leading portrait-painter in Bath] has been so charmed with this sweet boy's drawings that he intends sending him to Italy with his own son.

This house was full of books, as well as paintings, drawings, and music; and all the family seem not only ingenious and industrious, but amiable; added to which, they are strikingly handsome.

I hope we shall return the same road, that we may see them again.'

Towards the end of May Fanny Burney had another glimpse of the Black Bear, stopping 'to change horses at Devizes in preference to Chippenham, merely to inquire after the fair and very ingenious family of the Lawrences; but we only saw the mother and elder son'.

The visit to London, referred to by Miss Burney, took place at the invitation of Mr. Hugh Boyd, one of the supposed authors of *The Letters of Junius*. This gentleman 'was so enraptured with the beauty and cleverness of the child, that he invited the father, for the sake of the son, to his house in town—we think, in Berkeley Square. They stayed with him several weeks, during which he took the child to the homes of eminent persons, whom he delighted with his extraordinary talents, particularly with his pencil. His copying some stuccos, at the house of Mrs. Richard Lee, is spoken of as a very surprising proof of juvenile talent'.

During Lawrence senior's absences from home Mrs. Lawrence, with the assistance of Miss Lea, the future Mrs. Nalder, was presumably left in charge of the Black Bear. As most of Lawrence's biographers state that it was in 1779 that the family was obliged to leave Devizes, whereas Miss Burney's visit took place in the following year, it seems probable that Lawrence senior may have removed himself from the reach of his creditors and left his wife as *locum tenens* until the new landlord, a Mr. Halcomb, was ready to take over. Mr. Halcomb must have maintained, if not increased, the reputation of the Black Bear among the 'nobility, gentry and others', for on 16th September 1789 King George III and Queen Charlotte stopped the night there. The reasons for old Lawrence's failure are not far to seek. As his son's anonymous biographer acidly observes: 'Whilst the father was revelling in poetry and speeches, and attending to the drawings of his son, the hosts of the rival inns were attending to the drawing of corks, and to all the details of their business.'

III

BATH

IN THE notice of his discharge from bankruptcy which appeared in the *London Gazette*, 29th October—2nd November 1782, Thomas Lawrence senior is described as 'Innholder, dealer, and chapman'. It was to the latter occupation, as a hawker of his son's portrait drawings and as his agent and impresario, that Lawrence senior now devoted himself. When the family finally left Devizes their first move was to Oxford, where they were already well known. As Williams is our chief authority for what happened during this visit, the passage describing it may be quoted: 'Many of the heads of colleges, and the dignitaries of the University, had stopped at Devizes on their way to Bath for the fashionable season, and upon their return to the University, the beauty and talents of the child of Mr. Lawrence, the keeper of the Black Bear, had often been the topic of conversation. When he was known to be in Oxford, the father was much noticed, and the child as much caressed. He took the likenesses of the most eminent persons then at Oxford; but his pencil was not confined to grave sexagenerians; for many of the younger nobility and gentry were anxious to have their portrait taken by the phenomenon; and the female beauty of the dignified city and its wealthy neighbourhood equally pressed upon his talents.' Young Lawrence had recently had his portrait painted by William Hoare, R.A., then Bath's leading portrait painter, and engraved by Sherwin. The print, the price of which was 10s. 6d., was subscribed to by the Vice-Chancellor of Oxford University, the Bishops of Oxford and Llandaff, numerous peers and heads of colleges, and a large number of undergraduates. The success of this print indicates the amount of interest taken in the youthful subject of it. At Oxford there can be no doubt that Lawrence

44

senior extracted substantial sums of money from his son's activities. After leaving the city, the family went on to Salisbury and Weymouth, 'then the favourite bathing-place of our late sovereign [George III] and of a certain high class of the nobility and gentry. What occupation they gave to the young artist, or the exact time of his residence among them, it is now impossible to trace'. The stay at Weymouth could not have been long, for before the end of 1780 the Lawrences arrived in Bath, which was to be their home for the next six years. They lodged first at 14 St. James's Parade, but by 1782 the proceeds of the young artist's pencil were sufficient to enable them to take a substantial house, 2 Alfred Street, within a few yards of the upper Assembly Rooms, off the lower part of Lansdowne Road. This house, once known as Alfred House, had been previously occupied by Mrs. Catharine Macaulay, in her day a much admired historian, bluestocking and social figure. The Lawrences paid £100 a year for it, a high rent at that period, but a contribution to their overhead expenses was made by a Mrs. Alcock, 'sister to Mr. Cumberland the poet',[1] who boarded with the family as a friend, paying £120 a year for her board and that of her servant. The elder son, Andrew, who had now been ordained and had obtained the lectureship of St. Michael's, Bath, with a salary of £140 a year, also lodged with his parents and paid his father £80 a year for his keep. Young Tom's earnings as a fashionable portraitist were from the start considerable. At first his charge for an oval crayon likeness was a guinea, but this was quickly raised to a guinea and a half. As sitters continued to throng what Williams calls his 'atelier', the price of his half-lengths was eventually doubled, and as he regularly completed three or four portraits a week, his weekly contribution to the family exchequer must have varied between nine and twelve guineas. Twelve years earlier, when Gainsborough, then thirty-five years old, was in practice at Bath as a portrait-painter his price for a head in oils was five guineas, subsequently raised to eight guineas. Mrs. Siddons, when leading lady at Palmer's theatre in Bath, had to be content with a weekly salary of only £3. If the value of a pound sterling in the late eighteenth

---

[1] Richard Cumberland (1732–1811), a well-known dramatist.

century is multiplied by six, we shall get an idea of the young artist's earnings, in current terms, at this early stage in his professional career. That the house in Alfred Street was just as full of books, pictures and music as the Black Bear had been can be taken for granted and, from what we know of his character, we can be certain that the twice bankrupt innkeeper, out of the profits derived from his son's industry, did himself well, and lived in the style to which Mrs. Lawrence at least had been accustomed. 'Old Mr. Lawrence,' says Williams, 'placed his two daughters at an eminent boarding-school; the eldest, at the expiration of a year, became the companion to the three daughters of Sir Alexander Crawford; and the youngest soon after supported herself by a most laudable exertion of her talents, as head-teacher in a seminary at Sutton Coldfield, Warwickshire.' Although we hear no details of what happened to William Read Lawrence, we know that he was able to obtain his commission in the Army. The elder son, Andrew, as we have seen, was already earning his living as a clergyman. The comparative prosperity of the Lawrence family at this period was, however, due entirely to the skill and industry of young Tom. In justice to his father, it must be admitted that he seems to have shown some business capacity in the exploitation of his son's talents. On their first arrival in Bath they sought out Mrs. Siddons and Tom made two drawings of her, one as Euphrasia in *The Grecian Daughter*, the other as Zara in Congreve's *The Mourning Bride*. These Lawrence senior had engraved by J. R. Smith as well as a drawing of the artist, by himself, and published them, no doubt with considerable profit. The print of young Tom was inscribed 'To the Nobility and Gentry in general and the University of Oxford in Particular who have so liberally countenanced his pencil, this portrait of Master Lawrence is Inscribed by their most devoted and most grateful Servt T. Lawrence, Sen.'. Although Williams dwells with awe on the 'noted and great' who made young Lawrence's studio 'the resort of all the distinguished company of this splendid concentration of wealth and dignity', and lists among his patrons Lord Barrington, his brother Admiral Barrington, Lawrence's portrait of whom was also engraved, Lord Cremorne, the Bishop

of Durham, the Marquis of Ely and his brother, the Bishop of
Clogher, General Ross, Sir Henry Harpur and 'the beautiful
Duchess of Devonshire, the sister of the Earl Spencer, whose
union of beauty, intellect, rank and affluence rendered her at that
period nearly the most distinguished lady in the Courts of
Europe', it is refreshing to find that even in his Bath days Lawrence valued his real friends for their merits rather than for their
social importance. If ever a youth was tempted to become a snob,
a toady, a climber, a conceited young coxcomb and a spoiled
darling, it was this good-looking, precocious and singularly
charming boy. It has become a habit, in a 'de-bunking' age, to
discount claims made by biographers regarding the virtues and
good qualities of their subjects. In Lawrence's case, some writers,
in recent times, have assumed that the impression he made on his
contemporaries was too good to be true. Against this, it may be
pointed out that what is recorded of him is at least consistent with
his having possessed, in the fullest degree, the modesty, the
generosity, the loyalty to his family and friends, the devotion to
his art and the high sense of personal honour which his actions
appear to indicate. In Bath, if he made an excellent living out of
his socially distinguished patrons, and learnt to comport himself
in their company with ease and grace, combined with the necessary show of outward deference, it was quite another sort of
patron that he had the good sense to appreciate, cultivate and
learn from. In his *Literary Recollections* the Rev. Richard Warner
gives an account of two such patrons, Dr. Falconer and Miss Mary
Hartley, both of whom exerted a beneficent influence on the
young artist in the formative years of his adolescence. Of Dr.
Falconer, Warner writes: 'If it were highly honourable to the
character of Lawrence that, during this period, he maintained his
father and mother, by the exercise of his pencil; it was equally
creditable to my great and good friend, the late Dr. Falconer,
the patron of all that was ingenious and virtuous, to encourage
and befriend the young man in his career of successful effort,
stimulated by filial piety. Dr. Falconer gave him his advice;
assistance; and friendship. Most of Lawrence's leisure was passed
at the Doctor's house. Under his hospitable roof were begun

and completed many of the best of the artist's early drawings. Among others, I have contemplated with delight, two pencil ones, of Cassandra, and a Christ's head: every line of which is radiant with genius; and full of the promise of future excellence and fame. Lawrence, to his praise be it spoken, never forgot his obligations to Dr. Falconer.' Although, for his period, perhaps one of the darkest in British medical history, Dr. William Falconer (1744–1820) was accounted an able physician and numbered such men as William Pitt, Lord Chancellor Thurlow and the Duke of Rutland among his patients, he was also a man of all-round scholarship and erudition. 'Few students,' says Warner, 'had read more extensively or more successfully than this gentleman. His knowledge of the Latin language was uncommon: his acquaintance with general literature comprehensive: his intellect bright and quick; and his memory more than ordinarily tenacious.' Dr. Falconer, who concealed his kind heart under a peculiar brusqueness of manner, sometimes referred to as the Falconer temper, lived at 29 Circus. He was a sturdy Liberal in politics, though not, like Warner, an extreme pacifist, shared Burke's views on the French Revolution, wrote tracts on miscellaneous subjects and published essays on the Bath waters which were much valued in their day.

He was a man of good presence, dignified in manner, and a brilliant conversationalist. A pleasing picture of young Lawrence in Dr. Falconer's home circle is given in a letter written by Miss Sarah Thackeray to Miss Jewsbury, which is quoted by Williams. Evidently in answer to a request for information about Lawrence's early life, Miss Thackeray writes:

'My intimate acquaintance with Sir Thomas was confined to the last months of 1785 and to the first six months of the ensuing year; these I spent in the house of his friend and patron, Dr. Falconer of Bath. He passed several evenings in every week with us; and I scarcely recollect anything with more pleasure, than the little social circle that surrounded that joyous tea-table: he was one of its pleasantest members; and his appearance, which depended upon his inclination or convenience, was ever hailed

ELIZABETH FARREN

Exhibited at the Royal Academy, 1790, when the portrait was described in the catalogue as 'An actress'. It was engraved by F. Bartolozzi, R.A., in 1803, and is now in the United States.

JAMES BOSWELL
from a drawing in the National Portrait Gallery.

with delight. A kindred taste for the art drew him and Sir Sidney Smith together, and he sometimes, though more rarely, made one of the little party. I have seen the future President, and the future hero of Acre, drawing at the same table, the one tracing a human countenance, the other a ship. Sir Thomas was very engaging; he was kind and warmhearted, and his manners were graceful and easy. I am told they lost in warmth more than they gained in polish, in his after-intercourse with the world. He often recited long passages from Milton and Shakespeare, which he did even then with taste and feeling; and frequently sketched, for our amusement, the celebrated beauties, or the distinguished public characters he had seen at the Rooms the evening before. These he impressed upon his own memory, by tracing them with imaginary lines, upon the crown of his hat; he rarely failed to give, in a few hasty strokes, so correct a likeness, that we easily recognised the characters (when we afterwards saw them) from the representation. At this time he was painting portraits for three or four guineas a-piece in crayons. A mutual friend has a likeness of me in this style. He became acquainted with Bunbury, and he drew his portrait with one of his long caricatures depending from his hand—I believe his "Long Minuet". The drawings I possess of his are, two masterly sketches in black chalk, the one of a younger sister, the other of myself; and a personification of Contemplation from Milton's "Il Penseroso", a very highly finished and beautiful pencil drawing. He was remarkably handsome as a boy; he wore his collar thrown back, and his hair, which was beautiful, was so redundant, that its rich, dark curls almost obscured his face when he stooped to draw. You must remember, my dear Miss Jewsbury, I am describing the costume of half a century back. I was told he lost much of his beauty when he assumed the manly attire and reduced his fine hair to trammels of the stiff powdered fashion of that day; but I never saw him after. All this I feel is just nothing; but to supply the deficiency I will write to Dr. Falconer (son of the one above-mentioned) whose excellent memory and longer intimacy will supply, I hope, much that may be useful. His father and his uncle (the learned editor of the Oxford Strabo) were very kind to young

Lawrence, and fostered his early genius with the encouragement and assistance that even genius requires in its first efforts.'

It would be hard, indeed, to imagine a better preceptor and guide to budding genius than Dr. Falconer, and there is little doubt that Lawrence owed much to this erudite, kindly and distinguished man.

In Miss Mary Hartley, half-sister of the younger David Hartley and daughter of the eminent scholar, philosopher and metaphysician, Dr. David Hartley, young Lawrence was no less fortunate in finding a patroness who was not only an excellent amateur artist, but also, through her highly-placed friends and social connections, in a position to advance his interests. Warner says of this lady that she 'was indeed one of the most extraordinary women of her day: accomplished to a degree far superior to the generality of her sex. She, like her half-brother David Hartley . . . had enjoyed the high advantage of an education by her excellent parent; and imbibed all his piety, and much of his philosophical spirit. Her knowledge of the Latin language was considerable; her skill in the Italian and French critical. Every branch of the graphic art was familiar to her pencil; and, whether the subjects of her drawing were living or inanimate nature, she threw a grace and spirit into the delineation that manifested the taste and power of a master.... The superior talent of Miss Mary Hartley in drawing: her knowledge of its principles and skill in applying them; together with her extensive acquaintance and correspondence, with persons of rank, fortune and taste; rendered it highly desirable, to all the young artists in her neighbourhood, to obtain her notice, advice and patronage. It was her delight to confer these on every promising youth, when genius was associated with moral worth. The late Sir Thomas Lawrence, when he quitted Bath, to establish himself in London, benefited largely by her countenance, recommendation and advice'.

This amiable lady who had, in her youth, been engaged to a young man who died untimely, suffered much from ill-health, and towards the end of her life lost a foot and had to use a wheelchair, but preserved unruffled calm and sweetness of temper under all these afflictions. 'Diffidence and modesty,' says Warner, 'an humble opinion of herself and her endowments, combined with a glowing sensibility of heart; and an extreme gentleness and polish of manners completed a moral portrait as beautiful as it is infrequent.' From 1784, when her brother retired to Bath after the death of his friend, Sir George Saville, until her death in 1803, Miss Hartley lived with David Hartley at 37 Belvedere, which is now called Hartley House. David Hartley had sat in the House of Commons, where his speeches were notorious for their dullness, for fourteen years, and had been on intimate terms with the great Lord Chatham, William Pitt, the Duke of Portland, the Marquis of Rockingham, Edmund Burke, Charles James Fox, Sheridan and all the other eminent Whigs of his period. In 1783, at the end of the American War of Independence, the continuation of which he bitterly opposed 'not only from its *inexpediency* but from its *injustice*', he was made Envoy Pleni-potentiary at Paris to discuss terms of peace with Dr. Franklin and the other American delegates. 'He was,' Warner tells us, 'a real *patriot* and entered politics with no senseless love of power or thirst for *place* or *patronage*.' The two great questions with which he identified himself during his political life were the 'State of Ireland', that perennial anxiety to enlightened Liberals, and peace with the American rebels, but though he was in constant political opposition to Lord North he 'had a personal regard for his Lordship, which was cordially returned by the Premier'. Another friend of Hartley's was that enlightened Irish nobleman, the Earl of Charlemont. In a letter to the Rev. W. Gilpin, quoted by Warner, Mary Hartley records her affection for her brother, 'with whom', she says, 'I have lived for above forty years, in the most intimate and confidential friendship; and whose kind heart makes me full amends for every concession to his taste'. As his habits were somewhat eccentric and his staple diet bread and butter and tea, some concessions were, no doubt, needed. In his retirement David Hartley continued his interest in such Liberal or, as we should now term them, 'Left-wing', causes as the abolition of the slave trade, the State of Ireland and the progress of the fledgling American Republic. Warner says that Hartley spent the last twenty-five years of his life at Bath 'in philosophical investigations; ingenious experiments; mechanical inventions; and acts of frequent but unobtrusive benevolence'. His scientific attainments must have been great, for he did much work in association with James Watt and received a Parliamentary grant of £2,500 for his invention of fire plates. The type of high-minded, disinterested, humane and progressive Liberal patriot represented by David Hartley, though to-day almost extinct, exerted a beneficent influence on English political thought throughout the eighteenth and nineteenth centuries, and young Tom Lawrence could count himself lucky in having the entrée, as a boy, to circles so morally and intellectually distinguished as those of which the Hartleys and Dr. Falconer formed the centre. Of the more frivolous society, such as surrounded the glamorous Georgiana, Duchess of Devonshire, Lawrence saw at least as much as, possibly more than, was good for him, and it says a great deal for his native good sense and natural modesty that he never allowed his head to be turned by the flattery and 'caresses' of the fashionable world.

Although stress is laid by Lawrence's biographers on his lack of education in general and of instruction in drawing and painting in particular, it is hard to believe that any master in a provincial school of art would have taught him more or taught him better than Miss Mary Hartley, who must herself have received the best kind of academic training then obtainable. Moreover, we know that Lawrence was befriended by and frequently in the studio of William Hoare, R.A., then head of the arts in Bath, who once used the boy as a model for the head and bust of a figure of Christ. His versatile son, Prince Hoare (1755–1834), who, in addition to being an artist of some repute, wrote several successful plays and was made honorary foreign secretary of the Royal Academy in 1799, also took a friendly interest in the young artist and gave him useful advice. Another important influence on Lawrence's artistic development during his Bath period was 'the Honourable Mr. Hamilton, residing on Lansdown Hill, the uncle of the late Marquis of Abercorn', who made the boy free of the valuable collection of old master paintings at Rock House and encouraged him to copy any of them he pleased. The educational value of this privilege, as the Hamilton collection was unrivalled in this part of England, must have been considerable and Lawrence took full advantage of it. Among the pictures of which he made crayon copies were Raphael's 'Transfiguration', the 'Aurora' of Guido Reni, the 'Taking Down From the Cross' of Daniele da Volterra, the 'Vision of San Romuald' by Andrea Sacchi and 'Saul Receiving Sight from Ananias' by Pietro da Cortona. Williams states that Lawrence senior refused an offer of three hundred guineas for these copies. The copy of Raphael's 'Transfiguration' brought young Lawrence an unusual distinction from the Society of Arts which then annually awarded a gold medal as first prize and a silver palette as the second prize for the two best drawings submitted. It was a rule of the Society that a work to compete for the gold medal 'must be performed within one year prior to the date at which it is sent to the Society'. As Lawrence's drawing was dated 1782 and not submitted until two years later, it was automatically excluded from being taken into consideration for the higher prize. It was, however, thought of such extraordinary merit that the Society not only ordered the silver palette to be entirely gilded but also took the unusual step of voting the young artist a reward of five guineas 'as a token of the Society's approbation of his abilities'. The drawing was identified as the sole performance of young Lawrence by Prince Hoare. The artist was not, apparently, allowed to go up to London to receive his award in person, for the minutes of the Society record that 'Mr. W. R. Lawrence attended on behalf of Mr. Thomas Lawrence, Jun., to whom the silver palette, and five guineas, have been adjudged, as a bounty for a drawing of the "Transfiguration"; and received the same for his brother'.

Many years later Lawrence, in conversation with Samuel Rogers, the banker-poet, told a touching story about this award. He said that after he had received his prize 'he went with it into the parlour where his brother and sisters were sitting; but that not one of them would take the slightest notice of it; and that he was so mortified by their affected indifference, that he ran upstairs to his own room and burst into tears'. Their behaviour, no doubt, was due to a desire to prevent the boy from becoming conceited, although conceit was never one of Lawrence's failings.

Among Miss Hartley's protégés was a young landscape painter, Thomas Barker, who had come to live in Bath with a Mr. Spackman. It was from Barker, subsequently known as 'Barker of Bath', and from his friend and patron, Mr. Spackman, that Lawrence received his first instruction in the use of oil paints. Warner thus records the incident: 'It is highly creditable to that accomplished artist, my friend Thomas Barker, Esqre of Sion Hill, Bath . . . that he, in conjunction with Mr. Spackman, the architect and artist, who received Mr. Barker (before he went to Italy) into his house to study painting—first taught Sir Thomas Lawrence the use of oil colours; and showed him how to set a palette; or in other words, to dispose the various colours, according to the established arrangement, adopted by scientific painters. Mr. Barker informs me that when he had been about a week with Mr. Spackman, that gentleman came into the painting-room to him, and said: "I have had a visit from a young brother artist of yours, who called to ask me to show him the use of oil colours, and set his palette"; and that Mr. Lawrence accordingly came again in a few days, to Mr. Spackman's and was then instructed by that gentleman and Mr. Barker, in this preparatory stage to oil painting. Before this, Sir Thomas attempted nothing in this department of the art. All his portraits and fine fancy pieces, in the possession of my learned friend Dr. Falconer, are in crayon or pencil.'

Although Lawrence was kept hard at work turning out pot-boiling portraits for the benefit of his family, it would be a mistake to imagine that he spent his spare time only in being 'caressed' by society beauties, going to the theatre to admire Mrs. Siddons, or having his mind improved by intercourse with such people as Dr. Falconer and the Hartleys. He delighted in his boyhood in all forms of manly exercise and was remarkably active, even athletic. Although he never became a good horseman and 'never learned the *manège*', he was a good shot, an expert courser, an excellent fencer and a first-rate pugilist. 'When a boy,' Williams records, 'he had a fondness, an absolute passion, for pugilism;

and though it may shock the reader's imagination, yet I have not a doubt, if nature had stunted Lawrence's mind, and, leaving him only his corporeal energies, condemned him to be a boxer, he would have been one of the best of the "Fancy". I had this opinion from one who knew him when they trundled their hoops together, and this gentleman could have been no tiny playmate, for he is an uncommonly powerful man, and so well proportioned that he stood as the model of Lawrence's Satan. When they were boys about twelve years of age, Lawrence used to implore this companion lovingly to go out alone with him on holidays to some sequestered field, where, stripping themselves to the waist, they had it out in fair blows; my informant adds that he liked the amusement pretty well for a time, having the advantage of Lawrence in size and strength, but that the young artist improved so rapidly in skill and laid his colours on his future Satan with such potent strokes and touches, as to make him at last decline coming up to the brush.' Williams adds that 'all the athletic sports and boxing in particular, are indigenous to the Western counties of England, for which they have been celebrated throughout our history. Bristol and its neighbourhood have generally taken the lead in producing the champions of the ring; and certainly the casual boxing-matches that may be witnessed in the streets of that city, even among children, are astonishing to the inhabitants of other parts of the Kingdom. It is not surprising that young Lawrence caught the mania of this native town, and practised that in which it was the pride of all around him to excel'. In addition to his prowess at boxing, Lawrence had sufficient leisure at Bath to become a masterly billiards player, and continued to exercise the talent for reciting passages from the great poets and dramatists which his father had so sedulously fostered at the Black Bear. His boyish admiration of Mrs. Siddons, which no doubt his father shared, was increased by the opportunity afforded him of seeing her in all her leading roles.

Lawrence was a boy of only thirteen when Mrs. Siddons left Bath to make her first successful appearance in London, but the impression she made on him was indelible. Sixteen years later he wrote a copy of verses headed 'On Being Left Alone After

Dinner', in which he recalls his early rapture. The following are
the concluding stanzas.

> 'Up Bath's fatiguing streets I ran,
> Just half pretending to be man,
>   And fearful to intrude;
> Busied, I look'd on some employ
> Or limp'd to seem some other boy,
>   Lest she should think me rude.

> The sun was bright, and on her face,
> As proud to shew the stranger grace,
>   Shone with its purest rays,
> And through the folds that veil'd her form,
> Motion display'd its happiest charm
>   To catch th'admiring gaze.

> The smiting lustre of her eyes,
> That triumph'd in our wild surprise,
>   Well I remember still;
> They spoke it joy to give delight,
> And seem'd to say, "If I'm the sight,
>   Good folks, pray take your fill".

> And can it be that 'neath this roof,
> While I sit patiently aloof,
>   This watching form can be?
> Quick let me fly—avaunt my fears!
> 'Tis but a door and sixteen years
>   Divide this Fair and me.'

In addition to the drawings of Mrs. Siddons, to which allusion
has been made, Lawrence also made a drawing of a Miss Shakespeare, then the 'belle and reigning toast of Bath', who was pointed
out to him in an adjoining box one evening at the theatre. The

next day he executed a capital likeness of her from memory, which brought him considerable *réclame* and attracted other fair sitters to his studio. Lawrence was so fascinated by the theatre that, much to his father's perturbation, he became stage-struck and applied to Mr. Palmer, the manager of the company, to be admitted to a trial. As he was already earning a far bigger income than Mrs. Siddons, Lawrence senior was naturally horrified at the prospect of his son's abandoning his career as a portraitist in favour of one so ill-paid and so insecure. Accordingly, so Cunningham relates, 'he entered into a sort of ill-laid plot with Bernard, the comedian, to evoke the evil spirit of the sock and buskin wholly out of him'. The actor thus relates the plot and its success in his *Retrospections*: 'All the parties assembled: old Lawrence, and his friends, in the back parlour; young Lawrence, Mr. Palmer, and myself in the front. The manager was no sooner introduced than, with great adroitness, he at once demanded a specimen of the young man's abilities, and took his seat at one end of the room. I proposed the opening scene between Priuli and Jaffier. We accordingly commenced, I, Priuli, he, Jaffier: he went on very perfectly till, in the well-known passage, "To me you owe her", he came to the lines

"I brought her, gave her to your despairing arms:
Indeed you thank'd me, but . . ."

here he stammered, and became stationary. I held the book, but would not assist him; and he recommenced and stopped, reiterated and hemmed, till his father, who had heard him with growing impatience, pushed open the door, and said: "You play Jaffier, Tom! hang me if they would suffer you to murder a conspirator!" Mr. Palmer, taking young Lawrence by the hand, assured him in the most friendly manner that he did not possess those advantages which would render the stage a safe undertaking. The address did not produce an instantaneous effect; it was obvious that the young artist was of a reverse opinion. A conversation ensued, in which, I abusing the life of an actor, and other friends representing the prospects of a painter, young Lawrence at length became convinced, but remarked, with a sigh: "That if he had gone on the stage, he might have assisted his family much sooner than by his present employment." My reader can appreciate the affection of this sentiment, but I am unable to describe its delivery, or the effect it had upon every person present.'

A much more dangerous threat to Lawrence senior's pocket came from Lady Frances Harpur, a sister of the then Earl of Warwick, and her husband Sir Henry Harpur. Even before the arrival of the Lawrences in Bath, Lady Frances had intimated her willingness to adopt the young genius. This was followed by an offer from Sir Henry to lodge one thousand pounds in a banker's hands, to defray the cost of his education in Rome, on the ground that 'he would be the glory of our country, if he had the advantages of early study'. To this generous proposal, the father curtly replied that 'his son's talents required no cultivation'. The fact of the matter was that, without Tom to support them, the whole family would have been reduced to indigence. As no protest on the painter's part has been recorded, it is presumable that his loyalty to and affection for his parents made him acquiesce in what must, nevertheless, have been a bitter disappointment. At the same time, the presentation made to him by the Society of Arts must have stimulated his anxiety at least to exchange Bath for London and to get what teaching he could from the Royal Academy School. Cunningham says that it was in his seventeenth year that he 'first dipped his brush in oil colours, and began to free himself from the captivating facilities of crayons. . . . He copied, first, the style of Rembrandt; then that of Reynolds; and, lastly, he imagined he was imitating Titian. One of these pictures was audacious in subject; of its conception or handling no one has informed us;—this was Christ bearing the Cross, some eight feet high. He never was equal to the solemn grandeur which such a production required; his talents, first and last, lay with the soft, the graceful and the lovely. He was more at home in a portrait of himself of three-quarter size; it has been described as a wonderful work for one so young and so unacquainted with colours'.[1]

---

[1] At this period Lawrence painted the small portrait of Mrs. Kemble (mother of Mrs. Siddons), now in the Victoria Art Gallery at Bath, which is thought to be his earliest portrait in oils.

Lawrence's desire to try his fortune in the metropolis was actively supported by Miss Mary Hartley, who may have helped him to persuade his nervous parent to let him take the plunge. Some financial help to father and son came in the form of a loan from Dr. Kent, and from another patron, Mr. Edward Poore of Salisbury, a country gentleman fond of travelling in Italy and well acquainted with the colony of English artists in Rome. Writing to one of these from Salisbury in 1790, he says of Lawrence: 'We have a young face painter whom I once assisted in his outset who, I think, has the most extraordinary eye for colours since Titian; he is also a good draughtsman, more from eye and hand than theory, never having had a master. I left him just set up and actually gave my word for security for his lodgings when I left England.' On his way to London, in the summer of 1786, Lawrence appears to have spent some time in Salisbury, where he no doubt made Mr. Poore's acquaintance. Cunningham says he went on to London with his pockets 'full of the money obtained by crayon portraits there'. Lawrence senior accompanied him, for the anonymous biographer records that on their arrival in the metropolis 'His father immediately hired a very handsome suite of apartments (at four guineas a week) over a pastrycook's shop in Leicester Square. This at once indicates his love of display, and his possession of funds. These lodgings were within sight of the house of Sir Joshua Reynolds, whose study and drawing-rooms were daily visited by the nobility, and the wealthy and celebrated persons in London. This was a sight inspiring to a lad of real genius and laudable ambition'.

IV

FIRST DAYS IN LONDON

OF LAWRENCE'S first months in London, the chief incident recorded is his visit to the great Sir Joshua, for which the way had possibly been prepared by a word from Mrs. Montagu, the eminent bluestocking of Portman Square, and with more certainty by a letter of introduction from the amiable Prince Hoare. Lawrence senior, in any case, applied for an interview in a letter that no doubt reminded the great man of his son's early drawings which he had been shown at the Black Bear. The request was readily granted, an appointment made and the irrepressible father and the talented youth presented themselves in the painting-room of 'this favoured head and origin of the English School of Art'. Sir Joshua, we are told, 'was forcibly struck by the beauty and fine figure and graceful manners of the lad; and he received him with an attention and benignity that dissipated his apprehensions, and restored him to self-possession. As they entered, Sir Joshua was examining the specimen of another juvenile aspirant, who had evidently come upon the same object. The youth stood in trembling expectation of the decision of the oracle, which was to determine his course of life, and after some ominous hems and haws, some positive blame, and some condemning with faint praise, the Macaenas dismissed him with the negative encouragement, "Well, well, go on, go on." The situation of young Lawrence during this scene can be easily imagined'. Sir Joshua now inspected the self-portrait in oils which Lawrence had brought with him, was evidently much struck with the promise it revealed, and bestowed on it a very long scrutiny. 'At last he addressed the youth with an air of kindness, though serious and impressive: "Stop, young man, I must have some talk with you. Well, I suppose you think this is very fine, and this colouring very natural, hey, hey!" He then broke into a sterner tone, and began to analyse the performance, and to point out imperfections, sufficient in the alarmed imagination of the sensitive lad to destroy all hope of being a great painter. Presently, altering his tone, he began to show the "other side" of the picture—its merit; and he concluded in a mild manner, "It is very clear you have been copying the old masters, but my advice to you is, to study *nature*, apply your talents to nature, and don't *copy* paintings." He then took him by the hand, and kindly told him he was welcome, whenever he chose, to call. Young Lawrence was always well received by Sir Joshua from that hour to his last illness, which occurred four years after'.

The exact date of this interview, which was to have a momentous influence on the painter's career, is not known, nor indeed is it known for certain whether it was in the autumn of 1786 or the spring of the following year, that he took possession of the suite of rooms at 4 Leicester Square, then called Leicester Fields, which was his first London lodging. A letter of introduction written by J. Farr of Pierpont Street, Bath, on 13th March 1787 to Mrs. Poggi,[1] quoted by Layard, begins: 'The bearer of this letter, Mr. Lawrence . . . more than a year since . . . proposed going to London, which occasioned my giving him a letter. He is now again preparing for his journey (his first intention having been laid aside) and behold I am writing another letter; for I could not forgive myself if I did not endeavour to procure him the singular advantage and happiness of your acquaintance; and I am greatly mistaken if you do not find yourself highly gratified with his modesty, good sense and superior genius, which you will discover in his character'. Williams gives September 1786 as the date of the following very interesting letter from Lawrence to his mother, but Layard asserts that it was written in 1788. If this is correct, the self-portrait in oils referred to must be a different picture from the one which Lawrence showed to Sir Joshua on his first arrival, at the interview described above.

'MY DEAR MOTHER—I think myself much obliged to you for the books you sent me; and the shirts which, believe me, were very

---

[1] The wife of a well-known art dealer and interior decorator.

acceptable, as my stock was a little reduced. Rollin would be very acceptable; but perhaps Andrew cannot spare him. Having received no answer from Mr. Brummell I wrote to the Earl of Gainsborough, informing him that the picture was at his service, and I expect an answer soon. Lady Middleton said he was mad after it. I am now painting a head of myself in oils; and I think it will be a pleasure to my Mother to hear it is much approved of. Mr. P. Hoare called on me; when he saw the crayon paintings he advised me to pursue that style; but after seeing my head, and telling me of a small alteration I might make in it, which was only in the mechanical part, he said the head was a very clever one; that to persuade me to go on in crayons he could not, practice being the only thing requisite for my being a great painter. He has offered me every service in his power; and as a proof of fulfilling his word, I have a very valuable receipt from him, which was made use of by Mengs, the Spanish Raphael. His politeness has indeed been great. I shall now say what does not proceed from vanity; nor is it an impulse of the moment, but what from my judgement I can warrant. Though Mr. P. Hoare's studies have been greater than any paintings I have seen from his pencil, mine is better. To any but my own family I certainly should not say this; but, excepting Sir Joshua, for the painting of a head, I would risk my reputation with any painter in London. I hope you and Andrew will not be disappointed when you see it; for it will be sent that I may know your opinions. I have had the pleasure of seeing the great Mr. Barry; he did not recollect my name, nor did I wish to make myself known—as being ignorant of it, I became what I desired—a spectator. He is, in truth, a great man; to his wonderful talents for his profession he unites the classic truth of his scholarship, and the noblest and most sublime mind I ever met with. There is a clearness and precision in his ideas, together with a strength of language by which they are conveyed to you, so that even the most indifferent subject, when taken up by him, appears in a different light to what you ever before viewed it in. How great the pleasure, then, I received when that mind was employed, for the most part, in canvassing my loved pursuit, you may easily conceive. The large pictures, and the large books, would look well here, if you can spare them. I can think of no better present for my dear Mother. Uncle Codger must e'en sit for his portrait in oils, which shall not disgrace the original.—I now conclude myself, Your ever affectionate and dutiful son,

THOS. LAWRENCE.

Send the prose volumes of Miss Bowdler's works, unless wanting.'

The reference to 'Rollin', which presumably means the English translation of Charles Rollin's *Histoire Ancienne*, shows that the 'uneducated' young painter continued to improve his mind by the study of serious subjects unconnected with his art. Although at that period it was a handicap for a gentleman to be ignorant of Latin and Greek, many who had received the conventional classical training had far less knowledge of literature in general and that of their own country in particular, than Lawrence, with his father's early encouragement, acquired.

The James Barry referred to was Professor of Painting at the Royal Academy from 1782 until 1799, when he was expelled, with the King's consent, in consequence of his violent quarrels with, and accusations against, his fellow Academicians. Nothing appears to be known of 'Uncle Codger' nor of the contents of the letter which Brummell, whose arrogant ill-manners may perhaps be regarded as a form of compensation for his grandfather's lifetime of successful servility, neglected to answer.

From the letters written by Lawrence to Miss Hartley, which have been preserved, we can get an idea of the efforts made by his friends to provide him with useful introductions. The following is dated 6th April 1787 and the address given is 4 Leicester Fields.

'MADAM,

I do myself the honor of informing you that the letters you favor'd me with I have deliver'd, except the one directed to Lady G. Cavendish, being inform'd by the Dutchess D. of Beaufort, she does not come to Town till a fortnight hence. Lady T. Bathurst, I left, who was likewise out of Town but expected home in a week. Mr. Pepys did me the favor of a call, and politely offer'd to introduce me to Mr. Agar's Collection which I have heard is a very fine one. Mrs. Waddell has promised me every service in her power, I did myself the pleasure to call on Mr. D. Hartley, but was concerned to find a slight indisposition was the cause of my not seeing him, which I hope will be speedily remov'd. —The parcel of Feathers I deliver'd safely to Mrs. Montague, who return'd her best thanks to Miss Hartley for them, and would have wrote, but hop'd to be excus'd from the weakness of her Eyes, which alone should have prevented her. I had the honor of being shewn the elegant Mansion, by its elegant Mistress, but the room I most wish'd to see being then cleaning, I was unfortunately depriv'd of the pleasure of seeing. I nevertheless mention'd to Mrs. Montague the Improvement you propos'd which she approv'd of very highly, but express'd her fear that it could not be put into execution, as there were but two persons in London who could do the festoons of Flowers, and on that account it would be several years before the Work would be compleated, though herself much oblig'd in you thinking of her, said she would mention me to all her Friends, particularly Mr. Walsingham, and Sir J. Reynolds, and when the Room was set in order, would let me know that I might look at it. —I have experienced great pleasure in viewing the Works of Sir Ja, Mr. West, Mr. Romney, and Mr. Gainsborough. The former is, I think, evidently the first, yet there is a Classic Truth in Mr. R.'s Drawing, which I could wish united with that Elegance of Design and Brilliancy of Effect, so exquisite in Sir Jua. —With Mr. West, I was not at first so much pleas'd. The Gallery I pass'd through, without even turning my head to the right or left, as it ever was my wish to reserve the best Fruit for the Last! There is that hardness, that disgusting something in his coloring, which will ever strike with an unpleasant sensation those who have been so charm'd with the flowing pencil of a Reynolds, but his Drawings made me ample amends, particularly those which were the least finish'd, one of which was indeed most wonderfully Fine, the Triumph of Death was the subject and Terribly Glorious he appear'd.—

'PINKIE'. MISS BARRETT

Exhibited at the Royal Academy in 1795. The subject of this famous portrait, now in the Collection of the Hon. Andrew Mellon, became the mother of Mrs. Elizabeth Barrett Browning, the poetess.

BENJAMIN WEST, P.R.A.

Exhibited at the Royal Academy, 1811. In the Tate Gallery.

Mr. Gainsborough's Paintings I very much admir'd, but could with pleasure leave the Portrait for the Landscape Painter, the latter is really delightful. Yet there is one Person, in this case Flattery Madam cannot be laid to my charge, when I name Miss Hartley, whose Drawings I prefer to him, and here I must not omit my returning my particular thanks, for your kind Introduction of me to Mr. Prince Hoare to whose great politeness I shall ever think myself a Debtor, and with whom I saw the above Gentleman's work, as likewise the President's, and whose own paintings would do honor to the first Masters.—

I have to hope your goodness, Madam, will cast a favourable eye upon I fear the rash judgment I have made, as it was you who desir'd me to give it. Happy shall I account myself, if in the smallest degree it meet with your approbation, and in always testifying with how much gratitude I remain,

Madam,

Your oblig'd, and Obedient Ser't

T. LAWRENCE.'

Lawrence wrote again to Miss Hartley, on 23rd April, to thank her for her efforts on his behalf.

'MADAM,

I do myself the honour once more to address you; and again to express my thanks, for the trouble you have taken, in procuring me the sight of so many fine pictures; and particularly feel indebted for my introduction to Lady Middleton, who has kindly offered me the view of her pictures at all times, with the liberty of copying any that I wish, which I shall immediately avail myself of and take this opportunity to improve in the study of oils, which is what I much long for. Through the means of Lady Templedown, I have seen the small, but charming collection of Mr. Udney. Mr. Agar's I saw with Mr. Pepys. Mrs. Waddell I have the honour of seeing on Friday, who said she had spoke to the Duchess of Northumberland, and that orders were given to the porter, to admit me to see the paintings at any time.

I yesterday had the pleasure of seeing Mr. D. Hartley; who was pleased to express himself much pleased with your portrait, and said he should be glad to render me every service in his power; the copy of it I have finished, which I hope will meet with your approbation, Madam; than which there is nothing I shall be prouder of. One of the pictures, by the desire of Mr. Fisher, was sent to Mrs. Delany in St. James's Palace who, when I called there, behaved very politely to me; and desired I would write to Miss Hartley, informing her, a particular friend of Mrs. D. wished much for a copy; and to beg her permission for its being taken. I now, with sentiments of gratitude, which I hope it will ever be my pride to own, conclude myself

Madam,

Your obliged and obedient servant,

T. LAWRENCE.'

The Mrs. Delany referred to was frequently in Bath during its most brilliant period and for a time occupied Nash's mansion in St. John's Court. She had been the friend and correspondent of Dean Swift and was a great favourite of the King and Queen, to whom she introduced Fanny Burney. William T. Whitley, in his invaluable work *Artists and Their Friends in England*, says that 'Probably it was Mrs. Delany, then living in a house at Windsor given to her by the King, and in almost daily association with the Royal Family, who first brought Lawrence's portraits to the notice of the Court'. She died in 1788, but two years later Lawrence exhibited portraits of the Queen and Princess Amelia at the Royal Academy.

On his arrival in London, Lawrence, perhaps at his father's instigation, put up his prices for crayon drawings, without apparently mentioning the fact to Miss Hartley, who, in recommending him to her friends, had quoted the fees he had charged in Bath. This seems to have caused Miss Hartley some annoyance which a long letter dated 26th June 1787 is evidently intended to dispel.

'MADAM,

It is with some concern I feel myself obliged to apologize for my seeming inattention to your condescending letter; especially in that I feel more flattered by it, than by the numerous favours before conferred on me by Miss Hartley; but I hope the plea of being extremely hurried lately, will in some measure excuse it. I must now acquaint you, Madam, with the motives which induced me to make the addition in my price. When I had the honour of being first known to you, four guineas was the sum I had received for nearly a year; some little time before I left Bath, it was raised to five. When I arrived in town, I was advised by my family and friends, to make a distinction between those portraits, where only the head was seen, and those in which the arms were introduced; which advice I the more readily took, from knowing my expenses to be rather heavy, the lodging I am in now, being three guineas the week; but more particularly from this reason—the necessary time to be bestowed on the finishing of crayons (which I attempted), was such, that from proofs I found my receipts were more when I painted for two guineas and a half, than they were when I had five. At the same time, that I inform Miss Hartley of this, I must blame my own imprudence, in not making myself acquainted with the prices of the painters here, as it is my wish ever to be clear from the charge of presumption, which I fear I have incurred.

I am much honoured and obliged in the Duchess Dowager of Beaufort, and Mrs. M. Townshend, interesting themselves on my behalf, and Madam if [it] should be your advice and your concurrence should attend it, the lowering of my price shall immediately be done, with the greatest readiness and pleasure.

The exhibition, I have heard from several whose judgment I can trust, has failed much this year. Sir Joshua certainly maintained his superiority above the rest. His portrait of Sir H. Inglefield, was a specimen of the art, that, in my opinion, could not be excelled. The Death of Rizzio, by Mr. Opie, there are many fine parts in. He has studied, and that to a great degree, the beauty of *chiaro oscuro*, and fine colouring, but has not, I think, sufficiently attended to the great end of painting—the

67

expressing with truth the human heart in the traits of the countenance. The face of Mary has an expression of horror in it, but it is vulgar, and appears to be impressed with it simply by the deed, not from the victim being the object of her regard and affection. There is something which takes from the dignity of tragedy, in the arm of the principal assassin being bared for the purpose to the shoulder. It gives too much the idea of a butcher. The head of Ruthven is very fine; as is the effect of a torch, on the heads of those who are rushing in. The figure of David Rizzio is very good, but his figure is not seen in front, and you are presented with a full view of a silk night-gown. Still it has great merit. Mr. Northcote's picture of the Death of Wat Tyler, has some good painting in it, but not equal to the above. To have had that livid hue, his wound must have been given him at least eight days before.

There is a sketch of Mr. West's, in which there is a great deal of spirit, and wonderful design, in the composition. The group-ing of the figures is indeed very odd: they were from the bottom to the top of the picture. St Paul is placed at the top of a high rock, and does not appear with the calm dignity of faith; but seems much agitated in the act of throwing the serpent from him. Yet the pencil of a master is to be seen in every part of it.

Feeling highly honoured by your desire to know my real sentiments, they are thus freely given; but accompanied with a hope, that you, Madam, will kindly make allowances for the inexperience of that judgment, with which, he who gives it, has not yet vanity enough to be satisfied.

Having been so highly favoured, and under the obligations which I am to Miss Hartley, it cannot be wondered at, that I should be hurt at her continued ill health; for whom there is no one who esteems and admires goodness combined with such wonderful talent, but must be anxious.

Mrs. Delany and Mr. Fisher are both at Windsor. I shall obey your commands with pleasure, the moment I see them; and will endeavour to learn the person's name. I had the honour of being introduced to the Duchess of Rutland, at Bath. If, Madam, it could be hinted to the Duchess D. of Beaufort, her Grace sitting to me would be a great favour; and that you would be so good as to fix on a subject for a Drawing (My utmost wish in it being to please the lady for whom it is designed);—it would be still an addition to those feelings of gratitude, with which I ever remain,

Madam,

Your obliged servant,

T. Lawrence.'

Lawrence had exhibited seven of his crayon drawings to the Academy of 1787, but if he had anticipated that they would have a flattering reception, his vanity must have received a shock. Most of the critics ignored them, but one was unkind enough to remark that his 'Portrait of a Lady' (207) 'and two or three more by the same artist are beneath contempt'. The effect on an ambitious young man, aware of his own talents but no less aware of how much he still had to learn, by precept and experience, before he could hope to achieve success, of this reminder that the critical standards of the metropolis were very different from those of Bath, was certainly salutary. Throughout his career Lawrence paid attention to adverse criticism in the belief that he might have something to learn from it. He could well afford to possess his soul in patience and to sustain initial rebuffs from the critics with equanimity, thanks to the exceptional help he received from a wide circle of influential friends.

For the accomplished courtier which Lawrence was to become his early contacts with some of the greatest figures in the social and cultural life of his country, at a time when England was approaching its highest level of military prowess, political prestige and creative achievement in literature and the arts, can only be regarded as singularly fortunate. It was a theatrical age and its leading figures played important roles on the European stage, comported themselves with dignity, looked their parts and spoke their lines, sometimes with nobility and always with conviction. It was thus natural that many of Lawrence's portraits should have a theatrical quality. Whether, under altered circumstances, with a different kind of upbringing, and a more conventional professional training, his natural talents might have enabled him to become a greater painter than he actually was is a kind of speculation in which it now seems futile to indulge. Destiny controls these matters, and since it was Lawrence's destiny to become the official portrait painter to two monarchs and to leave behind him a pictorial record of many of the personalities, male and female, who added so much lustre to their reigns, we must take him as we find him. For the career on which he embarked, almost in infancy, his personal qualities made easier the success to which his outstanding gift for portraiture entitled him. Not only was he strikingly handsome, but he had all the social accomplishments, facilities and graces on which the aristocracy laid emphasis. He had a delightful voice, was a capital actor in private theatricals, a good dancer, fencer and boxer, a masterly billiards player, a good shot and an expert courser. A friend said of him that 'if Lawrence had been doomed to drive geese from Bristol to London he would have managed his flock more gracefully and dexterously than any other man'. In social intercourse, though prone to flattery, he had consummate tact and self-control combined with an 'unarrogant self-possession' which has always been considered the hall-mark of the aristocrat.

In 1787, when Lawrence began his London career as a boy of eighteen, it was undoubtedly the encouragement he received from Sir Joshua Reynolds which gave him his first foothold on the ladder of success. At the President's house in Leicester Square, although Garrick, Dr. Johnson and Goldsmith had passed away, he could not fail to meet people who, attracted by his agreeable manners and prejudiced in his favour by Sir Joshua's good opinion of him, were willing to do what they could to advance his interests. It says much for Lawrence's sterling character, his seriousness and native good sense that from the first he resisted the temptations which must have beset him to indulge in the dissipations of London Life and devoted himself with the most austere and praiseworthy determination to the task of establishing himself in the profession to which his life was devoted. The motives which inspired him to scorn delights and live laborious days were a combination of natural ambition to achieve success and fame, and a sense of financial responsiblity in regard to his family which,

to modern ideas, must seem astonishing. Nothing that his preposterous father could do to embarrass him socially, waste his
hard-earned money, or make him look foolish, seems to have
impaired his filial loyalty and affection. An example of old
Lawrence's possessive attitude in regard to his children's money
and his inability, as a provincial showman, to understand conditions in the metropolis, occurred during the first year of his
residence in London. In 1787 his younger daughter Anne came
of age and received a legacy of £200 under the will of Mr.
Zachary Agaz. No information has come down to us as to the
identity of this benefactor, but the writer has examined at
Somerset House the will of a London master weaver called
Zachariah Agace, who died in 1778. It contains no mention of
anyone of the name of Lawrence, but in addition to the ample
provision made for his widow, there is a special legacy of £600
for her charitable fund for the families of dissenting ministers.
Whether Zachary Agaz and Zachariah Agace, who was presumably of Huguenot descent and of strong Noncomformist
views, were one and the same person, and whether Mrs. Agace
was in some way related to the Rev. William Lawrence and made
this provision for his grandchildren, are matters for conjecture.
What is certain is that Lawrence senior prevailed on his younger
daughter to let him use her legacy 'for the good of the family',
and to 'turn it to good account'. His idea of a profitable invest-
ment was to purchase, as Williams records, 'a little Museum
then exhibiting in the Strand, and consisting of natural curiosities,
stuffed birds etc. etc., and to these he added his son's paintings,
such as his "Christ bearing the Cross".' This work of Lawrence's
adolescence was eight feet long and, though no doubt remarkable
as a curiosity, had little artistic merit, was an ambitious failure
and has not survived. 'The exhibition was', as we can well
imagine, 'daily a source of loss and vexation: it did not pay its
expenses; and he at last sold it for a mere trifle'. Not content with
throwing away his daughter's money in this ridiculous fashion,
'Mr. Lawrence', says Williams, 'induced his daughter, after this
loss, to refuse an offer of accompanying the family of Sir. A.
Crawford to Italy, and this accomplished young lady became the

companion and friend of the Countess of Lincoln, afterwards Duchess of Newcastle'.

On 13th September 1787 Lawrence was admitted as a student at the Royal Academy. Mr. Howard, who was secretary and Trustee of the institution at the time of Lawrence's death, informed Williams that 'his proficiency in drawing even at that time, was such as to leave all his competitors in the antique school far behind him. His personal attractions were as remarkable as his talent: altogether he excited a great sensation, and seemed, to the admiring students, as nothing less than a young Raphael suddenly dropped among them. He was very handsome; and his chestnut locks flowing on his shoulders, gave him a romantic appearance'. Lawrence does not seem to have spent very much time at the Royal Academy School—no doubt attendance at the classes interfered with his earnings—but his connection with it enabled him to form several valuable friendships. Among the youths of his own age with whom he now became intimate were the elder Robert Smirke, Samuel Lysons, subsequently a well-known antiquary, and his brother, Daniel Lysons, and Richard Westall, who became an R.A., together with Lawrence, in 1794.

Probably before the end of 1787 Lawrence gave up the expensive suite in Leicester Square and established himself in apartments at 41 Jermyn Street, immediately opposite St. James's Church and overlooking the churchyard. His parents, meanwhile, were installed nearby in rooms in Duke Street. The house in Alfred Street, Bath, was given up and Mrs. Lawrence came up to London to rejoin her husband. This enabled the young painter to take his meals with his mother, an arrangement which must have been of considerable advantage to his health and comfort. His Jermyn Street studio was now thronged with fashionable clients, ranging from celebrities like John Philip Kemble to reigning beauties of the town. Young Lawrence was already being talked about in the numerically small world which formed the two 'court circles' —that of George III and the rival circle surrounding the Prince of Wales—which between them constituted Society with a capital S. The Victorian phrase 'the upper ten thousand' accurately described the aristocracy and those with whom it associated in the closing decades of the Georgian era. This 'ten thousand', many of whom were linked by ties of kindred and relationship, all knew each other at least by sight and by name, and owing to their constant opportunities for social intercourse, gossip soon went the rounds and it was thus easily possible for some new actress, writer or portrait painter quickly to become 'the talk of the town'.

V

ROYAL PATRONAGE

WHEN Lawrence took up his quarters at 41 Jermyn Street he was able, for the first time in his life, to carry on his professional activities under a roof of his own and without parental supervision. The address was a good one, for the main part of the house was occupied by a fashionable milliner. The only drawback from Lawrence's standpoint was that the windows of his painting room overlooked the graveyard of St. James's Church, thus reminding his fair models of 'Time's wingèd chariot' and the impermanence of youth and beauty. At this period Lawrence still wore his beautiful chestnut hair in long curls which hung round his neck and was referred to by his numerous admirers as 'the wonderful boy'. It was not until 1789, by which time his door was daily thronged by a crowd which half-filled Jermyn Street, that he tied up his hair at the back and assumed a more adult appearance. To correct any impression of effeminacy which this may convey, it is advisable to remind the reader of Lawrence's prowess in all manly pursuits and his out-standing brilliance as a pugilist. The friend with whom he used to spar in the fields outside Bath is believed to have been none other than John Jackson, the famous 'Gentleman Jackson' who after becoming champion of England in 1795, set up a school of boxing in Bond Street and had Byron among his pupils. Lawrence had evidently kept in touch with his boyhood friend, for when Richard Payne Knight, the famous collector, con-noisseur and patron of the arts, commissioned him to paint an historical picture of 'Homer Reciting his Poems to the Greeks', he used Jackson as the model for the young victor in the foot race, in the foreground of the composition. Jackson's figure was large, but according to Williams 'his joints were small and knit in the manner which is copied so inimitably in many of the statues and paintings of Michael Angelo'. In 1796 Lawrence again used Jackson for his enormous picture, 'Satan Calling his Legions'.

To the Academy Exhibition of 1788 Lawrence sent six portraits, of which five were in crayons, but the sixth, No. 147, 'Portrait of a Gentleman' (Mr. Darsey), was his first commission for a portrait in oils. Lawrence, when he first came to London, had made the acquaintance of the engraver James Heath, later A.R.A., and, according to Heath, he reproached his friend for attempting nothing more ambitious than pastel portraits at five guineas each. Lawrence thereupon painted a study of himself in oils which he showed to Heath and on Heath's recommendation Mr. Darsey sat for the portrait exhibited in 1788. One critic said of it: 'This is a production in oils of a very young man whose crayon pictures we have mentioned (see 60 and 112). It is so very harmoniously coloured, that we confess ourselves at a loss whose style to recommend the artist to pursue.' The critic of the *St. James's Chronicle* described it as an 'attempt in oil possessing considerable point, but not comparable to his crayons, to which we would advise this young gentleman to adhere'.

Some days after the opening of the Exhibition a paragraph appeared in some of the papers which must have caused the young painter much embarrassment and mortification, all the more so as his well-meaning but irrepressible father was responsible for it. It ran as follows: 'Twenty guineas to one was publicly offered at the Royal Exhibition on Tuesday and Wednesday last, by an eminent miniature painter, that the portrait marked 147 was not painted by the artist mentioned in the catalogue. But his crayon paintings of the Transfiguration, the Descent from the Cross, Saul receiving Sight and the Aurora, with his heads from Milton (all for sale) are really more surprising; for they were painted at thirteen and fourteen years of age at the late Hon. Mr. Hamilton's at Bath, and now make a part of the Exhibition which adjoins to the above, being at the right door.' Mention has been made of Lawrence senior's purchase of a small museum of curiosities with his daughter Anne's legacy. The paragraph appears to be intended as a combined puff for his son's first portrait in oils and advertisement of this museum which was housed next door to the Academy. Throughout his singularly unsuccessful business career Lawrence senior had been a great believer in publicity. The following advertisement, written in his usual florid style, indicates both the nature of the exhibition and the character and mentality of the showman in charge of it.

'It is truly just to pay becoming tribute to merit. There is now added to the elegant exhibition adjoining Somerset House, in the Strand (consisting of Automaton Figures which move in a great variety of descriptions, by clockwork, with the Diamond Beetle, scarce and valuable paintings, Needlework, Shells, Flies, Water Fall etc., etc., so universally admired), some of the most beautiful and striking Pencil and Chalk Drawings in the Kingdom, by Mr. Lawrence, of Bath, now at 41 Jermyn Street.' It was indeed fortunate that the rising young Jermyn Street portrait painter was not a snob, otherwise it might have enraged him to have examples of his art exhibited with Diamond Beetles and Automaton Figures. The father, who seems to have regarded his son's productions as his own, is said to have gone about selling Lawrence's beautiful crayon drawings 'even at the low price of half a guinea'. The anonymous biographer adds that 'Sir Thomas, latterly bought up those drawings with great eagerness, whenever he could trace them. Let not pride conceal these facts. Sir Thomas, though he sometimes confidentially accounted for his straitened circumstances through life, by referring to his early burdens, never regretted them or murmured at the reminiscence'.

On 2nd August 1788 Gainsborough died at his house in Pall Mall, and in December of the same year Sir Joshua gave his famous address on the dead painter before a gathering of the Royal Academy, the delivery of which, according to William Seward, was 'interrupted by his tears'.

The Academy exhibition of 1789, to which Lawrence sent thirteen oil paintings and pastel studies, immediately established him as the coming portrait painter who overshadowed all his rivals, including the Prince of Wales's protégé, Hoppner. In popular favour, he even challenged the President himself, and one keen observer hailed him as 'the Sir Joshua of futurity not far off'. All London was talking about him and, as Williams puts it, 'business flowed in upon him in an extraordinary degree; and his industry and application, for his age, were exemplary'. The portraits which, according to Mr. Whitley, attracted most attention were the pastel studies of the Duke of York and Mrs. Hamilton; and the paintings of Lady Cremorne, William Linley (the younger brother of Mrs. Sheridan), Mr. Lewis and Miss Lennox. 'The portrait of William Linley (171) is probably,' says Whitley, 'the admirable portrait of him as a schoolboy with long curling hair, now hanging in the Dulwich Gallery.'

One impressive result of his success was the arrival, in September 1789, of his first Royal command. The letter conveying this signal honour is quoted by Layard and runs as follows.

'SIR,—I am commanded by Her Majesty to desire you will come down to Windsor and bring your painting apparatus with you.

Her Majesty wishes you to come down on Sunday next the 27 inst. to be ready for Her to sit to you on Monday morning.

She likewise desires you will bring some of your pictures with you in crayon and in oil.—I am, Sir, your most obedient, humble Servant,

        H. COMPTON.

Friday Noon.—Bring some primed cloths with you. When you arrive, enquire for me at the Queen's Lodge.

Mr. Lawrence.

Portrait Painter. Jermyn Street. St. James's. Near St. James's Church.'

Lawrence's perfect self-possession and polished manners have already been remarked on. An occasion which would have made many young men of twenty extremely shy and nervous seems to have caused him no embarrassment whatever. We hear of the King 'quizzing' him for flirting with Mrs. Papendieck, the wife of his German musician, and he quickly made himself popular with the Royal children. Princess Amelia was then in her seventh year, and Williams relates that 'on one occasion the child ran to her father telling him in grief, that she was sure that

Mr. Lawrence did not like her as much as her sisters, since he had given each of them two drawings, and only one to her. The child's sorrow prevented the progress of the portrait for that day, and until the presents were equalised'.

For his portraits of the Queen and the Princess Amelia, which were exhibited at the Academy the following year, Lawrence was paid sixty and fifteen guineas respectively. By some means, not known, the portrait of the Princess Amelia, many years later, passed into the hands of a dealer near Soho Square. When Sir Thomas, as he then was, got to hear of this he immediately bought it and it formed part of his property at the time of his death.

Towards the end of 1789 Sir Joshua lost the sight of his left eye, and his closing years were clouded by this calamity, although he was able to complete his portrait of the popular actress, Mrs. Billington, which was exhibited in the Academy the following year.

On 13th April 1790 Lawrence came of age and under the will of Mr. Zachary Agaz (or Zachariah Agace) became entitled, as his sister had been, to the sum of £200. According to Williams, 'he proposed to his father that he (the father) should take a house large enough to accomodate his friend young Westall, and a servant boy, and to fit up a room for painting, Mr. Westall having commenced certain paintings for Alderman Boydell's publications'. With his unerring instinct for a bad bargain, Lawrence senior took a house, 57 Greek Street, Soho, which had a most unsavoury reputation. It had been occupied by a surgeon who was suspected of malpractices similar to those of which the patrons of the body-snatchers Burke and Hare were to be accused half a century later. It had even been raided by the neighbours who had taken up the floors and searched the sewers in quest of hidden skeletons. The rent was £100 per annum, including taxes, which seems ample for a medium-sized house in a central but no longer fashionable neighbourhood.

When his son, who had for so long been a source of profit to himself, attained his legal majority, Lawrence senior seems to have taken steps to secure a share of his future earnings by inducing him to 'sign a sort of bond in favour of himself and family'. Williams, who records this, is shocked into observing that 'this was scarcely kind towards a son who had always been so dutiful, confiding and generous, and whose nature was bountiful to prodigality'. Although, apart from the museum, we have no details of the elder Lawrence's financial transactions during his closing years, his capacity for incurring debts had been fully demonstrated by his two bankruptcies and there can be no doubt that his son always met his father's liabilities, however difficult he found it to meet his own. In after years, when he was still harassed by recurring financial crises, he confided to a friend: 'The truth is, I began life wrongly. I spent more money than I earned, and accumulated debts for which I have been paying heavy interest'. That his father was the immediate cause of Lawrence's wrong start in life there can be no question.

Williams, quoting from 'a family document now before me', which he says was drawn up from memory after a lapse of forty years, states that when his parents set up house in Greek Street Lawrence allowed them £300 a year, for which sum he was boarded and his man-servant provided with his dinner. In addition to this, the eldest son, the Rev. Andrew Lawrence, continued to allow his father £80 a year while his younger daughter, Anne, whose legacy he had squandered in the manner already related, generously allowed him an extra £170 per annum. She had at that time several young ladies of title under her care and must have been doing pretty well out of them. From the talents and industry of his children Lawrence senior thus derived what at that period was the comfortable income of £550 a year. Richard Westall, who, with his servant, lodged with the family, made a further contribution to the household expenses.

Soon after his parents were installed in Greek Street Lawrence gave up his rooms in Jermyn Street and took a set of rooms at 24 Old Bond Street, which enabled him to live in a manner more befitting the fashionable and much-sought-after portrait painter which he had now become. In spite of his very large earnings he was financially harassed, but he had, by this time, secured the friendship of the wealthy and generous John Julius Angerstein, who came to his assistance. The arrangement was that the painter should pay the whole of his professional receipts to Mr. Angerstein's bankers until the sum advanced was liquidated. In the meantime Joseph Farington, R.A., the famous diarist and one of Lawrence's most valued friends, was authorised to draw £20 every week for the young man's household expenses, and no doubt did his best to teach him businesslike habits and prevent him wasting his money. This good action on Farington's part seems to have been the origin of Cunningham's extraordinary story that he acted as Lawrence's 'secretary' and was paid £20 a week for doing so. Farington, although his talents as a landscape painter were not outstanding, was an excellent business man and an important figure behind the scenes in Royal Academy politics. He was a man of good family and comfortably off. When he first interested himself in Lawrence's tangled affairs he was forty-three years old. Although Northcote, after referring to his great influence among the Academicians, declared that he 'cared nothing at all about pictures and his great passion was the love of power', Lawrence had every reason to be grateful to this influential friend and adviser whose 'watchful care and instant and unselfish devotion' never failed him. 'Once for all,' says Layard, 'it may be admitted as probable that, lacking his sound judgment and constant help, Lawrence would never have been able to maintain the struggle against his continuous pecuniary embarrassments. Beginning badly by anticipating his income in favour of his family, to the day of his death he was never clear of creditors, and his case would indeed have been desperate deprived of this level-headed friend, who spent himself in relieving him as far as was possible from his pecuniary anxieties.'

The rivalry and antagonism between Lawrence and Hoppner began when, at the Academy of 1789, the latter painter, who was eleven years older than Lawrence, found himself overshadowed by, and his work unfavourably compared with, that of the younger man. The St. James's Chronicle, after dismissing one of Hoppner's portraits as ungraceful and vulgar, added that 'this artist some years ago seemed an attentive pupil of Sir Joshua; but that character is resigned to young Lawrence'. Another writer, in the same

WILLIAM COWPER

This drawing, which is either a copy of the one exhibited in the Royal Academy in 1795 or a hitherto unknown variant of it, was presented to the Hon. John Fremantle by his brother-in-law, Lord FitzHarris, on the dispersal of the contents of Hurn Court.

RICHARD PAYNE KNIGHT

*This portrait of the famous collector, connoisseur and dilletante was exhibited at
the Royal Academy in* 1794. *It is reproduced by courtesy of the owner,
C. A. Boughton Knight, Esq.*

paper, in referring to Lawrence's portrait of Miss Lennox, said that it might 'easily be mistaken for one of the President's best heads'. These comments must have been particularly galling to a man who for some time past had enjoyed almost a monopoly of the business of portraying fashionable beauties, thanks to the fact that the young Prince of Wales, the *arbiter elegantiarum* of the smart world, was his generous patron. In 1790 Lawrence struck another blow to Hoppner's prestige and self-esteem by exhibiting his whole-length portrait of the immensely popular actress, Miss Elizabeth Farren, afterwards the Countess of Derby, which immediately became the picture of the year and still ranks as one of his acknowledged masterpieces. In 1911 it was acquired by Mr. Pierpont Morgan for a large sum, rumoured to be £43,000. Its companion on the walls of Somerset House was Sir Joshua's portrait of another well-known actress, Mrs. Billington, the last important work he was destined to complete. Whitley relates that Reynolds at the private view, looking at the two portraits hanging near together, 'congratulated his youthful rival in the most generous terms and predicted a great future for him. "In you, Sir," he said, "the world will expect to see accomplished what I have failed to achieve"'.

The judgment of the critics was for the most part favourable to the point of enthusiasm. The *Public Advertiser*, for example, said that 'such a portrait as that of Miss Farren might excite envy in the mind of the finest artist that ever existed. We have seen a variety of portraits of Miss Farren, but we never before saw her mind and character upon canvas. It is completely Miss Farren—arch and careless, spirited and engaging'. The critic of the *English Chronicle* declared that the best work in the Exhibition was that of Lawrence, whose portrait of Miss Farren was far superior to Sir Joshua's Mrs. Billington in spirit, colour and expression. 'He is a youth of extraordinary genius,' he adds, 'who has not only outstripped all junior artists but, in portrait-painting, may at this moment stand in competition with the President himself. The Queen of this young artist is an admirable portrait, and, independent of the strong likeness, has a multitude of beauties. Criticism could scarcely point out a fault in this picture. Her Majesty's nose, indeed, appears sore from taking snuff, but that is not the fault of the painter'.

Some critics of the Farren portrait took exception to the fact that although the lady appeared in a midsummer landscape she was dressed in a white winter coat, of the kind then called a 'John' coat, and carried in her hand a large fur muff. Lawrence expressed his annoyance at these carping criticisms to Edmund Burke and thus called forth from him the oft-quoted remark: 'Never mind what little critics say, for painters' proprieties are always best.' Although the portrait was engraved and had an enormous sale, which must have carried Miss Farren's beautiful features into drawing-rooms all over the country, various circumstances connected with it caused annoyance to the lady herself. In the first place, owing to a mistake in the catalogue, the picture was labelled 'Portrait of an Actress', instead of 'Portrait of a Lady', as Lawrence had directed. In the Georgian era the word 'actress', if unqualified by the adjective 'famous' or 'celebrated', had almost its modern police court connotation, and Lawrence was publicly accused of having committed an error of taste in using it. He hastily wrote Miss Farren a long letter of apology and explanation and when the catalogue was reprinted the picture was described as 'Portrait of a Celebrated Actress', in the hope of averting her displeasure. There seems to have been an understanding that the wealthy Earl of Derby, who was regarded as the prospective purchaser of the picture although he had not commissioned it, should be asked to pay the admittedly high fee of a hundred guineas. In a letter to Dr. Kent, quoted below, Lawrence senior mentions this as the agreed figure, but Miss Farren had other views. Layard quotes a waspish note in which she says: 'I must own that [I] never was more astonished in my life than on reading your letter this morning. You must have forgot that the last time I had the honour of sitting to you, you told me that the price of my portrait would be *sixty guineas*, and I then informed you that Lord Derby meant to be the purchaser.' Lawrence evidently stuck to his guns, for after the portrait had remained on his hands for two years the infatuated peer paid over the price demanded. After the portrait had been duly delivered to Lord Derby, Miss Farren, perhaps still resenting the fact that she lost the argument about its price, wrote expressing the dissatisfaction of her friends with certain of its details. The sprightly note, quoted by Layard, in which she pretends to convey 'the owner's' ideas, speaks for itself.

'Mr. Lawrence, you will think me the most troublesome of all human beings, but indeed it is not my own fault; they tease me to death about the picture and insist upon my writing to you.

One says it is so thin in the figure, that you might blow it away—another that it looks broke off in the middle: in short, you must make it a little *fatter*, at all events, diminish the *bend* you are so attached to, even if it makes the picture look ill; for the owner of it is quite distressed about it at present. I am shocked to teaze you, and dare say you wish me and the portrait in the fire—but as it was impossible to appease the cries of my friends, I must beg you to excuse me.'

Whether the over-worked painter paid any attention to this effusion is not known.

A good idea of how Lawrence senior regarded his son's success, and how scrupulous he was in using his son's money to pay debts which he himself had incurred, can be gathered from a series of four letters written by him to Dr. Kent at various dates in the spring and summer of 1790. It is characteristic, but perhaps excusable, in view of the number of children born to him, that Lawrence senior could not remember the date of his son's birth.

'Thomas Lawrence, Senior, to the Rev. Dr. Kent.
Rev. Dear Sir,—Although I begin with hoping most sincerely that you are well and happy, I wish to inform you that next Wednesday will be a very flattering day to my youngest son, from the opening of the Royal Exhibition to which Their Majesties mean to go to-morrow, and will see of his portraits of the Queen, of the Princess Amelia, the sons of Lord Ducie Moreton, sons and daughter of Lord George Cavendish, son and daughter of the Earl of Abercorne, Gens. Patterson, a Mr. Laskar in the East India Service, the celebrated Mrs. Carter, Mr. Locke,

Andrew Lawrence (the Rev. Andrew Lawrence, his brother) and Miss Farren, for which last he is to receive one hundred guineas, and he has now with the most general approbation raised his price to 20, 40, and fourscore guineas, with plenty of business to go on at these prices, being the highest ever known in this or any other kingdom at his age, who will be one and twenty the 6th May, on which day would you be pleased to have your money lodged with Messrs. Hoare, or remitted to you (with very grateful thanks!) by the post.

My son will continue in Jermyn Street, in the mean time we have taken an excellent house and a cheap at 100 guineas a year, taxes included, within two doors of Soho Square, in Greek Street, and have let a small part of it to a single gentleman at 60 guineas, and mean to furnish the remainder, neat and plain, as we conveniently can, and have always every convenience for your reception, when you shall be pleased to honour with your company (and for as long a time as you please) which I hope will take place in 3 weeks at farthest. I have other franks directed to you, viz for the 26th, the 30th, and May 6th, and will therefore close my present account with assuring you how very much

I am, ever your's
With the most perfect respect and gratitude
T. LAWRENCE.

Wife and children always join their best wishes and readiest services.'

'REV. DEAR SIR,—I received the favour of yours and am truly and very much concerned for your being so much troubled and distressed, and most sincerely wish a speedy end to all of them and a succession of blessed peace and perfect happiness.

I wished for your company yesterday at the Chapel of the Foundling Hospital, where the devotion, preaching and singing, work altogether for the benefit of the hearer, and leave the mind in a state of tranquillity and humble resignation to the divine will. Wednesday, will most assuredly become a day of triumph to our youngest son; for then, the Exhibition opens, but to-morrow is the public dinner, which will be held in the grandroom, where

Sir Joshua will sit at the head of the table, at his right hand the Prince of Wales, and on his left the Primate and Metropolitan of all England, and to which treat a much greater number are invited than was before ever known with only three excuses returned.

Their Majesties and the Princesses were there on Friday and expressed the highest degree of satisfaction, in short it is spoke of as the best.

All my son's pictures were received, being twelve in number, while many others were rejected for want of room.

I am informed that Sir Joshua dwelt in contemplation of the merits of one of his pieces for upwards of 20 minutes, and when it was told him that another artist endeavoured to copy of him in his manner, his reply was "They may all study after him, but in his opinion they would never overtake him".

It is the united wish of this family, to be favoured with your company, and in very deed I most sincerely hope it would prove a pleasing relaxation to all your care, which we, in our little way, but accompanied with our very best endeavours, would alleviate if we would not remove. Pray write more fully for so you have now promised.

I told you what wonders the Haunted Tower was like to enact: it is advertised for the four and fiftieth time.

The Nation is like to continue at peace, and the stocks continue to rise.

No payment for the Queen or Princess as yet, but his business increases most rapidly at 20 guineas a head, which is a greater price than was ever charged by Sir Godfrey Kneller—surprising at his age, but as Hamlet says, something too much of this.

Lady Lincoln for change of air is come to Sunning Hill near Windsor, and Lucy with her, who we expect soon in town for a short time, and Tom has given Nanny an invitation at his expense to give her the meeting, who pleads attention to duty an excuse. My son will inclose agreeably to your's, with the most grateful acknowledgments, on the 6th of May, and I am,

Ever so, Rev. Dear Sir,
THOS. LAWRENCE.'

26th April 1790.

'REV. DEAR SIR,—Words are wanting to express my sense of gratitude to Heaven and to the world, for the great name my son has so wonderfully acquired from the opening of the exhibition. That you may form a judgment of my reason for being thus thankful, I herewith present you with extracts from different papers of yesterday that I have seen. N.B. It opened on Wednesday.

The Diary says:

"Mr. Lawrence, young as he is, treads close already on the kibe of the most eminent of the profession. Such a head as that of Mr. Locke, painted as we understand at a single sitting, and such a portrait as Miss Farren's, might create envy in the mind of the first artist that ever existed.

We have seen a great variety of pictures of Miss Farren: but we never saw before her mind and character upon canvas. It is completely Elizabeth Farren, arch, careless, spirited, elegant and engaging."

The *Oracle*, after speaking of Sir Joshua's performances, proceeds:—

"If any picture from another pencil can do thus, it is the claim, we say this with astonishment!—of young Lawrence. For this delightful whole length of Miss Farren, which for winning ease, for expressive attitude, for the mind's eye, and that peculiar style of feature, so difficult to catch, of sweetness without insanity and spirit without distortion, can never be exceeded."

The Morning Herald:

"The portrait of Miss Farren, by Mr. Lawrence, possesses great merit, and is extremely characteristic. The background is very fine."

The *Morning Chronicle*, after speaking of Sir Joshua, says of Lawrence:

"The picture of Her Majesty, No. 100, is admirable in point of likeness. The drapery is well disposed, but the landscape will merit of improvement. The full length of Miss Farren, is an excellent production: he hath given all the richness and fascination of the original with exquisite effect."

"Of the other portraits, that of his brother the clergyman is by far the best. This picture, with respect to likeness and colouring is, we had almost said, unrivalled."

The *Gazetteer*,—"Mr. Lawrence hath this year fulfilled all the promises which he gave a year ago. We cannot speak with sufficient commendations of the beauties he hath exhibited. Miss Farren is one of the most delightful portraits we ever saw. The Queen is a most perfect likeness, and the small angel is a coloured jewel."

The *World*—"The best portraits in oil, are Mr. Cholmondley, Lord Malmesbury's daughter, Mr. Tomkins, Miss Farren, the Queen, little Lord Paisley, the Angel, and his Sisters head, the Princess Amelia, and No 268, by Mr. Lawrence." And again in the same paper—"Lawrence deserves the greatest encomiums for his portraits. That of the Queen by this artist, is certainly a performance of which Vandyke himself would have been proud."

London Evening—"Lawrence hath improved since last year, astonishingly! His portrait of Miss Farren yields to none in the room—That of the Queen has already been mentioned by the public; and these, with the other portraits, speak him one of the most promising geniuses of the age. That Lawrence bids fair to be the first portrait painter, in the kingdom, is not saying too much."

The *Times* to-day, (with which I will conclude) says of the portraits,—"Those of the Queen by Lawrence and Russell, and that of Miss Farren likewise, by Lawrence, appear to be the best."

You will perceive by the catalogue the great number of artists, and then judge of the grateful surprise of

Rev. Dear Sir, your most devoted Servant,

THOS. LAWRENCE.

30th April 1790.'

'REV. DEAR SIR,—This morning met B.D. Esqre. He has not been wanting in his polite attention towards us, consequently communicating your good wishes.

We went together to the Royal Exhibition, where I communicated to him a little of my intelligence extraordinary, and he in return uttered his thoughts respecting when the town would have occasion to mourn his absence, which would not be these 4 or 5 days, and that he would call at 57, Greek Street, in the intermediate space.

He was going to the habitation of the Prime Minister, where I, having no pretensions, we on that account agreed to bid farewell.

I cannot sufficiently express my satisfaction, and you believe me, at the great name my son has so deservedly acquired: he is, in a manner, become the theme of every applauding tongue. But more of this when I shall have the grateful pleasure of waiting upon you where your last favour was addressed, and where I hope you will sleep with the most pleasing composure, and attended with the most grateful welcome by all.

I am, Rev. Dear Sir, ever yours
T. LAWRENCE.

4th June 1790.
P.S. We have no encouragement to return for any impertinent enquiries that may be made. I will (may I not?) hope for the favor of seeing you very suddenly.

Tom is going this day, to drink the health of his Majesty, when Sir Joshua will be the toast maker.
The Rev. Dr. Kent. Whisley. Devizes. Wilts.'

The 'B.D.' referred to in the last letter, is believed to refer to Bernard Dickenson, of Bowden Park, near Devizes, who was intimately acquainted with both Dr. Kent and Lawrence senior.

The King showed his high appreciation of the Queen's portrait and his interest in the young genius who had painted it by a not very tactful suggestion to the President of the Royal Academy, whom he had always treated with a lack of civility almost amounting to insult, that Lawrence should be elected an A.R.A. According to a statement which appeared in the *Public Advertiser*, when the Academicians met on 1st November 1790, 'Sir Joshua informed them that His Majesty had spoken in very warm terms, in favour of Mr. Lawrence whose early display of genius has been so much admired, declaring that it was the Royal desire that the Academy should afford its countenance to such distinguished talents, and enrol the artist as soon as opportunity occurred among its highest members'.

There was considerable republican, or at least anti-monarchical, feeling in London in the year after the fall of the Bastille and freeborn Englishmen were in no mood to put up with the King's attempt to interfere with their private concerns. The Academicians ignored the Royal message and proceeded to elect Francis Wheatley, who had been exhibiting at the Royal Academy for the past ten years and was a man of forty-four. Wheatley received sixteen votes, Beechey four, Lawrence three, and Gainsborough Dupont one. In recording this result the *Gazetteer* observed: 'The fate of the King's request—the first of its kind—is truly honourable to the Academy, as it manifests the proper independence of the National School. This election is by no means an imputation on young Lawrence whose merits are of the highest order and will soon place him in the most elevated ranks of the English masters. But in the present day, when subserviency to Kings is made the topic of courtly praise, it raises the Academy justly high in the mind of every manly man'.

Lawrence was elected A.R.A. on 10th November 1791, when he was twenty-two, entirely on his merits. His 'official' biographer, Williams, writing in 1831, made the erroneous statement that Lawrence's election was only made possible by the suspension or contravention of a law, which the King himself had sanctioned, that was 'imperative against the admission of any Associate under the age of twenty-four'. Cunningham added the misstatement that 'he was elected a supplemental Associate; a sort of honour which no one has enjoyed either before or since'. Mr. W. T. Whitley, who searched the records at Burlington House, discovered that no 'supplemental Associate' of the Royal Academy has ever existed and that the law referred to by Williams was not passed until 2nd December 1796, five years after Lawrence's admission. The entry in the minutes on that date is decisive. 'Resolved. That no artist shall be eligible to be an Associate who is not twenty-four years of age.' The legend that Lawrence's early election was due to royal interference rather than 'to his

own talents and good conduct' was given wide publicity in a
lampoon by Peter Pindar entitled 'The Rights of Kings', of
which the following is a typical verse.

> Refuse a monarch's mighty orders!
> It smells of treason—on rebellion borders.
> 's death, Sirs! it was the Queen's fond wish as well
> That Master Lawrence should come in!
> Against a Queen so gentle, to rebel,
> This is another crying sin!

To be the subject of a lampoon by Peter Pindar (John Wolcot),
like being caricatured in *Punch* in a later age, at least afforded the
victim the satisfaction of knowing that he had become a public
figure and was something of a celebrity. It is, therefore, unlikely
that Lawrence took any offence.

Early in the year 1792 *The Morning Herald* published the melancholy news that Sir Joshua Reynolds was dying. The end came
at eight o'clock on the evening of 23rd February, when the
President was in his sixty-ninth year. He was buried in St.
Paul's Cathedral, at his own desire, and, as Fanny Burney records,
'nothing was spared, either in thought or expense, that could
render the last honours splendid and grateful'. His last public
appearance had been in the summer of 1791, at the dinner held
annually on the king's birthday when the Royal Academicians
entertained the exhibiting artists of the year. According to the
Public Advertiser, 'the guests numbered between two and three
hundred. James Boswell, Esq., was invited as a friend of the arts
and one whose works, though not actually exhibited at Somerset
House, have been lately exhibited to the world with general
applause. He was placed on the right hand of Sir Joshua Reynolds,
the President, who filled the chair with a most convivial glee,
and on whose left hand sat Sir William Chambers, between
whom and the worthy President it was evident that all misunder-
standings were forgotten'. Lawrence was, presumably, one of the
guests at this banquet which was held in the Freemasons' Tavern.
On 3rd March 1792, with his brother associates, he was one of

the mourners who followed the remains of his admired master and generous patron to St. Paul's Cathedral.

George III's ignorance of art, poor taste and lack of judgment showed itself not only in his obsession with the merits of Benjamin West, on whom he showered commissions, but even more in his ostentatious refusal to extend his patronage to one of the foremost men of genius in his reign. Sir Joshua Reynolds had been appointed Court Painter in 1784 at the reduced salary of £50, which carried with it the obligation to paint whole lengths of their Majesties for £50, instead of £200 which he received from every other sitter. Whether his dissatisfaction at the financial rewards of his post, which he had expressed in a letter to the Duke of Rutland, had been brought to the King's notice, and given offence, or whether the King merely disliked him on personal grounds and failed to recognise his merits as a painter, is not clear. Whatever may have been the reason for the omission, the fact remains that neither the King nor the Queen ever gave Reynolds a single order, and the only time he painted them was at his own request and at his own expense. Almost before the breath was out of the old President's body, indeed with a haste which seems almost indecent, Lawrence received the notification that he was to succeed Sir Joshua as Painter in Ordinary to His Majesty. Williams quotes the official letter.

'Lord Chamberlain's Office.

26th February 1792

Sir, I lose no time in acquainting you that I have appointed you to be Painter in Ordinary to His Majesty in room of Sir Joshua Reynolds, deceased; and you are requested to attend this office on Thursday next, at two o'clock, to be sworn in.

I am, Sir,

Your obedient Servant,

Salisbury.

Mr. Lawrence. Bond St.'

No time indeed was lost, as Reynolds had only been dead three days. Another appointment, rendered vacant by the death of

Sir Joshua, to which Lawrence succeeded, was that of Painter to the Dilettanti Society. This distinguished Society had been founded in 1734 by a number of noblemen who had made the Grand Tour and were desirous of encouraging a taste for the arts in Great Britain. One of its 'fixed and primary' rules was that 'no person was admissible as a member who had not crossed the Alps'. The fact that the rule was waived in Lawrence's favour was, like the appointment itself, an honour which any painter, however eminent, would consider highly flattering. Williams says that Sir Joseph Banks, when made president of the society, had proposed that the affluent William Hamilton, with whom Lawrence was then on intimate terms, should receive the distinction and that Hamilton replied: 'Portrait-painter I am none; my friend Lawrence, however, is the most proper person you can select; his talents are of the highest order and, though young, he will do honour to your appointment.' Another supporter of Lawrence was the influential Richard Payne Knight, who, some years before, had commissioned him to paint the historical picture, now at Downton Castle, of which mention has been made. Knight seems to have been conscious of an obligation to Lawrence senior and his family for helping him in his election campaign of 1784, which resulted in his being returned to Parliament as Member for Ludlow, and on that account was the more assiduous in backing his son. As Ludlow is near Tenbury, it is probable that Lucy Lawrence and her husband were on a visit to the Rev. William Read, Lucy's brother, with whom she had remained on friendly terms, while the election was being fought. If this was the case, the Read influence, if exerted on his behalf, must have been of considerable help to Knight.

Sir Joshua's successor as President of the Royal Academy was the King's favourite, the American-born historical painter Benjamin West, who was elected almost unanimously. The exhibition of 1792 was below the standard of recent years. Prince Hoare, referring to it, said that 'the death of Reynolds seemed to diffuse a momentary torpor over the arts, and the Exhibition wore a cold and lifeless hue'. Lawrence, who had sent eleven pictures to the previous exhibition, sent ten to this one.

The most important of them, from the standpoint of publicity, was a portrait of the King which hung next to a large historical painting by Benjamin West of Edward III crossing the river Soane, which the King had ordered for the Audience Chamber in Windsor Castle. The new 'Painter in Ordinary' had no excuse for complaining, like his illustrious predecessor, of any lack of orders and commissions from his Royal Master, or of any attempt to cut down his fees. In July 1792 he was commissioned to paint two elaborate whole-length portraits of the King and Queen to be despatched by our Ambassador, Lord Macartney, as a present to the Emperor of China. In September of this year he completed his whole-length portrait of the Duke of Rutland, for the Town Hall at Bristol, and finished, in the same month, another full-length portrait of the King, which the two Members for Coventry had ordered as a present to the Corporation. For the latter work, which was greatly admired, he received the then enormous fee of three hundred guineas. To the exhibition of 1793 Lawrence contributed nine portraits to Hoppner's one, and to that of 1794, when he was styled in the catalogue 'R.A. Elect', he contributed eight. His advancement to the rank of Royal Academician at the General Assembly held on 10th February of this year, when he defeated Hoppner by fifteen votes to thirteen, did not result in the improvement in Lawrence's position which he may have anticipated. In the eyes of the critics, who could not be expected to be interested in his full-length official portraits, he had done no work since 1790 to be compared with his masterly portrait of Miss Farren and he was no longer singled out as a rising genius and the destined successor of the great Sir Joshua. In the exhibition of 1795 the chief honours were carried off by Beechey and Hoppner, and the *Telegraph* spoke of the exhibition in general terms as 'the triumph of Beechey, Northcote and Hoppner'. *The Times* ignored the work of Lawrence altogether and in referring to the fact that Hoppner had been chosen to paint the first portrait of the new Princess of Wales remarked that his merit 'is so undoubted that his brother artists cannot reasonably complain of the preference given to him'. Although Hoppner had been the Prince's official painter for some years and could therefore naturally expect to be commissioned to paint the Princess, it is probable that Lawrence was not among the 'brother artists' who were entirely satisfied by the decision. The comparative neglect shown by the critics of the exhibition to the work of the new R.A., though mortifying to Lawrence, who had by this time taken the lease of a large house in Piccadilly, could hardly have upset him so much as an advertisement which appeared in several newspapers shortly after the Academy opened. Lawrence must immediately have recognised the authorship of this astonishing announcement which, in every line, is stamped with the character of his incorrigible old father.

'Royal Exhibition

Thomas Lawrence, R.A. Principal Painter in Ordinary to His Majesty, less indebted in years by many to those artists who have been so puffed off before and since the Exhibition was opened. Let any impartial judges examine and compare, with their background, the portraits numbered 75, 86, 168, 175 and 191, with a like number by any other artist, and then give his or their candid and fair judgment; notwithstanding the portraits of Lady Inchiquin and Lady Louisa Gordon are placed (which is surely not polite) out of the line of beauty and fashion.'

As the first of the portraits mentioned, No. 75, was that of Miss Moulton Barrett, later known as 'Pinkie', which at the sale of Lord Michelham's collection in 1926 fetched 74,000 guineas, posterity may think that, after all, the infatuated parent knew better than the critics, but to a man like Lawrence, so sensitive on the point of honour and so modest, courteous and diplomatic in his public dealings with the outside world, the advertisement must have caused an agony of mortification. Whitley, to whose researches we are indebted for this revealing episode, quotes the following letter which Lawrence at once addressed to the editor of the *Oracle*.

'Piccadilly, May 8th 1795.

SIR, It is to save myself from the interpretation of being a vain and contemptible coxcomb that I request you to insert my complete disavowal of an advertisement respecting my pictures which appeared in your paper of this morning.

To those who know me (and I hope to every candid mind) this may appear unnecessary—but yet, being exposed to such an imputation, I am under the painful necessity of declaring that instead of being the effort of malignity as it might naturally seem, it is the production of an injudicious friend, who with the best intentions towards me, and with qualities of the heart which I love and revere, is too apt by his officious kindness to lay both himself and me open to ridicule. But I think, Sir, you will not again be troubled with any correspondence on this unpleasant subject. The friend I allude to will no more give me cause to lament that imprudent zeal will render void every wish of affection, nor will he again heap on me the disgraceful effect of censure by such coarse and humiliating praise.

Your most obedient and most humble Servant
THOMAS LAWRENCE.'

We may gather from this that a considerable amount of plain speaking had taken place at 57 Greek Street.

VI

24 OLD BOND STREET

AN ENTRY in Farington's diary, dated 26th October 1793, tells us that Lawrence paid 200 guineas a year for his lodgings in Old Bond Street and that at that time his price for portraits was forty guineas for a three-quarter,[1] eighty guineas for a half-length and one-hundred and sixty guineas for a whole length. At these substantial fees he was kept busily engaged, so much so that it is difficult to understand how he could have found time and energy for the very full and, apparently, complicated social activities which his correspondence reveals. Croker said of him, after his death, that 'he had *at least* two distinct societies, the individuals of which never met the others'. Sir Max Beerbohm, in one of his essays, divides people into two categories, hosts and guests. Lawrence, throughout his life, was essentially a guest and, owing to his exceptional social accomplishments, always a welcome one. Unlike Reynolds, he very seldom entertained his friends to dinner parties, and though his generosity was proverbial he was the reverse of hospitable in the accepted sense. Williams explains this reasonably enough by his unremitting industry and observes that 'sometimes he would begin a head at ten in the morning, and finish it by four in the afternoon. Such exertions exhausted him, and he sought repose, not in conviviality, but in a change to milder occupations under his own roof, or sometimes in the *délassement* of an evening with a few private friends, who were selected with a taste that reflected credit on his discernment'. On the other hand, he frequently found opportunities of visiting his friends and patrons, William Lock of Norbury Park and John Julius Angerstein, who, in addition to

[1] This somewhat misleading term refers to the size of the head, not of the picture.

96

MOTHER OF SIR THOMAS LAWRENCE

From an engraving by F. C. Lewis, after the drawing made by Lawrence in 1797. In the Lawrence Collection, British Museum.

FATHER OF SIR THOMAS LAWRENCE

From an engraving by F. C. Lewis after the drawing by Lawrence in 1797, the year of his father's death. In the Lawrence Collection, British Museum.

his house in Pall Mall, had a country villa at Blackheath. In her book on *The Locks of Norbury*, the Duchess of Sermoneta says that 'Mr. Lock employed Lawrence to paint the portraits of practically all the members of his family. The artist spent a great deal of his time visiting his friends, passing from the Locks at Norbury to the Angersteins at Woodlands and on to the Boucherettes at Willingham in Lincolnshire. He loved them all and made countless sketches of them'. As early as 1791 we find an exchange of letters between Mr. Lock and the artist which indicates the former's generosity and his high appreciation of the young painter. Enclosing a substantial cheque, Lock writes: 'I beg your acceptance of the enclosed as an inadequate discharge of what I am indebted to you for my portrait.' Lawrence's reply was as follows:

'DEAR SIR,—I know not really what to say or how to thank you for your obliging letter. You have sent me a sum much beyond what my price was when the picture was bespoke, and greater than I now have. To return any part of it I fear would offend you. I must therefore consider it as a double payment.

I cannot but lament that I am deprived of the pleasure of feeling I have added, tho' in so small a degree, to the happiness of Mr. and Mrs. Lock without other reward. . . .'

John Julius Angerstein, whose important collection of old masters, housed in his private picture gallery in Pall Mall, was acquired by the State after his death, was a wealthy insurance broker, who was born in St. Petersburg in 1735 and brought to England as a youth by Andrew Thompson, of the firm of Thompson and Peters, Russia merchants, of whom, according to Farington, he was the natural son. He had a distinguished and profitable business career, played a part in the establishment of State lotteries and was noted for his integrity and public spirit. His son married a daughter of William Lock and his stepdaughter by his first wife, with whom Lawrence had a long and intimate friendship, became the wife of Ayscough Boucherette, a Lincolnshire landowner.

Lawrence painted his well-known portrait of Mr. Angerstein

and his first wife, which is now in the Louvre, in 1792; and, as has already been mentioned, Angerstein made him a considerable loan to tide him over some of his recurrent difficulties. In forming his collection of pictures Angerstein greatly relied on Lawrence's knowledge and usually unerring judgment. Another intimate friend of Lawrence's in his early days was the affluent and erudite William Hamilton, R.A., who had studied in Italy and was a friend of Antonio Zucchi, the husband of Angelica Kaufman. Hamilton, though an artificial and insipid painter, had important connections and considerable influence in art circles. His best-known portrait was that of Mrs. Siddons in the character of Isabella, with her son Henry as Biron's child, which was engraved by Caldwell. Until Hamilton's death, in 1801, Lawrence 'almost became one of the family', and Williams states that he and Lawrence passed happy evenings 'drawing from the antique statues at night, whilst Mrs. Hamilton read to them either poetry, history, or works of imagination'. Hamilton's friendship with Mrs. Siddons and her brother, John Philip Kemble, no doubt made a bond in common, and it is not unlikely that Lawrence renewed his friendship with the great actress and her brother through meeting them in Dean Street. Williams's assertion that Mr. Hamilton 'first introduced Mr. Lawrence to Mrs. Siddons and Mr. John Kemble, and laid the foundations of an intimacy which had a powerful influence upon the professional and private life and character of the artist', an assertion which has been repeated by later writers, is obviously mistaken. At Bath Lawrence had not only made portrait drawings of Mrs. Siddons, but one of his first known portraits in oils was that of her mother, Mrs. Kemble. It is probable that the two families knew each other intimately. In London, as both Lawrence and Mrs. Siddons were included in the Devonshire House circle, they had no need of any 'introduction' from the Hamiltons, and must have met in their house as old friends.

Although Lawrence had little taste or inclination for the frivolities of the fashionable world, there is no doubt that he maintained his footing in it and thus met many of his sitters on terms of social equality. Miss Croft mentions that during his Bath days he made a drawing of the celebrated Georgiana, Duchess of Devonshire, who took a fancy to the precocious boy, as did most of the great ladies who sat for him at that period, and, when he grew up and settled in London, 'always noticed and invited him to Devonshire House'. She adds primly that 'the morality of these parties, I fear, was grievously questionable; but in such society, consisting of all the men and women of taste and refinement and wit and learning of the age, his manners could not fail to improve, and attain the peculiar grace and urbanity which mark'd them through life'. It is perhaps to the influence of Devonshire House that we must ascribe the impression Lawrence made, as a young man, on Lavinia Forster, the daughter of the sculptor, Thomas Banks. 'His manners at that time', she wrote to Allan Cunningham after his death, 'appeared to me to be so frivolous, that I neither sought, nor supposed I obtained, his notice.' Undoubtedly his early social experiences combined with his physical attractions had made him something of a *petit maître* in the art of gallantry as it was understood in the period when he grew to manhood, though, from what we can divine of his character and temperament, it is doubtful whether his flirtations, before he met the Siddons girls, were ever serious. Layard says that the fact 'cannot be blinked that Lawrence was one of those men who, without dishonourable or cruel intentions, find their pleasure in hanging on to the skirts of this or that woman'. There seems little doubt that nothing of the enormous philoprogenitiveness of Lawrence senior was inherited by any of his three sons, none of whom married or left any known descendants. There is no reason to suppose that the handsome painter was impotent, like Count d'Orsay, or, as Greville suspected, that he was actively homosexual. There is much more likelihood that he suffered from that other form of sexual maladjustment, not uncommon at the beginning of the nineteenth century among men of heightened sensibility, to which Stendhal called attention in *Armance*. John Russell, in a brief note on Lawrence in *British Portrait Painters*, remarks that 'in his personal affairs he seems to have suffered from some malady of the will. So marked, in fact, is this that he seems to epitomise that *impuissance d'aimer* with which readers of *Armance* and *Adolphe* are familiar'.

Layard, after quoting a letter of heartfelt gratitude to Lawrence from the widow of the portrait painter, John Foldsone, for generously coming to her assistance, remarks that 'there were innumerable episodes of this kind in Lawrence's life, but fortunately all the distressed artists' wives whom he helped had not fascinating daughters'. In spite of his extreme discretion, his *amitié*, more of less *amoureuse*, for Miss Anne Foldsone got to the ears of the gossips and a paragraph appeared in the *Morning Herald* linking their names. 'A coalition of palettes, colours and brushes is talked of between Lawrence the portrait painter and Miss Foldsone the pretty enamellist. The affections of this female artist, though delicately pencilled in miniature, are expected soon to be matured at whole length; as from Lawrence's design, though but a hasty sketch, it is evident that he intends to place Hymen in the foreground.' There was not a word of truth in the rumour, which must have caused annoyance to both the victims of it. In a draft of a letter to someone unknown we find Lawrence taking strong exception to the scandalous stories put in circulation about him.

'Sir,—I have been informed by my friend Mr. Westall that some little time ago in a conversation which passed between you and him, you mentioned its having been told you by a friend that I had made proposals of marriage, or, in the common phrase, paid my addresses to Miss Anne Foldsone, which proposals had principally been rejected because a letter had been found belonging to me in which was enclosed a demand upon me for a gaming debt of a very considerable amount.

The first of these assertions tho' totally untrue has yet paid so elegant a compliment to my taste that I cannot in any other light than a friend of the lady be justly offended at it.

The latter falsehood, from my not mixing very much with the gay world, I consider an imputation on my character which it is ... incumbent upon me in my situation to maintain and defend....'

The tone of a letter from a Miss Anne Theresa Fleming of John Street, Bath, with its arch and ogling phrases, makes it clear enough that this style of amorous badinage had about as much connection with love as a set of drawing-room verses has with poetry. 'Fy on such promise breakers!' the lady writes. 'How can I depend on your safe delivery of the small pacquet that accompanies *this*, if you fail in the first favour I requested. *Once* more then I trust to your word, that you will with your own hand give to Miss Anne Foldsone the dictates of a sincere friend; if *you* can have interest enough to procure me her answer, I shall no longer doubt you have *some* influence over her and participate her affections.' In an idiom varying with the times young people at suburban tennis clubs habitually exchange this kind of badinage which 'doesn't mean a thing'. Whether Anne Foldsone secretly harboured deeper feelings for Lawrence than he was able to reciprocate we do not know. In any case, the lady soon after the incident married a Mr. Mee, who was said to have been unworthy of her. She became a successful miniature painter and outlived Lawrence by many years.

A friendship much more revealing of Lawrence's true character than his flirtations with pretty women had grown up between himself and William Cowper. Williams quotes the following letter from the poet, which shows the high regard which the old man entertained for the young artist.

'DEAR SIR,

As often as I have comforted myself with the hope of seeing you again soon, I have felt a sensible drawback upon that comfort, from the fear of a disappointment which, considering your profession and your just pre-eminence in it, appeared to me extremely probable.

Your letter, most welcome otherwise, gave me this most unwelcome information the moment I saw your name at the bottom of it. We all feel our loss, and much as I suppose you are beloved by my friend Rose, who has pretty acute discernment, I will venture to say he is not more mortified than myself. You do me justice, if you believe that my invitation did not consist of words merely: in truth, it was animated by a very sincere wish that it might prove acceptable to you: and once more I give you the same assurance that, at any time when you shall find it possible to allow yourself some relaxation in the country, if you will enjoy it here, you will confer a real favour on one whom you have already taught to set a high value on your company and friendship. I am too old to be very hasty in forming new connexions: but short as our acquaintance has been, to you I have the courage to say that my heart and my door will always be gladly open to you.

Mr. Rose is gone this morning to Newport, and does not know that I write. My cousin, whom you often heard me mention by the name of Johnny, is gone with him. Him Mr. Rose will introduce to you on his return to London; and though perhaps, being a little shy, he may not discover it in his manner when he has the pleasure to see you, he has already caught from me an ardent desire to know you.

Mrs. Unwin sends her compliments, and sincerely joins me in the wish that you will never hereafter consider us as strangers, or give us reason to think you one.

I remain, dear Sir, affectionately yours,

WILLIAM COWPER.

Weston, Oct. 18th 1793.

When will you come and give me a drawing of the old oak?
To Thomas Lawrence, Esq.
Old Bond Street. London.'

Shortly after the receipt of this letter Samuel Rose called on Lawrence, commissioned him to make a drawing of the poet and took him down to stay for a day or two at Weston Underwood while he did it. This portrait, probably the original sketch, was shown at the Royal Academy in 1795. It was engraved by Bartolozzi in 1799, and the print was distributed privately to Cowper's relations and friends. According to a correspondent to *The Times* (6th May 1930), Cowper's cousin Lady Hesketh, received her copy of "The incomparable Engraving from Lawrence's charming sketch" in January 1800. "Never did I see so perfect and so pleasing a likeness!" she wrote, "all who know him declare nothing was ever so like, and those who do not are sure it must be like him, as Soul and Genius and Goodness are visible in every feature!" Later on she came to take a less rapturous view of it. "Nothing can equal as a resemblance (in my opinion) the sketch done by Lawrence! If the painter had not lessened the softness of the resemblance by heightening the animation it would have been perfect".'

Two other engravings of the portrait appeared, one by Ridley in the *Monthly Mirror* for May 1801 and the other by Blake in the second volume of Hayley's *Life of Cowper*, in 1803. The original drawing was sent to Hayley by Lady Hesketh, for Blake's use, and after this it disappeared altogether. In 1950, a portrait of Cowper came into the possession of the Hon. John Fremantle, having been presented to him by his brother-in-law, Lord FitzHarris, on the dispersal of the contents of Hurn Court. The size of the pencil drawing, which has been photographed for this book for the first time with the owner's courteous permission, is $8\frac{1}{4} \times 6\frac{1}{2}$ inches. On the back of the frame is an old label bearing the following inscription:

'This drawing of William Cowper Esqre The celebrated Author of The Task and various other beautiful and instructive Poems was given me by my dear departed friend Lady Clarges the last time I saw her in the Spring of 1809—she had permitted me to have a *copy* taken of the drawing the year preceding, she now said that knowing how greatly I admired the superior talents and esteemed the admirable character of Mr. Cowper (tho I knew him only by his writings) she wished to give the *original* to a person whom she was pleased to think worthy of it—She was not certain whether the drawing was taken by Lawrence, or his Sister, but it is evident it is from a similar likeness the Engraving was taken which may be seen in the Quarto edition of Cowper's Poems, under which may be read T. Lawrence R. A. del^t

LOUISA MARGARET HARRIS.'

Mr. Kenneth Povey, of Liverpool University (the writer of the article in the *Times*, quoted above) who has examined the photograph of the drawing in Mr. Fremantle's possession, believes this to be a copy of the sketch from which Blake made his engraving. 'My reason for this opinion,' he writes, 'is that it omits much detail which Blake is unlikely to have invented, notably the inscription in Lawrence's hand. It was perfectly legitimate for Blake to engrave this inscription, but to copy it in a drawing would have been near to forging a signature.' It was Lawrence's practice, when taking a likeness, to make preliminary sketches before he was entirely satisfied. He did this when he was painting the Calmady Children, and gave the discarded first drawing to their mother. It is possible, therefore, that he made a preliminary drawing of Cowper, before completing the final one, to which he added his signature. Until the experts have pronounced judgment, all that can be said with certainty is that if Mr. Fremantle's drawing is not by Lawrence, the copyist must have had remarkable talent.

At the end of 1794 Lawrence, now a full R.A., felt sufficiently confident to move from his rooms in Old Bond Street to a house in Piccadilly facing the Green Park. Farington notes in his Diary that 'Fuseli told Lawrence a few days ago that he would probably become President of the Royal Academy—and ironically laughing while telling it to Marchant, said "He bore it"'. There is little doubt that he felt his new home was the proper setting for a man in the position he expected to occupy. Farington went with him on 21st December to look over the house, the landlord of which was the Hon. Mr. Butler. It had been built by Novosielski at a cost of £5,000 and the ground rent was ninety-three guineas a year. 'Lawrence,' says Farington, 'has a lease for 40 years from Christmas, with liberty to quit at the expiration of each successive 7 years'. The rent was 250 guineas and the taxes about £80 per annum. Farington adds that 'Dance says the House Lawrence has taken is ill built, and the offices below very bad and inconvenient'. He was not destined to occupy this house for more than three years, and the cost of furnishing it and the surrender of the lease must have involved him in a heavy loss.

VII

FAMILY AFFAIRS

THE HOPES and ambitions which encouraged the newly-fledged R.A., then twenty-six years of age, to establish himself in a large house in Piccadilly, were not destined to be realised. Although his royal portraits brought him in about £500 a year and the flow of other commissions continued unabated, his expenses must greatly have exceeded what, with careful management, would have been a satisfactory income, and there is little doubt that he got further and more deeply into debt. The critics, as has been mentioned, though they still for the most part treated his pictures with respect, had begun to show more interest in such rivals as Hoppner, Beechey and even Northcote, and his father's unfortunate advertisement, to which he had to reply from his new address, must have added to his secret mortification. Lawrence's attitude towards adverse criticism was the exact opposite of his father's, and nothing showed his good sense, his good manners and his essential modesty more clearly than the way in which he accepted it. In the previous year, like other painters much in the public eye, he had attracted the attention of John Williams, who, as 'Anthony Pasquin', had for some years enlivened the world of art by his witty, venomous but occasionally shrewd criticisms. He was no respecter of persons or reputations and his comments often verged on the libellous. Of Lawrence's 'Portrait of a Lady of Quality', exhibited in the Academy of 1794, he wrote that 'the face is chalky and sickly; the robe is so white and unencumbered by shadow that it might pass for an habiliment of porcelain texture. While I viewed it, I was betrayed from a recollection of the surrounding objects, and I momentarily imagined that if I cast a stone at the vestment I should shiver it to pieces'. The lady's family, the Hobarts, perhaps as a result of Pasquin's destructive criticism, refused to accept the portrait and Lawrence never afterwards painted any of its members. Lady Emily Hobart later married Lord Castlereagh. She was twenty-three at the time the portrait was taken and formed, as Williams observed, 'a lovely subject for the artist's pencil'. It was rare for Lawrence to fail in his portrayal of beautiful women, and the rejection of the portrait must have disconcerted him. Of his 'Portrait of a Gentleman', Richard Payne Knight, Pasquin observed : 'It fills me with the idea of an irascible pedagogue explaining Euclid to a dunce. . . . This is surely the saturnalia of vice and insignificance.' These acerbities filled Lawrence senior with rage, and the father's annoyance was evidently referred to in a letter from an unknown correspondent, to whom the son made a characteristically mild and sensible reply.

'SIR,—You must impute the warmth and resentment with which my father spoke to you upon the subject of Mr. Pasquin's critique to his warmth and affection for me, which make him distrust his Friend for being acquainted with those who withhold their approbation from his son. As the best proof, Sir, that I think justly of your conduct I will endeavour to convince him that his love for me has made him a little unreasonable to you. . . .

The critique I have not seen. . . . I have no doubt that it contains much good sense and wit and is a little too severe. This must be expected. Moderated satire, though I daresay it would suit Mr. Williams very well, would certainly be out of character in a Pasquin. I shall certainly get it, for I have found much benefit from the severest criticism. Something may be learnt, and the greatest improvement I remember to have made in my work was from seeing in a critique upon them that when I learnt to distinguish flesh from glass I might make a tolerable painter.'

Although the fashionable portrait painters such as Lawrence, Hoppner, Beechey and one or two more, were not greatly affected by the alarming events of the period, other English artists suffered severely during the last five years of the century. In the welter of alarm, excitement and discussion in which England was involved, before and after the French Revolution and during the years of war which followed, there was little chance or opportunity for the cultivation of the arts of peace. In his memoirs Raimbach, the engraver, wrote: 'Everything connected with them was at the lowest ebb—so low indeed that I remember, during Mr. Pitt's administration, the members and associates of the Royal Academy were expressly exempted from the operation of some war tax then levied, in consideration of the abject expiring state to which the fine arts had been reduced.'

The year 1795, which saw the acquittal of Warren Hastings and the ill-fated marriage of the Prince of Wales to Princess Caroline of Brunswick, was chiefly memorable to the common people on account of the shortage of food, and to the business community on account of the shortage of money. It was therefore very unfortunate for the parties most concerned that two important art sales took place in the spring of this year. The first of them, held in March, was the disposal by Christie of the Old Masters which had been collected and, in some cases, skilfully restored, by Sir Joshua Reynolds. Many of these pictures were knocked down at bargain prices. The collection had been offered by the executors in 1793 to the Empress Catherine of Russia, but without success. The sale was postponed until 1795 in the hope that the economic position of the country would have improved by then, instead of which it had grown worse, and the prices realised were considerably less than they would have been under more normal conditions. Even more important than the Reynolds collection was that of M. De Calonne which was put up for auction shortly afterwards by Skinner and Dyke, a firm which at that time rivalled Christie in public esteem, and realised only about £25,000.

Calonne, an enormously wealthy Frenchman who had made a hobby of collecting Old Masters over a period of more than thirty years, had been Prime Minister of France until his resignation in 1787. Foreseeing the approaching troubles in his country he had prudently transferred himself and his pictures to London, with the intention of settling permanently in England. He bought a large house in Piccadilly near Hyde Park Corner, entertained lavishly and soon began adding to his collection by purchases from English owners, his first acquisition being 'The Triumph of Time' by Nicholas Poussin which he bought from Lord Carysfort for eight hundred guineas. He was engaged in building a gallery near his house in which to display his treasures when the French Revolution broke out and upset all his plans. He thought it his duty to give up the prospect of a pleasant life in London and go to Coblenz to throw in his lot with the French *émigrés* established there. In order to assist them, his biographer records that 'he employed the capital of his fortune, sold his town and country houses and mortgaged that unrivalled collection, formed by a labour of thirty-five years and at an expense of above sixty thousand guineas'. Up till 1794 Calonne still hoped to get his pictures out of pawn, but this proved impossible and the mortgagees took them over. Although we do not hear of Lawrence making any purchases at either sale, possibly because of his financial difficulties, they must certainly have stimulated his collector's instinct. He was already beginning to interest himself in Old Master drawings, the collection of which was to become the most absorbing hobby of his life, and had also acquired a picture by Rembrandt, for whose work he had a profound admiration. Williams relates an anecdote which illustrates the generosity of John Julius Angerstein and his affectionate regard for Lawrence. Angerstein attended the Calonne sale and happened to overhear Mr. Lawrence's admiration of a female portrait, by Rembrandt. This was a half-length portrait of an old lady dressed in black, with a large white ruff round her neck, and a Bible hanging to her waist by a chain. The painting was knocked down to Mr. Angerstein for one hundred guineas. Mr. Lawrence at this time was in possession of Rembrandt's 'Rabbi', on which he had often bestowed the highest encomiums.

Mr. Angerstein, during the sale, approached Mr. Lawrence, saying: 'My reason for purchasing this portrait is that it will make a capital companion to your Jew Rabbi, to which you are so partial; and I beg the favour of your acceptance of it'.

Speaking of the influx of Old Masters into England at this period 'in consequence of their possessors being ruined by the events proceeding out of the French Revolution', Williams makes the apposite comment that 'had these superb paintings been segregated in a national gallery, how immediate, great and permanent might have been the consequences to our national taste! but, unfortunately, the mania for war had seized upon the nation, and they were bought by the affluent and hid in their mansions from the study of the artists'.

The Royal Academy of 1796 contained eight hundred and eighty-five pictures, of which Lawrence contributed eight portraits. In this year his younger sister, Anne, was married at St. Anne's, Soho, to the Rev. Richard Rouse Bloxam, a Fellow and master of Rugby. Although no details of the ceremony have come down to us, we can imagine that friends of the family, among them the Siddons girls from Great Marlborough Street and possibly their parents, were present in force and that Lawrence senior, who never spared expense when he did not have to foot the bills, saw to it that everything was done in a befitting style.

By this time, as we shall see presently, Lawrence had fallen in love with Sally Siddons and was, in varying degrees, emotionally entangled with the whole Kemble clan who, as a family, had much the same effect on those who came under their spell as the Terrys had in late Victorian days. Mrs. Siddons, probably without realising it, was herself more than half in love with the handsome young painter whom she had known since childhood, although her insistence that his engagement to her elder daughter should be kept secret was ostensibly based on a desire to see Sally's health established. She, herself, had had to wait two years before she was able to marry her Sid and no doubt thought it no hardship for Tom Lawrence and Sally to do the same. Lawrence, however, beneath his self-control and even temper, was a man who if he wanted a thing 'will have it'. Sexually he was a *cérébral*, a type more commonly found in women than in men, and it seems that one of his sisters, probably Anne, resembled him in temperament. I am indebted to Mr. Anthony R. Wagner, *Richmond Herald*, for the following passage written in a notebook by his late cousin Henry Wagner (1840–1926) about the year 1863, which sheds a revealing light on a characteristic the brother and sister had in common. 'My grandmother used to ask Sir T. Lawrence's sister to ye house

frequently out of a feeling akin to pity as she had been quite ill from ye violence of an attachment she had formed for my uncle John—she was a governess in the Duke of Newcastle or Somerset's family, in both of which he was tutor.' The 'uncle John' here mentioned was the Rev. John Henry Michell, 1759–1844, Fellow of King's College, Cambridge, and for forty years Rector of Buckland, Hertfordshire. Whichever was the sister referred to, her violent attachment to the tutor did not prevent her from subsequently making a happy and successful marriage. The obstacles which Mrs. Siddons put in the way of his courtship of her daughter seem to have produced something like a nerve storm in Lawrence, the effect of which, combined with his long-cherished ambition to paint something sublime, in the manner of Michelangelo, caused him to embark on a colossal picture on the Miltonic theme of 'Satan Summoning up his Legions'. This huge canvas was never sold and remained on Lawrence's hands until his death. In spite of the strictures passed upon it by Anthony Pasquin and the dry comments of Fuseli, the painter all his life regarded it as his masterpiece and had no doubt that posterity would value it at what he believed to be its true worth. After the disposal of Lawrence's estate it eventually found a resting-place on the staircase leading up to the Diploma Gallery, in Burlington House. For the principal figure, a nude Lucifer of gigantic size, Lawrence used as a model his old friend 'Gentleman Jackson', but the face was recognised as that of J. P. Kemble 'in a mask of rage'. 'The demon writhing upward from the pit at Satan's feet,' says Naomi Royde-Smith,[1] 'was given the unmistakable eye and profile of Mrs. Siddons herself'. Later on, whether after or before the picture was exhibited at the Academy is not clear, Lawrence painted a cloud of smoke over Mrs. Siddons, but Miss Royde-Smith affirms that the 'original figure broke through a little with time and can still be distinguished, when the light is good enough. . . ."
If the picture had some of the quality of a *roman à clef* and transferred to canvas a domestic drama in which the Muse of Tragedy and the enamoured painter played leading roles, there is no doubt that Lawrence put all he had into it and made a sustained effort to

---

[1] *The Private Life of Mrs. Siddons,* by Naomi Royde-Smith, p. 239.

achieve greatness in a form of art for which he was singularly unfitted. The result enabled Pasquin to produce one of his wittiest and most scathing comments. 'This picture,' he wrote, 'is a mélange made up of the worst parts of the divine Buonarrotti and the extravagant Goltzius. The figure of Satan is colossal and very ill-drawn; the body is so disproportioned to the extremities, that it appears all legs and arms, and might at a distance be mistaken for a sign of the spread eagle. The colouring has as little analogy to truth as the contour, for it is so ordered that it conveys an idea of a mad German sugar-baker dancing naked in a con-flagration of his own treacle; but the liberties taken with his infernal Majesty are so numerous, so various, and so insulting, that we are amazed that the ecclesiastic orders do not interfere in behalf of an old friend.'

In the same exhibition Lawrence showed portraits both of J. P. Kemble and Mrs. Siddons. Of the former, catalogued as 'Portrait of a Gentleman', Pasquin observed: 'This is another representation of Mr. Kemble the actor, of whose visage we have so many copies, that we are led to think that half his time is wasted in sitting for his multifarious portraits; but this at least is not in any way favourable to his character; or the reputation of his friend Lawrence. There is a black air of defiance in it, which does not argue a mind at peace either with himself or mankind.'

Of the portrait of Mrs. Siddons, catalogued as 'Portrait of a Lady', Pasquin said: 'It is no more like her than Hebe is similar to Bellona. We have here youth, flexibility of features, and an attempt at the formation of beauty, to denote a lady who is proverbially so stern in her countenance that it approaches to savageness,—so determined in the outline of her visage, that it requires the delusion of the scene to render it soft and agreeable, and who is so far from being young, that her climacteric will be no more.' As a description of the beautiful if flattering portrait of Mrs. Siddons now in the possession of the National Gallery, this to-day seems manifestly absurd, and the lack of sternness in the sitter's eyes, indeed, the melting tenderness in them, can be explained by reasons which, to Pasquin, were probably unknown. Mrs. Siddons, whether aware of it or not, was more than half in love with the young artist, who while painting her was also courting her daughter.

That the difficulties which Mrs. Siddons was making over of Lawrence's *affaire* with Sally were already exasperating him by the beginning of 1796 is shown in a letter from William Godwin, dated 20th February of that year, part of which Layard quotes. The philosopher-novelist, who was then about to run off with Mary Wollstonecraft and subsequently became Shelley's father-in-law, had a wide experience of affairs of the heart and was peculiarly fitted to understand and sympathise with Lawrence's troubles had he been the type of man who could confide, instead of the type who carries secrecy about his personal concerns to extravagant lengths. Godwin wrote:

'I have felt considerable anxiety about you. I could plainly perceive, when I breakfasted with you a few weeks ago, something extraordinary passing in your mind. It showed itself principally in a sort of listlessness, which might almost at first sight have suggested the idea of paralytic affection, but might easily be supposed to be disconsolateness and dissatisfaction, arising from some cause, not of a physical, but an intellectual nature. I longed I confess to probe you, but dared not . . .

And now you hint to me that your uneasiness is sacred, and that no one must intrude upon it. I am sorry for it. My sympathies, active and reactive, should have been much at your service . . .

I hope I am not to understand you literally, that your conceptions are "only proper to yourself". I hope you are not so finished a monopolist. Nothing is more inimical to the restoration of cheerfulness and activity than this obstinate silence. Let me add, that it seems a peculiar refinement of pride, of which I should not have suspected you, to resolve to be uneasy and that the world shall know nothing of the matter.'

As we have seen, something at least of the mental turmoil about which Lawrence was unable to unbosom himself to Godwin, he managed to work out of his system in his picture of Satan.

In May 1797 Lawrence lost his mother and he refers to this

MARIA SIDDONS

*The original portrait was taken by Lawrence in 1797. The litho-graph reproduction here was made from it in 1830, by R. J. Lane.
In the British Museum.*

SALLY SIDDONS

From a lithograph by R. J. Lane. Lawrence is believed to have made the original drawing in 1800. In the British Museum.

JOHN JULIUS ANGERSTEIN AND HIS FIRST WIFE
Exhibited at the Royal Academy in 1792. This picture is now in the Louvre.

event in a letter to his friend, Miss Sophia Lee, of Bath. Writing from Greek Street he says:

'I have mentioned other griefs in order to turn my thoughts from that pale Virtue, whose fading image I can now contemplate with firmness. I kiss it, and not a tear falls on the cold cheek. You can have no notion of the grand serenity it has assumed. I think, I cannot but persuade myself, since the fatal stroke, it seems as if the soul, at the moment of departure, darted its purest emanations into the features, as traces of its happier state. Have you seen death often? It cannot be a common effect. . . . But half an hour since, I had the dear hand in mine, and the fingers seemed unwilling to part with me. Farewell.

Let me know the day you come.—My father's and sisters' best respects.'

Farington's diary gives us several glimpses of Lawrence in 1797. His entry for 9th July shows that Lawrence's affairs were beginning to cause anxious discussion among his friends. 'We had much talk of Lawrence,' he writes. 'He has laid out on House in Piccadilly at least £500—His Academy room cost £150—a Cold Bath He made to supply it with water £5 a year tax and never was in it—put up Library cases for Books not 3 months ago.—Lawrence is very close—never speaks of his affairs to Hamilton but on emergencies. If his mind be set on a thing, he will have it, very proud. The Royal pictures produce him abt £500 a year.—His father is gone to reside with his sister in Gloucestershire. The other sister [Lucy] to set up a School with a Miss Bird from Birmingham. Lawrence to assist her is to give her value of his picture by Rembrandt—loses much time with Miss Lees of Bath when they are in town.' The Miss Bird referred to was, as we shall see later, the intimate friend of the Siddons girls and their confidante throughout their tangled love affairs with Lawrence. On 15th July Farington notes that Sir George Beaumont called. This influential art patron and amateur landscape painter had been a friend of Dr. Johnson and Reynolds and later became intimate with Scott, Wordsworth, Byron and

Coleridge. He was among those who helped in the foundation of the National Gallery, to which he presented some valuable pictures, but does not seem to have been particularly friendly to Lawrence, on first acquaintance, although later he came to have a high regard for him. The object of the call was to tell Farington that Lawrence had written to him 'offering his Rembrandt for 150 guineas on condition that He may have it back in 4 yrs if He chooses for 200 gs. Says he gave 400 for it. Sir George declined the conditions but offered 200 gs. for it, which Lawrence has accepted'. As Lawrence is known to have had several Rembrandts in his possession at different times, it is not certain which of them is here referred to, but there is little doubt that the object of the transaction was to provide funds to help his sister establish her school. Two days later Farington quotes Beaumont as saying that Lawrence's *manner* always made him uneasy. 'His compliments forced—the early reputation he had had was a dangerous temptation to overset his judgment.'

Later in the year, in a letter probably to Miss Sophia Lee, which Williams quotes, Lawrence makes it clear that he is endeavouring to get rid of his Piccadilly house, which was beyond his means and must have run him deeply into debt. He writes:

'Apropos, I have not yet let or sold my house, and matters in Greek Street are as they were. My father, at times, is much troubled with his cough; but I hope and believe he is not otherwise worse than when you saw him, but rather better. The country air, peace and content will, I trust, soon restore health, and gratify the wishes of his children to whom, whatever differences of character or disposition there may have been, his essentially worthy nature and general love for them make him too dear an object of regard, not to form the greatest portion of their solicitude. To be the entire happiness of his children, is perhaps the lot of no parent.'

The old man died some weeks later, in the month of October, and Lawrence's grief is shown by the brevity and simplicity of the letter in which he informs Miss Lee of his loss.

'MY DEAREST FRIEND,

The cause of my silence is a terrible one,—my father's death. He died before I could reach him; but he died full of affection to us, of firm faith and fortitude, and without a groan.

THOMAS LAWRENCE.'

Williams says that Lawrence was painting in his house in Piccadilly when a messenger burst into the room and announced that his father was dying. 'Lawrence, in the intensity of his feelings, ran out of the house, and proceeded through the streets without his hat; but notwithstanding the rapidity of his pace, he did not arrive until after his father had expired.'

A pencil drawing of his father, which Lawrence made in the year of his death and which was afterwards engraved by F. C. Lewis, shows him in a wig, with his waistcoat open at the neck and its last two buttons undone, seated on a chair and looking curiously solemn and also, as might be expected, rather silly.

John Bernard, author of a witty volume of memoirs called *Retrospections of the Stage*, tells a story of Lawrence senior which sheds some light on his curious character. 'Lawrence not only used to entertain his friends at home,' he writes, 'round a snug parlour fire, with his readings, but whenever a new play was announced, would come over to Bath and proffer his services to the actors to read their parts—a kindness which some who intended to sponge at his house would accept but others of more dignity declined.' He also says that Lawrence senior 'frequently brought his boy to the Green-room, and we would set him on a table and make him recite Hamlet's directions to the players.' Another anecdote recorded by Bernard seems to suggest that the old man had a prophetic instinct. He was asked by friends in Devizes to allow his son to attend a party and give his readings. The father consented on condition that the boy confined himself to the passages chosen for him. 'When the complimenting was over, he was asked what recitation he preferred in Milton. He replied "Satan's Address to the Sun"; but that his father would not permit him to give it. For that reason they were particularly eager to hear it, as they wished to discover whether Tom was a mere parrot, or a prodigy. His dutiful scruples, however, were not to be overcome, till they had promised to obtain his father's forgiveness. He then turned to the forbidden page, and a written slip of paper dropped from it; a gentleman picked it up and read it aloud. "Tom mind you don't touch Satan." ' It was perhaps a pity that he did not remember the parental injunction when, in later life, he attempted 'sublimity' by painting Satan summoning his legions. That Lawrence senior was a genuine eccentric and a personality cast in no ordinary mould is clear enough from what we know of him, but there is evidently much that we do not know. He must have had genuine talents, even if he did not know how to apply them, and we have his son's tribute to his 'essentially worthy nature', which would hardly have been paid unless there were good reasons for it.

The death of his parents led to Lawrence's abandoning his Piccadilly house and establishing himself at 57 Greek Street. Here, after making some alterations which included the removal of a floor to enlarge his painting room, he lived and worked for the next sixteen years. One advantage which, in the then state of his amorous emotions, the house possessed, was that it was within a few minutes' walk of the home of the Siddons family at 47 Great Marlborough Street.

VIII

SALLY AND MARIA SIDDONS

THE INTIMACY which had developed in Bath between the Lawrence and Siddons families was continued in London and was facilitated by the fact that they lived within a few minutes' walk of one another, separated by the beautiful gardens of Soho Square. The Lawrence girls and their friend Miss Bird, though older than Sally and Maria Siddons, had known them since childhood, and their respective parents were acquaintances of long standing. As for Lawrence, he not only met Mrs. Siddons on important social occasions, since both of them, as well-known public figures, were welcomed in the houses of the great, but as painter and sitter they spent hours in each other's company in circumstances which favoured the growth of the closest intimacy and understanding, perhaps of even warmer feelings. In 1790 Sally and Maria had been placed by their parents in a boarding-school at Calais, from which they were brought back two or three years later, when war threatened between England and France. The two girls, who were no more than children when they went abroad to be 'finished', now took their place in a social circle of which their famous mother, when her professional duties permitted, was the dominating figure. As early as May 1793, when the girls were aged eighteen and fourteen respectively, Mrs. Piozzi, better known as Mrs. Thrale, writes: 'We were at Ranelagh two nights ago, and staid till morning. Mrs. Greatheed and the young Siddonses with us. Sally quite outlooked her sister, by-the-by, and was very finely dressed.' A month later, in a letter to a friend, she says: 'The dear Siddons left me yesterday; she has charming daughters now, so have I, so we can see but little of each other. Sally is exceedingly well, and just as pretty as every pretty girl of the same age, and prettier than Maria, because her face looks cleaner.' Sally, in addition to her other attractions, was an accomplished musician, well-educated, serious and intelligent. Both girls were good-looking, but both were constitutionally delicate, and soon showed symptoms of the lung troubles which, aggravated by their too stimulating social activities and by defective medical treatment, were destined to cut them off in the flower of their youth. Sally's illness took the form of spasmodic asthma, a disease which she never managed to shake off and which eventually proved fatal. To Mrs. Piozzi we are indebted for a detailed account of one of the attacks from which she periodically suffered. Writing from Guy's Cliffe, the Warwickshire seat of the Greatheeds, she says: 'On the road hither . . . Sally Siddons was taken *illish;* I hoped it was the influenza, for cold she could not have catch'd, and I have kept her at all possible distance from my own girl ever since she threw up blood at Denbigh. Here, however, was she seized yesterday with such a paroxysm of asthma, cough, spasm, *any-thing*, as you nor I ever saw her attacked by. . . . She is in a state I know not how bad but, as God never leaves one deserted, here most providentially was found Mr. Richard Greatheed, who you know, practised physic for many years in the W. Indies, and under his care we are now existing, not living. . . . Sally in her bed desires to be remembered to you, who have so often watched her bedside. She has reason to adore Mrs. Greatheed though, who ransacks the country for relief to the dear creature, and we expect her mother every minute, to add to our agony.' Fortunately the attacks were not of long duration, and when she got over them Sally quickly recovered her gaiety and high spirits.

The Siddons' home in Great Marlborough Street was enlivened by the presence of two gay and good-looking young men, Charles Kemble and Charles Moore, younger brother of the General Sir John Moore who was to die years later at Corunna. Charles Kemble, though only a few months older than Sally, was the uncle of the Siddons girls and seems to have had a full share of the Kemble charm. Charles Moore, who was reading for the Bar, was one of those essentially shy and modest youths who conceal their tender hearts behind roars of laughter and are looked on by their friends as the very embodiment of cheerful good humour. It was only after Sally's death that he admitted that he had always been secretly in love with her, but knowing that her heart was engaged, had never confessed it. Others who attended the evening parties at Great Marlborough Street were Miss Sarah Bird, the friend and subsequently the partner of Lucy Lawrence, Amelia Lock, daughter of William Lock of Norbury, and, last but not least, Thomas Lawrence.

That Lawrence should find himself falling in love with Sally Siddons and should become, for a time, equally enamoured of Maria, was a foregone conclusion in view of the fascination exerted over him by their mother and indeed the whole Kemble clan. It is so common a phenomenon for a man to find himself in love, in varying degrees, with two sisters, that it is surprising to find Lawrence's biographers adopting a censorious tone about it. Charles Dickens had a similar experience and is thought to have discovered, after his marriage, that he had made the wrong choice. By temperament, character, disposition and accomplishments Sally, had she enjoyed robust health, was calculated to make Lawrence an ideal wife. Both were musical, Sally being a composer of songs, and both of them, though they enjoyed 'society', preferred quiet evenings at home. Sally would have been as much delighted to hear Lawrence, after his hard day's work, reading chapters from the novels of Jane Austen and Walter Scott, as the excellent Miss Croft was in after years. She was a kind, unselfish, good-tempered, highly intelligent and deeply affectionate girl who must have appealed to all Lawrence's best qualities as well as sharing and promoting all his most serious interests in life. There is no doubt that they fell deeply in love with one another, that they had come to an understanding and that Mrs. Siddons did not, in principle, withhold her consent to their eventual marriage. For what seemed to her good and sufficient reasons, however, she insisted that the engagement should be kept secret and refused to allow her husband to be informed of it. Lawrence's financial embarrassments must have come to her ears, and she may have reflected that a long engagement would both test the seriousness of his intentions and allow him time to get out of debt. On the subject of money Mrs. Siddons held rigid views, formed in the school of harsh experience, and as she was the bread-winner for her family, though her husband had control of her income, any provision made for Sally would have to come out of her earnings. Another reason which may have contributed to her reluctance to allow the engagement to be made known to her husband and her brother, John Philip, was her anxiety about Sally's health. An ailing wife, she may have felt, would prove a handicap to Lawrence in his career and no amount of tenderness on a husband's part could compensate for a mother's care. Where her children were concerned the great *tragédienne* was like a lioness defending her cubs, and her maternal instinct, combined with other subconscious emotions at which we can only guess, confused her judgment and made her play for safety by post-poning decisions.

Meanwhile there was no opposition to Sally and Lawrence meeting each other freely. No doubt Sally frequently visited the house in Piccadilly and gave her lover the happiness of drawing her for his own pleasure, in the intervals of painting portraits for his living. We can imagine them walking together in Green Park and through the squares and gardens in what was then a capital of incomparable beauty and splendour. Ugliness, except the ugliness due to lack of sanitation, human vice, bad smells and the contrast between dire poverty and excessive wealth, had then scarcely been invented. The contrasted beauties of the two dominating styles of Georgian domestic architecture, the simpler type of house with its plain façade, Grecian portico and elaborate fanlight and the more grandiose Palladian mansion with its marble cornices and fluted columns, combined to form a picture into the frozen poetry of which no jarring note as yet intruded. The carriages and sedan chairs with which the streets were thronged were in themselves examples of the most exquisite craftsmanship, horses were as well-groomed and finely bred as their riders, even the extravagant costumes of the *ton* were masterpieces of the tailor's and couturier's art. Above all, London was in those days a city of gardens. Even its meanest, most congested and filthiest districts were still within half an hour's walk of green fields and sylvan glades.

Two capable novelists, M. André Maurois and Naomi Royde-Smith, have exercised their imagination in regard to the tangled love affair of Lawrence and the Siddons girls, but the only basic facts on which we can rely are contained in the long series of letters reproduced by Dr. Oswald G. Knapp in his book *An Artist's Love Story*. It is on these, supplemented by the knowledge of the principal characters concerned derived from other sources, that we must base our interpretation of what took place. In 1795, when Maria reached the age of sixteen, she changed in a few months in a surprising fashion. Miss Royde-Smith says: 'She ripened quickly into a hectic loveliness, a bloom so soft and brilliant that, for a time, it was mistaken for the bloom of health'. In addition to her young beauty, she possessed a precocious vivacity combined with something, as M. Maurois puts it, '*de sauvage et de passionné*', which her sister entirely lacked. She was, moreover, vain, selfish, frivolous, totally lacking in moral scruples and fully conscious of her power to attract. All her life she had been petted and spoiled by her parents, her elder sister and their circle of friends. Of Sally's love for the dazzlingly handsome portrait painter whom her mother so much admired, she must, from the first, have been aware. Up till then the two girls had been constant companions, but now she found herself frequently left alone, when Sally and Lawrence went out together, and acute jealousy added to her sense of neglect, especially as she was already aware of her effect on male susceptibilities. '*Près d'elle,*' says Maurois, '*les hommes les plus forts se troublent. Elle sent que par un mot, par un geste, elle peut les faire pâlir. C'était un plaisir auquel Maria, dès qu'elle l'eut connu, sentit bien qu'elle ne pourrait plus jamais résister.*' It was thus inevitable, when she became conscious of her power, that she should endeavour to exercise it on her sister's lover. Not only was Lawrence, the painter, captivated by her adolescent grace and daring coquetry, but he found in Maria another example of that Kemble charm which he was never able to resist. Gradually Maria insinuated herself into the company of Sally and Lawrence, got herself included in their walks abroad and continued to be the recipient of kisses which became less and less brotherly or avuncular.

M. Maurois,[1] without quoting any authority for the statement, says that on many subjects the tastes of Maria and Lawrence coincided and were opposed to Sally's. Both, he says, desired an ostentatious life, brilliant receptions and fashionable salons, while all that Sally wanted was a little house, the care of children and a few friends. Sally cared little about money and wished Lawrence to paint every year a small number of perfect portraits, while Maria encouraged the natural taste of the young painter for slick portraits, quickly executed and well paid. He is on surer ground when he says that Lawrence became nervous, irritable and violent, but this condition showed itself before Maria began to set her cap at him and was caused by the objections raised by Mrs. Siddons to his engagement to Sally and is explained by Farington's terse comment, 'if his mind be set on a thing, he will have it, very proud'. I can find no justification for M. Maurois' statement that Lawrence sometimes treated Sally with incredible harshness and immediately reproached himself for doing so. When he makes Lawrence say to himself 'Truly, I am mad. She hasn't a fault, but can I bear it if the other girl escapes me', he is clearly exercising his talent for fictional biography. Maria's shameless attempts to cut out her sister in Lawrence's affections were greatly facilitated by the fact that in 1797 Sally fell seriously ill, was laid up for a long time and made a very slow convalescence. Although at first unsuspecting, she must have realised what was happening, and there is little doubt that her distress of mind aggravated her illness and delayed her recovery. Maria, meanwhile, seized her opportunity to carry on her intrigue with Lawrence, by means of private notes and clandestine meetings in the studio in Greek Street. Miss Sally Bird, who was staying with Lawrence and his sister Lucy, seems to have been the principal intermediary in this dangerous liaison. Lawrence at this time, as is shown by a letter to Mr. John Graham dated 17th October 1797, was, in addition to the turmoil of his emotional life, in very serious financial difficulties. John Graham was the Bow Street Magistrate and the letter

[1] *Meipe*, by André Maurois.

asks for a postponement of executions by the Sheriff against his effects. 'Having the strongest reason to believe that I shall have ample means in my power to satisfy the Executions against my Effects before the 30th instant,' he writes, 'I request that you will not proceed to remove or sell the same previous to that time and if not then paid you have my authority to sell the said Effects by Auction on the premises.' The letter was endorsed by the recipient twenty-two years later, as follows: 'What a strange diffce. The progress of merit, now Sir Thos Lawrence, the finest portrait painter of the age. Emperors and Kings, the Pope himself, subservient to his pencil. The suavity of his manners, his gentlemanly conduct, rendered him particularly estimable in the eyes of her R.H. The Princess of Wales and Mrs. Siddons.' The confusion in the household caused by his father's death, which occurred in this month, no doubt added to Lawrence's difficulties. We have no record of how he managed to overcome them, but the probability is that he once again borrowed what he required from one or other of his wealthy patrons.

It was in this nerve-racking and harassing situation that Lawrence made the fatal error of supposing himself more in love with the vain, selfish, empty-headed but entrancing Maria, a dark Venus *'toute entière à sa proie attachée'*, than with her loyal and sweet-natured elder sister. Dr. Knapp says that 'how he contrived to secure his recognition in the new role of Maria's lover, without bringing about a breach between the sisters or a rupture with their mother, can only be conjectured'. He discounts the story told many years later by Fanny Kemble, in her memoirs, that stormy scenes took place between Lawrence and Mrs. Siddons. 'It is much more likely,' he says, 'that Sally (whose judgment was sounder and whose feelings were more under control than those of her sister), finding that Lawrence's devotion was growing cool, and that Maria's affections were deeply engaged, allowed him to transfer his allegiance without protest. . . .' Fond as she was of Maria, she must have been aware of her defects of character and frivolity of mind and, with the insight into Lawrence's real nature which love had given her, she may well have thought that his infatuation would not last, and that the most dignified as well as the most sensible thing she could do was to let things take their course. The liability of essentially faithful husbands to form sudden, violent, but transitory attachments to pretty faces is something which married women have had to face throughout the ages. Just as jealousy and resentment have wrecked many marriages on this account, so restraint, forgiveness and loyal devotion have saved many more. Sally, though without experience of married life, had the wisdom of the heart which springs from depth of feeling. From what we know of her sad story we can discern that, until the day of her death, her love for Lawrence was, in the words of the old ballad:

> a durable fire
> In the mind ever burning,
> Never sick, never dead, never cold,
> From itself never turning.

There is no end to the self-sacrifice and self-immolation which such a love can sustain. To Maria all this was a closed book. She wanted her sister's man and was determined to get him. Lucy Lawrence and Miss Bird, who probably had only a dim idea of the real state of Lawrence's mind and were anxious to do everything they could to facilitate his courtship of Maria, were the recipients of letters from both the Siddons girls. Miss Bird, in particular, was assiduous in passing on notes from Maria to 'Mr. Tom', and fully in the secret of their clandestine meetings in Greek Street. After one of these, Maria wrote to Miss Bird, saying: 'I'm very glad you lik'd me in black; I did not see myself before I went out, for I came home so late that I went to my room directly, and would not ring for Candles that they might fancy I had been in a *great while. I felt* how to dress myself, absolutely, and came down about the middle of dinner, and my Father ask'd me where I had been. I told a *story*, and there was an end of it. Sally is getting better, I hope; she has been very ill, and is still very weak. She desires her kindest love to you, and thanks you for your letter; she begs you will come the first day you can, and she will thank you herself; you know *I* am always delighted to see you, and

you are *sometimes pleas'd to see me*, are you almost always? . . .
Give my love to Miss Lawrence.' Later she writes to Miss Bird
and Miss Lawrence, saying: 'Tomorrow morning we intend
calling on you between twelve and one; if it does not rain, if
you are not otherwise engag'd I mean'. Later she writes to Miss
Lawrence, saying: 'I am very sorry I shall not see your brother
before he goes. Tell *Mr. Tom* he shall hear from me tomorrow
morning, because my mother don't like to bear a letter.' The
letter for Mr. Tom was evidently conveyed to him by Miss Bird,
through whom, as usual, his reply was transmitted.

London in the winter was unhealthy even for people of robust
constitution, and particularly so for girls with a tendency to
consumption. There were thick fogs, necessitating the services
of link-boys, mud and slush on the unswept pavements, and the
whole atmosphere was tainted by the smells from open sewers and
rotting garbage. Miss Royde-Smith suspects that Maria, when
she went out in the raw winter weather to keep her assignations
with Lawrence, did so 'in ridiculous little sandals and the thinnest
of thin silk dresses under her coat and waited about in the fog',
but there does not seem any evidence that her meetings with her
lover took place in the manner described, or indeed that they
contributed in any way to her ill-health. If Lawrence had not
existed, it is almost certain, from what we know of her medical
history, that her constitutional weakness would have shown itself
when it did. In the course of the winter her parents became
seriously alarmed about her health, and Maria took advantage of
their solicitude to tell her father that she was in love with Lawrence and he with her, and to beg him to give his consent to
their engagement. As Mr. Siddons had been told nothing about
Lawrence's earlier understanding with Sally, the situation as
far as he was concerned had no complications except Maria's
ill-health and Lawrence's debts. Maria was his favourite daughter
and when he realised that her heart was set on marrying Lawrence
and that she was in too delicate a state to have her wishes thwarted,
whereas the prospect of a happy marriage might assist her cure,
he eventually withdrew his objections. As the family man of
business, he discussed settlements with his future son-in-law and

agreed to provide Maria with a dowry out of his wife's earnings, sufficient to pay his debts. Maria's triumph, which proved to be short-lived, was now complete. All that apparently remained was for her to get well and for the date of the ceremony to be fixed.

The situation was described in detail in a letter written by Sally to Miss Bird on 5th January 1798, in the course of which she said:

'I am sure you are impatient to hear how Maria is, and so I will defer all that I have got to say till I have given you an account of her health. She is, dear girl, to all appearance very much better, but Dr. Pierson does not say so; he seems entirely to rely on her pulse, and that goes (or at least did yesterday) at the same galloping rate that it has done for this week past. He says she is in a *very* doubful state, and has given us too plainly to under-stand that a Consumption may be the consequence. I cannot however see her so very much recover'd without great hopes that her youth, and the unremitting attention that is paid to her, may conquer this complaint. Do not for Heaven's sake breathe a syllable of this which may reach Mr. Lawrence's ears, for I suppose, if he could imagine her so seriously ill, he would be almost distracted, now especially, when every desire of his heart is, without opposition, so near being accomplished. For now, dear Miss Bird, I must tell you a piece of good news, which will I know surprise and please you; my Father at length consents to the marriage, and Mr. Lawrence has been receiv'd by him in the most cordial manner as his future son-in-law. Maria determin'd to speak to my Father when she was much worse than she is now; she did, and he, mov'd by the state in which she was, and con-sidering, no doubt, that the union must take place with or without his consent, thought it most wise to agree to what was inevitable. Some letters pass'd between him and Mr. L. and now all is going on smoothly, and he regularly makes us a visit every evening. Should not this happy event have more effect than all the medi-cines? At least I cannot but think it will add greatly to their efficacy. But what will our friend do without some difficulties to overcome? But perhaps in this pursuit he has found enough to satisfy him, and will be content to receive Maria, tho' there now remain no obstacles. Well, I rejoice sincerely that there is an end to all mystery, and I think Maria has as fair a prospect of happiness as any mortal can desire.'

The essential fact which emerges from this letter is that it was Maria, not Lawrence or Mrs. Siddons, who 'determin'd to speak' to her father and did so. She it was who took the initiative, and this fact must, in itself, have contributed to Lawrence's recovery from his temporary infatuation. He found himself trapped by and publicly affianced to an empty-headed girl who had used her illness to influence her parents and assert her claim on him. In a letter to Miss Bird, dated 28th January 1798, Sally mentions Maria's return to the drawing-room, 'where she has now been for several days, and is recovering her strength and good looks every day'. The doctor, however, ordered that she must remain there all the winter. 'But surely,' says Sally, 'if ever confinement was supportable, it must be to Maria, for she not only sees all our friends and acquaintances as usual, but the visits of her *first friend* are unremitted, and should (should they not?) console her for everything.' But what were Lawrence's feelings on these occasions? We can, I think, rely on the feminine intuition of Miss Naomi Royde-Smith to reveal them. She writes:

'To meet the lovely, excited, ardent little creature for a few stolen moments; to witness the delicious confusion his own perfections had stirred in her; to share a romantic and self-deceiving belief, that they too were lovers persecuted by grim and tyrannical parents, was one thing; but to sit by a feverish, little, empty-headed chatterer, in licensed courtship, under the chandeliers of a well-furnished drawing-room for an hour or two every evening of the week, was quite another, especially when a grave and lovely girl to whom he could now only pay the distant and limited attention of a prospective brother-in-law sat quietly at her tambour-frame in another corner of the drawing-room or, worse still, entertained Charles Kemble and Charles Moore and

other young men of their acquaintance with smiles and conversation in which Maria would not allow him to take any part.'

M. Maurois was clearly mistaken in suggesting that Lawrence
and Maria had tastes in common which Sally did not share. The
contrary was the case. Maria does not appear to have had any
intellectual interests, whereas Lawrence and Sally had many.
Both had an intelligent appreciation of literature, the drama, and,
above all, of music. Lawrence, although according to Miss
Croft he 'literally did not know a note of music', had a pleasant
voice, 'never sung a note out of tune' and was also a capable
violinist. Sally composed songs which were much appreciated
by her friends and also sang them to her own accompaniment;
she was well-read and could comment intelligently on acting and
the drama, which, as well as being her mother's profession, was
Lawrence's abiding passion. Everything indeed combined to
make Sally Lawrence's ideal companion, for not only had she the
qualities of mind which he admired but also the character and
temperament which accorded with everything serious and worthy
in his own nature.

In the second part of her letter, quoted above, Sally gossips
about 'the Charles's', one of whom, Charles Moore, had, as we
have seen, a more than friendly regard for her, and mentions
visits to the theatre. 'Since Maria has been so much better,' she
says, 'and has had so agreeable a companion, I have been out to
amuse *my*self two or three times. I have at last seen the Castle
Spectre,[1] and was delighted quite beyond expression when the
Spectre did appear, but what a deal of dullness one has to wade
thro' before she comes! And how ridiculous some of Mrs.
Jordan's attempts at the pathetic are! I could really scarcely forbear
laughing outright two or three times. I was at Drury Lane too,
the first night of Blue Beard; some of the Music is charming,
and the scene where Sister Anne (as she was call'd in the old story)
appears on the Tower, is capitally manag'd, and interesting to
an excess, the pleasure of which is almost painful! I was delighted

---

[1] *The Castle Spectre*, by 'Monk' Lewis, was a popular and horrific melodrama which ran
for sixty nights at Drury Lane.

MARIA SIDDONS

From a mezzotint by G. Clint after the picture by Lawrence. In the Royal Collection, British Museum.

MRS. SIDDONS

Lawrence's most successful portrait of Mrs. Siddons was exhibited at the Royal Academy in 1797. She is described in the catalogue as 'Lady'. In the National Gallery.

at that part of the piece, and very angry at, and very much tir'd with much of it; they have not told the story by any means well.'

Although we may be certain that Sally made no conscious effort to win back her lover, instinct prompted her to do all the things which were calculated to enable her to do so. Instead of wearing her heart on her sleeve and letting her manner betray her inmost feelings, she was gay and cheerful and showed every outward sign of satisfaction at her sister's happiness. The attentive friend-ship of Charles Moore, which, we may be certain, did not escape Lawrence's notice, must also have played some part in increasing his misery and exasperation. He began to look in at Great Marlborough Street before Maria had descended to take her place in the drawing-room, when he was certain of finding Sally alone. As the weeks went by he made his real feelings more and more clear to her, until at last there came the frank avowal. The situation thus created was one of appalling difficulty and painful in the extreme for all the characters concerned in it. Sally would not have been human had she felt that loyalty to Maria made it incumbent on her to reject Lawrence's renewed addresses. After all, Maria had not scrupled to use her sex appeal to undermine Lawrence's allegiance, so why should she reject him, now that he had recovered from his infatuation, out of solicitude for Maria's feelings? After watching them together, she found it impossible to believe that Maria really loved her man in the way that she herself loved him. Not much imagination is required to under-stand the emotional turmoil in the minds of Sally and Lawrence, a turmoil which was increased by the extraneous complication of Maria's illness. That Maria, herself, was aware of Lawrence's waning ardour is clearly revealed in a letter she wrote to Miss Bird on 16th February [1798]. 'My mother and Sally,' she says, 'are gone to Covent Garden to see a new comedy, and the famous Joan of Arc, and Dorothy Place is sitting with me; her company is very delightful to me in my confinement; it has been a very long one, and I am anxious to go out of the house for air, but I must not till April! I agree with you that nothing can be so delightful as the *unremitting* attention of those we love, but where shall we find constancy enough in this wicked world to make us always happy!' After many expressions of affection for Miss Bird and some gossip about Charles Moore, she remarks: 'Dorothy desires to be remember'd very kindly to you, and I daresay if Mr. Lawrence were here he would desire his respectful compliments.' No doubt Miss Bird drew her own conclusions from the fact that Maria had thought fit to mention that Mr. Lawrence was *not* there! Shortly after this the fat was in the fire. Maria became increasingly incensed by Lawrence's moody and erratic behaviour and complained to her mother about it. Of the scenes which followed various fancy descriptions have been given, based largely on the possibilities presented by the idea of the greatest tragic actress of her time playing a major role in a domestic drama, assisted by a richly talented supporting cast. The dazzlingly handsome *jeune premier*, whom Miss Royde-Smith credits with having 'a fiend's temper in leash behind his angel's face', was a brilliant amateur, Maria, as the *ingénue*, could be trusted to give a good account of herself, and if Papa Siddons was what might be described as a 'ham actor', his part of outraged heavy father was one in which he should have been reasonably adequate. Although Fanny Kemble had a mistaken view of what actually happened, the account she gives of the family row in her *Records of a Girlhood* is probably substantially accurate. She says that Lawrence had become 'deeply dejected, moody, restless, and evidently extremely and unaccountably wretched'. Violent scenes of the most painful emotion, of which the cause was inexplicable and incomprehensible, took place between himself and Mrs. Siddons, to whom he finally, 'in a paroxysm of self-abandoned misery, confessed that he had mistaken his feelings . . . and ended by imploring permission to transfer his affections from one to the other sister'. Neither Fanny Kemble or, for that matter, William Siddons, knew the whole story, as Lawrence's first engagement to Sally had been kept a secret. To Mr. Siddons what had happened was that Lawrence had shamelessly jilted poor Maria, who, although not 'on her death-bed', was certainly in a dangerously weak condition. As he had consented to the engagement, in the first instance, in the hope that it might have a beneficial effect on Maria's health, his outraged feelings on her

account can easily be understood. His action in forbidding
Lawrence ever again to darken the doors of 47 Great Marlborough
Street was what might have been expected of him in the circumstances, and it is of course possible, as Miss Royde-Smith
suggests, that he 'spoke of the defaulting Lawrence in those terms
borrowed from the stableyard which middle-aged gentlemen are
wont to employ when enraged by their juniors'. As for Mrs.
Siddons, she, we may well believe, was driven almost distracted
by her emotions, and it is tempting to imagine, as Miss Royde-
Smith does, that 'her performance . . . was said, by those who
witnessed it, to give an inkling of what her King Lear might be'.
Unfortunately, however, she does not produce these witnesses,
and it is therefore safer to rely on the guarded account given of
the affair by the most self-controlled, truthful and level-headed of
the parties concerned. In a letter to Miss Bird on 5th March 1798,
Sally explains her not having written before by saying:

'I was at first prevented by indisposition and since by circumstances that have indeed almost entirely engross'd my
thoughts, and which have made me neglect almost everything
else. If you could guess these circumstances, how would you
be amaz'd, and yet, perhaps, you would not, for you seem to be
well aware of the mutability of *men and things*. A great, great
change has taken place in our house; when you write to Maria
avoid, if possible, mentioning Mr. Lawrence, at least for the
present; all that affair is *at an end*. Are you astonish'd? Had you
been present for some weeks past you would not be so much
surpris'd. Maria bears her disappointment as I would have her,
in short like a person *whose heart could never have been deeply
engag'd*. Mr. Lawrence has found that he was mistaken in her
character, his behaviour has been evidently alter'd towards her, as
I told you, for weeks; his letters, too, she said, were as chang'd—in
short, we see him no more. I long to be with you that I might
tell you *all* and *everything*, for I am sure you are much interested
in this affair, but cannot write half I would say. It is now near a
fortnight since this complete breaking off, and Maria is in good
spirits, talks and thinks of dress, and company, and beauty, as

usual. Is it not fortunate? Had she *lov'd him*, I think this event would almost have broken her heart; I rejoice that she did not. You will say nothing of all this when you write to her, perhaps she may herself tell you of what has happen'd.

We are become quite gay, I assure you, for as Maria cannot go out, we try to make her confinement as pleasant as possible, and therefore have frequent parties of an evening. Dorothy Place is spending some time with us, she is a sweet girl, and a chearful companion. I have not been out scarcely these six weeks, of course Maria keeps us very much at home, but this week I shall be very gay, I am going to no less than three parties, but one of them I shall, if possible, decline. I think I need not tell you that I take no great delight in these sorts of visits; nobody enjoys *society* more than I do, nobody has less delight in *company*.'

She concludes with references to the Charles's, and to her mother. 'What a merry creature Mr. Charles Moore is, I think I never saw anyone laugh so heartily in my life; it is impossible not to join him, even tho' one is ignorant of the cause of his mirth.' Of Mrs. Siddons she writes: 'You see by the Papers that my Mother has begun to play again; she was a good deal fatigued after her Play on Saturday night; and was very indifferent all day yesterday, but she has comforted me this morning by saying she feels much better. I am writing to you before breakfast; Maria is not yet up, or I should be charg'd with her love and thanks for your nice letter. Adieu, dear Namesake, keep the balance even in which you weigh your love for me and Maria, for if it leans ever so little to her side I should be jealous.'

If the entanglement with which we are dealing had occurred in a suburban family living, say, at Surbiton or Pinner, no particular astonishment would be felt. Tom Lawrence, though deeply in love with Sally Smith, was led up the garden path, when Sally was away ill, by her younger sister, Molly. That sexy little piece, having provoked Sally's boy-friend into making a declaration, promptly told her father and got his consent to their engagement. Luckily Tom then came to his senses, realised that he had made a fool of himself, and backed out of it in good time. Now everything is straightened out, Sally is happy again and Tom more devoted than ever. The only complication is that Molly has developed T.B., which of course she would have done in any case, and excites everyone's sympathy on that account. But she never really loved Tom and only made passes at him out of vanity, to demonstrate her sex appeal, so what has happened serves her right. If she had any decency she'd be the first to admit it, instead of reviling poor Tom and complaining that he jilted her. After all, she didn't have any compunction about making him jilt Sally.

Told like that, in simplified terms, the story would make a commonplace plot in contemporary fiction, and since the liability of males to be temporarily carried off their feet by designing and physically attractive minxes is well understood—it happens so often—readers would be inclined to sympathise with the hero in his unfortunate predicament. The fact that the leading roles in the Siddons drama were played by two great artists, in whose careers posterity has shown an abiding and well-deserved interest, has led to a mystery being made of what was an essentially human imbroglio, in which those concerned behaved as people normally do behave in an emotional crisis. Everyone was partially to blame for what occurred. Mrs. Siddons, who had a violently possessive love for her daughters, and a more than maternal feeling for Lawrence, and was also harassed by the demands of her exacting profession, seems to have lost her head and behaved foolishly. Lawrence gave an impressive exhibition of what can happen to a man of strong emotions, who habitually exercises an iron self-control, when the control breaks down. Maria, the real cause of all the trouble, can be excused on account of her illness and her youth. Only Sally came through the ordeal with dignity, good sense and undeviating honesty, but even she might have shown more strength of character when the drama reached its concluding stages. On the whole, therefore, it is a case of *tout comprendre, c'est tout pardonner*, and although we do not know all the details of the story, we know enough to exonerate Lawrence, hitherto regarded as the villain of the piece, of the charges which Dr. Oswald Knapp and others have brought against him.

In her letter to Miss Bird, dated 14th March 1798, Maria referred to the state of her health in a way which could hardly fail to arouse her friend's sympathy and even at this distance of time cannot leave any reader unmoved. 'A relapse', she says, 'is always worse than the original illness, and I yet think I shall not live a long while, it is perhaps merely nerveous, but I sometimes feel as if I should not, and I see nothing very shocking in the idea; I can have no great fears, and may be sav'd from much misery.' It was natural enough that the poor girl should associate her broken engagement with the distress of mind caused by the ravages of the disease from which she suffered, but the way in which she does so reveals the innate selfishness of her character. 'You know I suppose,' she says, 'the cause of too much of my misery, therefore I shall be spared the hateful task of mentioning it. Yet from the love I have for you I cannot bear that you should think I have been in the wrong, ah no, indeed, he himself, if it is possible any feeling can remain in him, will acknowledge how little he deserv'd the sacrifices I was willing to make for him.' One of these 'sacrifices', indeed the only one of which we have any knowledge, was her sister's happiness, but of this she makes no mention. How different was Sally's attitude when Lawrence transferred his affections to Maria!

The remainder of the letter is devoted to conventional gossip about the social activities in Great Marlborough Street, in which, as usual, the popular and high-spirited Charles Moore played a leading part. 'I saw your favourite Mr. Charles Moore here on Sunday evening; we had a great deal of company that evening, and among them was pretty Miss Ogilvie, looking very well indeed. The party was so large that it a little tir'd me, but I was reviv'd by being assur'd I look'd not at all like an invalid, but as well as ever I did in my life. How deceitful one's looks sometimes are then, for I was far from being well or in good spirits. Mr. C. Moore is very much entertain'd with Dorothy's natural manner, and laughs in such *peals* it quite frightens the lookers-on, for fear he should go into fits. He is a very pleasant creature indeed, and seems always in equal good humour.'

She goes on to complain, with good reason, of being confined to the house 'on these beautiful sun-shine days' and says that she so longs to go out that she envies 'every poor little *beggar* running about in the open air'. She says that she expects to go to Clifton in the summer but looks forward to it with no pleasure as Sally and her mother will be in Scotland and she will be separated from them. On the other hand, she has pleasant memories of Clifton, and thinks she is more likely to get well there than in any other place in England. 'It is a lovely place, and I never was more delighted in my life than I was the first time I ever saw that walk there is between the rocks; a river runs through it, and when we were there it was evening, and there was one late boat coming home, and music in it.'

The folly of the medical treatment to which Maria was subjected, obvious to everyone in the present age of comparative enlightenment, was not lost on a sensible woman like Mrs. Piozzi who expressed her mind on the subject in her usual forthright terms. Writing on 27th March 1798 to Mrs. Pennington she says: 'We dined, in Mr. and Mrs. Whalley's company, at Mrs. Siddons' last week . . . Maria dined in the room, and looked (to me) as usual, yet everybody says she is ill, and in fact she was bled that very evening while we were at the lecture. Shutting a young, half-consumptive girl up in *one unchanged air* for three or four months would make *any* of them ill, and ill-humoured too, I should think. But 'tis *the new way* to make them breathe their own infected breath over and over again now, in defiance of old books, old experience and good old common sense.'

In Maria's next letter to Miss Bird, dated 8th April 1798, she is more cheerful in tone and relates a piece of gossip which shows the anxiety felt in London about the progress of the war with France. 'Mr. Windham was here last night; and really he frighten'd me out of my wits about the French. He says they will certainly come and kill us all, *or worse*: I never heard anything so dreadful as his account of their intentions, and he says they will be here in six weeks perhaps, you, I daresay, are not so much alarm'd, at a distance from London, as we are.'

Sally wrote again to the beloved Miss Bird on 16th April and relieved her anxieties respecting Mr. Charles Moore, for whom

Miss Bird had evidently conceived a tender passion. '*I see him come with pleasure, and depart without regret,*' she says, adding, to comfort her, that she does not believe that the 'object which charms' Miss Bird 'is any more interested respecting us than we are about him. He laughs and talks with unceasing gaiety and good humour, I never saw him otherwise, and these are not the tokens by which I discover a love-sick heart'. She tells her friend that she has been composing songs lately, 'one or two of which are much approv'd of' and that Maria has at length burst from confinement, has been 'three times out in the carriage', has walked a little, and that her spirits are greatly mended. She then refers in very guarded language to the fact that she is 'surrounded with doubts, fears, and perplexities, from which I see not how to extricate myself. . . . Oh, you cannot guess my situation, but you pity me, I am sure. . . . You give me credit for some philosophy; could you know the history of my life for the last two years, you would not call back your praise. . . . Miss Lawrence is, I suppose, by this time with you; pray mention me kindly to her: have either of you heard from Mr. Lawrence? I once took it in my head you corresponded. How strange Miss L. must think this last affair; this time last year—good Heavens!—what changes have I seen since that time. Do tell me if it does not appear to you almost impossible for that violent passion, of which you were so close a witness, to be entirely vanish'd? And yet so it must be, or would the treasure, almost in his possession, have been resign'd? Ten weeks ago, who could have foreseen this? . . .'

Her anxieties as to the whereabouts of her lover were very soon set at rest. Sally and Lawrence, after an enforced separation, met again and came to a complete understanding, as the letters which follow make clear. They were apparently not available to Dr. Oswald Knapp. Their importance lies in the fact that they supply the essential clue to everything which happened between the time that Lawrence received them and Maria's death. The letters were among the Lawrence papers bequeathed to his friend and sole executor, Mr. Keightley. If included in the five immense volumes of letters, by and to Sir Thomas Lawrence, which were placed at the disposal of Mr. G. L. Layard by Mr. Keightley's daughters, they were not quoted by him in his book *Sir Thomas Lawrence's Letter-Bag*. They were first given to the world by Lady Priestley, in an important article entitled 'An Artist's Love Story' which appeared in *The Nineteenth Century and After*, for April 1905. I am able to reproduce them here through the courtesy of Mr. John G. Nicholson, almost the only direct descendant of Mr. Keightley, and the grandson of his daughter, Lady Nicholson. The first of the letters is without address or date, but both were evidently written in the second half of the month of April 1798.

'Friday Morning.
Our friend in Dorset Street (Mrs. Semple) is a good and kind friend, and you may, if you please, tell her all; and that will not, I imagine, be more than she suspects, for I believe I thank'd her a little too warmly when she put your letter in my hand. He is such a creature (says she), there is really no denying him any-thing. Ah! Mrs. Semple, thought I, and do *you* feel his strange, resistless power? No wonder, then, that Sally is thus led on, step by step, to feel and to confess that she is again upon the point of surrendering that heart which (plaguing thing that it is!) was lost for a great while some time ago, and now is teasing and tor-menting her to let it go where it is sure of being well receiv'd. And, besides, it is jealous of *another heart*, which it declares it sees plainly enough I do "to every heart prefer"; and so I have a good mind to bid it begone, and rid myself of its importunity, especially as it has the generosity to assure me that, delighted as it shall be with its new abode, *it will obey my call* and, should its rival prove inconstant, will immediately return to Sally. Yet I think I should consult some friend before I make so dangerous a change. What do you think of it? I know you will tell me of *friends averse*, of *circumstances embarrassed*, of the *time that must elapse in secrecy and anxiety*, and, above all, of the *inconstancy of man*. My good friend, I have thought of all this twenty and twenty times. Your last is indeed a serious (forgive me if I differ from you and say I think it is the only) objection, for constancy and perseverance may surely overcome the others. The time that must pass before we could avow our sentiments may

be employ'd by him (you know who I mean) to extricate himself from all pecuniary difficulties, for *do not suspect me of being so mad as to add to the embarrassments of him I love by giving him a wife to support. Indeed, you wrong me if you do. The more I love him the stronger will be this resolution.* But tell me, you who are his friend and mine—and tell me, I charge you, the truth, for I know you can—will his exertions, if he perseveres, enable him at last to marry one who will have nothing but a heart to offer? I know that this must be the work of perhaps years. I do not start at the idea, for *I know myself*; but will he be constant for *years?* I do not mean that we are to pass all this time situated as we are at present. I wait but for the time when Maria shall be evidently engaged by some other object to declare to her my intentions, and then there will be no more of this cruel restraint and we may overcome the objections of those whose objections are of importance. And now, having finished my letter to *your friend*, I will begin one to you. You cannot be in earnest when you talk of being soon again in Marlborough Street; *you know it is impossible.* Neither you, nor Maria, nor I could bear it. Do you think that tho' she does not love you, she would feel no unpleasant sensations to see those attentions paid to another which once were hers? Could you bear to pay them, could I endure receiving them? Oh no! banish this idea. Your *absence* indeed affects Maria but little—so little that I am convinced she never lov'd—but your *presence*, you must feel, would place us all in the most distressing situation imaginable. I was told that you pass'd thro' our street yesterday; I did not see you. If chance should ever bring you this way at nine o'clock in the morning and if it should occur to you to look towards our house, you might see a friend of yours at one of the parlour windows, where she is generally writing or reading at that hour, and where she now is, the clock just striking nine. I went last night with my father to a fine party where there were between fifty and sixty people—not one that I ever saw before or ever wish to see again. I was seated by one of the card tables. "You seem very attentive to the game, Miss Siddons" said a gentleman to me. "Are you learning or criticising?" "Neither, Sir," replied I. And in truth, tho' my eyes might be fix'd on the Cards, my thoughts were employ'd by a much more serious game, upon the event of which depends my happiness or wretchedness. How much better would Mr. Burke's speech suit me than you! If I have any merit, believe me, it consists in this. Not that I know much—far, far from it—but that *I am desirous of knowing more.* I will not suffer you to rate me too highly. I cannot bear the thoughts of your deceiving yourself in this respect. It seems like mockery when you talk to me of being *my pupil.* No, no; I have too much pleasure in the hopes of becoming yours to make any such agreement. I know that, should the prospect I now have before my eyes ever be realised, you will be much employ'd. So much the better. The more I see of men that have nothing to do, the more I wish that my husband may be oblig'd to do something. This temporary separation will, in my eyes, have many advantages. I can find employment for a morning as well as you. It is my choice to be alone in the morning; no one in an evening has greater delight in society. Need I tell you there is *one (if he is but constant)* whose company I would prefer to all the world? I inquire after you whenever I have an opportunity, and I am rejoic'd to hear that you paint diligently, and that the "Coriolanus" is likely to leave all behind it at the exhibition, as "Satan" did last year. I recall my words. Yes, I will suffer a rival: I permit you to be almost as much devoted to your divine Art as to Sally. When I hear of your attention and perseverance in painting I will consider it as the proof of your attachment to me. I have thought of something. It is of vegetable substance, *very white at present,* but you may cure it of that defect very soon. I have set you the example. Can you guess? Adieu! In the present circumstance your plan of secrecy is an excellent one. Nobody need know what passes; from me they certainly will not. I will try to make myself easy, since my conduct is no secret to her whose approbation is as dear to me as my life; but I shall have much to endure. I foresee it. I am not one of those who can set at nought the opinions of my friends. But you should be the better pleas'd that I am not, for is it not a sacrifice I make you? Oh, then, judge me not by others; think not that when you have won my heart you may abandon me and I shall soon recover. I tell you now, before you proceed any further, that *if I love you again* I shall love more than ever, and in that case *disappointment* would be *death.*'

This letter bore no signature, and was addressed to 'Mr. Lawrence, Greek Street', on the back. The second letter is dated

'Tuesday morning. 12 o'clock
[24th April, 1798.]

And did I indeed see you, speak to you, last night? Good heavens! was it not rather a dream? No, no, it was reality. How short, how cruelly short, did the time appear! It seem'd to me that I had a thousand thousand things to say to you, and yet, I think, I said nothing. But was it necessary to *say*? Oh! could you not read in my eyes the ecstacy of my heart? I could scarcely imagine it was reality; and yet "such sober certainty of waking bliss I never felt (*but once*) before".

You will not be surprised at my writing to you; you will guess that the cause which oblig'd me to resign this pleasure is *in part* remov'd. I will tell you more on Thursday. Yes, I will *tell* you; for if it is fine I mean to walk before breakfast, as I have done every fine morning lately. I shall be in Poland Street before nine. You have a key of Soho Square: shall we walk there? Oh time, time, fly quickly till Thursday morning! But alas! as hours last night appeared but moments, so will moments now be long, *long hours.*

I looked for you all over the pit last night, and had almost despair'd of seeing you; but I found you out before you saw me. You were on both sides up one pair of stairs; then in the stage-box, where I believe Mr. Lysons pointed me out. Sunday and Monday—happy days! They have repaid me for a month of anxiety. I can hardly hope that I shall be so happy as to see you, as I intend, on Thursday. If I should, Thursday will acquire another charm for me. *One o'clock*—how often, how impatiently do I look at my watch from breakfast till that hour! And when it comes—tell me, tell me—do you think of Sally? I sit where you have sat; I stand where you have stood; I look round on those Shakespeare prints, I try to recollect your observations on them. And which do I look on longest, most intently? *Orlando—dear Orlando!* And then I write. Would you know what? You shall *read.*

I can no longer continue my Journal as I us'd; I dare not write my thoughts now; but, since I am forbid to express the feelings of my heart in my own words, I transcribe those lines, wherever I find them, which best accord with my own sentiments and situation. *This* is what you shall read. Have you taken your ring to Cowen's? But do not learn the puzzle of him; let me only teach it. Do you know its name? Have they told you it is a True Lover's Knot? I bought it for you. I have worn it, kissed it, and waited anxiously for an opportunity to give it you. Last night, beyond my hopes, it presented itself. You have it, keep it, love it, nor ever part with it till *you return me my letters.*

You like my locket. Your hair and my mother's are in it—think if I prize it! I wear it always, but . . . [torn] . . . When you go to see Miss Bird you will hear my songs and see the fashions. The first I think you would like if you did not love me; the *last, miserable as they are,* you will look at with pleasure because I did them.

You have sometimes praised my singing and my compositions. I remember, too, you once observ'd I was improv'd since you first heard me. Well I might. I never should have sung as I do had I never seen you; I never should have composed *at all.* Have I not told you that the first song I set to music was that complaint of Thomson's to the Nightingale? I compos'd it at Harrow Weald. You then liv'd in my heart, in my head, in every idea; every moment your image was present. *You did not love me then.* But now! Oh, mortification, grief, agony are all forgot!!!'

The effect of these letters on Lawrence can easily be imagined. Coming from Sally, whom he regarded as the incarnation of sincerity, they must have afforded him the most complete assurance that his love was returned.

His subsequent actions can only be understood if we realise th
although obstacles were put in the way of their meeting or con
municating with one another he was convinced of Sally's fidelit

A letter from Maria to Miss Bird, written on 6th May, sugges
that that perspicacious young school mistress had more than a
inkling of the true character of the younger Siddons girl.
am a little angry with you', Maria writes, 'for some part of yo
letter, when you wish I may resume my favourite employme
of *conquest-making*. You are deceiv'd, I assure you, I have a
abomination of it. Some people may do it innocently enough, b
I particularly feel how wrong it is, and I hope I shall always sh
it. I am very serious, you think, but I always am when I a
suppos'd, even in joke, to be a *conquest-maker*.' She goes on
speak of Sally's new songs, particularly of 'When Summer
burning heats arise', and says that she thinks Sally's voice h
improved and that she 'never heard singing that delighted me
hers does'. From this we may gather that at this period Sal
was happy in her love and still hopeful that her romance woul
have a happy ending. Maria goes on to mention that 'We are a
to leave Town the beginning of next month, I believe, for Clifto
and most happy shall I be to turn my back on this place, whe
I have suffer'd so much, and be permitted to stroll about in th
beautiful lanes by myself'.

Sally's next letter to Miss Bird was written from 'Prince
Buildings No. 6, Clifton', and is dated Wednesday, 15th Jun
1798. She says that 'Maria is not at all the worse for her journe
and I hope this fine and famous air will soon restore her entirel
to herself:—indeed I have no fear of her (not) doing very we
during the Summer, but I shall dread the return of Winter, it wi
I fear, be a great trial to her. She begins to-day to drink th
Waters, and to ride double.' Other items of news, besides th
usual arch references to the Charles's, are that she is going wit
her father to Bristol, 'to try if I can find a Piano Forte' and th
her parents intend to stay at Clifton a month. After that, she say
'if Maria is pretty well, and in good spirits, I shall accompany m
Mother, who wants a companion sadly in her Summer excu
sions'. In a later letter Sally mentions that she is going to a Ba

and that 'Miss Lee brings Miss Tickell from Bath on purpose to go with me'. The reference to Miss Lee is one of many indications of the intimacy which existed between Sally and Maria and some of Lawrence's closest friends. Miss Bird, as we have seen, was the friend and partner of Lucy Lawrence, and references which occur in the correspondence to Amelia Lock, who subsequently married John Angerstein, to Samuel Lysons and others, show that the Siddonses were on familiar terms with these members of what may be described as the inner circle of Lawrence's acquaintances. The Miss Lee referred to here was probably Miss Sophia Lee (1750–1824), one of two literary spinsters living in Bath to both of whom Lawrence was greatly attached. Sophia Lee was able, out of the profits of her comedy, *The Chapter of Accidents*, to establish a school for girls at Belvedere House, Bath, to which Mrs. Siddons subsequently sent her youngest daughter, Cecilia. Harriet Lee (1757–1851) was also a well-known novelist and dramatist, whose chief work, *The Canterbury Tales*, was appearing at this time. In the same year, 1798, Harriet refused an offer of marriage from William Godwin. The two sisters were the daughters of John Lee, an actor and adapter of plays, who had been associated with Garrick and was manager of the Bath theatre in 1778–9.

Sally's letter contains also a revealing description of her mother's close friend, Mrs. Pennington, the kindly but rather ridiculous woman who received Maria into her home at Clifton and looked after her with great devotion until her death. As Penelope Weston, she had been a member of the artistic and literary coterie which surrounded Dr. Johnson's friend Anna Seward, the famous 'Swan of Lichfield', and included Mrs. Piozzi, Harriet Lee and others. For the past six years she had been married to William Pennington, a prominent local figure and minor Beau Nash who had been 'inducted to the office of the Master of the Ceremonies at the Clifton Hot Wells in 1785' and continued to preside over the entertainments of the visitors to the Spa for nearly thirty years. Their home was at Dowry House, Clifton. Sally confesses to Miss Bird that she finds this excellent couple a little overpowering. They are going, she says, 'by water to dine at a Gentleman's House who lives near King's Weston, where we shall stroll about, and return again by water. It will be very pleasant, and I should like it much better if our friends Mr. and Mrs. Pennington were not to be of the party, for her incessant talk is rather fatiguing, and the beauties of Nature call forth such a *torrent of eloquence* that there is no possibility of enjoying them in her company. It seems to me quite impossible she can feel the sensations she finds such fine language to explain. When I am most affected I am most silent!' She refers later to her delight in dancing and says that 'my partner must be odious indeed if I am not pleas'd to dance; if he is agreeable, the pleasure is double. I wish it may be my lot to meet with such a one on Tuesday, though I trouble myself but little about that, since, if I dance, I am *satisfied*'. She concludes by mentioning that she must go and get ready 'for a Gentleman who is to call, and take me out in an open carriage'. The letter contains no hint of what she must have been feeling and thinking about her lover and seems designed to throw dust in Miss Bird's eyes and make her think that she is heartwhole and free from care.

Shortly after the letter was written Sally set off with her mother on a tour of the Midlands, which included appearances in such towns as Cheltenham, Gloucester, Worcester, Hereford and Birmingham. Mrs. Siddons's letters to Mrs. Pennington naturally show great anxiety about Maria's health, although she seems not to anticipate any immediate danger and still hopes that the air of Clifton will do her good. Sally writes to Miss Bird that Maria has been 'allowed to go to two balls, tho' not to dance' and that she herself has passed her time 'very pleasantly at Cheltenham; we made two or three agreeable acquaintances, I went to one Ball, and danc'd all that was to be danc'd, but I'm an indefatigable, and three hours will not satisfy me'. Shortly after this, Sally fell ill, and her harassed mother, in a letter to Mrs. Pennington, though she does not explicitly mention Lawrence, gives very clearly one at least of her reasons for opposing his wish to marry her ailing daughter. 'How vainly did I flatter myself,' she writes, 'that this other dear creature had acquired the strength of constitution to throw off this cruel disorder. Instead of that, it returns with increasing velocity and violence. What a sad prospect is this for her in

REV. ANDREW LAWRENCE

When this portrait was re-lined, the date 1804 was found painted on the stretcher.
Lawrence exhibited an earlier portrait of his eldest brother at the Royal Academy
of 1790. The picture reproduced here is by permission of Mr. Christopher Norris of
Polesden Lacey.

PRINCESS CAROLINE OF BRUNSWICK, WIFE OF GEORGE IV

marriage? for I am now convinc'd it is constitutional, and will pursue her thro' life! Will a husband's tenderness keep pace with and compensate for the loss of a mother's, her unremitting care and soothings? Will he not grow sick of these repeated attacks, and think it vastly inconvenient to have his domestic comforts, his pleasures, or his business interfered with by the necessary and habitual attentions which they will call for from himself and from his servants? Dr. Johnson says the man must be almost a prodigy of virtue who is not soon tir'd of an ailing wife; and sad experience has taught even *me*, who might have hop'd to have assured that attention which *common gratitude* for a life of labour in the service of my family shou'd have offered, that illness, often repeated, or long-continued, soon tries a man. To say the truth, a sick wife *must* be a *great misfortune*.'

While there is much truth and common sense in Mrs. Siddons's observations, it must be said, in fairness to Lawrence, that he was a very different type of man from William Siddons. He showed exceptional solicitude whenever any of his friends, relations or servants fell ill and did everything he could for them, often at considerable inconvenience to himself. Had he been permitted to marry Sally it is impossible to doubt that his care for her would have been unremitting. So loyal a son, so loyal a brother, so loyal a friend, could not have failed to make a devoted and constant husband.

IX

THE DEATH OF MARIA

WHAT Lawrence was doing in the months immediately following the receipt of Sally's love-letters we have no means of knowing except through the letters of Mrs. Siddons and Mrs. Pennington. He must have been in a high state of excitement, which evidently turned to apprehension when Sally ceased to write. As his renewed understanding with her was still a secret, the only questions he was able to put to John Philip Kemble, whose portrait in the character of Coriolanus was among the six pictures which he exhibited in 1798, were connected with the health of Maria. He and Kemble had become close friends, but not close enough to enable Lawrence, who in any case never discussed his private affairs, to take him into his confidence. No doubt he heard stray bits of gossip about what was happening at Clifton from Miss Sophia Lee, and possibly from his sister Lucy, who would have heard from Miss Bird the scraps of news conveyed in Sally's and Maria's guarded letters. As Lucy was his favourite sister and stayed with him in Greek Street while he was courting the Siddons girls, she must have had a pretty shrewd idea of her brother's feelings.

There were ample grounds for Lawrence's fears that influences were being brought to bear on Sally which were inimical to his hopes. Poor sick Maria, having nothing to do but think about herself, had been confiding in the garrulous and gushing Mrs. Pennington and had played upon her sympathies by giving a distorted picture of her *affaire* with the wicked Mr. Lawrence. In an effort to cheer up the invalid Mrs. Pennington had taken to reading aloud to her from the novels then in vogue. One of these was Mrs. Sheridan's *The Memoirs of Miss Sidney Biddulph*, the hero of which, Orlando, is represented as having trifled with the affections of another lady, while courting the heroine. Maria, not being an actress's daughter for nothing, at once saw herself and Sally in the role of these cruelly treated young women and proceeded to play her part for all it was worth before her susceptible hostess. She expressed to Mrs. Pennington the horror and repugnance she felt at the idea of her sister ever becoming Lawrence's wife. She pretended to be convinced that any such union would be fatal to Sally's happiness. In the evidently long and detailed account of these conversations which Mrs. Pennington at once wrote off to Mrs. Siddons, she claimed to have pleaded with Maria that Sally should be left free to follow her own inclinations in the matter, but without in any way altering Maria's views. In her long reply, Mrs. Siddons, who was then at Birmingham, praises her friend for having 'developed' Maria's character 'with a depth of penetration, a delicacy of perception, and sweet indulgence, that at once astonishes and charms me'. We may, however, be excused for thinking that both Mrs. Siddons and Mrs. Pennington allowed their tender hearts to deceive them as to Maria's true character and motives. 'Sally is well again,' Mrs. Siddons writes, 'and I thank you most sincerely for the sollicitude you have so kindly evinc'd for her future happiness. I *have* done *all*, my dear friend, that it is possible to do; for before your last and most excellent letter I had suggested to her my doubts, my fears. The GOOD SENSE and TENDERNESS it was evident had *needed no prompter*, and while she ingenuously confessed her predilection, she was as well aware of Mr. L's blameable conduct as anyone could be and declar'd that (Maria *totally out of the question*) she felt the weight of many other objections that seem'd to preclude the possibility of the dreaded event.'

In view of the fact that only a few months previously Sally had fully forgiven Lawrence for his 'blameable conduct' and declared her passion for him in terms which, for the period, were amazingly outspoken, this attitude on her part, if her mother reported it correctly, betrays a weakness of character which it is difficult to admire. Admittedly her position was both painful and embarrassing, since her devotion to her mother and sister was, in a way, no less strong than her devotion to her lover, nevertheless she does not appear to have extricated herself from it very creditably. In a postcript, Mrs. Siddons adds: 'What relates to Mr. L. and Sally in this hasty scrawl you may perhaps think it right to communicate to Maria. *That* to your own discretion—*never enough* to be ADMIR'D.' In view of what followed, this admiration is difficult to share.

Mrs. Siddons's movements during the next few weeks cannot now be followed in detail, but she evidently paid a flying visit to Brighton, for she writes from there to Mrs. Pennington, perhaps in August. From her letter we gather that Sally has recovered from an attack of her complaint, but 'My poor Husband', she says, 'is quite lame, absolutely walking on crutches. Something is the matter with his knee, but whether Rheumatism, or Gout, or what it is, heaven knows; and the terrible, yet not irrational dread of becoming a cripple makes him very melancholy—Alas! alas!' In spite of all her anxieties and afflictions, the indomitable, Immortal', as Lawrence once called her, 'played twice to fine Houses and the Prince frequents the Theatre with great attention and decorum'. He commanded her to have supper with him at the Pavilion, which she at first declined, from a disinclination to meet the scandalous Lady Jersey, who was then the Prince's mistress, but 'when I came to talk it over with Mr. Sid, he thought it best that I shou'd recant my refusal'. She seems to have overcome her repugnance for Lady Jersey who, she says, 'certainly wou'd look handsome if she wou'd not affect at forty-eight to be eighteen'. Mrs. Siddons, herself, was then forty-three.

Maria's health now began to change for the worse and her condition was rapidly becoming critical. After her return to Birmingham, Mrs. Siddons sent Sally, in charge of Mr. Macready, the manager of the theatre there, by post-chaise to Clifton, to be with her sister. 'By this means, too,' she says, 'we shall avoid the distress of meeting with Mr. L. who is come here, I understand, upon a visit to his sister. This charming girl has determined, and this day I told him so, to put an end to his expectations. It is two o'clock—I am harass'd, fatigued to death, body and mind, and feel a heaviness that I will encourage—It is long since I have slept.' Lawrence, like any other man in love who has received the clearest proof that his feelings are reciprocated by the object of his affections, was driven half demented by Mrs. Siddons's announcement that Sally had rejected him and refused to accept his dismissal as final. In a later letter to Mrs. Pennington, Mrs. Siddons throws more light on what must have been a stormy interview. 'My dear Soul,' she writes, 'I know not if Sally has told you that this Mr. L. was at Birmingham when she left me. He has left this place without letting a soul know whither he is gone. His hopes with regard to Sally, I, with her own concurrence, told him were entirely at an end, representing at the same time the situation of her sister. I suppose he is almost mad with remorse, and think it is likely that he may be at this moment at Clifton. I pray God his phrenzy may not impell him to some *desperate action!* What he can propose by going thither I know not, but it is fit they should both be on their guard. Mr. S. knows nothing of *all this*, the situation of dear Sally, when one recurs to her original partiality for this wretched madman, placing *her* in so delicate a situation, we thought it best to keep the matter entirely conceal'd, as it was *impossible* that anything cou'd come of it, if ever, NEVER, she was RESOLV'D, till her sister shou'd be perfectly restor'd. I hope it will always be a secret to Mr. S. as it could answer no end but to enrage *him* and make us *all* still more unhappy. . . .' She adds, in a postscript, what effectively disposes of the calumnious assertions made by some of Lawrence's detractors, that his treatment of Maria caused her death. 'If he *shou'd* be at Clifton and be impell'd to make an éclat of this business, he will *ruin himself for ever*, and make us the talk of the whole world—it is dreadful to think of, and the effect on my *poor Maria!* Oh God! His mind is tortured, I suppose, with the idea of hasting her end. I REALLY, my dear friend, do not think so, and if one knew where he was, to endeavour to take this poison from it, he *might* be persuaded to be quiet. Dr. Pearson premis'd from the *very beginning* all that has or is likely to happen to her. But the agonies of this *poor wretch*, if he thinks otherwise, *must* be INSUPPORTABLE.'

As Lawrence knew perfectly well, from Sally herself, that Maria had never really loved him, and he would have been a fool had he supposed that her illness had any connection with the broken engagement, Mrs. Siddons's diagnosis of his 'phrenzy' as being due to 'remorse' was evidently mistaken. It is hard to understand how so experienced a woman could ever have made such a blunder. As for Lawrence, who has been so frequently represented as an inconstant flirt, incapable of deep and genuine feeling, it can only be said that his actions in the ensuing weeks are impossible to reconcile with such a conception of his character and it seems that Sally herself did him less than justice. He behaved exactly as any man might behave who was passionately in love and believed, what was in fact the truth, that unfair pressure was being brought to bear on Sally by her mother and her dying sister to force her, against her will, to give him up.

At this point it may be well to consider on what evidence the often repeated charge that Lawrence habitually trifled with the affections of young women and paid them insincere attentions actually rests. Lawrence, like Mrs. Siddons, had a brilliantly successful professional career which brought him public fame and rendered his appearance in what may be called 'court circles' almost obligatory. The fashionable portrait painter, like the renowned actress, dined with the Prince of Wales, attended balls and functions and played the parts allotted to him on the stage of High Society to which his talents had given him the *entrée*. Both of them kept their personal or private life separate from their public lives, both chose their inner circle of friends from people connected with their respective professions and from what may be termed the middle-class intelligentsia. Mrs. Siddons, we can believe, was more herself when she was hobnobbing with such friends as Mrs. Pennington, Dr. and Mrs. Whalley or Mrs. Piozzi than when, for professional reasons, she was dining with the Prince of Wales in the company of Lady Jersey. Similarly Lawrence, although his good looks and charm of manner made him a sought-after figure in the world of rank and fashion, was much more himself when he was dining quietly with men like Samuel Lysons, Farington and the Smirkes, or spending an evening in Dean Street with Mr. and Mrs. Hamilton. In our own day no less than in the days of the Regency famous painters appear to exercise a peculiar fascination over young women.

There can be no doubt that, from his boyhood in Bath, Lawrence continued, at least through the early part of his life, to be pestered with the attentions of empty-headed females and it is more than probable that, as a measure of self-protection, he developed a manner which both flattered them and, at the same time, kept them at arm's length. His real friends he chose with care, for their qualities of heart and mind, and it is noticeable that these very rarely belonged to the aristocracy of birth. He seems to have been as nearly free from the vice of snobbery as any Englishman can be, and, except for his aberration in regard to Maria, who was after all half a Kemble, and had her share of what, for him, was the Kemble glamour, there is no recorded instance of his ever having loved a woman, however beautiful, who could not share his intellectual interests. Not only were his friends, both men and women, people of exceptional character and intellectual gifts, but his friendships were lasting and his loyalty in this relationship was no less outstanding than his loyalty as a son and brother. Inconstancy, save only in the one tragic instance of Maria Siddons, is the very last charge that can with any degree of fairness be brought against him.

Mrs. Siddons's fears that Lawrence might be intending to hurry off to Clifton in the hope of finding out for himself what it was which had caused Sally to renounce him were fully justified. After leaving her, he made straight for the Hot Wells, put up in an hotel there under an assumed name, and began operations by writing a long, involved, but almost frantically sincere letter to Mrs. Pennington. He wrote:

'My name is Lawrence, and you, then, I believe, know that I stand in the most afflicting situation possible! A man charg'd (I trust untruly in their lasting effect) with having inflicted pangs on one lovely Creature which, in their bitterest extent, he himself now suffers from her sister!

I love—exist but for Miss Siddons, and am decisively rejected by her.

If I have touch'd her heart—would I knew I had—her present conduct is the more noble, correct and pure as every thought and action of her sweet character! If founded on the consideration I hope it is, I will not, dare not rail, hardly murmur at the decision which exalts the Object of my love.

Be assur'd, Madam, the Paper I have enclos'd has in it nothing contrary to this sentiment, and it is therefore I have confidence in requesting that you will, at a fit but speedy moment, *give it into her own Hand.*

I know, Madam, that secresy should always be justified by Reason; and the reasons for it in the present case are very obvious. Miss Maria's situation is, I know, a very dangerous one. *If it is* REALLY *render'd more so by feelings I may have excited, the least mention of me would be hazardous in the extreme.* If it is not, and her complainings on this head are but the weakness of sick fancy, perhaps of Hope, wishing to attribute her illness to any other than the true fix'd and alarming cause, still it will be giving an additional distress to her sister, and afford another opportunity for wounding me with a real, THO' NOT INTENTIONAL, injustice. I know her rectitude and worth!'

Lawrence's diagnosis of Maria's complainings as being due only to 'the weakness of sick fancy' was undoubtedly correct and he would not have been wrong had he described the fancy as 'spiteful and malevolent' as well as sick. The letter continues at great length in a mixture of agony, high-mindedness, stilted phraseology and genuine emotion, which might have melted a heart far more stony than that of plump and gushing Penelope Pennington. 'That Hour of severe distress in which Affection for the lamented Object invests every Thought and Action with Angelic Purity,' he says, 'when the querulousness of sickness becomes the Complaint of Injur'd Virtue; when Hints are Commands, and implied Wishes (however irrational or fancifully construed) binding as the most sacred duties;—should that moment soon arrive—God! God! avert it!—how dangerous will it be to that trembling Hope which, half-broken as it is, my heart still cherishes as its sole spring of Life!' It is evident from this that Lawrence had guessed from what Mrs. Siddons had let fall that Maria intended to use her dying energies in preventing his marriage with Sally. That there was something fiendish in Maria's disposition, notwithstanding her angelic purity, was certainly not lost on him, though he writes with the ingenuity of a man fighting desperately for his future happiness and is careful to say nothing which could put Mrs. Pennington against him. Her reply to this letter has not been preserved, but she consented to see him, though not in her own home, and gave him a conditional promise of an interview with his 'dear angel' Sally. The interview seems to have taken place, though what the lovers said to each other can only be imagined. Mrs. Pennington promised to give him frequent reports of Maria's condition, and Lawrence returned to London by way of Birmingham, where he had two more stormy interviews with Mrs. Siddons. These she describes at considerable length to Mrs. Pennington in undated letters.

'I shudder to think on the effect this wretched madman's frenzy has had on you. *I* know the effect too well, for he well knows he has TERRIFIED me into *toleration* of his love for Sally by the horrible desperation of his conduct; and if his own words are to be believed, I have more than once shut upon him the Gate of SELF-DESTRUCTION by compromising (thou' without that self-possessing wisdom) as you have now done. Yes, that dear Sally, is indeed an Angel and, my dear Friend, she lov'd him; think then on the tremendous situation I was placed in, and let my tenderness for his feelings be the excuse for my weak indulgence.'

That Mrs. Siddons was torn with conflicting emotions, among which something very much like love for 'this unhappy man, on whom an EVIL FATE *seems to attend*' played a part which she is unwilling to recognise, is evident throughout this agonised letter. 'That so many excellencies,' she continues, 'should be thus alloy'd by ungovernable Passion is lamentable indeed. A duteous Son, a tender Brother, a kind and zealous friend: all these he is. I have *seen* him, and I bless God and you that you have reason'd him out of some extravagance that might have been dreadful in its present or future effects upon my POOR GIRLS or on himself. He appeared to be extremely repentant, and I was impell'd not only by policy and commiseration to treat him with more lenity than I thought I cou'd have done. I gave him my sincere forgiveness and calm advice, but told him positively that he had NOTHING MORE to hope from ME except my good wishes for his success and happiness. Oh, may I never have the painful part to play again!' That both she and Lawrence, whose histrionic gifts have been noted, gave an unforgettable private performance we can well believe, but this does not imply that their emotions were not deep and genuine. Quite ordinary people, in moments of crisis, speak, act and write in a manner which appears theatrical in contrast with their normal behaviour, so that it is hardly surprising that two people so closely connected with the stage as Lawrence and Mrs. Siddons adopted theatrical clichés when they were both profoundly moved. In a postscript Mrs. Siddons says: 'Mr. L. set off for London last night after pacing about here for three hours in agonies that brought me almost to fainting three or four times. He went off calmly, however, and with resolutions to be all that cou'd be wish'd. I hope for his own sake he will, for *we* I trust have seen the end of our sufferings from him.'

In a note written on the following day, she tells Mrs. Pennington that she 'was so shaken by his wild transports yesterday that, on rising to ring for some hartshorn and water, I should have fallen upon the floor if he had not fortunately caught me at the instant, and was totally incapacitated to play last night'. In the course of another long outburst to Mrs. Pennington, dated 'Fryday', the great actress again pours out her heart to the 'dearest, wisest, best of creatures', who must have felt highly flattered to be so described, about Lawrence's violence and what she regards as the weakness of character of a man who 'at the age of Thirty appears to have so little control over himself'. As, throughout his life, except only during this harrowing period, when he was almost driven insane by the violence of his frustrated passion, Lawrence was remarkable for his self-control and for the circumspection of his conduct, it seems that once again Mrs. Siddons proved a poor judge of character. She has the grace, however, to remark: 'Oh! that caprice and passion shou'd thus obscure the many excellencies and lofty genius of this man!'

After his return to London in a calmer mood, Lawrence wrote another long letter to Mrs. Pennington, dated 29th August, which occupies six pages of print in Dr. Knapp's *An Artist's Love Story*, in the course of which he seeks to convince her 'how reasonable has been every act of madness of which I am accus'd, and how very rational every wild Chimera that threaten'd me with the loss of this dear Girl'. Sally was gone, and he flew after her 'because I could neither know peace nor rest till I had seen her, or at least had such an explanation from her as satisfied me that I ow'd the loss of her Society to Necessity, and not to Choice'. Any man in love might be expected to act in the same way. A curious passage in this letter is a burlesque reference to the interview which took place between himself and Mrs. Pennington, on a broiling day, in a field behind the Bear at Clifton. Only a middle-aged woman with a very keen sense of humour could have read such a description of herself as Lawrence gave without being incensed, and it is odd to find so tactful and diplomatic a man running such a risk of giving offence to a woman whose help he needed so desperately. He begs her to let him hear that he is still loved, that 'in some pause of Sorrow one of the purest Hearts in the Creation yet beats for me, though hardly daring to tell itself the cause of its vibrations. . . . My Sally's truth I rest upon as on my Rock. *My* constancy is now not doubted'. He goes on to implore Mrs. Pennington to work on his behalf, with all the energy of her character. '*Think of my Gratitude!*' he says. '*Think that you are working out the happiness of two Beings destin'd (yes, with all my frailties), destined for each other by Love and Mind, by every feeling and perception of Heart and Intellect.*' At the end of the letter he refers to a drawing he is making of Maria, evidently in the hope that, when shown to her, it will soften her heart and render her hostility to his union with Sally less implacable by assuring her of his still warm if now fraternal affection. It was one of the crayon heads in which Lawrence excelled, and in view of the circumstances we may well believe that it was the best he ever did. It was duly forwarded to Clifton, but it has now vanished.

From now onwards Mrs. Pennington started making copies of

her answers to Lawrence's letters, and her literary style, influenced
by memories of the Swan of Lichfield, becomes more laboured,
pompous and selfconscious. It will have been noted that all the
actors in this domestic drama vied with one another in the expression of lofty sentiments and if there is much exposure of the
agony of wounded hearts, it is invariably, to the last degree,
high-minded and accompanied by the most virtuous protestations.
In the case of Lawrence and Mrs. Siddons, though they adhere as
far as possible to the epistolary manner at that period in vogue,
their agitation frequently gets the better of them and betrays
them into undisciplined, at times almost incoherent, utterance.
Mrs. Pennington, her emotions not being deeply involved, is
more controlled, and as we read her letters, which were from now
onwards intended for other eyes than those of the recipient, we
understand what Sally meant when she complained that it was
'impossible she can feel the sensations she finds such fine language
to explain'. She constantly exhorts Lawrence to govern his
passions, to exercise a rational discretion and not to indulge in the
excess produced by his emotions. 'Love this dear Girl (Sally),'
she writes, 'but love her with a sacred and reasonable devotion:
with that love which shall consecrate her true interest in your
heart superior to all selfish considerations: which not only leaves
her in the present distressing crisis in the unmolested, conscientious
discharge of her duties, but prompts her to the performance of
them.' The rest of the letter is a prolonged lecture to Lawrence
on the extravagances of his conduct, in the course of which she
conveys a reproof from Sally and asks him 'what less can a man
of sense and principle expect from a creature of rectitude and
intelligence like S.S. than that if he was weak enough to shock
her with the horrible idea of *Suicide*, she should assume energy
enough of Character to give him the reproof he merited, by
showing him she despised the threat? And by so doing she paid
him a much higher compliment than by admitting the possibility
of such an atrocious act, even for a moment, or flying with
frantic folly to save the ideot or Madman from his Fate?' In a way
which any woman less obtuse than Mrs. Pennington would
have realised must drive Lawrence half demented, she later

observes that 'We talk often of you—sometimes with a kindness that would be flattering—often in a style that you would not at all approve; because we lament that so many good Gifts as you possess, should be rendered in a great measure abortive by the eccentricities that shade your character; and instead of the excelling Thing you *might* be, leave you the mere Slave of Passion'. Lawrence's natural reaction on receiving this would be: 'I don't believe Sally ever said anything of the kind.' The letter, with unconscious sadism, makes clear that Mrs. Pennington did not at this time regard Sally's rejection of Lawrence as either final or conclusive. 'You have much to do, and to *undo*, my friend,' she remarks sententiously, 'before you can be deserving of this excellent Creature, should fortune and circumstances ever favor you so far as to put the prize within your reach.' Lawrence's reply to this exasperating effusion has not been preserved, but the nature of it can be gathered from Mrs. Pennington's next letter, dated 4th September. Before it was received Lawrence had completed his portrait of Maria and forwarded it to Clifton with a short and formal covering note.

Mrs. Pennington writes: 'You have favoured me with a Letter compounded of ingenuity, wit, and sarcasm. These are very amusing qualifications in a Correspondent; in a Lover, perhaps, I should not be very fond of tolerating the licence, and in a husband I should certainly fear, as much as I might admire, the spirit: but I am inclined to think great part of what lies before me is rather written *at* dear Sally than *to* me; and it is only honest to tell you, that she has the firmness to resist taking any part in this correspondence, and will neither peruse, nor hear read, your letters, nor my Replys.' It appears that Lawrence had referred to the possibility of his having a rival in Sally's affections, and for this suggestion he is roundly taken to task. It is possible that what prompted him to talk about a rival was the thought that by so doing he might force Sally to break her long silence. Another effort to force Sally's hand was, no doubt, Lawrence's remark, which he expected Sally to be told of, that he had exposed her 'two last letters to the perusal of his dearest Friend'. This produced from Mrs. Pennington, who was not, as we are, aware of the contents of the 'two last letters' which provide the clue to Lawrence's subsequent conduct, the comment that he had 'voluntarily and in a cool hour, abused the confidence of the woman he loved . . . a transaction that, situated as the person I allude to is with S.S., nothing can justify. There is no mind that could be candid enough, under circumstances so recent, to reconcile to her honour and advantage, an intercourse with the apostate Lover of her Sister'. Lawrence's 'dearest Friend', to whom, as we have seen, Sally addressed the greater part of one of her love letters, was, of course, himself. If Mrs. Pennington had shown this passage to Sally, as Lawrence obviously believed she would, the girl would have grasped its meaning immediately. On the subject of Maria's feeling for Lawrence Mrs. Pennington writes with more perspicacity than usual although what she has to say can only have increased Lawrence's apprehensions. 'With your knowledge of that degree of self-love which is interwoven into most of our characters, and which was certainly a prominent feature in this sweet creature's, you may well suppose that her *most favourable* sentiments of an unfaithful and inconstant Lover must ever be indignant:—that they are so, and *not tender*, you should hear with a sort of generous pleasure, or at least satisfaction. She said once, lately, she "wished Mr. Lawrence no ill, and freely forgave him the uneasiness he had caused her"—make your own comment on these words, and spare me further on the subject.'

Mrs. Pennington refused to show Maria Lawrence's idealised drawing of her, which might have soothed her vanity, afforded her some secret satisfaction and possibly lessened her desire for vengeance, on grounds that seem highly questionable. 'I know it was intended as a peace-offering to Maria,' she writes, 'and am persuaded the present is not a fit season to mention the subject. She would connect it with the idea she so recently entertained, of your having been here, and had an intercourse with her Sister: this idea seems to have again subsided, and its revival could produce no other effect than an increased irritation, ever most injurious to her. If she lives to return to London, she shall know of this gift in your most graceful manner. The drawing has the stamp of a great Artist and, what I prize more, a striking resemblance of features for which I shall always retain a fond and tender remembrance; and once more, I sincerely thank you, dear Sir, for this treasure.'

As her illness progressed Maria completely lost her looks and the vain girl could have gained nothing but misery from seeing herself in the glass. The satisfaction of gazing at Lawrence's portrait of herself as she had been, in the flower of her beauty, was denied her and the 'treasure' was not even preserved. A memorandum in Mrs. Pennington's handwriting, attached to the letter quoted above, conveys more of her real sentiments and shows that she is now actively set on keeping Lawrence and Sally apart.

'This torment of a man again importuned me to prevail on Sally to receive his letters, and renew their correspondence, and I was compelled to return him the following concise and rough reply—"The Being you persecute is not sufficiently impassioned to go the length of your heroics, and you are too *Pindaric* a genius to be at all content to love and go on like 'Folks of this world.' You will therefore continue to torment each other for a while, and then, weary of this 'delightful anguish', by mutual consent, give up the point. Much more time is necessary to give the past to Oblivion than your impetuosity and restlessness of temper is disposed to admit, and Sally will not lose of what she owes to herself and others; and therefore I think I know perfectly *what the end must be.*"

Again—"Your having been tempted, by *any* motive or consideration, to expose dear Sally's letters to the observation of anyone but Mrs. Siddons, is a bar to the renewal of correspondence not to be got over. Here, then, the matter must rest; I positively will no more enter on the discussion of these points".

The 'bar' to which Mrs. Pennington refers was of her own and not of Sally's making, and her remarks prove how untrustworthy she was as 'medium through which poor Sally chose to transmit her sentiments and feelings to Mr. Lawrence'. Lawrence got to hear through his friend Mr. Twiss, the husband of Frances Kemble, Mrs. Siddons's younger sister, that Sally had once more fallen a victim to her congenital illness, and his anxiety on her account induced him to write again to Mrs. Pennington. The date of the postmark is 7th September 1789. He says: 'How *can* I be silent when I know that this dear Creature is ill!' and begs for a line telling him how she is. 'Never have I lov'd her more, never with so pure an ardour, as in the last moment of sickness I was witness of (the period she must remember) when, in spite of the intreaties of her dear Mother and Maria, I stole into her room, and found her unconscious of the step of friend or relation; her faculties ic'd over by that cursed poison, [laudanum] and those sweet eyes unable to interpret the glance that, at that instant, not apathy itself could have mistaken. No, my dear Mrs. P., if her days of sickness *trebled* those of health, still she should be mine, and dearer than ever to my heart, from the sacrifice of this distrustful and selfish delicacy to confidence and love; from this generous pledge of her esteem and trust in the *heart* of the man she loves. In ardour I fear it is beyond her own—in tenderness, truth and constancy it shall not be behind it. Never! never! never!'

This obviously sincere and moving letter prompts the reflection that Lawrence, had Mrs. Siddons and Mrs. Pennington understood his real character, could have been relied upon by them to make their dear Sally happy during whatever years might remain to her. Their obtuseness and Maria's malignancy, as we shall see, combined to inflict the most intense suffering on two young people, deeply in love with one another. On Sally's side there was undoubtedly a certain weakness of will, caused partly by her illness, but more by her intense devotion to her mother and to Maria and the overpowering influences thus brought to bear upon her. In a letter to Sally Bird, written on 15th September, less than a month before Maria's death, she refers to Lawrence in a way which reflects not her own feelings but the ideas which had been sedulously put into her head. She says:

'What aggravation to my present misery are my reflections upon that unfortunate affair! Heaven grant that restless being may be quiet, at least with respect to us. That he can ever be happy is, I fear, impossible. His strong genius and disposition impel him to seek for and to conquer difficulties; the object of his desires,

LADY GEORGIANA FANE

Exhibited at the British Institution in 1830. Engraved by C. Turner in 1828. In the Tate Gallery.

THOMAS CAMPBELL
In the National Portrait Gallery.

once obtain'd, *becomes indifferent*, some new idea fills his imagination, more danger must be encounter'd to fulfil his wishes, and
thus, I greatly fear, a life will be pass'd, which might have been
spent, *oh, how differently!* with more steadiness and consistency
of character, joined to talents and fascination which no mortal
ever was so highly gifted with!'

If the last clause in this sentence can be regarded as expressing
Sally's real feelings, the remainder of it can be dismissed as 'pure
Pennington'. No one could have shown more steadiness and
consistency of character than the recipient of Sally's love-letters.
She concludes by saying: 'Thank Heaven, dear Maria's mind is
perfectly tranquil concerning him, she thinks not of him, or if
she does, it is only to hope that I will never have anything to do
with this, *our common enemy*, as she calls him.'

Maria now got rapidly worse and Lawrence was forced to renew
his correspondence with Mrs. Pennington in the hope of hearing
news of her condition. In one of his letters he says, with bitter
sarcasm which must have been lost on the recipient, 'be not
apprehensive about my composure: it is now so fix'd that the
most trifling matters can engage my attention . . . I could amuse
myself last night with the letters of Miss Siddons'.

In reply Mrs. Pennington makes it clear that Maria is dying,
and says: 'Shall I dare tell you, that I have kept my faith?—that
the drawing has been mentioned, not seen; that both Mrs. S.
and myself have spoken to *her* of *you*; and that I request you to be
satisfied with the assurance, that SHE awards you what is generally
understood as CHRISTIAN forgiveness, and to entreat that you will
enquire no further?' On the same day Sally wrote to tell Miss
Bird that Maria had been removed in a sedan chair from Mrs.
Pennington's house to a lodging-house on the opposite side of
the square and had borne the exertion better than was expected.
'My Mother and I sit by her all day; she takes great quantities
of laudanum, which keep her in a continual stupor.'

On 3rd October Lawrence wrote another of his long, agonised
letters to Mrs. Pennington, in the course of which he says: 'I have
never believ'd that Maria's nature was unrelenting; and when

you tell me that I am awarded Christian forgiveness, I receive it as indisputable fact; for I could believe it, had I violated her person, and struck at her very life. A wretch at the gallows would have had it.' He adds that 'Mr. Kemble is very much afflicted for Maria, and Mrs. Kemble equally so; but the former with more delicacy, which dear Miss Siddons will readily believe. How is she—Sally?' On the following day he wrote again and sent 'a thousand grateful remembrances to my beloved Mrs. Siddons for the effort she made for me'. Other letters followed in quick succession which reflect Lawrence's grief at Maria's hopeless condition, as well as his personal anxieties, which are expressed in a request that no detail of Maria's passing should be hid from him. 'I would know *everything*.' Mr. Siddons had been summoned to Clifton when Maria's end was approaching. She died on 7th October and was buried two days later in the old Parish church of Clifton, which has since been pulled down. The marble tablet to her memory was removed and placed in the west porch of the present church. Mr. Siddons, according to Mrs. Piozzi, was overcome with grief. His wife, the Immortal, at least had the consolation of being able to express her feelings through the medium of her art. A fortnight after her daughter's death she reappeared in London as Isabella in *Measure for Measure*.

On the day before the funeral Mrs. Pennington set herself to the not uncongenial task of complying with Lawrence's wish to be informed of everything that took place in Maria's death chamber during her final hours. She evidently regarded this letter as being an occasion for the exercise of every scrap of literary talent she possessed and was no doubt highly gratified with the result. Although it occupies seven pages in Dr. Knapp's book she made at least one, if not more, copies of it with which, no doubt, under a pledge of secrecy, she later regaled her intimate friends. Miss Royde-Smith justly describes her effusion as a 'masterpiece of self-deluding cruelty', and the effect on Lawrence when he received it was to drive him to the verge of insanity. After describing how Maria received the news of her approaching death, Mrs. Pennington continues:

'She spoke as never girl of nineteen spoke, or thought; it was inspiration of the Divinity, who permitted her to live till her nature was purified and perfected.

But how am I to proceed? How tell you that *all* which you *fear'd* HAS HAPPENED.

In her *dying* accents, her last solemn injunction was given and repeated some hours afterwards in the presence of Mrs. Siddons. She call'd her Sister—said how dear, how sweet, how *good* she was—that one only care for her welfare pressed on her mind. "Promise me, my Sally, *never* to be the wife of Mr. Lawrence. I *cannot* BEAR to *think* of *your* being so." Sally evaded the promise; not but that a thousand recent circumstances had made up her mind to the sacrifice, but that she did not like the positive tye. She would have evaded the subject also, and said, "dear Maria, think of nothing that agitates you at this time". She INSISTED that it did not agitate her, but that it was necessary to her repose to pursue the subject. Sally still evaded the promise, but said: "Oh! it is *impossible*" meaning that she cou'd *answer* for *herself,* but which Maria understood and construed into an impossibility of the event *ever* taking place, and replied: "I am content, my dear Sister—I am satisfied".' After this Maria inquired when her end was expected, and 'desired to have Prayers read', which her 'angelic mother' accordingly did.

After this interlude, the dying egotist's thoughts reverted to Lawrence for whom her diseased mind was evidently filled with an almost fiendish hatred. Lawrence had apparently assured Mrs. Siddons that he had destroyed her letters and there is no reason to doubt that he did so, but Maria was unsatisfied and made her mother promise to procure them from him or have their destruction confirmed. '*I* have no opinion of his honour,' she said, 'and I entreat you to demand them.' We come now to the salient passages in Mrs. Pennington's letter which dealt the last shattering blow to Lawrence's hopes. It is hard to believe that Mrs. Pennington did not feel a certain secret satisfaction in announcing to 'this torment of a man' that Sally had finally thrown him over. She knew that this was what the great Mrs. Siddons, whose friendship was so flattering to her self-esteem, had from the first desired and, knowing that her letter would be read with close attention by Sally's mother, added her own sententious comments on the scene she described, with the most brutal indifference to the effect they must produce on the distraught man who read them.

'She [Maria] then said Sally *had promised her* NEVER to think of an union with Mr. Lawrence, and appeal'd to her Sister to confirm it, who, quite overcome, reply'd: "I did *not* promise, dear, dying Angel; but I WILL, and DO, if you require it". "Thank you, Sally; my dear Mother—Mrs. Pennington—*bear witness*. Sally, give me your hand—you promise never to be his wife; Mother—Mrs. Pennington—lay your hands on hers" (we did so).—"You understand? bear witness." We bowed, and were speechless. "Sally, sacred, sacred be this promise"—stretching out her hand, and pointing her forefinger—"REMEMBER ME, and God bless you".

And what, after this, my friend, can you say to Sally Siddons?' she continues, on a note which scarcely conceals her feeling of triumph. 'She has entreated me to give you this detail—to say that the impression is sacred, is indelible—that it cancels all former bonds and engagements—that she entreats you to submit, and not to prophane this awful season by a murmur.

If you can sanctify passion with friendship, still you may be dear to their hearts and, at some future time, but even that far distant, enjoy their society. If you *cannot* do this, never approach or, if you can help it, think of them more. I think Sally will not lightly or easily, if ever, make another election; but *yours* she NEVER *can*, never WILL be. She is wonderfully well and wonderfully supported; feeling all that she can and all that she ought.'

The impudence of this provincial busybody in announcing the terms on which Lawrence may hope, in the future, to enjoy the society not only of Sally but of her mother, whom he had known intimately since boyhood, speaks for itself. Mrs. Pennington goes on, at enormous length, to expatiate on the 'divine composure' of Maria, and 'the heavenly expression' which Mrs.

Siddons notes 'in her countenance', but somewhat mars the effect by narrating some of the spiteful and vicious things which Maria had said about Lawrence to her mother just before her death. She closes her letter with a laboured attempt at fine writing which shows how conscious she was of having played an important part in the lives of people more eminent than herself. 'We have read the death-bed scenes of Clarissa and Eloisa', she says, 'drawn as they are by the hands of genius, and embellish'd with all that skilful and powerful fancy could give them to touch the imagination; believe me, they are faint sketches compared with those last hours, that have enriched the memories of us who attended Maria Siddons, where nature supplied touches that art cou'd never reach.' Two short notes followed this major epistolary effort, in the last of which she offers Lawrence her 'constant friendship and tender sympathy'. The effect of these communications on the distracted lover would have been anticipated by anyone less insensitive and less blind than Mrs. Pennington. Lawrence was evidently unprepared, after having heard so much about her 'Christian forgiveness', for Maria's last shocking act of vengeance and can hardly be blamed for believing, what was in fact the case, that pressure had been put on Sally by Mrs. Pennington as well as by her mother, to weaken her resistance to it. His savage reply, subsequently referred to as his 'diabolical letter', is reproduced in facsimile in *An Artist's Love Story*, from which the factual evidence in this account, but not the conclusions drawn from it by Dr. Knapp, is taken. The handwriting is that of a man driven half out of his mind by the violence of his emotion. The postmark is dated 13th October 1798 and the address given is Charles Street. The text is as follows:

'It is only my Hand that shakes, not my Mind. I have play'd deeply for her, and you think she will still escape me. I'll tell you a secret. *It is possible she may. Mark the End.*

You have all play'd your parts admirably!!!

If the scene you have so accurately describ'd is mentioned by you to one *Human Being*, I will pursue your name with execration.'

By the same post Mrs. Pennington received a letter from Mrs. Siddons, then in London, in which she says: 'Of our wretched friend I hear only that he is miserable. May your wise and sweet counsels operate to soothe and purify his mind! I have received, and thank you for your beautiful letter to him.' Mrs. Pennington lost no time in informing Mrs. Siddons of the effect which her 'beautiful letter' and her 'wise and sweet counsels' had produced on 'a DARK and DESPERATE character, to which I do not *chuse* to fix the *proper* name'. In her brief and excusably indignant reply to Lawrence's explosive outburst she ended by saying that 'any further letters from your hand will be return'd unopened'. When Lawrence had recovered his self-control, he wrote to her twice again, and his letters were not, of course, returned, but forwarded to Mrs. Siddons, though Mrs. Pennington does not appear to have replied to them. In the second letter he said:

'You would not have borne with me so far, if your heart cou'd not pardon the madness I have been guilty of, which, indeed, your letter was as certain of producing as any cause its un-avoidable effect.

From your preceding letter, and the account of Maria's state of mind, I was led to expect the *very opposite* of the chilling fact you have announced to me, and it is no wonder that my excessive astonishment at it shou'd have generated suspicion.

My mind, however, is so far quieted by your intelligence, that Remorse is no longer its inhabitant. My crime, I thought, was to Tenderness—I cannot give its expiation to Revenge.'

Lawrence's exact meaning, like that of the other correspondents whose letters form the documentary evidence from which this love-story must be elucidated, is often obscure, owing to his preference for using veiled language, but it is not very difficult to understand that Maria's last actions saved him from feeling any remorse on her account. To the three women, who found it natural to regard a young girl, dying of consumption at the age of nineteen, as an 'Angel', particularly a girl for whom they had so tender an affection, Maria's last words and deeds seemed not only sacred but 'Divinely Inspired'. Lawrence, on the other hand, who had a much clearer insight into her character, could be excused for regarding her in an altogether different light. Young devils are just as susceptible as young angels to the ravages of tuberculosis. In addition to the idealised drawing of Maria which Lawrence made in 1797, when he thought he was in love with her, and the later drawing sent to Mrs. Pennington, of which there is now no trace, there exists another portrait, the date of which may safely be placed as soon after the receipt of Mrs. Pennington's letter. The face is the face of a maenad, an incarnation of hatred, malice, and malignant purpose. The nostrils of the dominant Kemble nose are drawn in, the lips tight-set, the eyes implacable and ablaze with a lust for vengeance. Only the head, with its tangled mop of dark hair, and the neck are completed, the dress being roughly indicated by a few savage brush strokes which reveal the violence of the artist's emotion. A mezzotint engraving of this unfinished masterpiece was made by George Clint. The original is in the Royal Collection at the British Museum.

X

THE DEATH OF SALLY

THE SERIES of letters from Mrs. Siddons and Sally to Mrs. Pennington, and Mrs. Pennington's replies to them, which followed Maria's death would afford rich material for analysis by an expert in feminine psychology. Even a lay observer can detect that they are largely made up of sentiments which the writers of them believe the recipient would consider appropriate, though every now and then, when the self-imposed censorship is relaxed, we are afforded glimpses of what they really think and feel. The assertions by Mrs. Siddons, and by Sally herself, that she has definitely and finally rejected Lawrence, continue with renewed vigour, but Mrs. Pennington, who by this time had developed a hatred of 'that *wretched man*' only less violent than Maria's, still has her doubts and is determined to do everything she can to strengthen Sally's resolution by poisoning her mind against her lover. In a letter to Mrs. Siddons, written immediately after the receipt of Lawrence's furious note, she advises Mrs. Siddons at all hazards 'to put the affair at once into the hands of Mr. Siddons', also to consult with Mr. Kemble. She thinks it necessary that Sally should be placed 'under the protection of those who are naturally inclined and able to afford it her. While *he* thinks he has ONLY the *timidity* of WOMEN to operate on, and to oppose him, there is no saying *what* he may not *attempt*. . . . *What a wretch!* My nerves and my nature shudder at this man. What will you do to save yourself, and above all, dear, dear Sally, from him?' After continuing for some time in this strain, she says: 'I could wish dear Sally's mind kept quiet; yet surely she *ought* to know of this *outrage*, which I shou'd imagine must cast him from *her* heart for *ever*. Much am I mistaken if there is not more wounded *Interest* than *Love* at the bottom of all this. *It is desperate*, because his FORTUNES *are so*.' It is something to find Mrs. Pennington at least admitting the possibility of error. Not only was she much mistaken but she showed herself a complete fool into the bargain. If Lawrence's 'outrage', which she is so anxious should be shown to Sally, really had the effect of casting him from her heart for ever, then she affords the first recorded instance of a girl who is horrified, instead of being deeply moved, by the evidence of her lover's passion. As for her idea that Lawrence's 'INTEREST' was wounded because his fortunes 'were desperate', it could only have been entertained by a woman who was completely ignorant of the man whose character she was bent on smearing. While it is true that Lawrence's financial difficulties, aggravated by his emotional turmoils, were more than usually acute, his prospects were brilliant and, as all his friends had predicted, he was about to begin a period of his career which continued, with unbroken success and increasing public fame, until the day of his death. No consideration other than love could have induced him to wish to marry an ailing girl, with no money, and nothing to bring him in a social sense which he did not already possess.

Sally, who now takes her mother's place as correspondent, fills her letter with all the sentiments and opinions which Mrs. Pennington would naturally expect her to express. She deplores Lawrence's 'ingratitude' to Mrs. Pennington and says she believes he is at times 'quite mad'. Having said this, a hint of her real feelings escapes her. 'Poor, wretched creature! let him inflict still further torments on those who love and are interested for him, he will still be the most tormented.' As if afraid that this remark may arouse Mrs. Pennington's suspicions of the real state of her heart, she hastens to reassure her. 'Do not fear on my account, dearest friend! where can there be any danger, since I am myself more unwilling to put myself in his power than any of my relations can be? Am I NOT BOUND BY A PROMISE, THE MOST SOLEMN, THE MOST SACRED,—is not that sufficient to preserve me, even should my own treacherous heart dictate a thought in his favour! *But that it does not*, even when I thought of him as unhappy and resign'd I did not regret my promise given. But now, his shocking violence at such a time, to such a friend, has thrown him more from my heart than anything else in the world;—*It may be love, but such love as I never wish to inspire; I fly with* HORROR *from such a passion!*' After more in this vein, poor Sally continues: 'I will not say *that weakness shall never return* . . . We cannot, you know, quite conquer all our *feelings*, but virtue and reason may regulate our *conduct* and, with the help of heaven, I fear not for myself in that respect; whatever I may *feel* I will *act* as I HAVE PROMIS'D.' Sally protests far too much for anyone of normal intelligence to be taken in by it, and it is doubtful if even Mrs. Pennington, now determined to use every means in her power to keep Sally and Lawrence for ever apart, was convinced by her assurances.

Mrs. Siddons, writing from London on the same day as Sally, 7th October, shows welcome signs of returning common sense and is evidently not disposed to follow Mrs. Pennington's advice to take her husband and Mr. and Mrs. Kemble into her confidence. After saying that she has heard from Mr. and Mrs. Twiss that the 'infatuated creature, whose diabolical letter you have astonish'd me with this morning', has, after 'every species of frantic behaviour', become 'PERFECTLY COMPOS'D and determined, by a course of proper conduct, to deserve the blessing he hopes for', she gives her reasons for maintaining a discreet silence where her husband and brother are concerned. 'I wou'd follow your advice implicitly,' she says, 'but that Mrs. Kemble, with a thousand good qualities, is so fond of talking over other people's concerns, and that so indiscriminately, that it is no exaggeration to say this affair would be known in every milliner's shop in Town, had she the least intimation of it. The confidence between Mr. S. and my Brother is unbounded, and I fear, were I to acquaint my Husband of it, there is no doubt of the forenam'd consequences. Mr. S., too, is unhappily so cold and repelling, that instead of tender sympathy I shou'd expect harsh words, "unkind reproof and looks that stab with coldness".' She adds: 'There is nothing to fear from Sally, you know, and L is resolv'd to be *quiet* at present.'

On the same day Mrs. Pennington wrote to Mrs. Siddons enclosing the letters from Lawrence which she did not return unopened, and continues her railing accusations against him. In her reply Mrs. Siddons says: 'All here is calm and quiet, God grant it may continue! for my very soul is weary of these turmoils. If our Tormentor will but cease his persecutions, we shall not only be content, but happy; for my dear, sweet Sally still assures me that it is impossible *she* should be otherwise while I am with her. And while she acknowledges (what we all feel) the powerful fascinations of this creature, she is as well aware as any of us that to be his wife would be to be *completely wretched*.' From this we may gather that at the bottom of her heart Sally realises that to be his wife would make her completely happy. Mrs. Siddons adds that 'I hear from Mrs. T. [her sister, Mrs. Twiss] that he [Lawrence] has resumed his composure, and even cheerfulness—to whom he has said, "the possession of such a woman as Sally is worth all efforts"; and he is determin'd to [deserve] her by a course of conduct worthy of her and of himself'. The difficulty of reconciling this with the charges of inconstancy brought against Lawrence, seems to have occurred to Mrs. Siddons, for she continues: 'In the first place, I *doubt* his resolution', which means that she cannot help being impressed by it, 'and think Sally will have good courage if she *ever* accept him, after what she has experienced of his character. Though she contended the other day that what *we* have seen of him *lately* has not been the *character* of the man, because it is so unlike all that we have seen of him *heretofore ourselves*, and all that we ever *heard* of him. . . .' In a later letter, dated 'Saturday', she gives further evidences of a changed attitude towards Lawrence which Mrs. Pennington must have regarded as showing an exasperating weakness on her part. 'All is still quiet,' Mrs. Siddons writes. 'I am astonished at it, and so is Sally. He goes to the Play, and in all respects appears quite easy. Mr. Lysons tells me that he talks of going a journey of two hundred miles for the pleasure of spending only two days with some friends in Lincolnshire; and when Lysons urg'd the greatness of the expense and trouble for so short-liv'd a pleasure, his answer was that, among other inducements, Miss Amelia Locke was to be of the party he was to meet. Oh! wou'd to heaven she, or any other, might divert his

attentions from us.' Amelia Lock, the daughter of William
Lock of Norbury Park, later became the wife of John Julius
Angerstein. The 'friends in Lincolnshire', were the Boucherettes
of Willingham. Although Lawrence was on terms of the closest
intimacy with both the Locks and the Angersteins and with their
family circle, there is not the slightest reason for supposing that
his feelings for Amelia were ever anything but fraternal.

If Mrs. Siddons was anxious to cure Sally of her love it seems
curious that she did not arrange for her to stay anywhere but
in London. If the Swiss mountains, at that time the recognised
retreat for persons suffering from emotional disturbances, were
rendered inaccessible by the war with France, she had friends in
Dublin, in Edinburgh and in Bath to whose care Sally might
have been confided. In London where, in the social, theatrical
and artistic circles in which they both moved, everybody knew
everybody, it was impossible for Sally to avoid the risk of some
chance encounter with her lover.... 'When I talk'd of the importance of *their first meeting anywhere*,' Mrs. Siddons continues, 'she
told me it was impossible for her to treat him with coldness or
neglect: poor thing! ... She is not likely to meet him anywhere
in private, except at Mrs. Semple's, where she assures me she
will not go without me, and has promis'd that if she shou'd be
at the Theatre etc., she will seem not to see him. Her Father or
myself will always, I hope, be able to accompany her on such
occasions, and, by these precautions, I hope he will be tir'd of the
pursuit. I wish, and so does Sally, that we had her letters out of
his hands, for he may think, perhaps, their being suffer'd to
remain with him is a sort of tacit encouragement, yet, on the
other hand, we sometimes think it best not to awaken the sleeping embers of those passions that may again, *upon a breath*, break
forth to torment us. I perceive he has interested Mrs. Twiss very
much, though she is convinc'd of the imprudence of Sally's
listening to him; she sees no chance of happiness with such an
impetuous creature in the first place, and appears to feel that his
circumstances and Sally's unfortunate constitution all combine
most powerfully to operate upon a sober mind against such a connexion; for, as to Maria's injunction (to my great surprise), she

seems to say an *extorted* promise goes for nothing. This, I fear, is his opinion too. Sally does *not* think *so*, yet thinks her sister shou'd not have exacted such a promise, and that she was actuated as much by resentment for *him*, as care and tenderness for *her* in it.'

This welcome sign of good sense in Mr. and Mrs. Twiss, together with Sally's belated understanding of Maria's motives, evidently infuriated Mrs. Pennington. In her next letter, after saying that the *horrors* which 'that strange and unworthy man' excited in her mind are subsided, but that her agitation has brought back an old complaint in her stomach, she returns with vigour to a theme which has now become an obsession. The news that Sally has again been taken ill prompts the comment that 'with such a constitution, Lawrence out of the question, there is hardly a matrimonial connexion possible for her to make that would not be death to all her comfort and happiness'. Present-day readers, with the example of Robert Browning and Elizabeth Moulton Barrett fresh in their memories, may well doubt this assertion. The only thing which might have improved Sally's expectation of life was marriage to the man she loved. Even if marriage and fulfilment did not give her the strength to keep her illness in check, it would at least have made her remaining years supremely happy. Mrs. Pennington does not wait long before getting her knife into Mrs. Twiss. She says that 'dear Sally, *though in love*, proves a much sounder casuist than Mrs. Twiss; for certainly Sally's promise to her dying sister, being *voluntary*, is as binding as any human engagement CAN be. No promise can be "*extorted*" but by authority, at the peril of one's life, or some great and important forfeiture . . . Sally was free to have *remained silent*, or to have refused her sister whose fate was fixed . . . and if Sally chose to give her the satisfaction she required, it *was voluntarily* done on her part, and in all truth and justice she must abide the consequence, and will ever have reason to bless the impulse, which I am confident was *divine* interposition, to save an innocent and valuable creature, through the organs of that dying Angel, from *certain ruin*.' Mrs. Siddons had informed her that Mr. Twiss, though remaining friendly to Lawrence, had forbidden him further mention of the subject of Sally. She now has the effrontery to say: 'I wish all your near connexions would go one step further, my belov'd friend, and *exclude the man.*' Her excuse for this request is that, probably through her own indiscretion, 'the subject has spread much more widely than we any of us suspected', which presumably means that, at the Hot Wells, people had started to gossip about Lawrence and Sally. She concludes by reiterating her demand that Sally should once again convey to Lawrence that 'she was fully determined *never to be his*'. An interesting point about this vicious letter is that the writer admits that she knows that Sally is 'in love' with Lawrence, but does not, in spite of that, hesitate to use all her influence to force the poor girl to ignore the promptings of her heart. In view of the value to the Kemble family, from what might now-adays be termed the 'publicity' standpoint, of Lawrence's friend-ship, her attempt to persuade Mrs. Siddons to exclude from their circle the leading portrait painter of the age, is surprising, even from such a self-important nonentity as Mrs. Pennington. Had Mrs. Siddons been fool enough to act on this advice it would certainly have increased the scandal she was anxious to avert.

Sally's long reply to Mrs. Pennington, written on Wednesday, 7th November, does credit neither to her heart, her good sense, her character, nor her loyalty. After endlessly reiterating her 'firmness' and once again assuring Mrs. Pennington from the bottom of her soul, in capital letters, that she can never look favourably on Lawrence as a Lover again, she says that she 'saw him for the first time last Sunday—he was standing opposite our windows, and looked earnestly towards them. I no sooner perceiv'd him than I instantly retired from the window, and return'd there no more. This, if he expected anything, must be some check to his expectations.' It was part of Sally's tragedy that she appears to have had no sensible friend of her own age who could expose Mrs. Pennington in her true colours and advise her to tell the good lady to mind her own business. She was too lacking in spirit, a rare defect for a Kemble, to stand up for Lawrence and be true to herself in face of the older woman's bossy interference. 'No, kindest, best of friends,' she writes, 'I do not impute a line of your (I fear) too true delineation of his character to *pique*. All your development of the real feelings of this man coincide[s] but too exactly with the opinion I must myself at length embrace. I do not shut my eyes to conviction; *I see him as he is.* Yet, oh pardon me, if I sometimes cast over him that brilliant veil of enchantment which conceal'd his errors from our fascinated eyes—I do indeed. I cannot help viewing him sometimes as *he was*, or rather, such as he appear'd to be; and I then think that the world does not contain another creature who could so answer my idea of perfection. *But that creature was ideal!* such as my heart imagin'd it, IT NEVER EXISTED—hard, hard task, to return to the reality! . . . I do not think I shall ever so love again as I have lov'd that man, but this is most certain, I LOVE HIM NO LONGER. The creature *I would have liv'd and died for*, EXISTS NO MORE or, as I have said, *never did exist*. Time and circumstances have discover'd to me a character which nothing could tempt me to unite myself to.'

There is much more in this strain which, though the letter was written when she was still weak after an attack of asthma, does little credit to her heart or head. When we reflect that, after the receipt of her two long love-letters, all that Lawrence had done was to give rather too extravagant evidence of the passion they had aroused in him and to write, under extreme provocation, a rude letter to Mrs. Pennington, Sally's wholesale condemnation of his character, on such ridiculous evidence, seems to suggest that she was much more the offspring of her fish-like father than of her magnificent mother. If she expected her fascinating Tormentor to behave with all the reason and decorum of a ham actor, devoid of talent, who aspires to the hand of the manager's daughter, her judgment must indeed have been at fault. Moreover, her own conduct, in not finding a way of communicating with Lawrence after she went to Clifton, largely contributed to the extravagance of his behaviour. She could not have been so inexperienced as to suppose that she could write burning love-letters and follow them by an unexplained silence, without disturbing the equilibrium of a man as deeply attached to her as Lawrence was. Nor could she expect him to take a letter which she wrote from Birmingham, obviously under the influence of her mother and Mrs. Pennington, assuring him that 'there must be a total end of all intercourse between us', as final and irrevocable. It was natural that he should wish to see her, face to face, and if possible alone, and receive his dismissal from her own lips. This would at least have given him a chance to defend himself and to clear up all misunderstanding between them, but Sally, distrusting her 'firmness', as well she might, had not the moral courage to agree to it. Writing to Miss Bird in her usual 'Pennington' vein, Sally made the assertion that 'I should, on my own account, rejoice to hear that he had given up all thought of me, and was in love with Miss anybody else', which Miss Bird may or may not have taken at its face value.

On Sunday, 19th November, Mrs. Siddons wrote to Mrs. Pennington telling her that 'Last Sunday we saw the unhappy disturber of our peace at church, whose self-love was naturally wounded by our total inattention to his presence. He went to Mrs. Twiss's and was betrayed into his usual excesses of passion. He persuades himself that Sally still loves him, and is only operated upon by some powerful influence to *appear indifferent* to him'. She goes on to say that she has after all taken Mr. Siddons into her confidence and told him the whole story in order to provide Sally with 'the strong fence of a Father's care and caution. I only wish he would *write* to Sally,' she adds, 'that he might be convinc'd, if anything can convince him, that it is possible for the terrors of *pecuniary distress*; its natural attendant, a gloomy mind; and, tho' last, not least, THE DISAPPROBATION OF FRIENDS, to resist the happiness of being *miserable* with *him*, which he, perhaps, thinks impossible.—There is a corner yet left in my heart that feels for this unhappy creature, and still yearns towards him, when I think of the hours we have all spent together under this roof,—and the happiness I proposed to myself in spending the last hours of my life in the bosom of that domestic peace, which my fond imagination had pictured in his virtues and rare endowments, as the husband of my child.—Poor creature!'

On 23rd November Sally again wrote to Miss Bird and reiterated her protestations that it is 'as impossible for me ever to think

MRS. WOLFF

Exhibited at the Royal Academy in 1815. Now in the Art Institute of Chicago.

MARY DIGGES

Exhibited at the Royal Academy in 1826. In the National Gallery of Scotland.

of a union with him, *as if he were dead*', so that Miss Bird may well
have wondered if she ever thought of anyone else. 'I have not the
least doubt of seeing an end of his misery concerning *me*,' she
goes on, 'for, heaven is my witness, I am far from believing myself
mistress of sufficient attraction to attach a being of such noted
inconstancy, even if I had the power;—as it is *this* passion cannot
be of long duration.'

Shortly after this, Mrs. Siddons writes to tell Mrs. Pennington
that her husband had received the information she gave him about
Sally 'with that coldness and reserve which had kept him so
long ignorant of it, and that want of an agreeing mind (*my*
misfortune, though not *his* fault) that has always check'd my
tongue and chilled my heart in every occurrence of importance
thro' our lives'. He would not have spoken to Sally if Mrs. Siddons
had not 'represented to him how strange such reserve must appear
to her; whereupon he testified his total disapprobation, nay,
abhorrence of any further intercourse with Mr. L., whom he
reprobated *with the spirit of a just man* ABOVE *the* WEAKNESSES
which are the misfortunes of the Race in general'. We can be
sure that Mr. Siddons gave his usual dull and second-rate performance. She opens her letter to tell Mrs. Pennington that
'Mr. L. has written to Sally, and that she has answered it in so
decisive a manner that she has only to let him see she continues
in the same mind, to extinguish in a short time all hope: and I
fancy the sentiment of constant love without *that*, even if it did
exist, is now quite obsolete'.

On 19th January [1799] Sally wrote to Mrs. Pennington to say
that the date is fixed for her parents and herself to visit Bath and
that her friend Patty Wilkinson is going with them. The references to Lawrence, though in the usual vein, are much curtailed.
'All I can tell you,' she says, 'is that *I am just as firmly determin'd
as when I first determin'd, and that he is, I fear, still guilty of loving
me too well.* Why will he not give us one more proof of his inconstancy? But we must have patience, it cannot fail to happen soon.'

On 23rd January she wrote to tell Miss Bird about the approaching journey of her family to Bath and asks: 'Have you had the
promis'd visit from Mr. L.? But I rather think you have not, for

I have not heard of his going so far from London. I saw him one night last week at Covent Garden Theatre, and was very much distress'd to be oblig'd to pass close by him.'

On 8th February she wrote another letter to Miss Bird, this time from Bath, in which she mentions having seen Mrs. Siddons in the role of Zara in *The Grecian Daughter*, refers with gratification to her mother's success and popularity, and says she has been to two musical parties at Miss Lee's. She spent about a month at Bath where, in spite of illness, she was frequently in the company of Mrs. Pennington and Mrs. Piozzi.

On her return to London she again wrote to Miss Bird and comments on a piece of gossip she has heard about Lawrence in a way which shows clearly that her mind is still obsessed by him. 'I never heard of the report of Mr. L. till your letter told it me. I wish most sincerely it may be true. Whether the Lady is to be married to him, or whether her possessions are extensive, is yet a secret to me, but that there *is* a Lady who engages all his attention, and who paints extremely well, *I know*. She lives at Clapham, where he for some weeks has pass'd almost all his time. I was told by a person who does not credit the report, that there are two sisters who both paint, and that it is merely *this talent* which attracts him. He might admire them extremely, but would never devote his whole time and attention to such *ancient artists*. If you should hear any more of this affair, do not fail to let me know, for entirely as I have refus'd every sollicitation, I can never cease to be interested in the fate of this singular being.'

In a letter to Mrs. Pennington, dated 5th March, Sally again refers to Mr. L.'s imaginary engagement. 'You may imagine my happiness at having my friend Dorothy [Place] with me once again, and what a painful pleasure we find in talking over the past. She has never seen or heard anything from Mr. L., which I rejoice at extremely, and most heartily wish the report I hear is in the Newspapers may be true; it says he is shortly to be married to a young Lady of distinguished talents and extensive possessions. It is very certain that he spends almost all his time with a family at Clapham, where I understand there are two young Ladies who paint extremely well.'

178

Writing to Miss Bird on 23rd March, Sally again refers to Lawrence's rumoured engagement. 'I have heard no more of Mr. L. since my return to town, but am told that he denies any *particular attraction* being the cause of his frequent visits to Clapham, and he has certainly not yet sent me the proof which I have solemnly demanded to receive whenever he is contented to think of *me* merely as a friend. If he was indeed going to be married, I think he could not deny my request, which was *that he should return me all my letters.* Tell me whenever you hear of him for, separated as we are for ever, I must, while I have sense or feeling left, be more interested in the fate of that being than I ever was, or perhaps shall be, in the fate of any other.' Few men in London had better chances of marrying an heiress, had he wished to do so, than Lawrence. At this period it was considered no more than ordinary common sense for an eligible bachelor to pay his attentions to a girl who, in addition to her other attractions and talents, had the advantage of 'extensive possessions.' It was therefore not in the least unlikely, had Lawrence been as changeable and 'inconstant' as Mrs. Pennington and Sally herself pretended to believe, that the rumours about the Clapham young lady, which caused Sally so much agitation, should prove to be correct. That Lawrence was not only the last man to contract a mercenary marriage but also, once he knew his own mind, the most constant, loyal and devoted of lovers, would have been obvious to Sally if, instead of basing her opinion of Lawrence on that of biased elders, she had used her own judgment. As it is, we can see from the changed tone of her letters that the rumour that Lawrence intended to console himself by marrying a girl who was rich as well as talented, had shaken her more than she cared to admit. She could not but be aware that the 'wretched man' from whose passion she had professed herself as flying 'with horror' in so many letters, the 'creature' who, she said, 'never existed' and whom she protested that she loved no longer, was managing to conceal the villainies attributed to him with remarkable success. Not only was his professional reputation as the leading portrait painter by now established, but his wide circle of friends seemed to value the 'madman', denounced and rejected by Mrs. Pennington, Mr. Siddons and by Sally herself, more highly than ever. Both Norbury Park, the Locks' hospitable home, and 'Woodlands', the Angerstein's equally hospitable house at Blackheath, contained wealthy and attractive young women whom Lawrence sketched and painted and with whom he was on terms of agreeable intimacy. Gossip, again without foundation, coupled his name with one of these beauties, Miss Jennings, whose portrait he had painted. In a letter to Miss Bird, dated 3rd June, Sally mentions the rumour and, while admitting her beauty, fails to find in Miss Jennings 'that expression of an intelligent mind, without which all beauty is, in my eyes, defective. . . . You know I have resign'd all thoughts of Love, or Jealousy, but if I had not, I do not think Miss Jennings would make me jealous. I have once or twice seen Mr. L. by chance, and I thought I should have dropp'd the Sunday before last, in Kensington Gardens, when I passed him so close that I might have touch'd him! Whenever I meet his eyes with that glance that pierces thro' and thro' one, it is like an electric stroke to me, and it is well I had hold of Dorothy's arm. I pass'd his door too, the other day, and my heart sank within me when I pass'd the windows of that Parlour where we have pass'd so many pleasant hours! Ah, my dear friend, these are sad recollections, and such vain regrets will follow, that I always strive, and now must, to banish them from my mind'. She ends this letter by begging Miss Bird to send a quick reply containing all the news she hears 'from a certain quarter'. On 11th June Mrs. Siddons resumed her correspondence with Mrs. Pennington and in the course of a long letter, mostly about the way in which Sheridan has appropriated her money, she says she wishes she could persuade herself that the Lawrence affair is ended, as he 'has been perfectly quiet now for some months. And, good God! a man *must* be out of his senses to build his happiness on the possession of a poor creature who brings such an affliction for her *portion*; for I believe her Father's mind is irrevocably fixed on that subject, if she herself were dispos'd, which I am sure she is not, to think of marrying him'.

As Lawrence grows calmer and regains his habitual self-control, it is Sally's turn to become increasingly agitated and disturbed by jealous fancies, fears, misgivings and regrets. In July Sally accompanied her mother to Edinburgh, where her uncle Stephen Kemble was manager of the Theatre Royal. Writing to Miss Bird on 15th July she says: 'I hope that you are well, I was going to say happy but tho' I am not very old, or very experienc'd, I have learnt that *happiness* is the lot of but *very* few, and that to be content is all that most of us must aspire to. My mother told me last night of a circumstance which I must hope is true; it is that *our friend* thinks of me now ONLY AS A FRIEND. Before she left Town she wrote to him to make one more attempt for the restoration of our letters. His answer was, she tells me, that *when he married*, her letters and his *dear friend* Sally's should be returned, but that that event he believ'd to be at a great distance; and after a great deal more, some of which was in his ambiguous style, he desires his kind remembrances to Sally, and begs my mother to tell me they are *those of friendship*. From his late quiet behaviour I am inclin'd to think his passion is indeed expiring, yet why will he not, as I conjur'd him, confirm this idea, and his own assertion, by restoring me my letters? I must however be as easy as I can about them; may he be happy, and forgetting me, fix his affections *for the last time* where no obstacle will arise to his wishes. You will tell me what you hear of him, my dear girl, for from you I wish not to conceal the interest I must ever feel in all that concerns him.' Mrs. Siddons's northern tour, which included visits to Glasgow, York, Wakefield, Sheffield and Hull, as well as Edinburgh, occupied some months and must have afforded Sally welcome distraction from her anxieties on Lawrence's account. She had a severe attack of illness at York in August, but in late September, while her mother was playing at Wakefield, they spent a week in the country house of Mr. Smyth, whom Sally describes to Miss Bird as 'the most clever and amiable man I ever met'. A month later they paid a visit to Sir William Milner at Nun Appleton. 'Monk' Lewis was one of the house party, and Sally says she was 'quite provok'd at his arrogance' and mocks at him for having 'no more ear or voice . . . than a croaking Raven. . . . You may imagine what charming duetts we have had together'.

Alas, how unlike the 'tormentor' with whom she once sang duets in Great Marlborough Street! On 11th November 1799 Mrs. Siddons writes to Mrs. Pennington from Hull to tell her that Mr. Siddons 'has arrang'd his affair with Mr. Sheridan' and that she is returning to London to play in his 'Pizarro'. Referring to Lawrence, the inexhaustible topic, she says: 'Not a word have we heard of Mr. L. but I shall not at all wonder to hear that the old sport of ogling and sighing at the Theatre had begun again. I find Sally blesses herself that she is "OUT OF THE SCRAPE", and she told me a few days ago that if he did think proper to amuse himself in the old way, he would find himself mistaken. Poor Soul, she thought, I suppose, (naturally enough for her), that his adoration was to last for ever, even against Hope, and I think is rather piqued to find that "these violent transports have violent ends". I hope to God we have nothing more to fear for him, and that he will be quiet himself, and never more disturb the peace of my poor child!'

On 24th November Sally wrote to Mrs. Pennington to express the hope that she was recovering from a recent illness, and to tell her about her mother's flattering reception, by a 'brilliant audience', in the part of Isabella, but as usual cannot refrain from dragging in the subject of Lawrence. After saying that 'the flow of spirits' in the intervals between the attacks of her complaint 'is no longer checked by tormenting regrets, by dangerous, but seducing, recollections', she continues: '. . . I seem a new creature, my mind is so at ease, that it helps me thro' confinement and sickness has lost half its terrors. . . . Tell me, my kind friend, that you participate in my *restoration*, and it will add to my pleasures:—but though I own myself completely cur'd of that *disease*, A TENDER PASSION—I shall never like to hear the object I once looked up to as the standard of perfection, *vilified, abus'd, execrated*. I wish him well and happy, *and rejoice that his welfare and his happiness no longer depend upon me.*' How far Sally genuinely deceived herself when she made these protestations must remain a matter of conjecture, but Mrs. Siddons was certainly right when she told Mrs. Pennington that her daughter was 'rather piqued' at the thought that Lawrence's devotion had definitely cooled. Which was the silliest of the three women, as regards their attitude towards Lawrence, is, at this distance, difficult to decide. Mrs. Siddons had occasional flashes of insight, as the example just quoted indicates. Sally appears weak, well-intentioned, lacking in spirit, incurably foolish and rather hypocritical, while Mrs. Pennington solemnly plays the knave in a tragi-comedy which, whenever she appears on the scene, is apt to degenerate into farce.

At the end of the year, when their pupils were presumably on holiday, Miss Bird and Lucy Lawrence planned to stay with Lawrence in Greek Street. This, naturally, threw Sally into a state of pleasurable perturbation and she is evidently afraid that if she sees too much of her friend her mother's suspicions may be aroused. Writing to Miss Bird on 15th December she says: 'If my mother is not yet convinc'd that I have acted with truth and consistency, she never will be convinc'd. Even when I confess'd that my heart and my reason were at variance, I was guided by my duty; she was the confidant of all my feelings, all my resolutions. Thank Heaven I no longer have such feelings to confess, and is not Mr. L. as perfectly at ease concerning me? I know he is, and that conviction first help'd to restore me to myself. I hope, however, that my Mother will continue in her present tranquillity respecting this subject. She has frequently said she never believ'd Mr. L. *lov'd me; what could be the interest* strong enough to make him so successful an hypocrite, I cannot find out. I should be tempted to think, perhaps like her, if I had been mistress of a fortune considerable enough to tempt any man to such an extraordinary conduct; but were I to marry, I should at least have the pleasing certainty that I was courted for *myself.* I have always been told that I was to expect but little in the case of such an event, and this, I believe, was pretty well known.'

Miss Bird arrived in London early in the new year and Mrs. Siddons, although unwilling to call on her at Greek Street, gave her an interview at the theatre and seems to have conveyed, through her, friendly messages to Lawrence to which he responded. On 7th February 1800 we find Mrs. Siddons writing to Miss Bird: 'Will you be so good as to ask Mr. L., where I can get some very fine carmine? I find it the best Rouge, cover'd with a little hair-powder; but I can get none at all equal to some he gave me about two years ago.' Shortly after this Mrs. Siddons and Lawrence met one another and the interview seems to have been entirely normal on both sides. This impelled Sally to say, in a note to Miss Bird: 'I am glad my Mother has seen Mr. Lawrence, I mean talk'd with him, as I think the composure of his manner the most likely method to convince her of his sincerity. I have not entertain'd the smallest doubt of it, but I am perhaps better able to judge in this case, as I *know from myself* what a change may take place in one's feelings in the course of some months.' From such glimpses as we are able to get of Miss Bird's personality, she emerges as the sort of kindly, sympathetic, level-headed young woman to whom the mothers of young ladies could safely entrust the care of their daughters. Had she not been both sensible as well as accomplished, Lucy Lawrence, who seems to have been highly valued as a schoolmistress and had excellent connections, would hardly have taken her into partnership. As the intimate friend of the Lawrences, with whom she frequently stayed on her visits to London, it was natural that she should do her best to be helpful both to Lawrence and Sally, in a difficult and complicated situation. She had already acted as confidante and go between in their affairs, and on the present occasion she continued to convey messages of a harmless nature and probably suggested that the two 'friends' might now meet each other as rational social beings and stop making everyone feel uncomfortable and ill at ease. Unfortunately for Sally, the more she heard of Lawrence's resumed calmness, sangfroid and general cheerfulness, the more her much trumpeted 'firmness' began to weaken. In a letter written to Miss Bird on the eve of the latter's departure from London, she gives herself away completely. 'It seems to me,' she says, 'I had many things to ask of, and to say to you, that I have neglected, but perhaps these things are best *unsaid, unheard* . . . I have been very triste ever since you left me. In your departure I think I lose *two* instead of one. You will not be sorry that I blend your idea with one for whom you know I have so true a regard, so lively an interest. While I am writing this I cannot help cautioning you not to let it be seen, for what I have said above, might by *some* be misconstrued, but *I trust I am writing to yourself only.*' Miss Bird evidently made some kind of 'proposal', regarding the future relations between Lawrence and Sally, perhaps that they should meet occasionally in the presence of third parties, though its precise nature is not revealed. Continuing, Sally asks: 'Who now will tell me *I am remember'd!* or say that *I do not forget?* I think I have never said as much to you before, but the idea of your being lost to me for so long a time has made me melancholy, and awaken'd feelings which it is the study of my life to stifle and extinguish. Generous Girl! I admire you for the sentiments you express'd this morning, but I should not like to make trial of you at the expense of my own piece of mind. It should be my constant prayer to be *always kept at this same distance from that being, whose fascination I have not the power to escape, should I be drawn within the circle of his magic.* Time and absence have work'd wonders in me, let me then not seek to counteract their salutary effects. My heart is so restor'd that, can I but keep clear of *that one rock,* it will, I think, split on no other. . . . Do not forget to say something *kind and friendly* for me to Mr. Lawrence;—what does he say to your proposal?'

The mystery of the 'proposal' is deepened in a later letter in which Sally again refers to it. 'I have never heard or seen anything of our friend since you left Town, but perhaps you have, are you to be correspondents? I did not imagine indeed, my dear girl, that our joke was likely to be realis'd; such a proposal, as you observe, can never come from you, and indeed if it had from *him,* you would have been a bold woman to have accepted it.' Later, on 31st May 1800, Sally writes to tell Miss Bird that the family are going to spend two months at Broadstairs, followed by two at Brighton, and mentions that she has seen the Royal Academy Exhibition and was delighted to witness Lawrence's 'complete superiority and success'. Sally and her parents returned to London for the Drury Lane season on 26th September and she writes to tell Miss Bird that 'at the Play on Tuesday last I saw our Greek Street friend, looking, I thought, very pale and ill'. The indisposition must have been of very short duration, for his old friend Miss Lee with whom, as Farington noted, Lawrence always 'wasted a lot of time' when she was in London, told Sally later that he was 'quite well, quite gay, and she believ'd, just at present, *heart-whole*'. This information must have caused Sally a good deal of secret heart-searching, and she was also disturbed to discover that her mother and Lawrence were now meeting frequently. All this and much more she pours out in a letter to Miss Bird, written on Christmas Eve. 'You may have heard (and it is true),' she says, 'of Mr. L. being in Mrs. Kemble's Box, and with my Mother. I fancy she often sees him at the Theatre, but you have indeed been misinformed by those who told you he was ever of *our party*. All I ever see of him is now and then at the Theatre, when he just appears for a minute, as if *purposely* to make me a formal bow, and then he generally goes away, to some other part of the house, I suppose. My Mother told me the other night that he was very well and in very good spirits, which will, I sincerely hope, continue. I am less likely than any one to inform you how he spends his time. All I know of him is that he is painting, or means to paint, my Uncle as Hamlet, and that my Mother says the sketch is *very beautiful;* that he is very frequently at my Uncle's house, and I believe scarcely ever misses a night when my Mother performs, when he generally pays her a visit in her dressing room. This I hear not from my Mother, for unless I force her to it, she never mentions him, but if she would give me an opportunity I would tell her something which I know would greatly please her, which is that I am now *at last myself perfectly convinc'd* that he is become *entirely indifferent* towards me. Of this change, *time* and *himself* alone could have convinc'd me.' This 'conviction' on Sally's part would have been better described as an agonised fear that Lawrence had ceased to care for her, a fear for which, in fact, there was not the slightest justification. Her morbid railing against Lawrence's alleged 'inconstancy', in face of convincing proof that, in spite of the way she had treated him, he remained the most constant of lovers, suggests that the unhappy girl took a delight in self-torture. Mrs. Siddons, from motives at which it is possible to guess although she herself may not have realised them, lost no opportunity of assuring Sally that Lawrence had fully recovered from his 'madness'. In a letter to Mrs. Pennington written on 19th December, she says: 'Our Knight errant is tir'd of fighting Windmills, and is very peaceable. He has a great deal to do, which is the best thing that can happen.'

That Lawrence's peaceableness was no more than a mask, worn to conceal his real feelings, was proved a few weeks later when he and Sally had a full-fledged 'lovers' quarrel' which at least revealed that their feeling for each other was unchanged. In recounting the whole affair at great length to Miss Bird Sally, for once in a way, stops pretending and expresses her feelings without ambiguity or humbug. As the letter is of great importance in the elucidation of a love story which has been much misinterpreted by some of Lawrence's biographers, it requires to be quoted in full. Lawrence had been staying at Rugby with his married sister, Mrs. Bloxam, and, while there, had naturally taken the opportunity to see Lucy Lawrence and Miss Bird. Writing on 23rd January 1801, Sally says:

'It was but a day or two before I received your letter, my dear namesake, that I heard of your friend's visit to Rugby. I dare say you were all much delighted to see him, it is *not easy to forget the pleasure of such society!* and *you* may enjoy it without the dread of consequences, and the fear of displeasing those whom you wish to make happy. And so he mentioned the coldness of my salutation; believe me, my dear, he himself set the example; I could not endure to think that he should fancy me more delighted than he *wishes me to be* at the sight of him. It is very very seldom that I *can* see him, and as I told you, *his* manner has been so cold, so repelling, that I am determined to learn the lesson he seemed to wish to teach me, and accordingly, I confess the last time I saw him, I made him as distant a Curtsy as he made me a Bow. I know my Mother sees him often, and I know she cannot cease to look upon him with the partiality she always did, and always I believe will feel for him, yet she never mentions him to me, never tells me he has spoken of me, or desires to be remembered to me,—perhaps indeed he never *does* think or speak of me—but can I ever forget the days that are past? Is it easy, is it *possible* to wish to be quite obliterated from a heart which I once thought it the extreme of happiness to possess? Ah! no, no, I feel it is not possible, and however *right* I may think it that we are separated, I would not have him *forget me!*

I know that his is an unconstant heart, that he has lov'd many, yet I think there were circumstances attending my attachment to him and his to me, which (though love be gone) should ensure me *for ever* a portion of his recollection and his tenderness. As for *my heart, it is a single and a constant one,* it never gave itself *but once* away, and I believe it *incapable* of change.

You cannot imagine how near I was meeting him in a *private party* and *without my Mother* last night at your friend Mr. Westall's. After having met him and his sister at a Lady's house twice, we liked each other so well, and they gave Patty and me so pressing an invitation to spend an evening at their house, that we could not refuse, nor had we indeed any inclination, for they are both very pleasant and good humour'd. But when my Mother heard of this she did not like it at all, and after some time said that perhaps we were not aware how very likely it was we might meet one artist at the house of another. We had heard the Westalls speak of Mr. Lawrence and so thought this no impossible event, but it would indeed have been a most distressing one to all parties, so with my Mother's approbation Patty called upon Miss Westall and told her from some circumstances that had happened in our family, it would be very distressing to us to meet Mr. L. and therefore if he was engaged we would wait on her some other evening. She said it was very lucky Patty had just then mention'd it, as her brother was to dine with Mr. L. that very day and had certainly intended asking him, so you see what a narrow escape we have had. What do you think would have become of us if we had met. I don't imagine he would have accepted of the invitation if he had known *I* was to be of the party, for my Mother would have heard of it of course, and would have been so much displeased, that it would cost him some time and trouble to bring her back to her present kind dispositions towards him. I have done nothing but think all this day, that had it not been for my Mother's representations I should have

ound myself in company with him to-night, and then what
hould I have done all the evening?—I was not quite well, and
ho' I tried to sing, succeeded very indifferently . . .'

Thus Mrs. Siddons again intervened, from a mixture of motives
which it is improbable that she herself ever faced and analysed,
o destroy her daughter's last chance of happiness with the man
hey both loved. Since their reconciliation, her feeling for Law-
ence had certainly become far deeper and warmer than mere
riendship, and this only intensified her determination to keep
aim and Sally apart. Whether the meeting at the Westalls'
which so nearly took place, had been carefully planned by Law-
ence, or whether the circumstances were as fortuitous as Sally
upposed, we have now no means of knowing. Lawrence's anger
hat Sally refused the invitation as soon as she discovered that he
was to be present at the party suggests that he had worked out
he whole scheme in detail, with Westall's connivance, and
ttached the utmost importance to its success. If she still cared for
aim, he may have asked himself, why did she not jump at the
chance of spending an evening in his company in the presence of
congenial friends and under conditions which must have absolved
aer of the slightest blame? His exasperation at her failure to grasp
he opportunity thus offered is hardly surprising and the coldness
of his rage at her conduct, for which he could not have known
hat Mrs. Siddons was responsible, was a sure indication of the
till unabated warmth of his love. It found expression in a scene
at the theatre which Sally described, with great perturbation,
n a letter to Miss Bird, dated 13th February 1801.

'I write, my dear namesake, to tell you my grievances, and
because I think by your means I may gain some information I
very much wish for. I was last night at Drury Lane where I saw
Mr. L.—for the first time these *many, many weeks*. Well, as soon
as I thought I perceiv'd his eyes turn'd towards me, I bow'd to
aim; he did not return my salutation, and I supposed I had been
mistaken in thinking he was looking at me. I waited a little,
and then feeling sure his looks were fixed upon our Box, I bow'd

three times, still he took not the least notice. I began to feel a little surpris'd and almost to fancy he *would* not see me; to be certain of this I took an Opera Glass, caught his eye, and immediately repeated my salutation *three times,* he actually star'd me in the face, without even once smiling, or answering me by the smallest inclination of his head. This behaviour *astonishes and grieves* me; tell me, my dear namesake, (for you only can) to what I am to attribute this amazing change. I cannot believe he means to insult me—nor do I know in what I can have offended him. You can find this out—and I entreat you do. Separated for ever as we are, I would still live in his memory as a friend he esteems and regrets, and to think that he can quite forget me, and after not seeing me for so long a time behave to me as he did last night, gives me great uneasiness. Be diligent to send me an answer. I know you sometimes write to him, ask him *from me* what I have done, for I would rather think him angry than suppose he wish'd to make me understand I was more forward than he desired I should be to acknowledge him. I need not tell you how impatient I shall be to hear from you, and do not write till you can resolve my doubts—neither you nor he can *misconstrue* my feelings. I have never ceased to express the interest I take in him, in his fortunes, in his sentiments, and I had flatter'd myself that tho' every former hope was *by both of us resign'd,* I should not in passing from his heart, be mixed with the many who had gone before and were forgotten.'

Miss Bird, as usual, did her best to help her friend. She got in touch with Lawrence and passed on Sally's message. According to Dr. Knapp, who omits to supply any documentary evidence for his statement, Lawrence wrote a letter, forwarded by Miss Bird, in which he charged Sally 'with some fancied wrong', by which he probably means that he expatiated with some bitterness on the Westall incident. Sally's reply, which is unfortunately not quoted in extenso, seems to have contained an indignant denial that she had ever injured him in thought, word, or deed, and an assurance that she would never more trouble him with her 'ill-timed salutations'. Thus, instead of making the soft answer that would have turned away Lawrence's wrath, she jumped on her high horse, and, in doing so, increased her own distress of mind.

Dr. Knapp, apparently on the strength of a letter which he has read but does not quote, says that 'she announced to Miss Bird her fixed determination to omit from her letters for the future, a subject which she had resolved to banish for ever from her thoughts'. As one of her principal reasons for writing to Miss Bird so frequently was the relief it afforded her to be able to discuss freely her feelings with regard to Lawrence, the correspondence between the two girls now lapsed. Having voluntarily deprived herself of the consolation of confiding in Miss Bird, Sally yielded to the urge to tell her mother how greatly she resented Lawrence's conduct. In the course of conversation the cause of Lawrence's strange behaviour—her refusal of Miss Westall's invitation, and especially the manner of it—was no doubt referred to, and it is probable that Sally made it clear that when answering Lawrence's angry letter, she had let him know that, in avoiding the meeting, she had merely been obeying her mother's wishes. As Mrs. Siddons was by this time herself more than ever infatuated with her daughter's lover, she was naturally annoyed with Sally for having put the blame for what took place where, in fact, it belonged. She vented her agitation on the unfortunate Miss Bird whom, Dr. Knapp says, she suspected 'of having broken her promise of non-interference, and of having been actively working to bring about a renewal of intercourse between Lawrence and Sally. She had an interview with Miss Bird on the subject while playing at Birmingham, in the summer, and several stormy epistles, couched in a high tragedy vein, passed between them'. Miss Bird succeeded in allaying her suspicions, and peace was restored. Silence and oblivion now rest upon the tragic love story of Sally and Lawrence. If further letters passed between them, if the quarrel was forgotten and more bows were exchanged by the separated lovers at Drury Lane, we shall probably never know. Writing to Mrs. Pennington on 7th January 1803, the year of her death, Sally says: 'If I could but have foreseen how much better my health was to be than it has been for many, many years, how rejoic'd should I have been to have gone with her [Mrs. Siddons] upon this expedition.' At the end of the letter she writes: 'Do you read in the papers of the gaiety of the Marquis of Abercorn's family at his seat *the Priory*, near London?' It is significant that she makes no reference to the fact, which the newspapers recorded, that Lawrence was one of Lord Abercorn's guests and took a prominent part in the private theatricals which contributed much to the 'gaiety' of the house party. Lawrence played Lord Rakeland in *The Wedding Day* and Grainger in *Who's the Dupe?* and acquitted himself with his usual success. This, so far as is known, was the first occasion on which he employed his talent for declamation by acting on a stage, and it must have required some control on Sally's part to avoid mentioning it.

Sally's health continued satisfactory during February and her brother George, who went to Ireland to say goodbye to his Mother before taking up a post in India, was able to give good news of her. On 10th March, however, Mr. Siddons wrote to his wife's companion, Patty Wilkinson, telling her that Sally was ill but asking her not to inform Mrs. Siddons. He did not wish the profitable Irish tour to be abandoned. Two days later he wrote telling Mrs. Siddons to set her mind at ease and fulfil her engagement to appear at Cork. Some days later she received a further and more unsatisfactory report of Sally's health and at once abandoned her tour and hurried to Dublin, where her crossing was delayed by easterly gales. When she at last succeeded in reaching England she was met on the road by a letter from Mr. Siddons admitting Sally's serious condition. News of her daughter's death, which occurred two hours after this letter was written, reached her the same day.

There was no Mrs. Pennington to record the end of this unhappy girl. We do not know who was present by her bedside when she expired or who attended the funeral. Mrs. Siddons reached London on 16th April 1803, three days after Sally's death which occurred on her lover's birthday. That Lawrence's grief was overwhelming cannot be questioned. No one ever took Sally's place in his heart and it is equally true that no one ever took the place of Lawrence in the heart of Mrs. Siddons. The

SATAN CALLING HIS LEGIONS

This enormous picture, which the painter regarded as his masterpiece, remained in his possession until his death. It was exhibited at the Royal Academy in 1797. At the Lawrence sale, June 18th 1831, it fetched £504, and was subsequently acquired by the Royal Academy.

GENERAL SIR JOHN MOORE, 1761–1809
In the National Portrait Gallery.

fact that Lawrence idolised the Kembles, constantly painted and drew portraits of members of the famous clan, and had an undying admiration for her mother cannot be seriously adduced as proof that his love for Sally was any less sincere and deep than this story discloses. To the end of his life Lawrence always dressed in black, used black sealing wax to seal his letters, and underneath his surface gaiety and social charm, there was a settled and deep melancholy, which his self-portraits reveal.

XI

THE DELICATE INVESTIGATION

IN SPITE of all the emotional disturbance caused by his frustrated passion for Sally Siddons, Lawrence's industry and application showed no signs of slackening. Always extremely reticent about his personal affairs, he seems to have confided in no one, outside the Siddons family circle, on the subject which must have filled his thoughts. Even Farington heard nothing which he thought of sufficient interest to record in his Diary. In the entry for 2nd January 1797 he mentions that he called on Lawrence, and found his sister and a clergyman there. He observes that 'His 2nd portrait of Mrs. Siddons I think his best female head'. On the following day he quotes an illuminating remark of Samuel Rogers, the banker and poet, on the difference ' in Mrs. Siddons when she is in a small familiar party from what she appears in a large company where she is reserved and cautious.—Speaking of herself she says it is the effect of *timidity* —that is she has a character to support and is afraid of losing importance.—The Siddons—Kembles and Twiss's—sup together frequently in parties, and Rogers has met there Lord Derby and Miss Farren—but it has been remarked that though Lord Derby sups at Twiss's and at Siddons, He never asks them in return'. He makes no mention of Sally and Maria. The death of Sally Siddons in April 1803 passes unrecorded.

On 2nd March 1804 Farington noted that Samuel Lane, his former pupil who had become Lawrence's assistant, told him that 'Mrs. Siddons sat to Lawrence for a *whole length last night by lamplight*, till 2 o'clock this morning,—Lawrence got up to-day a little before ten'.

This picture, a full-length, had been commissioned by Mrs. McHugh, Mrs. Siddons's ardent admirer, and proved, by general

194

consent, to be a failure. It is in the possession of the National Gallery, but is not generally shown. Farington records on 5th April, some opinions on it expressed by brother artists. 'Bourgeois sd. He was much disappointed in Lawrence's Mrs. Siddons.— West told me that Lawrence was grown careless. Bourgeois sd to me "I always speak my mind abt Lawrence's pictures. I wd not give 6d for that of Mrs. Siddons.—It neither represents Her body or mind".' On 20th June Farington mentions that there is 'much wicked allusion abt Lawrence and Her (Mrs. Siddons) in public papers'. He heard this from Lysons, in whose company and that of Dr. Burney he dined at the Ship Tavern at Greenwich, having gone there by water. 'Our dinner was good and everything very cheerful, but Dr. Burney made it very expensive by calling for Champagne, Hock, etc.—Lysons told me that Mr. and Mrs. Siddons have acquired £40,000 and that Mr. Siddons has lately settled upon Her £20,000 which He will also leave and all the rest at *Her disposal*. Her £20,000 brings in £1,000 a year. . . . Mr. and Mrs. Siddons are not suited to each other. While the daughters lived they went on tolerably.' It seems clear from this that neither from Lysons, who knew the whole story of Lawrence's love affairs, nor from Lawrence himself, had the gossiping Farington received any information about them. The chief events of Lawrence's public life, after his removal to Greek Street, were the portraits which he exhibited at the Academy. He sent in six, in 1798, including one of Mrs. Allnutt of Clapham, and one of Kemble in the character of Coriolanus which Williams says 'was never much admired by the profession'. In 1799 he again sent in six portraits, one of them being that of the beautiful Miss Jennings, afterwards Mrs. Lock, which is now in Paris, and another that of his friend Samuel Lysons. In 1800 Lawrence exhibited seven portraits. These were Mr. Boucherette's children, Curran, the famous Irish lawyer and patriot, J. P. Kemble in the part of Rolla, the Rev. Mr. Pennicotte, Lord Eldon and Mrs. Twiss. The latter may have been a reward for her patience in listening to the painter's passionate outbursts on the subject of Sally. Curran, an ugly little man, whose face Williams describes as 'the most unfortunate specimen of the coarsest Irish features', was the despair of portrait painters. In repose, there was nothing much to be done with a countenance so ill-favoured, but when he was excited, his inimitable humour and keen intelligence lent a brilliance to his eyes which transformed his whole appearance. Lawrence's first attempt was a failure. He tried again and, in one sitting, he succeeded in making a spirited likeness of this remarkable man. For the enormous figure of Rolla, Lawrence once again, as in his Satan, used Gentleman Jackson as his model. The child, much the most pleasing part of the picture, was a portrait of Sheridan's small son.

In 1801 Lawrence again exhibited six portraits of which the most noteworthy were the two daughters of the recently ennobled Lord Templeton of Antrim, the Hon. Sophia and the Hon. Caroline Upton, who were frequent visitors to Norbury Park, and another full-length portrait of Kemble, this time in the part of Hamlet. In this year Lawrence's rival, Hoppner, owing to increasing ill-health, exhibited nothing. The portrait of Kemble was greatly admired by contemporary critics and since it verged on the kind of historical painting for which Lawrence thought himself specially gifted, he also regarded it with satisfaction. In a revealing letter to his 'dearest Mrs. Boucherette', he says:

'I am very glad that, after the Two Friends, you like my Hamlet which, except my Satan, I think my best work. I must now try, though, to give something much better (for the low centre of your pier); for I begin to be really uneasy at finding myself so harnessed and shackled into this dry mill-horse business, which yet I must get through with steady industry, well knowing that this is the very season of my life when it is most necessary.

How good you are to tell me of those friends who become dearer to me every hour in my life, and, I think, in exact proportion as I begin to see the real blessings of existence, and to prize what is valuable as I ought; only I have been a dreamer, and wake too late. I have lived half my life; and though Death may not divide me from the being that I love, Circumstance (a creature of some potency) may as effectually do it, with more bitterness, if not equal sorrow. I am not fanciful enough to expect it otherwise.'

This reference to his ill-fated passion for Sally Siddons and the consolation he finds in the friends 'who become dearer to me every hour in my life' contains in it the secret of his heart. Denied, first by circumstance and later by death, of the fulfilment of his one great love, he was rewarded by the affection and esteem of his friends, among whom his brothers and sisters, not to speak of his nephews and nieces, were happily included. In saying that he had 'lived half my life' he proved an accurate prophet. The interest of the second half of his career, apart from his artistic achievements, largely centres in the fact that during an historical period which has for us a retrospective glamour, he had a wide acquaintance among the leading figures of his time and was scarcely less successful in the art of friendship than in that of portrait-painting. The essential constancy of his nature, his freedom from snobbery, his generosity, his loyalty and his gift of sympathy all found expression in the friendships which he made and retained. That he had need of steady industry in his 'millhorse business' of portrait-painting, which at least prevented him from rivalling Haydon's attempts to become an historical painter in the Grand Manner and saved him from producing any more Satans, is shown by a brief entry in Farington's Diary on 18th March 1801. 'L's [Lawrence's] circumstances are now so notoriously bad as to be common talk—£400 to Middleton [artists' colourman],—£40 to Poole etc. etc.—said to be 30 actions against him and it must end in Bankruptcy.' Bankruptcy, which at this time was so usual a solution of financial embarrassments as to be almost fashionable, would have relieved Lawrence of his worries and six years later his friend Thomas Coutts, the banker, strongly urged him to file his petition. The idea of letting down his creditors was repugnant, however, both to his sense of honour and his personal pride, and he preferred to struggle on, confident that by increased application he would at last be able to extricate himself.

Towards the end of 1800 and the beginning of 1801 he spent

some time at Montague House, Blackheath, the residence of the Princess of Wales, whose portrait, and that of her daughter, he had been commissioned to paint. His visits had embarrassing consequences, which will be referred to later.

Owing to the fact that the Princess had been too unwell to sit, Lawrence was late in finishing his portrait of her and, partly owing to Hoppner's ill-tempered objections, the Council of the Academy refused to allow him the necessary time to complete it. Lawrence called on Farington to tell him about this and talked of withdrawing all his pictures, which Farington, with his usual good sense, advised him not to do. 'Lawrence sat with me,' he goes on, 'till one o'clock, we had much serious conversation.—He requested me to urge him to exertion saying that at times He is incapable of any, at other times is full of it. He alluded to the state of his affairs.—I told him there was only one way which was to look his situation fairly in the face and to acquire a habit of regular application which He might obtain by each day taking up that picture which required finishing that he felt most inclined to work upon. He said He was sure his picture of [Kemble as] Hamlet had not taken him more than 10 days to paint it, supposing each day to be from 9 o'clock till 5.'

The exhibition of 1802 contained nine portraits by Lawrence and only one by Hoppner. Among Lawrence's were his portraits of the Princess of Wales and Princess Charlotte. In 1803 Lawrence exhibited five portraits of which the most notable were those of Lord Thurlow, Miss Lamb and Lady Charlotte Campbell. Early in this year Lawrence took part in the private theatricals at the Marquis of Abercorn's house, The Priory, Stanmore, to which Sally Siddons alluded in one of her letters to Mrs. Pennington. In a letter to his sister, Mrs. Bloxam, dated 28th January 1803, he gives an account of the party, which seems to have received an unusual amount of press publicity. He writes:

'You have seen in the papers an account of a theatrical fête at the Marquis of Abercorn's. . . . It was projected by a woman of great cleverness and beauty, Lady Caher,—very young and full of talent, with Lady Abercorn, and the rest of the female party; and of course it was acceded to by Lord Abercorn, who, whatever character of pride the world may have given him, is just as pleasant and kind and gentlemanly with his family and friends as a man can be.

It was determined to do it in a quiet way and more as an odd experiment in the talents of the party, than anything else;—but this and that friend would be offended; and at last it swelled up to a perfect theatre (in a room) and a London audience.

The Prince, the Duke and Duchess of Devonshire, Lord and Lady Melbourne, (their sons of the party), Lord and Lady Essex, Lord and Lady Amherst, with a long *et cetera*, and amongst the rest, Sheridan, were present!

A play was first thought of, and I was for Miss Barley's Comedy "The Trial" . . . At last, however, the pieces fixed upon were the "Wedding Day" and "Who's the Dupe?" In the first the characters were thus:

Sir Adam Contest	Mr. J. Madox
Mr. Milden	Mr. Madox
Lord Rakeland	Your Brother
Mr. Contest	Mr. G. Lamb

Ladies.

Lady Contest	Lady Caher
Hannah	Hon. Miss Butler
Mrs.—	Mrs. J. Kemble
Lady Autumn	Lady C. Lindsay

Who's the Dupe?

Old Doiley	Mr. J. Madox
Sandford	Mr. Lamb
Grainger	Your Brother
Gradus	Mr. G. Lamb
Servants	The Lords Hamilton

Ladies.

Miss Doiley	Hon. Miss Butler
Charlotte	Mrs. J. Kemble

I was obliged to be in town, and at first neglected my Parts, but not being coxcomb enough to do it wholly, I made good sail at the last and was perfect. The day at last came, and was very pleasant from all its distractions and inconveniences. The Prince was to dine at six, and in the same room that the performers dined in, who, of course, had an earlier hour, half-past three. We all sat down like a Rugby school party, but rather more vociferous, huzzaed our Manager, and hissed our Hostess off for talking of the Prince and hours.'

After describing the orchestra, which he says was perfect, and referring to the 'admirable scenery', he goes on:

'The Prince then came in, and of course the orchestra struck up, God Save the King; then a little terrifying bell rang, the curtain drew up, and the Wedding Day began. At first, I will own to you, Sheridan's face, the grave Duke of Devonshire, and two or three staunch critics, made me feel unpleasantly; for I opened the piece. However, this soon wore off. Our set all played extremely well, like persons of good sense, without extravagance, or buffoonery, and yet with sufficient spirit. Lady Caher, Mr. J. Madox and G. Lamb were the most conspicuous, the first so beautiful, that I felt love-making very easy.

A splendid supper closed the business, and the Prince, the Devonshires, Melbournes, Westmorlands, etc., etc., slept at the Priory.

Wednesday it was determined to act it again; but I have unfortunately prevented it by my illness, and they knew of it only on the morning; so that I occasioned great inconvenience, and have just been of consequence enough to frustrate a pleasant scheme. At Easter, if not before, it will be done again. You know me too well, dear Anne, to believe that I should be of such a scheme under any but very flattering circumstances; as it was I was right to join in it. Lord Abercorn is an old Jermyn Street friend—a staunch and honourable one, and particularly kind to me in real services and very gratifying distinctions. These all formed one strong reason for joining in the thing; and another secret one was, that whatever tends to heighten a character for general talent (when kept in prudent bounds) is of use to that particular direction of it which forms the pursuit of life. I have gained, then, and not lost by this (to you) singular step. I am not going to be a performer in other families, I stick to Lord Abercorn's; and for the rest, I pursue my profession as quietly and more steadily than ever.'

The apologetic note on which this letter concludes almost suggests that Lawrence still regards himself, after having been for so many years the family breadwinner, as in some way responsible to his relations. That he distinguished himself on this occasion is proved by an entry in Farington's Diary in which he records that 'Heath told us that Sheridan called on him to-day and told him that he had been to the Marquis of Abercorn's where He has seen the play by amateur performers. Lawrence performed the part of [Lord Rakeland] and was a very good actor. Heath asked whether He meant considering him as one who attempted. Sheridan replied No, but really a *very good actor*. —He added that Lawrence had painted several pictures there, but He did not much like them. He preferred his acting to his painting'.

The squabbles, commotions, intrigues and jealousies which shook the Royal Academy before Lawrence became its President would fill several volumes if any attempt were made to describe them in detail. A statement in the *Morning Post* of 15th April 1803, to the effect that the President, Benjamin West, contrary to the Academy's rules, had shown a picture of 'Hagar and Ishmail in the Wilderness' which had actually been painted and exhibited in 1776, resulted in a conflict among the academicians to which a brief reference must be made. West's explanation, that he was in the habit of altering and repainting his pictures and that he had done so in this case, adding the date 1803, was accepted by the Council of the Academy, of which neither Lawrence nor Farington were members. The General Assembly of the Academicians, however, refused to accept this excuse for the infringement of an important rule and showed their disapproval by electing the Architect Wyatt to the Presidency in place of West. The result was that George III, who was an ardent admirer of West, intervened on his behalf, and ordered the Resolutions passed by the General Assembly to be expunged. The revolting Academicians, of whom Farington was one, thereupon swallowed their pride, acceded to the King's recommendation, obeyed his desire 'to see peace and harmony restored in the Society' and, as Williams suggests, were reconciled, shook hands and hated each other ever after. In this affair Lawrence was torn by a conflict of loyalties between West, whom he liked and respected, and Farington, for whom he had a deep affection. Lawrence, as Williams rightly says, never 'imbibed the bitter spirit of the disputes, or at all entered into the cabals of the artists'. On this occasion, as on others, he was an advocate of peace at any reasonable price. Layard gives the draft of a letter written to Farington in August 1803, in which he says: 'When I tell you that I voted with you last night against my own opinion, I but tell you what you know. You will always guide and direct me if you *chuse* to do so, and I can hardly conceive that *possible* case in which you may not.' In a revealing passage he says: 'You are not Young, and will die before me, and I say the truth which is in my Heart when I say that except Mr. Lock *no* one will be so mist, so regretted by me.' All the same, he was uneasy about the line Farington had taken and after West was restored to the Presidency remained firm in his support. The following letter, written 9th December 1805, shows that in spite of all the hand-shaking the cabal against West was still active although, by this time, Farington seems to have modified his hostility. Lawrence writes:

'My DEAR FRIEND,

Much as we have reason to be disgusted with the very name of the Academy, I still think (and with no *affected* feeling) that where there is a fair chance of saving it from degradation we should be wanting in a *Duty* not to attempt it. You seem'd to think that Mr. West might be still secur'd in the chair, and with credit to himself. Surely in the present circumstances there can be no measure so beneficial to the Academy, or honourable to those who have its Welfare at Heart, and are known to have had the confidence of the President.'

The situation was complicated by West's 'democratic' opinions and his expressed admiration for Buonaparte, but it would occupy more space to go into this in detail than the subject warrants.

In the summer of 1803, about two months after the death of Sally Siddons, Lawrence and Farington went to dine with Doctor Charles Burney at Greenwich and Farington records some examples of Lawrence's table talk on that occasion which show how valued a guest he must have been in the homes of intelligent and cultivated people. Recalling his visit to Cowper at Weston in 1793, Lawrence said: 'Cowper's manner seemed to him to answer the description given of Addison by Steele:—It was pleasant with a tendency to delicate satire.—His appearance was that of a gentleman, but rather of a former fashion, what is now called "*The Old Court.*"—He avowed himself to be what the world would call a *Methodist;*—on the window seat of his sitting room, Lawrence found a heap of 3 penny and sixpenny pamphlets, published by various Methodistical enthusiasts.—Lord Thurlow, the old companion of Cowper, when they were students in the Temple, proposed to have visited Cowper, but He declined receiving his Lordship from apprehension it was believed that their manners would not suit each other. He had heard that Lord Thurlow was accustomed to swear, and be very decissive. Mrs. Unwin,—Cowper's valuable female friend, said little. Once she remarked, while the Company were speaking of Dr. Johnson, "That He seemed to have been born with '*No, Sir*', coming out of his mouth." '

Throughout 1803 and during the following years, until the danger was dispelled by the victory at Trafalgar, considerable apprehension was felt by the upper classes and by the well-informed, who seem to have constituted only a small percentage of the population, about the danger of a French invasion. Farington records a vivid dream he had 'of seeing the French boats approach in the utmost order, and myself surrounded by them after their landing. . . . It seemed to me that they came upon the country quite unprepared and met with no resistance . . . The only conversation yesterday that assimilated with my dream was occasioned by Marchant [R.A.] saying that Coll. Turner who was in Egypt, gave his opinion that England could not now be safe but by the *People* becoming *military*'.

On 7th October Lawrence told Farington, on the authority of Kemble, that 'Invasion is expected within a fortnight and the attempt wished for by many, that a defeated enemy may give up false hopes'. Some days before, Lawrence had dined with 'Baron Wolf the Danish Minister and went there with a Danish gentleman. In conversation much respect was expressed for this country, but he could perceive a jealousy of its naval power and desire to have it lowered'. As Nelson had won the battle of Copenhagen two years previously, which led to the conclusion of peace between England and Denmark, this jealousy was not unnatural. The Wolffs, father and son, were wealthy timber merchants and shipbrokers. George Wolff, the elder (1756–1828), came to London from Christiania in 1759 and settled in Wellclose Square, near the old Danish Church. In 1760 he married an Englishwoman, Elizabeth Gorham, and in 1767, the year when his son Jens was born, he became a naturalised British subject. In the same year he established his business in partnership with his brother Ernest. In 1783 the brothers took into partnership John Dorville of Ravenscourt Park, Hammersmith, and the firm became known as Wolff and Dorville. In due course Jens Wolff joined it and, in 1793, he and his father were appointed joint Danish consuls.

The Wolffs must by this time have become very rich for, after his marriage to one of three beautiful sisters, Jens Wolff established himself in a large house at Battersea called Sherwood Lodge, which adjoined two Royal residences, York House and Tudor House. Both he and his wife were interested in the arts and they made their home a centre of hospitality for artists and literary men, among who were Lawrence and Fuseli. The younger Smirke afterwards Sir Robert, built a gallery as an annex to the house, in which was displayed a fine collection of casts, mostly from the antique. The effect of the war was disastrous to the Wolffs' business they failed, and in 1812 Sherwood Lodge was sold to Mrs. Fitz herbert. She disposed of it in 1824. Later in the nineteenth century all three houses were pulled down and the site occupied by candle factory. Mr. and Mrs. Wolff, for reasons not disclosed, agreed to separate about ten years after Lawrence first met them and Mrs. Wolff, who had a son named Herman St. John, went to live with her sister at Charing, in Kent. She spent the last eight years of her life in Herefordshire, near Monmouth, where, according to Williams, she 'was known and beloved by the most respectable families in the neighbourhood'. Miss Croft says that two or three years after her first meeting with Lawrence, which took place at Dr. Heathcote's in Charterhouse Square about the year 1800, her friend Mrs. Wolff 'sat to Mr. Lawrence, in consequence of Mrs. Hill having seen a portrait of Mrs. Twiss (the sister of Mrs. Siddons) at Ross which struck her as the most graceful and pleasing likeness she had ever seen'. Miss Croft adds that Lawrence told her long afterwards that 'although he considered Mrs. Wolff very beautiful and even very clever, it was some time before he entered into the merit of her character; but as their acquaintance improved, he did the most ample justice to her genius and many amiable qualities, and their friendship only ended with her life in June 1829. He became one of the most intimate friends of Mr. and Mrs. Wolff and her two sisters, Mrs. Marshall and Mrs. Hill; and I had the honour and happiness of being admitted into a society which constituted the chief pleasure of my life, till I found myself in 1830 the sole survivor (expect Mrs. Marshall) of the party who had so long lived in affectionate and uninterrupted intimacy'. Lawrence's beautiful portrait of Mrs. Wolff which is now in America, was exhibited at the Royal Academy in 1815.

In view of the licentiousness of court circles and society generally during the Regency and the corresponding prevalence of salacious gossip, it was inevitable that it should be taken for granted by outside observers that Lawrence's relations with Mrs. Wolff were those of lover and mistress. The Earl of Egmont, an undoubted authority on the subject, since the number of his bastards was almost beyond computation, once said that when he came into the world 'there was hardly a young married lady of fashion who did not think it almost a stain upon her reputation if she was not known as having cuckolded her husband and the

only doubt was who was to assist her in the operation'. Illegiti
macy of birth was so common that no stigma seems to hav
attached to it. Among Lawrence's friends, John Julius Angerstein
the first William Lock, and the estimable Ayscough Boucherett
were said to have been irregularly conceived. The Diaries of Lord
Glenbervie and the Greville Memoirs abound in scandalous storie
which show how great, at this period, was the relaxation of mora
standards, at least among 'the best people'. The Prince of Wales
and his brothers and sisters, themselves set an unedifying exampl
which many of their entourage were only too glad to follow.

It was inevitable, in such conditions, that a man as goodlooking
and agreeable as Lawrence should be credited, by those who judged
others by themselves, with making full use of all his opportunities
Lawrence, however, although he had the *entrée* to the highes
social circles, and was evidently quite willing to engage in ligh
flirtations, had firm principles of middle-class morality. Hi
reputation as a Lothario seems to have been largely based on the
rather spiteful comments of ladies who had tested this morality
and found it disconcertingly invincible. As Williams says, 'ir
affairs of love, Sir Thomas had need of the fortitude of St
Anthony, for he was often tempted, and was more sinned agains
than sinning'. A woman friend of his wrote after his death tha
he was 'oftener wooed than wooing' and 'never gave pain
wilfully, to any human being, or flirted for the gratification o
his own vanity'. Another lady, writing of his *liaisons* rather les:
kindly, said that 'it cannot be too strongly stated, that his manner.
were likely to mislead without his intending it. He could not writ
a common answer to a dinner invitation without its assuming the
tone of a billet-doux: the very commonest conversation was held
in that soft low whisper, and with that tone of deference and interest, which are so unusual, and so calculated to please. I an
myself persuaded, that he never intentionally gave pain. He wa
not a male coquette; he had no *plan* of conquest'. All of thi.
seems to indicate that Lawrence, fond as he was of women, had so
repressed or sublimated his natural appetites that he never realised
that those to whom he paid polite and, to himself, meaningles.
attentions, might be physically more susceptible. The lady who

supplied this last piece of evidence, which has been quoted over and over again without scrutiny, had evidently been disappointed by his lack of enterprise and knew of others who had been similarly 'misled'. No woman could possibly write in such terms of a fascinating rake and experienced 'solvent of feminine virtue', as he has since been called. What the testimony really proves is that, in an age when, at least in court circles, feminine virtue was rarely impregnable, Lawrence often caused chagrin by his failure to make assaults upon it. When he fell in love, it was a serious matter, his heart and mind were engaged, and his intentions 'strictly honourable'. Apart from Sally Siddons, we know only of one other girl whom he wanted to marry, and she refused to accept him on account of the difference in their rank. According to Williams, who gives no details and supplies no dates, 'he fell *éperdument amoureux* of the Honourable Miss Upton, sister of Lord Templeton'. There were two Miss Uptons, Caroline and Sophia, daughters of one Clotworthy Upton who was given an Irish peerage for services not thought worthy of record by the *Dictionary of National Biography*. Lawrence met them at Norbury Park and painted their portraits, which were exhibited in the Royal Academy of 1801. Williams does not state which of the two was the object of his passion, only that it lasted for two years, which he regards as 'a tolerable duration for unrequited love'. Lawrence considered that the lady coquetted with him and trifled with his feelings, and wrote a long and bitter poem about 'the cold coquette', which possibly relieved them. That she was certainly a snob, and possibly rather a fool to miss the chance of raising herself from obscurity by marrying the future President of the Royal Academy, can be guessed from Lawrence's verses, which indicate that she had succeeded, at least, in inflaming normal desires. The concluding lines of the poem are worth quoting for the light they throw on his character:

> Urg'd by no passion, Reason only blames,
> Cold in thyself, to guide the fatal flames,
> With nice discernment touch the starting nerve,
> And every torment curiously observe;

Affect to soothe, but to inflame the pain,
And drive the poison faster to the brain;
And when no more thy victim can endure,
But raging, supplicates thy soul for cure,
Then, act the timid unsuspecting maid,
And wonder at the mischief thou hast play'd.

Unjust one! dost thou scorn the wand'ring wretch,
Forced on the pavement her cold limbs to stretch?
From generous weakness first her errors flow'd,
Some sacrifice the direful curse bestow'd;
The hardness of her sex her sorrows spurn'd,
And but from want to wickedness she turn'd,
And dost thou triumph no such crimes are thine,
No stain in thee pollutes thy boasted line?
That lost one at the throne of God shall rise,
And supplicate thy entrance to the skies;
Give to thy youthful vanity the blame,
Take from the worst of crimes its hateful name,
And ask of Heav'n in mercy to forget
The mean ambition of the cold Coquette.

Lawrence first met Mrs. Wolff in 1803, and it will be remembered that Miss Croft said that it was 'some time' before he 'entered into the merits of her character'. If we regard 'some time' as meaning about five years, the period during which he was under the subjection of the 'cold coquette' must have been between 1803 and 1808. He is hardly likely to have begun paying marked attentions to Miss Upton during Sally's life-time, even after their last quarrel, as, had he done so, she would undoubtedly have got to hear of it. What Williams calls 'his more intellectual attachment to Mrs. Wolff' began after he had recovered from his unrequited love for Lord Templeton's daughter. A 'discreet friend of the parties', probably Miss Croft, told Williams that his friendship for Mrs. Wolff, 'undoubtedly, innocent as it was, absorbed all his feeling and his time, and left no room for other attachments. If he made conquests he was not vain of them, for I am sure his most

GEORGE IV

This painting was probably completed in 1822. Lawrence wrote that it was 'perhaps my most successful resemblance'. In the Wallace Collection.

WARREN HASTINGS
Exhibited at the Royal Academy 1811. *In the National Portrait Gallery.*

trusted friend, after Mrs. Wolff (Mrs. Hayman) has no idea of them.' The first letter from Lawrence to Mrs. Wolff which has been preserved, dated 14th October, 1803, is concerned with a point of literary criticism and it is certain that, however tender their friendship may have become, things of the mind took a pre-dominating place in it. James Grieg, the Editor of *The Farington Diary*, in a footnote to an entry in the third volume, rightly observes that Lawrence's friendships with women, including even the wife of the Prince Regent, 'always made gossip active'. He, however, swallowed this gossip without making much attempt to sift or verify it. 'He [Lawrence] was a born philanderer,' Grieg says. 'None of his kidney in fiction surpassed him in callousness. Except, perhaps, in the case of Mrs. Wolff, he was never really in love with any one of the women he deluded, tragically in the case of the Siddons family.' This nonsense is appended to a reference by Farington to a disgraceful libel connecting Lawrence with Mrs. Siddons. On 27th November 1804 a certain Captain Thomas called on Farington and related gossip about 'Mrs. Siddons being gone off with a young man, an artist, who had courted two of Her daughters in succession, both of whom had died, and now had addressed the mother.—I surprised him by strongly reprobat-ing all that related to His going off with Mrs. Siddons, and told him it was a foul calumny'. The rumours were evidently so widely circulated that they got to the ears of Mr. Siddons who was forced to issue a denial of them. On 1st December Farington records that 'In this mornings paper the following advertisement appeared. It proves to what length the reporters of the wicked calumnies against Mrs. Siddons and Lawrence have carried their endeavour to asperse their characters and impute to them their having formed an illicit connexion. The object undoubtedly has been double, viz: to drive Her from the Stage and from Society, —and to injure him in his profession. Mr. Siddons, Her husband, being lately returned from Bath has thus publickly come forward to counteract the infamous attempt.——

'Having been informed on my recent arrival in town, that the most wicked and injurious calumnies have been circulated of late respecting Mrs. Siddons I do hereby offer a Reward of One Thousand Pounds, for the first discovery and conviction of any Person, who had been, or shall be concerned, directly or indirectly in the Circulation thereof.

WM SIDDONS

Upper Terrace. Hampstead.   Nov. 30th, 1804.'

'The calumny,' Farington adds, 'is shocking. Mrs. Siddons has been a long time confined by a sort of rheumatick complaint.'

'Mr. Sid's' drastic action does not seem to have entirely squashed the rumours for in the following August Farington notes that Lawrence is 'uneasy abt reports arising from paragraphs', concerning Mrs. Siddons and himself. Farington gave him the sensible advice to 'disregard them and to *live against* all Calumny so as to disprove it'. The calumny regarding Mrs. Siddons was not the only one which Lawrence had to refute during this period. Farington notes, on 20 September 1804, that he called on Lawrence, with Lysons, and that Lawrence 'read to me a note which He had recd from Mr. Coutts His *Banker* who is His Friend, who states that He had recd. several anonymous letters warning Him against Lawrence, accusing Lawrence *as a Gamester* and the danger of being connected with Him.— Lawrence told me that when young at Bath, He played remarkably well at Billiards, *but never for money*. That, when he came to London, He did sometimes for the first year or two occasionally play at a Billiards room on Exeter Change, but never for money. That he knew only how to play at Whist, and Cassino, and never saw Hazard played in his life, and at no time had ever lost 5 guineas at any game'. Lawrence, on several occasions, expressly denied that his debts were due to any form of loose living, gaming, or personal extravagance of the kind then in vogue, and in the absence of any evidence to the contrary, we have no reason for disbelieving him. Carelessness amounting almost to imbecility in regard to the use of money, can fairly be charged against Lawrence, but the vast sums which many of his contemporaries lavished on expensive mistresses or threw away at Hazard, were in his case devoted, as we shall see later, to his collection of Old

Master drawings which, by the time of his death, was the finest in Europe. To this must be added, his personal generosity to his relations, his friends, needy members of his own profession and indeed anyone who appealed to him for help. In considering Lawrence's affairs we have to remember first that financial recklessness was part of the behaviour-pattern of the age in which he lived. His embarrassments were no greater than those of Sir Walter Scott, Lady Blessington, Sheridan, Brumell, Charles James Fox and a number of other eminent men. Secondly, we must remember that the penalty for failure to meet even comparatively trifling obligations could be, in certain circumstances, imprisonment. As Lawrence had a strong sense of personal dignity, as well as professional pride, fear of arrest over some carelessly overlooked demand was quite enough to account for his recurrent crises and agitations. In the eighteen months subsequent to the panic of December 1825 as many as 101,000 writs for debt were issued in England. In the year ending 5th January 1830 7,114 persons were confined in the various debtors prisons of London alone. A picture familiar to all of what happened in these prisons is given us by Dickens in Little Dorrit. The attention paid by Lawrence's biographers to the supposed 'mystery' of his unending worries seems to be traceable to chance remarks made by the Prince of Wales, Samuel Rogers and others who had on different occasions supplied him with money, but had no intimate knowledge of his always involved affairs. It has been suggested that there was some dark secret in his life, due to homosexual or other unavowable proclivities, which rendered him the victim of blackmail, but no shred of evidence has come to light to support such charges and, if there was any basis for them, it seems incredible that Farington should have had no inkling of it. There is a good deal of truth in the proverb that a man should be judged by his friends and of Lawrence it may be said that those who knew him best were those who valued him most.

In November 1804 Farington mentions that Lawrence was at Lord Abercorn's, at the Priory, Stanmore, 'on Saturday last, till Monday. Mr. Pitt, Lord and Lady Darnley,—Lord and Lady Hawkesbury—Lord and Lady Charlemont, Lord and Lady

Castlereagh,—The Attorney and Solicitor General, were there. —Lawrence noticed how high above the rest Mr. Pitt appeared to be in the consideration of the whole party. It did not prevent social conversation, but all seemed to be impressed with an awe of him. At times it appeared like Boys with their Master. When He spoke it was not extended to much talk, but rather pithy remarks and frequently sarcastic observations.—Lawrence observed that Mr. Pitt was taller than Lord Abercorn, and that he must be six feet high. Mr. Pitt told Lawrence that He wd sit to him for a portrait for Lord Abercorn'. Later in the year Lawrence told Farington that 'Lady Hester Stanhope . . . was at Lord Abercorn's yesterday and told Lawrence that Mr. Pitt had spoken of him very handsomely and would sit to him. She also signified that to enable Him to be better prepared for painting His portrait He should have opportunities of being with him in a domestic capacity.—Lawrence said Lady Hester has the understanding of a man'.

Pitt died in 1806 and Lawrence's portrait of him, exhibited in the Academy of 1808, was not painted from life, but partly from a bust chiselled by Nollekens from a post-mortem cast, and partly from a portrait by Hoppner. The portrait, which was a remarkable *tour de force*, was highly praised by contemporary critics, one of whom wrote that 'it is Mr. Pitt taken in his happiest mood, and represented rather in the dignity of his action, and the elevation of his great mind, than in the faithful portrait of his person. It is a portrait in the epic style of painting, and worthy of going down to posterity'. Lawrence, as a letter to Farington on the subject of the death of Nelson clearly indicates, had a full appreciation of the importance both of the historic events and of the outstanding personalities involved in them, which were raising England to new heights of glory and power. The romantic side of his nature responded to the stimulus of his country's victories on land and sea. If his professional commitments made it impossible for him to achieve, or to attempt to achieve, his lifelong ambition to paint historical subjects in the grand manner, at least he could commemorate the amazing period through which he was living by painting personalities destined to figure largely in England's history, in a manner worthy of them. With the portrait of Pitt, Lawrence, the painter of the Regency, the painter of Kings and Princes, of illustrious warriors and of the beautiful women who graced the Court, began consciously to realise his destiny. If fate had designed him to be a Court painter, he would adorn royal palaces and public buildings, not with lifeless canvases, but with works of art which, if theatrical in conception to modern ideas, were inspired with a 'sense of the present', no doubt, an ambition and to be recognised and applauded by posterity.

Although, as has been noted, it would be impossible for any fair-minded person to call Lawrence a snob, he would have been inhuman had he not been affected by the favour shown him by Royal personages. This perhaps accounts for the indiscretion he displayed in his dealings with the Princess of Wales.

He had seen a good deal of this unfortunate woman when he stayed at Montague House to paint her portrait and that of her daughter, and the friendship, if not intimacy, then formed, was continued in later years. Farington notes, on 10th April 1803, three days before the death of Sally Siddons, that 'Lawrence was to have gone at one o'clock to the Princess of Wales at Montague House, Blackheath, in consequence of the request sent to him by Miss Garth on Saturday, the 2nd inst. by order of the Princess, and a chaise was at the door for that purpose but He had reasons for not going'. Anxiety on Sally's account may well have been the cause of his refusal.

Over a year later, on 17th November 1804, Farington records that 'Lawrence told me that the Princess of Wales was sitting to Him in Greek Street a few days ago, when a letter from the King was brought to Her. After reading it she threw it open upon the table, and indicated to Lawrence that He might read it, which He declined. She sd that in it the King expressed that He knew it wd give her pleasure to be informed of anything that was agreeable to Him and then stated His reconciliation, and interview with the Prince of Wales.—This to us seemed strange, considering the apparently irreconcilable state He [the Prince of Wales] is in towards the Princess, and that He shd have mentioned such a subject had an odd appearance'. The incident at least shows the degree of intimacy which existed between Lawrence and the Princess. Three days later Lawrence called on Farington and told him that he had dined the previous day 'at Blackheath with the Princess of Wales. The dinner was at a quarter past 6, and he remained there till past two o'clock in the morning'.

By this time scandalous rumours were in circulation about the conduct of the Princess of Wales and these later became so serious and so widespread that it was decided to set up a Commission to make what was called a Delicate Investigation into the allegations against her character and morals. The Prince of Wales, to his credit, does not seem to have had any responsibility for this action. Lawrence was one of several men whose names were mentioned in connection with the Princess's alleged unsuitable levity of conduct and he was so much annoyed by it that, on 24th September 1806, he swore an affidavit on the subject, before the magistrate at Hatton Garden, in the following terms:

'I, Thomas Lawrence, swear, that in the year 1801, I did sleep several nights at Montague House, and that, frequently, between the close of the day's sitting and Her Royal Highness dressing for dinner, I was alone with the Princess. That I saw her in the evening, and remained till twelve, one, or two o'clock, but never alone, except in one single instance, and that for a short time, when I remained with Her Royal Highness in the blue room, or drawing-room, as I remember, to answer some questions that had been put to me. I cannot recollect the particulars, and solemnly declare that I have not the least objection for all the world to have heard or seen what took place; that I never was alone with Her Royal Highness in any other place; that I never was with the door locked, bolted or fastened, otherwise than in the common or usual manner, which leaves it in the power of any person on the outside to open it. So help me God.

THOMAS LAWRENCE'.

The Report of the Commission had completely exonerated the Princess of the charges of immorality, although Williams says 'her manners and conduct were impugned as of more levity than was acceptable in the society of this country'. The King wrote to express his full conviction of his daughter-in-law's innocence and ordered her accusers to be indicted for perjury. They were, however, 'screened from the hand of justice'. Lawrence's affidavit was sent to the King together with the statement made by the Princess in her own defence, which contained the following passages referring to her relations with him:

'What I recollect, then, is as follows:—He began a large picture of me and of my daughter, towards the latter end of the year 1800, or the beginning of 1801. Miss Garth and Miss Hayman were in the house with me at the time. The picture was painted at Montague House. Mr. Lawrence mentioned to Miss Hayman his wish to be permitted to remain some few nights in the house, that, by early rising, he might begin painting on the picture, before the Princess Charlotte (who, as her residence was at that time at Shooter's Hill, was enabled to come early) or myself came to sit. It was a similar request to that which had been made by Sir William Beechey, when he painted my picture. And I was sensible of no impropriety when I granted the request to either of them. Mr. Lawrence occupied the same room which had been occupied by Sir William Beechey; it was at the other end of the house from my apartment.

At that time, Mr. Lawrence did not dine with me; his dinner was served in his own room. After dinner, he came down to the room where I and my ladies generally sat in an evening. Sometimes there was music, in which he joined, and sometimes he read poetry. Parts of Shakespeare's plays I particularly remember, from his reading them very well; and sometimes he played chess with me. It frequently may have happened, that it was one or two o'clock before I dismissed Mr. Lawrence and my ladies. They, together with Mr. Lawrence, went out at the same door, up the same staircase, and at the same time. According to my recollection, I should have said, that in no one instance had they left Mr. Lawrence behind them alone with me, but I suppose, it did happen, once, for a short time, since Mr. Lawrence so recollects it, as Your

Majesty will perceive from his deposition, which I annex. He stayed in my house two or three nights together, but how many nights, in the whole, I do not recollect. The picture left my house by April 1801, and Mr. Lawrence never slept at my house afterwards. That picture now belongs to Lady Townshend. He has since completed another picture of me; and, about a year and a half ago he began another, which remains at present unfinished. I believe it is near a twelve-month since I last sat to him.

Mr. Lawrence lives upon a footing of the greatest intimacy with the neighbouring families of Mr. Lock and Mr. Angerstein, and I have asked him sometimes to dine with me to meet them. While I was sitting to him at my own house, I have no doubt I must often have sat to him alone, as the necessity for the precaution of having an attendant, as a witness, to protect my honour from suspicion, certainly never occurred to me. And upon the same principle, I do not doubt that I may have sometimes continued in conversation with him after he had finished painting. But when sitting in his own house, I have always been attended with one of my ladies. And, indeed, nothing in the examination states the contrary. One part of Mrs. Lisle's examination seems as if she had a question put to her, upon the supposition that I had been left alone with Mr. Lawrence at his own house, to which she answers that she indeed had left me there, but that she *thinks* she left Mrs. Fitzgerald with me.'

The Princess's statement, evidently written for her, as she was unable to express herself in grammatical English, has been given here in full because of the interesting light it sheds on the way in which the upper classes normally passed their evenings at the beginning of the nineteenth century, when the standards of English culture and education were at their highest. That a section of society should revolt against the rather insipid form of post-prandial diversion here described was natural enough. The reckless gambling at Clubs like Watier's, the hard drinking and sexual debauchery which figure so largely in Regency memoirs, were a form of compensation for a pattern of behaviour and a high-minded regard for things of the intellect which many found extremely irksome. The age was, indeed, one of extravagant contrasts of vice and virtue, poverty and wealth, learning and licence. It is important to remember that Hannah More and Emma Hamilton were contemporaries, and that Lawrence's 'sympathetic female friends', Miss Croft, Mrs. Wolff and the two Miss Lees, existed in the same period as the vivacious Harriet Wilson. John Cleland's pornographic classic, *Fanny Hill*, appeared in 1750, ten years after John Wesley preached his 'free grace' sermon at Bristol and eleven years before the Countess of Huntingdon established her first regular dissenting chapel at Brighton. The contrasting traditions of full-blooded profligacy and almost over-powering religious 'enthusiasm' flourished side by side during the Regency and were not infrequently found co-existing in the same person. In many gentlemen's libraries a copy of *Fanny Hill* might have been found tucked away behind a row of calf-bound Sermons. In the Princess of Wales, as in her husband and first cousin, Europe's 'First Gentleman', there was an undoubted streak of mania, as well as a conflict of discordant elements in her character and disposition. Thus, although she may sincerely have enjoyed quiet evenings with her ladies, enlivened by Shakespeare readings by her handsome young portrait-painter, there was a strong element of 'levity' in her make-up which, during her travels abroad, seems to have amounted almost to nymphomania. This 'levity' certainly showed itself in her relations with Captain Manby, by whom she had a child which was frequently on view at Montague House, and possibly with Sir Sidney Smith, whose acquaintance Lawrence had made when they were boys together in Bath. Lawrence seems unwisely to have preened himself, in a letter addressed possibly to Miss Hayman, on the fact that the Princess was much more partial to his society than to that of her other visitors, and Williams states that a private letter in his possession, from one of the ladies mentioned by the Princess, alludes, in very affectionate terms, to the great danger that Mr. Lawrence was in 'of losing his head'. The evidence of one of the witnesses examined by Lord Grenville, Thomas Cole, a servant of the Princess, implicated Lawrence on all the facts which he had denied in his affidavit, but Thomas Stikeman, a Page of the

Princess, contradicted Cole on all the points in which Lawrence was concerned. Lawrence's personal servant was also examined, by Lord Eldon. Williams records that shortly after the examination 'Lord Eldon, in conversation with Mr. Lawrence, said to him, "Sir, you are a very fortunate man indeed". "Why so, my Lord?" "Because you have the most faithful, clever and prudent servant, who has served you cunningly at the hour of need."' Contemporary opinion does not appear to have been at all censorious in regard to Lawrence's behaviour with the Princess, and his denial of the charges brought against him was generally accepted. The affair, like Hoppner's charge that the ladies of Lawrence show a gaudy dissoluteness of taste and sometimes trespass on moral as well as professional chastity, certainly did not impede the flow of female sitters to his studio.

There remains the question of why Lawrence took the unusual course of volunteering to make an Affidavit before his conduct had been called in question by the Commissioners. Three possible answers suggest themselves. He may still have been courting Miss Upton at the time and he was certainly becoming more and more intimate with the blameless Miss Croft and with Mrs. Wolff and her sisters. He had recently been calumniated in connection with Mrs. Siddons. He may therefore have felt it incumbent upon him to do something to clear his name and publicly refute the rumours that he was a man of loose morals. Another reason may have been that he had only just realised that the scandal about the Princess was true, that the whole 'Delicate Investigation' was in fact a whitewashing affair, and the 'Report' an elaborate fraud to deceive the public and restore a measure of respectability to the mother of a future Queen. What Lord Glenbervie confided to his journals as 'a secret that must be at least a century old before it ought to be whispered', was probably suspected by everyone in the Princess's circle and must have come to Lawrence's ears. 'During one of those *têtes-à-têtes* lately,' Glenbervie wrote, early in 1807, 'Little Willy, as the Princess calls him, concerning whose parents the enquiry was during the *Delicate Investigation*, was in the room after dinner, as, it seems, is usual on such occasions, and was playing with an orange which Lady Glenbervie [lady-in-waiting to the Princess] had given him, when the Princess, in a sort of reverie, after looking at him steadfastly said, in her imperfect English, "*It is a long time since I brought you to bed, Willy*". The boy not hearing distinctly showed that he did not by some gesture or expression, on which she said again, "*It is a long time now since I brought you to bed*". Still not understanding what was meant he seemed to have thought she said it was a long time since he ought to have gone to bed, for he replied that he would go to bed immediately and went out of the room.'

From what we know of Lawrence's character, particularly his Presbyterian prudishness, it is reasonably certain not only that his conduct with the Princess was as blameless as he claimed it to be but that, notwithstanding his respect for the Royal Family, he was horrified at the idea of having his name associated with the amours of a notoriously licentious woman. If, as alleged, he was foolish enough at one time to preen himself on the special marks of favour shown him by the Princess, he must have regretted it as soon as he realised the danger he was in.

XII

LAWRENCE IN GREEK STREET

SOHO SQUARE and the streets radiating from it had long ceased to be fashionable when the Lawrences first acquired the lease of 57 Greek Street. Carlisle House, where the famous Teresa Cornelys gave masquerades which drew all London, had been pulled down; the Venetian Residency, where Casanova called in 1763, had disappeared; the magnificent mansion built for the Duke of Monmouth, designed by Wren, had fallen into disrepair and been demolished, and the fine house of Alderman Beckford at the east corner of Soho Square and Greek Street was used by the City of London as the headquarters of the Commissioner of Sewers. Soho Square, like Greek Street, had become a business as well as a residential centre. James Newman, the artist's colourman, Dulau's French book-shop, John Trotter's Soho Bazaar and, later, Richard Hetley, the pioneer of the window-glass industry, introduced a note of commerical prosperity to compensate for the square's vanished social glories. In Lawrence's day, however, several distinguished people still lived in the square, among them the hospitable Sir Joseph Banks, President of the Royal Society, and his early friend and patron, Richard Payne Knight. Banks, whose portrait Lawrence painted, lived with his wife and his erudite sister in a beautiful Adam style house, No. 32, the destruction of which in 1937 was rightly described by Mr. John Summerson as a 'national scandal'. In this famous house, where Dr. Johnson had been a welcome and appreciative guest, the unconventional Sir Joseph entertained people of intelligence from all ranks of life, at parties which had become a recognised institution. It can be taken for granted that Lawrence, who was equally independent in his attitude to the fashionable world, occasionally attended them.

220

Richard Payne Knight, a typical eighteenth-century dilettante, ved at 3 Soho Square, next door to Trotter's Bazaar, amid his rge collection of antique bronzes, cameos, intaglios and coins. Ie was immensely erudite, 'an insatiable reader', but, like many ollectors, a better judge of the things in which he specialised than f art in general. His judgments in regard to sculpture and paint-1g, though delivered with assurance, were, unlike Lawrence's, lmost invariably wrong. He was born in 1749, the son of a :hurch of England clergyman, had been educated entirely at ome and, having as a youth inherited a large estate, travelled xtensively in Italy and Sicily with Philipp Hackert, a German ainter admired by Goethe. He went to Italy a second time, 1 1785, to add to his collections, and spent some time at Naples vith his friend Sir William Hamilton. It is possible that he :ayed long enough to make the acquaintance of the fair Emma, vho had become Sir William's mistress and joined him in Naples in 1786. In 1802 she and Nelson stayed with Knight t Downton Castle, his country seat in Herefordshire. A clue o the nature of some of Knight's studies is provided by the itle of his first published book, *An Account of the Remains of he Worship of Priapus lately existing in Isernia, to which is added ' Discourse on the Worship of Priapus and its connexion with he Mystic Theology of the Ancients*, which appeared in 1786. Knight owned several good pictures, including a Rembrandt, nd was a generous though not always discriminate patron >f struggling artists. As we have seen, he befriended Law-ence in his early days, although Lawrence came to distrust his udgment and, like others, does not seem to have admired his :haracter. Knight died in 1824, at the age of seventy-five, and >equeathed his collection to the British Museum. Edward Edwards, in his book *The Founders of the British Museum* (1870), hus sums him up. 'He was one of the many men who, in all >robability, would have attained more distinction had he been ess impetuous and more concentrated in its pursuit. He went in or all the honours. He aimed to be conspicuous, at once, as irchaeologist and philosopher, critic and poet, politician and Jictator-general in matters of art and taste. He was ready to give

judgment at any moment and without appeal, whether the question at issue concerned the decoration of a landscape, the summing-up of the achievement of a Homer or a Phidias, or the system
of the universe.' Charles Kemble came to live at 31 Soho Square
in 1824, but by that time Lawrence had long left Greek Street.

Greek Street, Dean Street, Frith Street, and the other connecting
streets which to-day make up Soho, had been laid out towards the
end of the seventeenth century and, since they were first built
had gradually descended in the social scale. In addition to a large
number of foreign residents, among whom the French pre-
dominated, they were inhabited by actors, journalists, artists no
of the first rank, shopkeepers and professional men. From 179?
until his departure to Russell Square at the beginning of 181.
Lawrence seems to have been the only person of any social importance who lived in Greek Street and his fashionable visitors mus
have thought it odd that he was content to occupy such comparatively humble quarters. It is interesting to recall that a
the time when the Princess of Wales was driving up in her coacl
to No. 57 to sit for her portrait, Thomas de Quincey, then a yout
of seventeen who had run away from his school in Manchester
was taking shelter in No. 58. This house, which was empty o
furniture, belonged to a down-at-heel attorney who called himse
'on most days of the week, by the name of Brunell, but occasionally by the more common name of Brown'. According to de
Quincey it stood at the north-west corner of Greek Street, 'being
the house on that side of the street nearest to Soho Square'
'Towards nightfall,' he writes, 'I went down to Greek Street, an
found, on taking possession of my new quarters, that the house
already contained one single inmate—a poor, friendless child
apparently ten years old; but she seemed hunger bitten . .
The house could hardly be called large—that is, it was not large o
each separate storey; but having four storeys in all, it was large
enough to impress vividly the sense of its echoing loneliness
and from the want of furniture, the noise of the rats made a
prodigious uproar on the staircase and hall.'

Both Lawrence and Farington were on very friendly term
with Lady Thomond, Sir Joshua Reynolds' niece, to whom he lef

the greater part of his property. Lady Thomond seems to have been struck by the unsuitability of the house in Greek Street for a portrait-painter of Lawrence's eminence, and accordingly intimated, through Farington, that she would be prepared to let him Sir Joshua's house in Leicester Square. Lawrence's inability to accept this offer, owing to his mounting load of debt, must have caused him disappointment. In a letter to Farington declining it, dated 17th August 1807, he writes:

'MY DEAR FRIEND,—I beg the kindness of you to express the sense I have of Lady Thomond's goodness in communicating to me through you the terms on which I might have the House in Leicester Square. It is on many accounts so desirable a situation and from its having been the residence of Sir Joshua so interesting to a Painter's mind that nothing but the serious consideration of Expense would make me hesitate to embrace the offer.

That however effectually prevents it and till the lease of my present House is out I have determin'd to remain in it, having expended some money in alterations to make it tolerably convenient to my purpose, tho' as you know it is still inadequate to my wants. I relinquish the Proposal with sincere regret and intreat that you will communicate my answer with my expression of my Respect and Thankfulness for this attention which Lady Thomond and the Marquis have been pleased to shew me. . . .'

It is necessary now to give some more detailed attention to the subject of Lawrence's debts which by 1807 had reached nearly £18,000. Coutts, his bankers, were the principal creditors, but several of his wealthy friends and patrons, including Lock and Angerstein, had advanced him substantial sums. In a letter, dated 19th February 1807, the beneficent Thomas Coutts, who, it is evident, has almost reached the limit of his patience, says: 'I have perused with infinite grief and concern the statement of your affairs.' After pointing out that even if Lawrence kept his personal expenditure down to £850 a year, 'still the sinking Fund would not clear you in less than twenty years and upwards'. He concludes by saying that 'In short, there is no means of extricating you except by a Commission of Bankruptcy. Sorry am I to name it, but you will find, if you can make up your mind to submit to the humiliation for a short period, it will save you an infinity of future mortification, and you may, when it is over, make a great sinking Fund, and do justice to those who are losers by you at the moment, which may clear all in time, and add a lustre to your name and character hereafter that will never be obscured'. Lawrence, on receipt of this, turned as usual to Farington, to whom he undertook to reveal his exact position, and various involved and ambiguous letters are quoted by Layard which, since we have no means of knowing what precisely they mean, need not be reproduced here. There is no ambiguity about a letter to his eldest brother, the Rev. Andrew Lawrence, which it must have grieved him immeasurably to have to write.

Greek St. August 31st 1807.

MY DEAR SIR,—I have received your letter in which you request me to accomodate you with £100 for the purpose of enabling you to enlarge your House, a measure render'd necessary by the increase of your Pupils.

It is very painful to me to inform you that difficulties which have been long accumulating have plac'd me in a situation which no longer allows me to gratify the wishes I have always felt to assist those who have a natural right to my affections.

Many circumstances with which they are unacquainted, the *amount* of my embarrassments with which I myself till lately was unacquainted.

A confidence ill plac'd when difficulties have occur'd and endless imposition on my inexperience in money transactions have together subjected me to a weight of demands upon me which only length of time and very strict economy and constant Industry can enable me to answer.

Thus situated and *pledg'd for the application of all the money I receive to the liquidation of those claims*, you will yourself see that it is out of my power to afford you the assistance you require.

In stating this to you I suffer more than I hope you will do from the disappointment. It is a very bitter and mortifying reflection

THE COUNTESS OF BLESSINGTON

*This much-admired portrait was exhibited at the Royal Academy in 1822. It was
engraved by S. W. Reynolds and by Samuel Cousins R.A. In the Wallace Collection.*

FIELD-MARSHAL PRINCE BLÜCHER

Exhibited at the Royal Academy, 1815. At Windsor Castle and reproduced by gracious permission of His Majesty The King.

to me that I cannot now tender those benefits to my Family which in my earlier Life was my strict endeavour.—I am, my dear Sir, your sincere Friend and Brother.

THOS. LAWRENCE.'

It seems evident from this that Lawrence had hitherto concealed his money troubles from his relatives, otherwise this request could scarcely have been made. That he was imposed upon by tradesmen who took full advantage of his carelessness in regard to personal expenditure can be taken for granted. Farington once noted in his Diary, as proof of 'how wastefully things are conducted' that Lawrence showed him a bill of £14 for turpentine, 'for the sole purpose of cleaning his brushes. He asked me How I managed that matter. I told Him I always cleaned them with *soap* at scarcely any expense'.

Lawrence was now thirty-eight. He had worked tirelessly in his profession, with steadily growing success and increasing public fame. In spite of this, through his generosity, ignorance of the handling of money and, as Layard admits, constitutionally procrastinating nature, he found himself sinking deeper and deeper into debt and facing bankruptcy. His pride and his personal honour prevented him from taking what would have been the sensible, if humiliating, way out of his difficulties, which Coutts had advocated. He could not endure the thought of bankruptcy. He preferred to set to, with redoubled energy, to clear himself by unremitting toil, even though it might require twenty years of labour before at last he found himself free. The documents printed by Layard are enough to prove that no scandalous mystery attached to Lawrence's embarrassments and the fact that at the end of his life his assets were insufficient to cover all his liabilities needs arouse no surprise. The effort he made was heroic and the fact that even his 'pot-boilers' were done with care and skill is proof of his integrity as an artist.

When Coutts reluctantly abandoned the control of his finances, Lawrence turned for help to a new patron, Sir Francis Baring, a merchant prince who was then one of the richest men in England. As usual Farington acted as his adviser and intermediary. Under

Farington's direction he drew up a statement of his affairs which, he says, 'has made my Heart ache, but Sir F. shall know it all That is a point on which I am decided, and would to God that a false shame years ago had not prevented the like confidence towards you'.

Farington, in a letter dated 17th November 1807, computes the total amount of his friend's debts as £20,569, and says: 'It is for you from your recollection to specify as exactly as you may be able to do whatever can be opposed to this amount.' Farington in a note sent to Coutts had calculated Lawrence's annual income as £2,700, but he now says that he is fully convinced that

'if it be calculated at £2,400 it would be as much as you would obtain till you have worked off much of the heavy load of unfinished pictures begun at lower prices than you have at present. . . .

In doing this [viz., explaining his financial troubles to Sir Francis Baring] you will do yourself the justice to represent to him the manner in which you began to incur debts—the family claims you had upon you, your inexperience in everything that related to money concerns, and what heavy expenses the necessity of having recourse to the law has subjected you to.—You can also justly add, that though not in many respects provident, yet that you have never by gaming, or by licentious expenses, brought yrself into difficulties.

My dr friend, very truly yours,

JOS. FARINGTON'.

With this letter we can leave any general discussion of Lawrence's debts, though references to occasional acute financial crises will occur at intervals as the record of his life proceeds. That Coutts remained actively friendly towards Lawrence is shown in a letter he wrote in June 1808 asking him to paint portraits of his three daughters, Lady Burdett, Lady Guilford and Lady Bute. Knowing Lawrence's habit of beginning portraits with energy and leaving them for long periods unfinished, the banker remarks: 'I have desired [Lady Burdett] to sit to you? and if you undertake it I hope you will exert yourself and finish it out of hand and well!'

Lawrence's unceasing toil was accomplished by an effort of will which made him overcome a constitutional weakness which he thus describes to Farington.

'On the third day and while my cough was on, he [the Doctor] gave me *Bark!* which the next day he discovered was wrong and recurr'd to the lowering system.

Now I do know *from internal sensations* that mine is not a case (common as it seems) to be trifled with at this stage. I have no *stamina* of Constitution, to resist Disease as you must have had at my Age. My habitual temperance has kept it from me, but not my strength, for half of my past inertness has been constitutional Languor, I think one of the heaviest visitations that Man can have'.

Lawrence's body-servant Robert, presumably the one who had served him so well at the time of the Delicate Investigation, fell ill shortly after this and Lawrence writes to Farington on 22nd August 1808 to express his anxiety and regret. 'You will be sorry to learn that poor Robert's thoughtlessness will so soon be terminated. I do not think he can survive. He is confin'd to his Bed, and with the very worst symptoms of rapid Decline. I shall miss him more, much more, than abler Servants, for he had a guileless Nature and an affectionate Heart—his Worth his own and his faults his Master's.'

Later he says: 'Robert's is a confirmed consumption. He may, *will* linger, but I fear it is a hopeless case, and all that regard for an honest Nature, and return for zealous tho' imperfect Service can do, is to make peaceful his closing hour, and in this thank Heaven I am greatly assisted.'

Lawrence was invariably kind to servants and Williams records another instance of his ready sympathy. An old woman servant fell into a rapid decline while he was living in Greek Street and he was advised to send her to a hospital. He would not hear of it but had her nursed in the house, attended by his own doctor and for the last three weeks of her life gave up his own bedroom to her, sleeping himself at a neighbouring lodging house. Such incidents as this throw sidelights on Lawrence's character which should cause embarrassment to his calumniators.

Among the events in the art world in the first decade of the nineteenth century were the foundation of the British Institution in 1805, the establishment by the Government of a Committee of Taste, the death of John Opie and Noel Desenfens in 1807, the death of Hoppner in 1810 and the death in the same year of Lawrence's friend and patron, William Lock. The British Institution 'for the encouragement of British artists' held exhibitions of pictures 'by the old masters, deceased British artists and others' in a gallery in Pall Mall which had been erected by Alderman Boydell. It was opened to the public on 18th January 1806 and continued in existence up till 1867. Williams ascribes to Sir John Leicester, afterwards Lord de Tabley, a discriminating patron of the arts whose beautiful wife Lawrence painted, the origin of the British Institution, but its inception is usually attributed to the philanthropist, Sir Thomas Bernard. No doubt several eminent people had a hand in its establishment. George III, with his blundering obtuseness about everything to do with painting, made Lawrence extremely indignant by expressing the opinion that artists 'should not have any concern with the management of the British Institution', an opinion hardly calculated to influence Royal Academicians in its favour. The Committee of Taste which the Government set up in 1807 had among its first tasks the selection of the models for the monuments voted by Parliament to the memory of Pitt, Nelson and Cornwallis. The idea of forming such a Committee had been under discussion for some years and Farington records a meeting at Mr. Angerstein's house, at Blackheath, in August 1805, at which Payne Knight's attitude towards the proposal to consult members of the Royal Academy came in for sharp comment. Various people, including Sir Joseph Banks, expressed their opinion of Knight's taste and 'Lawrence observed to them that Mr. Knight's taste was just that which shd not be adopted. It was founded on sensual feeling.—The simplicity of Raphael, His purity etc. afforded no gratification to Knight.— His pleasure was derived from the luxurious displays of Rubens. Wm Lock sd He had noticed this at the Marquiss of Staffords where Knight was profuse in his admiration of a sensual picture by Rubens but did not notice pictures by Titian to which Rubens would have bowed'. So great, however, was Knight's influence in official quarters that his views seem to have prevailed.

The death of John Opie at the early age of forty-five, which occurred on 9th April 1807, removed a portrait painter who, though never Lawrence's equal in popularity, had qualities which earned him the respect of his contemporaries. He was a Cornishman by origin and the best of his portraits were those of country characters. Lawrence does not appear to have known him well and was not among the brother Academicians who attended his funeral, although he was not the kind of man to be deterred from doing so by Opie's spiteful remark that 'Lawrence makes coxcombs of his sitters and his sitters make a coxcomb of Lawrence.'

Noel Desenfans earned for himself a distinguished position in the history of British art through his unsuccessful efforts to form a National Gallery and his generous bequest which led to the foundation of the Gallery at Dulwich. The Dulwich Gallery, opened in 1814, was the first free collection of pictures in England and preceded the National Gallery in Trafalgar Square by twenty-four years.

Desenfans was born at Douai, educated there and at the University of Paris and, driven by poverty, came to London as a teacher of languages. One of his pupils, Margaret Morris, fell in love with him and on their marriage brought him a dowry of £5,000. On his wedding tour he bought a picture by Claude Lorraine and this initial purchase started him on his successful career as a dealer in works of art. He was also a writer of some distinction and the author of a treatise defending Fénelon against an attack by Lord Chesterfield, for which he received a letter of thanks from the Paris Académie des Belles Lettres.

In 1799, having on his hands an important collection of pictures intended for the King of Poland, he proposed to the British Government the foundation of a National Gallery, offering to endow it both with pictures and money. The offer was refused. Shortly afterwards he and his wife shared a house with their friend Sir Peter Francis Bourgeois, R.A. Desenfans made a will in which he expressed his wish that Bourgeois and his widow should continue to reside together and that his collection of pictures should be retained by them and not dispersed. Bourgeois died in 1811 and bequeathed the pictures to Dulwich College, after the death of Mrs. Desenfans. A new gallery had to be built to receive them, at a cost of £14,222, of which sum two-thirds was contributed by the Bourgeois estate and by Mrs. Desenfans. The architect was Sir John Soane. Mrs. Desenfans died in 1814, and a year later the three founders of the Gallery were buried in sarcophagi in the mausoleum which formed part of the building.

The death of William Lock was a cause of great grief to Lawrence, which he expressed in letters to Miss Croft. 'I shall tomorrow,' he writes in one of them, 'attend the funeral, and then seek my usual occupations. I am not afraid of forgetting this dear man; and know that I am the better for his life, and for his death. It is thus a blessing, as well as a distinction, to have known him. . . . Mr. Lock is to be buried, by his own accurate directions, in the simplest manner, and exactly as his mother was—a walking funeral, and the coffin borne by his labourers.' William Lock was seventy-eight at the time of his death, which occurred shortly after that of Sir Francis Baring, for whom Lawrence had also a high regard. An obituary of the former, which appeared in the press, is generally attributed to Lawrence, owing to the fact that his name is not mentioned in it. 'In addition to the loss of Sir T. [F.] Baring', it runs, 'we have now to communicate, with deep regret, the death of W. Lock, Esqre, of Norbury Park, Surrey, the most zealous protector of the arts, and (out of the profession) perhaps the most enlightened and perfect judge. Mr. Lock distinguished himself, in early life, by his choice collection of pictures, models and fine works in sculpture, and still more by his liberality and taste. He, of all the lovers of the arts, was considered by its professors as their arbiter, their advocate, and common friend—the compassionate benefactor of the humblest, the revered associate or patron of the most celebrated artists of his time—of Sir Joshua Reynolds, Mr. Barry, Mr. Hoppner, and Cipriani; of Wilson, Barrett and Sandby; of many now living; Mr. West, the President of the Academy, Mr. Fuseli, who benefits it by the instruction of its youth, and other of its members, who will hear of Mr. Lock's death with unfeigned sorrow, and an admiration inseparably connected with his remembrance,—for so much acuteness and sensibility—such various knowledge—such solid yet unpresuming judgment, with taste so pure, elevated and enlarged—a man, in short, so gifted and accomplished, so just and admirably good— they can seldom hope to know. He will be more generally regretted by the highest circles in society, for that extensive information, and those simple manners, which made him so fine an example of an English gentleman; and for attainments of the scholar which procured him, in earlier life, a public testimony from Johnson; but especially, and most deeply will he be lamented for those many charities and virtues that have given to Norbury, the spot where he resided, a sacredness, a peculiar sentiment of blessing and respect. He died 5th October 1810, at the age of seventy-eight, and is survived by Mrs. Lock, and a family whom he lived to see in that happiness and respectability of connexion, which their characters and stations claimed. His son, Mr. W. Lock, succeeds him in his estate, the known inheritor of his work, and himself of distinguished powers.' This tribute is characteristic of Lawrence both in the warmth, generosity and 'loftiness' of its sentiments and the touch of pomposity in its style. Many have accused Lawrence of shallowness, of insincerity, of always acting a part, of being by nature a flatterer and a courtier. Much of this may have been true as regards his 'public' life and his manners in what he describes as 'the highest circles of society'. It is unquestionably untrue of his behaviour towards his intimate friends, with whom he was always unaffectedly sincere, kindhearted, affectionate and generous. His fondness and respect for the great abstractions—Angelic Purity, Steadiness of Principle, Honour, Integrity and so forth—which might have aroused ridicule in cynical aristocrats like Lord Glenbervie or Charles Greville, were equally genuine and derived from the traditions which he had inherited. He was, we must remember, the grandson on his father's side of a dissenting minister and, on his mother's side, of a country parson. Layard quotes a letter from Lawrence to

Farington on the election of his friend Robert Smirke, the architect, to the Academy, which reveals this aspect of his character. 'The more I see of Robert Smirke,' he writes, 'the more I am certain that no Election for many years will have prov'd so creditable to the Academy. He seems to have fix'd Integrity of Character, with great simplicity, and (what belongs to the Tone of his Understanding) an even Steadiness of Principle, that will never lead him to prefer the Expedient to the Right, or at least as seldom as can be expected from our imperfect Natures. As he gets on, I think he may have Pride, and Ambition belongs to his Talents; but they will both be regulated by Honor. This is a true impression on my Mind, and not an idle flourish of the Pen.'

John Hoppner, Lawrence's most formidable rival and his, at times, embittered critic, died in January 1810. Williams has a note saying that Lawrence 'called several times upon Mr. Hoppner during his illness, in the spirit of kindness and friendship, but the latter always denounced the visits as merely the gratification of a rival's joy at his approaching dissolution. Assuredly no such feeling ever actuated Lawrence, whose kindness to Mr. Owen, and to all his friends in sickness, was excessive'. It seems more probable, from a letter to Farington which Layard prints, that he would have liked to have paid such visits but was afraid they might be misconstrued. 'I could say a great deal on this subject,' he writes, 'that wretched Northcote would pronounce to be insincere; amongst other things, that it is a pain to me, *when in my Bed*, not to have call'd on him, and ended our long competition in peace—but to the last, I found that his soreness to me, and his amiable Friends, would have prevented the good I wish'd, and turn'd it on me as Evil.'

In the year before his death Hoppner contributed nine pictures of the Academy exhibition and Lawrence none at all. He was probably engaged, with Farington's encouragement, in finishing off a large number of pot-boiling portraits which he had begun before raising his prices. Up till his death the Prince of Wales and his circle continued their patronage of Hoppner. His departure from the scene enabled Lawrence to step into his shoes as the Prince's most favoured portrait painter.

In reporting his illness to Miss Lee Lawrence said that Hoppner 'has always been afflicted with bilious and liver complaints (and to these must be greatly attributed the irritation of his mind) and now they have ended in a confirmed dropsy. . . . You will believe that I can sincerely feel the loss of a brother artist, from whose works I have often gained instruction, and who has gone by my side in the race these eighteen years'.

In a later letter to Miss Lee he wrote that 'the death of Hoppner leaves me, it is true, without a rival, and this has been acknowledged to me by the ablest of my present competitors; but I already find one small misfortune attending it, viz. that I have no sharer in the watchful jealousy, I will not say, hatred, that follows the situation. At this (in all but historical painting) advanced period of the arts, it is quite impossible—it would have been to Sir Joshua—to get so far beyond rivalry as to leave it hopeless. There are too many ingenious men, if not men of genius, to make this attainable; and that defect of understanding that I have shewn in the necessary and just conduct of Life, has deprived me of that great advantage—independence, which gives such full security to professional station. This in some measure stimulates my exertions and gives my competitors hope that it may do so; but still, as I find my health better than I ever had it, my faculties not decaying, and I hope, and indeed know, my knowledge in my art increasing, as I think I have more of what gives elevation to it, than they at present possess, I shall go forwards as resolutely as I can, and as long as I can, trusting with patient confidence to the result'.

Hoppner's work is so poor in drawing and in composition, he was such a weak imitator of Reynolds, Gainsborough and, at times, of Lawrence himself, that in spite of his gift for prettiness and his occasionally pleasing colour, it is difficult to see why he achieved so much fame in his lifetime and gained the admiration of so discerning a judge as the Prince of Wales.

Although Lawrence worked regularly in his studio, from 'sunrise to sunset', as Miss Croft says, and only occasionally took a few days off to visit friends in the country, he continued to be an ardent theatregoer and rarely missed a play in which any of the Kembles were performing. The sensation of the theatrical world at this time was the sudden rise to fame of the actor Betty, called 'the young Roscius', who had first appeared in London at Covent Garden on 1st December 1804, when he was thirteen. Farington reports Lawrence as saying that 'it was astonishing to what an extravagant pitch the admiration of him [the young Roscius] had arisen and that among those who have been esteemed good judges of theatrical merit'. On the following day the two friends went to see Betty perform the part of Glenalvon in John Home's play *Douglas*. Farington thought him 'superior to any actor of the present day' and told Lawrence that his acting 'much exceeded, in my opinion, His performance on Saturday last; to which He replied, 'that He had never before seen him play so well, and that He was now decided as to His superiority over all except Mrs. Siddons'. Betty's success, as was to have been expected, had a disturbing effect on J. P. Kemble, who, in the following February, Lawrence reported as being very thin, suffering from a bad cough and looking extremely ill.

Covent Garden Theatre had been burnt down in 1808, when Handel's organ and MSS. were destroyed. It was rebuilt after the designs of Robert Smirke and reopened in September of the following year. Lawrence, who had secured a box, invited Mr. and Mrs. Wolff to dine with him and attend the opening performance. In three long letters to Farington he gives a vivid and detailed account of the famous O. P. (old prices) riots which continued for a fortnight until the proprietors at last submitted to the public demands. The riots took place because Kemble tried to put up the prices in the new theatre. As this belongs to theatrical history, the letters are not quoted here. Two years later, on 20th December 1811, we find Lawrence inviting Farington to go with him to see *Coriolanus*. 'The Town is fashionably and I had almost said rationally mad after it,' he writes. 'I have seen it but once. It will give you the best specimen of Kemble, and a fine one of Mrs. Siddons. It is a long time since I saw you, but my fair and true excuse is occupation; in the Days and the Evenings. An invitation from whatever quarter has with me three chances for refusal to one for acceptance, and this to excess is wrong, I know; but there is no enjoyment like that held out to us by our Art however we pursue it.'

Three days later, on the night of the performance, he wrote to invite himself to dine with Farington instead, and makes the revealing observation: 'I need not tell you that anything you like is best food for me. For the love of simple living I can match myself even with the simplest.'

Apart from theatre-going, necessary appearances at the houses of the great, quiet evenings with Miss Croft, and occasional dinners with the Wolffs at Sherwood Lodge, Lawrence's time and energy were almost entirely absorbed by the harassing task of making enough money, by continuous work, to keep his creditors at bay. Miss Croft says that 'from the year 1810 to 1821, Sir Thomas was in habits of the most constant and intimate intercourse with me and my friends at Hart Street, dropping in at all hours and especially of an evening, when too tired with the labours of the day to accept the invitations of gayer and more exalted friends. He used to express the comfort of coming, where he could without offence sit silent till he felt sufficiently rested to join in conversation. Frequently he would bring with him the novel or periodical of the day, and enliven our work-table by reading it aloud—and who ever read like him!' No one was in a better position than Miss Croft to deny the ill-founded rumours that Lawrence's inability to finish his portraits promptly was due to laziness or pleasure-seeking. 'During all this period', she writes, 'I can with truth report that he painted from sunrise to sunset, except in the hours he devoted to the correction of engravings and those of his hurried meals—and at this time I used to hear him accused of indolence and dissipation as the causes of his pictures being so long in hand; but he could only paint all day long, and he equally seemed to neglect his friends and strangers, for Mrs. Wolff's portrait was not gone on with for twelve years. I have known him admit four sitters for two hours each in bright summer days; and in the early part of his career he used to paint by lamplight. When he was without sitters, and finishing his pictures, he used to send for me very frequently to read to him.'

In view of his devotion to Mrs. Wolff, his failure to complete her portrait in reasonable time seems extraordinary. By 1814 Mrs. Hill, Mrs. Wolff's sister, had become so hurt and offended at the long delay that Miss Croft felt it necessary to intervene. Lawrence, she says, 'was quite distressed at my report, and promised the very next time Mrs. Wolff came to town he would certainly complete it. She sat only five or six times for the portrait in white satin, and it was finished after she left town, myself and my cousin sitting for the drapery. It was exhibited in 1815 with the portraits of Blucher, Platoff, and the Duke of Wellington, and the papers said of it that "the lady reading by lamplight was indeed a miraculous picture" '. This portrait, which was engraved by Cousins, is now in the Art Institute, Chicago. It is entirely free from Lawrence's besetting fault of pose and artificiality, and the look of tenderness in the lady's eyes as she bends over a book of engravings after Michelangelo, is rendered with masterly skill.

When Lawrence was able to escape from London he usually visited the Locks at Norbury or the Angersteins, but he also went several times with Farington to stay with Lord and Lady Thomond at Taplow and occasionally made more extended visits to his friends, the Boucherettes, at Willingham, in Lincolnshire. From the latter house he wrote a letter to Miss Croft, on 3rd. November 1810, shortly after Mr. Lock's death, in which he showed how greatly he valued her friendship. 'I must', he says, 'have appeared most blameably negligent, my dear Miss Croft, kind, dear friend, in not acknowledging your recent care of me, and very gratifying letter; but my time is so occupied here, with riding, and walking and eating, and all the genera of idleness and good living, that I have fewer moments to myself, than when up to my ears in business, in that Greek Street which you were so anxious for me to quit. You wished me to have air and exercise; the former has given me as good, coarse, tight and distended a skin as a man ought to have, and if to have all my bones aching with the latter be any satisfaction to you, you may securely enjoy the comfort. I am at home in all country exercises, coursing, shooting etc. and have so thorough a knowledge of an estate, that all I have now to do is to get one; for as to managing it, I flatter myself I can do that as well as the dear widow Blackacre, or farmer Smith himself. I feel, however with all of comfort, hospitality and friendship around me,—I feel the want of those friends sharing them with me, who are now the great essentials of the happiness of all of Life that is to be given me—you would both of you like to share them, as would both be respected and loved by all who are now here. Our party is composed of Mr. and Mrs. Boucherette, and three daughters; Mrs. and Miss Lock; Mr. and Mrs. J. Angerstein and family; Mr. Angerstein and your obliged friend. I cannot conceive beings who would be more in unison with all your feelings, than this circle, and it is quite ungrateful in me to find it incomplete: but I will own to you that I pine to be nearer that spot which I have left, and those good and inestimable partners that endear it to me.'

On his return to London Lawrence received a letter from Warren Hastings, then nearly eighty years of age, whose portrait he had begun to paint. 'The length of time that has passed since I first sat to you for my portrait,' says the courteous old man, 'begins to press upon my mind with the consciousness of something like a culpable neglect, to you for the trouble which I have ineffectually given you, and to another for a promise unperformed.' Further sittings were arranged to suit the painter's convenience and the picture must have been completed with unusual celerity, for it was exhibited in the following year. It is now generally regarded as one of Lawrence's finest male portraits.

The eight volumes of Farington's diaries, which cover a period of twenty-five years and were continued without cessation until his death in 1821, contain constant references to Lawrence's social activities, financial troubles, table talk, opinions on men and things, manner of painting, prices, pupils and minor details of his daily life. Farington's friendship for Lawrence also causes him to note down the views regarding his work of his professional rivals, the jealousy of Hoppner, the dislike expressed by such men as Thomson, a forgotten R.A. whom Lawrence cordially detested for his 'cold, distant, reserved manner,' and Constable's remark that 'Lawrence stood unrivalled in the opinion of all'. Reading over the innumerable entries in which Lawrence figures, we note that in October 1806 he went with Mr. Angerstein to stay at Sir Francis Baring's house in Hampshire, Stratton Park, to paint portraits of Sir Francis, his brother and his son-in-law and partner (Mr. Wall) in one picture. He asked only 260 guineas for this conversation piece, but was paid £300, which Farington thinks was only a moderate recompense for his 'loss of time and inconvenience'. We find Lawrence admiring Rembrandt's 'Woman Taken in Adultery' at Christie's and driving off at once in a chaise to Mr. Angerstein at Woodlands to induce him to bid largely for it. The diarist quotes a remark of Payne Knight's about Richard Wilson's pictures, then fetching high prices, 'though we had *better painters now living, Turner and the younger Barker of Bath*'. Lawrence felt the injustice of this reflection on Wilson, and said: 'Oh! no, not Barker surely.' Rogers, we hear, remarked that Knight 'is of a very obstinate disposition', but Lawrence qualified this by saying that he was 'very different in private and when with only one person could be worked upon successfully'. There is a brief reference, in 1808, to a visit by Farington, Lawrence and the Smirkes to the Elgin marbles, in the subsequent acquisition of which Lawrence played an important part, much talk of Lawrence's professional application—he once worked on his pictures ten hours a day for three days—and a note that Lawrence had bought from Boydell, 'as a guide', Sir Joshua Reynolds' portrait of Lord Heathfield, for £300, and thought it the best of Sir Joshua's portraits of men. In the summer of 1808 Lawrence and Lysons attended a dinner party and rout at Mr. Angerstein's at which the Princess of Wales was present. She stayed until half-past three and Lysons remarked that she had 'grown very coarse and that she dressed very ill, shewing too much of Her naked person'.

Canning sat to Lawrence in July 1808 and Lawrence reports him as saying that he thought Mr. Windham 'the best bred man in England'; and 'do you not think he knows it,' Lawrence retorted. Canning had a remarkable physical resemblance to Lawrence. The painter thought him modest because he blushed when looked at intently. They talked about Kemble, who, like Sheridan, the first pint of wine makes drunk, 'but Hew ill afterwards go on' and is, not surprisingly, thought to be gouty. In September of this year Lord Castlereagh sat to Lawrence, soon after having received 'the dispatches from Sir A. Wellesley, informing him of his retreat from Truxillo', and Lawrence observes that he never saw any man who appeared to be so sunk in his spirits, he seemed to be 'a figure of woe' and Lawrence observed him more than once to wipe his eyes.

A brief entry mentions the fact that Sir John Moore was killed at Corunna and that his brother Charles, one of those 'two Charles's whose constant laughter cheered the Siddons girls, is insane. In the following year, after references to the death of Hoppner, there is a note about Lawrence's mortification 'at the manner in which Payne Knight has written of the collection of Antiques brought over by Lord Elgin', and a good deal about the Academy squabbles, in which Farington and Lawrence could not escape being involved. Towards the end of the year 1810 we hear of Robert Smirke and Lawrence going to East Grinstead to see 'the pugilistic contest between Cribb the Champion of England in Boxing, and a Blackman. The former after a contest of 55 minutes proved the Conqueror, but both were dreadfully beaten'. An entry in January 1811 gives the surprising information that Lawrence says that the Prince of Wales is 'supposed to be affected by Methodistical notions and that Rowland Hill, the Methodist preacher, has been with him a second time'. Later Farington records that, in the course of one of his many candid talks to his friend, he told Lawrence that the characteristic feeling of his mind is a 'love of point'. He thought this was shown in his taste in conversation, in his art and in his reading and that it was 'so prevalent as to have caused Him till He studied His art more deeply, to give in to that metally, glittering, vicious practice which had been so much objected to. He allowed it, but reminded me how much he had for many years past strove and studied to get the better of this peculiarity, which I fully acknowledged, and that the great success of his endeavours had been manifested in his better works'.

At the Varnishing Day, on 25th April 1811, after Lawrence had completed his pictures, Farington says that 'His superiority appeared to me so manifest, and I found such a sense of His power in the art prevailing in the minds of the members . . . that I told Him this was the time for Him to have 300 guineas for a whole length and the smaller size in proportion'.

At the Royal Academy dinner, on 27th April, the Prince of Wales delivered a speech 'in a manly and graceful manner and it made,' says Farington, 'a very strong impression'. In the course of it the Prince said that 'others might be more able to judge of the excellence of works of art, but could not exceed him in his love of the arts or in wishes for their prosperity'. The proceedings seem to have been unusually successful, the Prince was in good spirits and 'conversed with those within His view with great freedom and cheerfulness, and left a very agreeable impression on the minds of the whole company, as was visible and expressed by many'. In this year the Prince of Wales was formally appointed Prince Regent and (after signing his name 14,000 times) remarked to Lord Dundas that 'playing at King is no sinecure'. His father, though better in bodily health, had become hopelessly crazy, sometimes imagining himself to be talking to the Earl of Bute and Lord Chatham, on other occasions carrying on conversations with Henry VIII and Cardinal Wolsey.

In September 1811, after seeing Mrs. Siddons in the part of Lady Constantine in King John, Lawrence told Farington that he thought it was time for her to retire from the stage. Apparently she thought the same, for she gave her farewell performance, as Lady Macbeth, on 29th June in the following year. Her brothers, J. P. Kemble and Charles Kemble, supported her, Covent Garden Theatre was 'crowded in an extraordinary manner in every part' and the heat was very great, but the performance was 'most excellent'. Mrs. Siddons, dressed in white satin and wearing a long veil, made her farewell address at ten o'clock precisely. The party in Farington's box included Lysons, Lawrence, Mrs. Wolff —but not Mr. Wolff, from whom she was by now separated— and 'several other Ladies and Gentlemen'.

Lawrence's interest in criminology and what Miss Croft calls his 'insatiable curiosity as to the countenances of murderers and persons capable of great crimes,' is shown by the fact that he got

HENRY FUSELI, R.A. 1741–1825
In the Musée Bonnat, Bayonne.

CARDINAL GONSALVI

Painted in Rome in 1818. *At Windsor Castle and reproduced by gracious permission of His Majesty The King.*

Farington's brother to help him procure an order of admittance to the prison at Cold Bath Fields, 'where he saw the dead body of Williams, the murderer of Mr. and Mrs. Marr etc., who, that morning, had hung himself in his cell.—On his return Home He made a drawing of Williams, which He assur'd me was a very strong likeness of Him. This drawing', Farington adds, 'He sent to me last night and I was much struck with it as having every appearance of being a faithful likeness—. We talked of a print being made from it, and He sd that He wd tomorrow morning apply to Condé, the Engraver for the purpose.—In what manner to publish it was deferred for further consideration.' The drawing was never engraved and was sold after Lawrence's death for £5 10s.

Miss Croft, to whom Lawrence also showed the drawing, says that 'I never saw a more beautiful head. The forehead the finest one could see, hair light and curling, the eyes blue and only half closed; the mouth singularly handsome, tho' somewhat distorted, and the nose perfect. I ask'd what became of the science of physiognomy, when such features could belong to such a monster; for he destroyed not only the father and mother, and I think a maidservant, but an infant a few weeks old in its cradle—and all this for the purpose of rifling the till in a little haberdasher's shop! Sir Thomas admitted the perfect beauty of the head; but said it was very singular that in all the three heads of murderers that he had seen and drawn, the formation of the lower jaw was precisely the same—very square, with a peculiar shortness of chin, and partaking more of the tiger than the human jaw. He instanced Governor Wall, who was executed for flogging a negro girl to death, and a Mr. Fillipo, who was tried and acquitted for one murder and afterwards hung for another. Phrenology was not known at this period, at least not very generally, but Sir Thos. became reluctantly but progressively a convert to it in his latter days. He said to me of a servant he dismiss'd, "Poor fellow I believe I must take him again, for he has the organ of destructiveness so strongly defined that I fear he will never get another place." '

In connection with Lawrence's interest in crime and criminals, Miss Croft relates one of the very numerous instances of his benevolence which may be quoted as a characteristic example of the generosity which added so greatly to his financial difficulties. 'A poor young man at Stratford was taken up and tried for coining, into which he was led by some well-known coiners in consequence of being a coach-harness-plater, which made him useful in their practises. It was proved that he had never seen the men till about half-an-hour before he was taken up, but this did not prevent his being condemn'd to death! We were all deeply interested about it, but could have done nothing without Sir Thomas's aid. After much trouble and labour he did succeed by the aid of Lord Sidmouth in getting the sentence commuted for transportation for life. He not only supplied this poor fellow with the means of comfort on his voyage, but paid the passage of his wife to follow him, and even made a slight drawing of him (now in Mr. Keightley's possession) for the consolation of the family. By obtaining letters to the Governor of Botany Bay, and by his excellent conduct, this same James Wright rose to situations of trust and confidence and continued to write the most grateful and satisfactory letters to Sir Thomas, till he was deprived of his generous and indefatigable patron in January 1830.'

The great events of the Napoleonic war were a frequent subject of conversation between Lawrence and Farington, the former, through his contacts with eminent persons, being exceptionally well-informed and often having the latest news before it was printed. It is pleasant, in this year, to find Sir George Beaumont, whose comments on Lawrence both as a man and as a painter had in the past been somewhat hostile in tone, now changing his opinion. He told Farington that Lawrence's painting had 'greatly improved in the last three years and that his portrait of Major-General [Lord] Stewart was a very complete and fine picture and that He had got the better of much of that metallic appearance which formerly prevailed in his pictures, which seemed to be owing to His admitting too many lights into His faces . . . Sir George sd He should like to know more of Lawrence: that He was a very gentlemanlike and a very clever man'.

In July 1813 Lawrence gave a dinner to some of his men friends, including Robert Smirke and Farington, and the conversation turned first on the relations between Lady Caroline Lamb and Byron, a perennial subject of gossip at this time, and later on Wellington, about whose mannerisms he gave some interesting particulars from first-hand observation. 'It has been observed', said he, 'that when thoughts of military movements rise in His mind while He is in society He has a habit of taking His left elbow into His right hand and sitting in that posture;—and that when He is dissatisfied with the management of the Commissariat or other concerns He covers His nose with His hand and on seeing this token of His disapprobation those officers who are concerned get out of His way as much as they can.'

About a month after this West and Lawrence were overturned in a chaise on Blackheath when returning at nearly midnight from a dinner at Mr. Angerstein's. 'Lawrence said it was remarkable to see the tranquillity of Mr. West on that occasion. He did not appear to be at all agitated.'

Neither of them could have been much hurt, for a few days later they set off in a coach and four, with Raphael West, Smirke and Farington, and proceeded to Greenwich, where they stopped some hours. 'We first looked at the Basso Relievo executed at Coade's manufactory from a design by Mr. West in Honour of Lord Nelson in the pediment of a Portico', Farington records. Afterwards they went to the Painted Hall in Greenwich Hospital to see the ceiling 'of which Sir James Thornhill has the credit, but it was executed by a foreigner of the name of Andrea, employed by Thornhill. It was much admired by all present.' They then went into the chapel and looked at West's large picture over the altar, and were joined by the two portrait painters, Thomson and Owen, and by the younger Robert Smirke. The party being now complete, they went on to the inn at Shooter's Hill, where they had arranged to have dinner to commemorate West's first dinner in England fifty years before. The President discoursed on the state of artists in this country, compared with what it was when he arrived in England, 'in respect of their personal manners and the degree of estimation in which they were and are held. Mr. West said that in 50 years they had become a different description of men, so much more decorous in their deportment and in their reception in Society'. There was a good deal of criticism of Northcote's *Life of Sir Joshua Reynolds* which had recently appeared. (In a later conversation Lawrence said that Northcote had made Garrick a blackguard. 'He had expected more from Northcote—He had felt very much disgusted while reading the book.') The party stayed at Shooter's Hill drinking coffee and tea till nearly eleven o'clock when they returned together to London in their coach and four. The bill at the Inn amounted to six pounds eighteen shillings and the waiters received five shillings. West, 'who desired it might be considered *His dinner*', paid it.

A family bereavement which must have caused Lawrence great distress occurred in 1813, the death from consumption of his elder sister, Lucy, who Miss Croft says was his favourite sister. She had married John Meredith, a Birmingham solicitor, and left a daughter, Lucy Louisa Anne, who married John Aston of Birmingham.

Early in the following year, Lawrence left his house in Greek Street and installed himself in 65 Russell Square.

XIII

65 *RUSSELL SQUARE*

LAWRENCE, though attached to his old home in Greek Street for sentimental reasons, had for some years found the accommodation it provided too restricted for his requirements. In October 1811 he wrote to Farington about his need for a large room in which he could show his pictures, and as the letter contains a revealing passage about the largest of them, his 'Satan', it deserves quotation. Fuseli once said of this picture that it was certainly 'a damned thing, but not the Devil', but until the end of his life nothing would convince Lawrence that it was not a work of genius and his supreme masterpiece. He wrote:

'I have miss'd a good opportunity of getting a large Room near me in Dean Street, which might have made my present residence very comfortable—the Auction Room opposite Mr. Lane's. One good Room in which I could well show my Pictures and finish them would make me contented with this House, for its comparative retiredness is both pleasant and advantageous. The free communication of one's thoughts and feelings is one of the greatest blessings of Friendship, and as I am now one and forty, I shall neither speak nor write with the deference of Youth, but only with that sincere regard and respect which your confidence in and kindness to me and your Character demand.

Since I wrote the first part of this Letter I have been out with Lord Mountjoy (sitting to me this morning) to shew him my Picture of Satan and to see Cosway's drawings etc., and I am return'd most heavily Depress'd in Spirit from the strong impression of the past dreadful waste of time and improvidence of my Life and Talent.

I have seen my own Picture with the Eye of a Spectator—of a Stranger—and I do know that it is such as neither Mr. West, nor Sir Joshua, nor Fuseli could have painted. I will request *you* to go with me and confirm this judgment.'

He goes on to accord high praise to Cosway's work, a 'little Being', of whom he admits, 'we have been accustom'd never to think or speak but with contempt'.

By December 1813 the business of preparing the house in Russell Square for his reception was well in hand, and he writes to tell Farington that his house

'goes on admirably, with great zeal and kind attention from our Vitruvius, and as much Economy as is consistent with usefulness and just Taste; by which I mean that which is at once suited to my Circumstance and necessary appearance. I look for our first Dinner in it with the GREATEST pleasure; and as the tendency of my Nature and Habits is rather to limit (perhaps too much) the circle of my Friends, it is a most solid Comfort and Delight to me to have them of such Character and Principle, for if I go even to that class of [word missing] that belongs more to the Patron and Acquaintance, such as Lord Abercorne and Mountjoy, there are in them, with all their alloy, such essential qualities as must be valued by every honorable and worthy Mind.

The feeling in which I write this is of one species of Egotism, I confess; but at least it is one of the most pardonable and that which leads to the best result'.

The 'Vitruvius' referred to is assumed to be Robert Smirke. Russell Square was laid out by James Burton for the Duke of Bedford, and as it was not completed until 1814 it is possible that Lawrence may have been the first occupant of his spacious new premises. The Square never seems to have been fashionable, but was inhabited by persons of wealth and importance, including several eminent lawyers. Sir Samuel Romilly, who committed suicide in 1818 after his wife's death, lived at No. 21. Lawrence's house was pulled down in 1910 to make way for the Imperial Hotel.

One of the first letters written by Lawrence from his new address was to his brother William, then with his regiment at the Cape of Good Hope, congratulating him on his promotion, which he had secured through the good offices of the Prince Regent's Irish protégé, Colonel McMahon. The casual methods by which such affairs were conducted at this period is amusingly revealed in the letter to Lawrence from the Colonel, which Layard quotes.

'My Dear Friend,—If the circumstances are such as Mrs. Stuart has stated to you, and the Vacancy of a full pay Majority in the 72nd made in Consequence, the Duke of York has just made a Knot in his Handkerchief, and promised me that your Brother shall *positively have it*. Ever sincly yours J. McMahon.

PS. The P.R. don't leave Town till Thursday next.'

To Farington Lawrence wrote a detailed account of the arrangement of his principal rooms and the placing of his collection of casts from antique statuary.

'Group of Laocoon—beyond it the Bacchus Torso, and lastly next the Door the Venus de Medici. I have Floor Cloth round the Room and in the Centre a Turkey Carpet, on which my circular Dinner Table will be always plac'd—there will be perhaps half a dozen Chairs in the Room.

My back parlour will be a common Living Room very neatly furnish'd and strictly in that Character. The small Room to the right of it is for Edward, and all his luxury of Oils, Varnishes, Colors etc. etc.

There is beyond it a still smaller Apartment—a mere temporary sitting-Room appropriated exclusively to no one.

My Front Room is my Show-Room, over the Chimney of which is already plac'd my Cato. [A portrait of Kemble "In the character of Mr. Addison's Cato", exhibited at the Academy in 1812.] This is the only part of my House about which I feel disquiet, for I do not like to appear unreasonably fastidious to Robert Smirke and Farington, and thus I suffer a Yellow Paper to remain that I know is hurtful to my Pictures. I should have suffered it in my Painting Room but for looking at a man's Countenance, when by closing my Window-Shutters I had made it a Study, and that determin'd me to have it chang'd. It is now a rich crimson Paper with a Border, one gold Moulding of this size [here is a small drawing] fix'd to an Inch Flat of Black.

My little Room beyond it is fitted in the same way, and is a sweet, precious Room, or would be, if the lonely was not its Inhabitant. But enough for the present of my House. It will never be completely mine till you have enter'd it.'

The next letter to Farington, dated 11th January, is remarkable for the changed attitude it shows toward Napoleon, '*The Tiger*', whom Lawrence had previously denounced in very emphatic and uncompromising terms. He writes:

'MY DEAR FRIEND,—I date my letter from Russell Square, because I am writing in it and paint and sleep in it; but I am not yet entirely remov'd to it, and even your continued absence is on this account pleasant to me—when the little things still necessary to be done are finally completed, I shall regret every Day that you remain at Hastings . . .

All who have seen are pleas'd with my new Residence; and its obvious professional advantages (distance alone excepted) appear fully to justify my choice, and the increas'd expense which may be *suppos'd* to accompany it. I enter it at the most unfavourable time, the most vacant and comfortless Season, and the bitterest Weather; and still it is comparatively cheerful.

What intelligence we have from the Continent!

You will not mistake the source of my Feelings tho' at first you may wonder at them, when I tell you that the vastness of the sacrifices of the last Twenty Years, the enormous waste of Human Blood and Human Suffering, with the suddenness of this change, which makes the whole so visionary, so empty in its result, if only to restore Profligacy and Imbecility, gives an oppressive and gloomy feeling to my Mind, by showing the *Nothingness* of this scene of exertion, toil, and misery, and folly!

The "*Tiger*", is indeed gone, but with him that exciting power that has rous'd one's faculties, and seem'd indeed to have shot new activity into the human Mind. Great part of his Career had in it something grand, noble, and comprehensive. It seem'd to embrace all that is splendid and wise in Government, all but that happiness of a People that can only arise from virtuous Freedom, and with it the safety of surrounding Nations.

Art and Science (from whatever craft or Policy) never were so distinguished as under him; till the cursed thirst of universal Power swallow'd up every other effort of human Genius, in the bloody necessity of military strength and the savage carelessness and ferocity that accompanies it. He now appears in his last throes, and it seems impossible for him to escape his Fate.

He dies then, and "the Monkey" [Louis XVIII] takes his place (I mean no allusion to the Individual) and one consequence of it will most probably be the breaking up and dispersing the most magnificent Collection of the most difficult (and with sculpture one may almost say the most ennobling) of all arts that the World has ever seen.

I appear to write with impressions on this subject different to that of many on our side of the question, with whom it is all matter of triumph and rejoicing; but I never write to you with affected feelings, and what I have now said has arisen from real pain of Mind, perhaps a little arising from being too much alone, and not partaking of the joyfulness of Friends . . .'

Farington and Robert Smirke dined with Lawrence in his new home on 5th March and both expressed their pleasure at the way it had been furnished. In the following month Napoleon abdicated and was sent to Elba as King. The ensuing Armistice enabled Lawrence to visit Paris for the first time. Like other English art lovers he was eager to see the priceless works of art assembled in the Louvre, before they were taken back to the countries from which Napoleon had looted them. In Paris he was warmly welcomed by his close friend Lord Stewart (Castlereagh's half-brother, who later became the third Marquis of Londonderry) and was just in time to see the masterpieces before their removal.

Writing in May to Miss Croft, he says: 'Had I delayed my journey a day longer, I should have lost the view of some of the finest works of this Gallery, the noblest assemblage of the efforts of human genius that was ever presented to the world. It very much surpassed my expectations, and particularly in its most celebrated pictures. The Transfiguration is still the very first. A few days will see the whole taken away; and much as we ought to reprobate the injustice by which the greater part of them was obtained, it is impossible to witness their departure without regret, —at least I know not how to check this feeling.' At the end of a letter somewhat overloaded with lofty sentiments, he tells Miss Croft that 'pleasure, and not innocent dissipation, has here all the activity of high Change in London. I see, however, and smile at it. Let those plunge into it, who are not scared from its contagion by superior enjoyment. I live with military men, but my mornings are spent in viewing works of art, my evenings at the Opera, or French Theatre, and at Lady Castlereagh's, or a walk through some other English house. All this terminates sufficiently soon to keep health unimpaired, and early rising habitual'. He concludes by conveying the news that he has lost 'a kind friend, and from his good-nature and worth, a most valuable man,—poor Mr. Boucherette, who was killed by a fall from his curricle'.

Miss Croft, who naturally heard the whole story of Lawrence's experiences in Paris when he returned home, gives a more detailed account of them than this letter contains. In her *Recollections of Sir Thomas Lawrence*, she writes that 'when Lord Stewart tempted him to visit Paris, before the stolen treasures of the Louvre were restored, he felt it so difficult to emancipate himself from the trammels of business, that he was very near missing the object of greatest interest. The Apollo Belvedere was actually packing, but his friend Blücher had it replaced on its pedestal for Sir Thos's inspection. . . . Lord Stewart (his constant and attached friend) made him a present on his arrival at Paris of a beautiful little Spanish horse called "Azor", which he, Lord S., had ridden at the battle of Dresden. The very morning after his arrival he accompanied his friend to a review of 20,000 Austrians at some distance from Paris, and very humourously described his dismay when, on reaching the ground, his white charger was led up to the carriage door with that of Lord Stewart. He said, "My Lord, I shall certainly disgrace you and your beautiful horse, and you will soon see the poor painter sprawling in the dust". Fortunately he had been an excellent horseman in his youthful days, as he had excelled in most other manly exercises; but he had long since discontinued riding for want of time. Azor played him every possible wicked trick, kicking and jumping up all-fours, and made many efforts to charge with the Cavalry, which he once nearly accomplished by getting the bit between his teeth; but Sir Thos in desperation stood up in his stirrups, and with his fist knocked the bit into the proper situation. The Duke of Wellington congratulated him on this happy effort. . . . Poor Azor once jump'd from under him at Charing Cross, while he had his hand on Mr. Angerstein's carriage window, and a dray touched the horse behind. He was very much hurt and shaken, but went out to dinner, and on his way called on his female doctors in Hart St. [Miss Croft and her cousin] to know what remedies he should use'.

Lawrence's stay in Paris was cut short by an urgent and flattering summons from the Prince Regent, in whose good graces he was by this time firmly established. In the previous month Lady Anne Barnard (the author of the song 'Auld Robin Gray') had written a long letter to the Prince proposing to him, as Farington records, that 'as the Emperor of Russia, and the King of Prussia were expected in England that the opportunity be taken to have a picture painted in which those Monarchs and the Prince Regent should be introduced; and that it should be a picture of a kind to commemorate the great events which had taken place in which these high characters had appeared so conspicuous. The Prince Regent was pleased with the proposal, and after some conversation with Col McMahon adopted the recommendation of Lady Anne Barnard that Lawrence should be the painter employed.' Later, Lady Anne wrote to Lawrence at considerable length telling him what scenes she thought should be pictorially recorded, but in spite of his thwarted ambition to become an historical painter, he does not appear to have taken the gushing lady's advice.

Writers of fiction, when kindly offered plots for their novels in similar circumstances, seldom find their creative instinct set in motion. Instead of painting such touching historical episodes as Louis XVIII taking from his shoulders the Order of St. Esprit and throwing it over the neck of the Prince Regent, in accordance with the Prince's orders he wisely confined himself to painting the portraits of historical persons.

As soon as the Crowned Heads and illustrious generals of the victorious allied nations arrived in England the Prince enjoined on Lawrence that he should take the likenesses of the Tsar of Russia, the king of Prussia, Prince Blücher and the Hetman Platoff 'in a manner', says Williams, 'that might not only commemorate their visit, but transmit the state of British art to future generations'. Williams was certainly right in saying that 'nothing could be more fortunate to a great artist than his living at a period of such extraordinary events; for the latest posterity to the end of time, will derive their ideas of the persons of these great characters, from the pencil of Lawrence'. It was in this way that Lawrence's life-long ambition to achieve fame as an historical painter came to be gratified. In addition to those of the foreign notables, Lawrence's first portraits of the Prince Regent and the Duke of Wellington date from this period. As the programme of the visitors was a full one, 'it required the utmost vigilance and importunity of Mr. Lawrence to obtain even short and irregular sittings'. The monarchs appear to have been painted in a part of St. James's Palace which was shortly afterwards pulled down, but Blücher and Platoff came to Russell Square and the cossack bodyguard of the latter, 'mounted on their small white horses, standing sentinels at the door while he was painting the portrait of their General', attracted admiring crowds. When it became known that Blücher also was having his portrait taken, the mob in Russell Square, says Miss Croft, 'rushed in, in a frightful manner . . . lining the staircase and filling the gallery; and at length it was scarcely possible to keep them out of the painting room, except by the aid of Bow Street officers'.

A happy chance enabled Miss Croft to be of great service to Lawrence on what must have been an embarrassing occasion.

She had called on Mrs. Bloxam, who happened to be staying with her brother, and the servant, Holman, informed her that Mrs. Bloxam was out and that his master was engaged with the 'Field Marshal'. She left her card and 'had only proceeded a few yards, when Holman came running to say his master begg'd I would return. Sir Thomas came down to me looking harassed and distressed, and said: "They have sent Blücher to me without any attendant or interpreter; he has been travelling all night from Portsmouth and is evidently 'half-seas over', and consequently falls asleep the moment I cease talking to him; and, moreover, being somewhat deaf, I can only make him hear by going quite close to him". I asked on what pretence I could be introduced; and Sir Thos. said, "As my sister, for such I consider you, and my real sister must have done me this service had she been at home." ' As Blücher only spoke German and very bad French and Lawrence was no linguist, Miss Croft's intervention must have seemed providential. 'It was very convenient,' says Miss Croft, 'that he did not understand our English, as Sir Thomas prompted me as to the best means of keeping him awake.' This was to talk about the Duke of Wellington. She spoke of the Duke's worn and altered appearance and Blücher answered as if it was impossible for a soldier to experience bodily fatigue. 'He went on to observe that Wellington was a boy to him, for he added, "I have been fifty-six years an officer". We calculated afterwards that as he was certainly raised from the ranks by Frederic of Prussia, he must in all probability be full seventy-six years of age when he fought so bravely. The fact of his having been a common soldier is, I believe, denied by his biographer, but Lord Stewart assured Sir Thos. that Blücher was rather proud than otherwise of it. In the commencement of my office Sir Thos. imposed a difficult task on me, which was to request he would curl up his moustaches so that they might not cover his lower as well as upper lip—this with my bad French I found difficult to make him comprehend, but I at length accomplished it more by signs than words, and putting his filthy fingers into his mouth, he brought them out plentifully wet, and curled the moustaches into a proper compass.'

Early in July the Duke of Wellington came to sit for his portrait, a whole length, which had been commissioned by the Prince Regent. 'He came on horseback,' says Farington, 'attended by the Old Groom, and [dressed] in the plainest manner, wearing a Blue Coat and a round Hat.—Nobody was apprized of his coming and the few people who were passing had no knowledge of His being the Duke of Wellington.'

7th July 1814 was Thanksgiving Day and a service was held in St. Paul's Cathedral, attended by the Prince Regent, Prince Blücher, the Duke of Wellington and other notables. Farington went with Lawrence and describes the scene as 'very fine and highly interesting'. A fortnight later a grand 'Fete' was held at Carlton House, to which Lawrence was invited. Farington noted down the exact wording of the card of invitation, which was as follows:

'The Lord Chamberlain is commanded by
The Prince Regent
to invite Mr. T. Lawrence
to a Dress Party on Thursday evening the
21st July at ten o'clock to have
the Honor of meeting
Her Majesty the Queen.
A Ball.'

Lawrence arrived 'at about three quarters before 12 o'clock' and, as Farington tells us, was much with Mrs. Boucherette and her daughters and 'had occasionally conversation with many of the first characters present'. We may well believe that this ball was 'a very splendid scene', as the Prince Regent was an accomplished host, understood the art of entertaining on a grand scale and on this occasion was no doubt anxious to impress his foreign guests. A hot supper was served at 3 a.m. and Lawrence 'came away a little before 5 o'clock at which hour the Queen remained there'.

The proposal was first made in this year by Lord Stewart, who had just been appointed our Austrian Ambassador, that Lawrence should accompany him to Vienna, at the time fixed for the Congress, to paint the portraits of the Emperors of Austria and Russia.

The Hundred Days, however, intervened, and Lawrence was not to set out on his 'Grand Tour' till four years later. Before his departure for Vienna, in October, Lord Stewart suggested to the Prince Regent that it might be advisable that Lawrence should be knighted, as the title 'Chevalier' was useful abroad. The Prince agreed and the honour was accordingly conferred on him on 22nd April 1815, just before the opening of the Royal Academy Exhibition. Lawrence's portraits in this year included those of the Prince Regent, Blücher, Platoff, Metternich, Wellington, Mrs. Wolff and R. Hart Davis, Esqre. The latter was highly praised by Williams who calls it a 'surprising portrait' and says 'it is masculine and severe, and totally devoid of any of the tricks of art to produce effect, or to catch the fancy of the ignorant'. The portrait of the Duke of Wellington, on the other hand, he condemns as 'full of glare, with a light showy view of St. Paul's in the background, whilst the Duke seemed unconnected with aught around him'. In his later portraits of the Duke Lawrence was more successful. His full-length portrait of the Prince Regent was shown to Farington before completion, and as usual Farington made valuable criticisms and suggestions of which Lawrence at once took advantage. The result was a brilliant example of 'Court' portraiture, which, though in the circumstances excusably flattering, is handled with masterly skill. Even Hazlitt, who had been dropped by Perry, the editor of the *Morning Chronicle*, for a damaging criticism of Lawrence's portrait of Castlereagh, which he said was not a likeness and had 'a smug, smart, haberdasher look', though still critical, is forced to admit the painter's competence. In a review of the Academy, contributed to the *Champion*, he makes fun of Lawrence for representing a corpulent man in his fifty-third year as he might have been twenty years before the portrait was taken. 'Sir Thomas Lawrence,' he wrote, 'has with the magic of his pencil recreated the Prince Regent as a wellfleshed Adonis of thirty-three; and, happy as we always are to contemplate the innocent happiness of others, even when it is not referable to the most philosophic sources of human satisfaction, we could not, as we stood before this very admirable picture (No. 65) but derive a high degree of goodnatured pleasure from imagining to ourselves the transports with which His Royal Highness must have welcomed this improved version of himself. It goes far beyond all that wigs, powders and pomatums have been able to effect for the last twenty years.'

To outside observers, indeed to all except his creditors and a very few intimate men friends, Lawrence must have seemed, at this moment of his career, to have reached a pinnacle of success which any artist might envy. His new honours and the congratulations showered on him by his friends and colleagues, however, can only have added to the distress of mind caused by the desperate state of his finances. In the past eight years he had paid off £10,000 from the sum total of his liabilities and considerable sums were owing to him, the prompt payment of which he could not ask for without betraying his embarrassment. The move from Greek Street to Russell Square must have involved a heavy initial outlay, while his visit to Paris, which interrupted his mill-horse toil, caused a corresponding diminution of his earnings. Whatever may have been the exact nature and extent of the demands which brought matters to a head, the crisis was sufficiently serious to make him write to tell Farington, on 6th April 1815, that 'the past temporary expedients have but retarded the general Ruin that I am told by W. and Mr. J. A. [ngerstein] is now not to be averted, but to be met in the wisest way. If it is, tho' occasioning present Affliction and very painful Feelings and exertion of Mind, the final result—the future may yet be happy, and complete release from thraldom. . . .' As Lawrence was never made a bankrupt, it is certain that once again his troubles were not met 'in the wisest way', but that further 'temporary expedients', possibly borrowing at high interest, were resorted to. The following truculent letter is an example of the wasp-stings to which, admittedly to a large extent through his own carelessness and imprudence, he was subjected only too frequently.

'MY DEAR SIR,—If you will have Honors conferr'd upon you, you must pay for them; I enclose you my card that you may know in what capacity I have call'd upon you. Send me a Draft before Eleven o'clock tomorrow morning for £108.2.8d, upon the

LADY ELIZABETH FOSTER

Exhibited at the Royal Academy, 1805. Lady Elizabeth married the fifth Duke of
Devonshire after the death of Georgiana, Duchess of Devonshire. In the National
Gallery of Ireland.

PRINCE METTERNICH

Exhibited at the Royal Academy 1815. Engraved by S. Cousins, R.A., in 1829. At Windsor Castle and reproduced by gracious permission of His Majesty The King.

receipt of which directions will be given for your Knighthood to be announc'd in the *Gazette* tomorrow Evening—Ever yours faithfully

W. MASH.'

Towards the end of the year, for ever made memorable by the victory of Waterloo, England was honoured by a visit from the Marquis Canova, the famous sculptor who was at that period regarded as the greatest living artist. He was entertained by the Prince Regent, who presented him with a snuff-box set with diamonds, by members of great families, who, when making the grand tour, had been introduced to him in Italy, and by the Royal Academicians, who gave a dinner in his honour in the Council Room at Somerset House. One of his reasons for visiting England was to see the Elgin Marbles, regarding which he completely endorsed the admiration which had been expressed for them by Lawrence and Haydon. The latter considered himself primarily responsible for their acquisition by the State, although the evidence given by Lawrence in their favour, in view of his position, his influence, and his ability to catch the ear of the great, probably had much more to do with it. Haydon, a disappointed and disgruntled man, was fond of telling rather spiteful anecdotes about people who had befriended him, of whom Lawrence was one. In May 1814 he wrote to Lawrence, saying: 'I feel great pleasure in telling you who have so kindly interested yourself in my favor—that my picture is sold. I cannot conclude without saying, that your conduct throughout has been noble and generous in the highest degree, and I shall always feel and always acknowledge it as long as I have existence.' In the summer of 1815 the directors of the British Institution got together a splendid collection of Old Masters, the first Exhibition of the kind to be held in England, to which the Prince Regent, Mr. Angerstein, Sir George Beaumont, the Governors of Dulwich College and other owners lent their finest masterpieces. Haydon, whose hostility to the Royal Academy, though not unnatural, was inordinate, left it on record that the Academicians were greatly annoyed with the directors for holding the exhibition, and even pretended that his benefactor Lawrence—of all people!—was rendered furious by the sight of Vandyck's portrait of Gevartius, now in the National Gallery. 'Lawrence,' he says, 'was looking at the Gevartius when I was there, and as he turned round, to my wonder, his face was boiling with rage as he grated out between his teeth, "I suppose they think we want teaching". I met Stothard in my rounds, who said, "This will destroy us". "No," I replied, "it will certainly rouse me." "Why," said he, "perhaps that is the right way to take it." On the minds of the people the effect was prodigious. All classes were benefited, and so was the fame of the Old Masters themselves, for now their finest works were brought forth to the world from odd corners and rooms, where they had never perfectly been seen.'

The passage is interesting for the light it sheds on the mind of the unfortunate Haydon and serves as a warning that his statements, particularly about Academicians, should be carefully checked. While there is plenty of evidence that Lawrence had a hot temper, which he did not always keep under control, there is still more evidence that he could not conceivably have made the remark which Haydon puts into his mouth. Lawrence was strongly in favour of the foundation of a National Gallery and hoped that the Angerstein collection to which the Gervartius belonged, and in the formation of which he had played so active a part, would be acquired for the public. He was the last man to suppose that he had nothing to learn from Vandyck. Whatever may have been the reasons for Lawrence's rage, they were certainly not those which Haydon attributed to him.

In June 1816 Parliament voted the sum of £35,000 for the purchase of the Elgin Marbles after a Select Committee of the House of Commons had recommended their acquisition. From the time the Marbles were first on view in London, in 1808, Haydon loudly acclaimed their merits and is entitled to respect for having done so. When he wrote his famous article on the Marbles which appeared in the *Examiner* and the *Champion*, Lawrence very generously said: 'It has saved the Marbles, but it will ruin you.' As it happens, however, Lawrence was the only painter, apart from the President of the Royal Academy, whose opinion was consulted by the Committee. Although Canova, when he saw the Marbles in 1815, had pronounced them of priceless value, the evidence of such sculptors as Flaxman, Nollekens, Chantrey, Westmacott and Rossi was contradictory and confusing. Lawrence was examined on 5th March 1816, and in view of the fact that he was known as the expert adviser of such eminent collectors as Mr. Angerstein and the Prince Regent, it is probable that his evidence proved decisive. The following questions and answers are extracted from the shorthand report which Williams prints in full:

' "Are you acquainted with the Elgin Marbles?"
"Yes, I am."
"In what class of art do you consider them?"
"In the very highest."
"Do you think it of importance that the public should become possessed of those Marbles, for the purpose of forming a school of art?"
"I think they will be a very essential benefit to the arts of this country, and, therefore of that importance."
"In your particular line of art, do you consider them of high importance, as forming a national school?"
"In a line of art which I have very seldom practised, but which it is still my wish to do, I consider that they would; viz. historical painting."
"Have you had opportunities of viewing the antique sculpture which was formerly in Italy and recently in Paris?"
"Very recently at Paris."
"Can you form any estimate of the comparative merit of the finest of the Elgin Marbles, as compared with the finest of those works of art?"
"It is rather difficult; but I think that the Elgin Marbles present examples of a higher style of sculpture than any I have seen."
"Do you conceive any of them to be of a higher class than the Apollo Belvedere?"
"I do; because I consider that there is in them a union of fine composition, and very grand form, with a more true and natural

expression of the effect of action upon the human frame, than there is in the Apollo, or in any of the other most celebrated statues."

"Are you well acquainted with the Townley collection of Marbles?"

"Yes, I am."

"In what comparative class should you place the Elgin Marbles, as contrasted with those?"

"As superior." '

Among the amateurs examined were Payne Knight, Wilkins the architect and various private collectors, who, as might have been expected, vociferously contradicted each other. Payne Knight 'gave the preference to the Apollo, and thought the Theseus a spurious addition by Hadrian and that some of the Metopes were "very poor".'

His evidence on the Elgin Marbles emphasises the fact that Lawrence was far and away the best all-round judge of artistic merit of any painter of his period, one might almost say of any period. His judgments, both of the work of the Old Masters and of that of his contemporaries, was remarkably sound, and when he detected genius, as he was quick to do in Turner, he was generous in proclaiming the fact. He was devoid of petty jealousy and did not allow his personal likes and dislikes of individual artists to distort his views of their capacity and achievements. He was, moreover, openhanded in his encouragement of obscure and neglected artists whose work showed promise. Mona Wilson, in her *Life of William Blake*, quotes an extract from the Diary of Lady Charlotte Bury (dated 20th January 1820) which illustrates the false ideas which superficial observers were apt to form of Lawrence's character and motives, while the sequel to it brings into sharp relief what he 'really thought'.

'I dined at Lady C. L.'s [Caroline Lamb's]. She had collected a strange party of artists and literati and one or two fine folks, who were very ill assorted with the rest of the company, and appeared neither to give nor receive pleasure from the society among whom they mingled. Sir T. Lawrence, next whom I sat at dinner, is as courtly as ever. His conversation is agreeable, but I never feel as if he was saying what he really thought. . . .

Besides Sir T., there was also present. . . . Mrs. Mee, the miniature painter . . . there was another eccentric little artist, by name Blake. . . .

I could not help contrasting this humble artist with the great and powerful Sir Thomas Lawrence, and thinking that the one was fully if not more worthy of the distinction and fame to which the other has attained, but from which *he* is far removed. . . . Sir T. Lawrence looked at me several times whilst I was talking with Mr. B., and I saw his lips curl with a sneer, as if he despised me for conversing with so insignificant a person. It was very evident Sir Thomas did not like the company he found himself in, though he was too-well-bred and too prudent to hazard a remark on the subject.'

Lawrence may have had his own reasons for despising Lady Charlotte, though it is improbable that they were the ones she attributed to him. His dislike of the company in which he found himself at Lady Caroline Lamb's dinner-table may have been partly induced by the fact that Mrs. Mee, *née* Anne Foldsone, formed part of it. It is always disconcerting for a man, after an interval of nearly thirty years, to be confronted unexpectedly by an old flame, even if the parting has been amicable.

Lawrence again met Blake, two years later, through Linnell, and proved his admiration for Blake's genius by buying copies of *Songs of Innocence* and *Songs of Experience* and two drawings, 'Queen Catherine's Dream' and 'The Wise and Foolish Virgins', at fifteen guineas apiece. The latter is now in the Tate Gallery. A friend of Lawrence, whose name is not divulged, noted in his diary that the 'Wise and Foolish Virgins' was 'Sir Thos' favourite drawing' and that 'he commonly kept it on his table in his studio, as a study'.

Work poured in on Lawrence in his new quarters, he was overwhelmed with commissions and, as a result, the quality of the portraits which he exhibited at the Royal Academy in 1815 and the three succeeding years seemed to some of his critics to show a falling-off from his usual high standard. As before, we must turn to Farington for sidelights on his private life during this period. Napoleon abdicated on 26th June, eight days after his defeat at Waterloo, and on 14th July Lawrence called on Farington and gave him many particulars about the battle which he had received from 'persons in official or military situations'. Lawrence told him that all the troops behaved well except a Corps of Hanoverians called Prince Ernest's (the Duke of Cumberland's) Hussars. The Colonel of the Corps received the order to charge 'but doubted the correctness of it, saying that "*the attack ordered would be attended with danger*" '. The italics are Farington's. We are given a good idea of the intimacy which now existed between the Prince Regent and Lawrence through an account which Farington gives of a conversation between them, when they were alone together in Lawrence's studio, on the subject of the unpopularity of the Duke of Cumberland. The Prince alluded to 'the report of *Senlis* having been murdered by him which had been current with many and remarked upon the improbability of there being any just foundation for such a report'. The Prince visited the Academy after the Exhibition was closed to the public and Lawrence was asked by Colonel McMahon to attend on this occasion and found there Benjamin West, Fuseli and Howard. The Prince was much pleased by the exhibition and 'particularly noticed Lawrence's portrait of Mrs. Wolff. He was delighted with it as exhibiting fine female beauty and taste'.

Farington dined with Lawrence on 15th August and notes that he appeared to have a bias 'against the Allies doing otherwise than granting to the French nation the same terms [as] they [gave] at the Peace of Paris in 1814 . . . With respect to B. himself, His feeling appeared to be more favourable to Him than agrees with the common impression of his character. He thought Him so constituted as to have an insensibility to human suffering and distress, but not a disposition to cruelty. He seemed to think highly of his abilities and of the daring frankness of His mind, and He gave credit to Him for possessing a power which enabled him instantaneously to see into the nature of every character and person who might be brought before Him'.

On 15th September Lawrence called on Farington to tell him that he was going immediately to Paris at the request of Lord Stewart, who added that it was also the wish of Lord Castlereagh. The visit was of short duration, for he was back in London and having dinner with Farington by 28th October. Lawrence tells him that he found Baron François Gérard, the French history and portrait painter, in very high repute in Paris, that Lady Castlereagh's evening parties were attended 'by the first Political and High personages', and that he prefers English women over French and German ladies, for 'modest delicacy and *beauty*'. Lawrence now raised his prices to 500 guineas for a whole length.

On 5th December 1815 a farewell dinner was given to Canova, who expressed himself as much gratified with his reception in London.

At the beginning of January 1816 Lawrence was informed at the Lord Chamberlain's office that it had been proposed to discontinue giving portraits of the King and Queen as a perquisite to Ambassadors and that Lord Amherst, who was preparing to go to China in that capacity, was not to have them. As this meant a diminution of Lawrence's income, Farington pressed him to apply for compensation for the loss of this employment. Gossip at this time includes such items as that Princess Charlotte of Wales is to be married to the Prince of Saxe Coburg, that the Duke of Norfolk, 'a cold-hearted sensualist', did not leave Captain Morris a shilling, that great affection subsists between Lord and Lady Liverpool although they had no children, and that the 'Banking House at Liverpool of which Mr. William Roscoe, the eminent literary character is at the head, *had failed*'.

Later we find Lawrence, who always had first-hand information from unimpeachable sources about people and events, discussing the unhappy separation of Lord and Lady Byron. 'Having heard a statement of the Case from a relative of Lady Byron,' says Farington, 'he was induced to think more favourably of Lord Byron than the world feels on this occasion.'

Whether Lawrence had, at this time, actually made Byron's acquaintance is uncertain, but they certainly met some years later, for Byron records having spent an evening in his company on

5th January 1821. 'The same evening I met Lawrence, the painter, and heard one of Lord Grey's daughters play on the harp so modestly and ingeniously that she looked music. I would rather have had my talk with Lawrence, who talked delightfully, and heard the girl, than have had all the fame of Moore and me put together. The only pleasure of fame is, that it paves the way to pleasure; and the more intellectual, the better for the pleasure and for us too.' Byron greatly admired Lawrence's portrait of Lady Blessington and refers to it in the first verse of a poem which, though familiar, is hardly up to his usual standard.

> *Were I now as I was, I had sung*
> *What Lawrence has painted so well;*
> *But the strain would expire on my tongue,*
> *And the theme is too soft for my shell.*

Mrs. Wolff was an ardent admirer of Byron, and in one of Lawrence's many letters to her, in which Byron's work was discussed and criticised, he included a verbal portrait which shows how closely he had observed him. It must always be regretted that our great romantic painter never had the opportunity of painting our great romantic poet. 'Lavater's system,' Lawrence writes, 'never asserted its truth more forcibly than in Byron's countenance, in which you see all the character: its keen and rapid genius, its pale intelligence, its profligacy, and its bitterness; its original symmetry distorted by the passions, his laugh of mingled merriment and scorn; the forehead clear and open, the brow boldly prominent, the eyes bright and dissimilar, the nose finely cut, and the nostril acutely formed; the mouth well made, but wide and contemptuous even in its smile, falling singularly at the corners, and its vindictive and disdainful expression heightened by the massive firmness of the chin, which springs at once from the centre of the full under-lip; the hair dark and curling, but irregular in its growth; all this presents to you the poet and the man; and the general effect is heightened by a thin spare form, and, as you may have heard, by a deformity of limb.'

Returning now to Farington and the year 1816, we read that the indomitable Mrs. Piozzi, still going strong at seventy-five, is thought likely to last another ten years, though actually she died in 1821. Sheridan died on 7th July of this year and Farington records his deathbed joke. The Prince Regent, some days later, asked Lawrence to give his opinion about arranging the pictures at Carlton House and afterwards showed his friendliness by coming *alone* to Russell Square 'at 5 minutes before 4 o'clock and remained with Him till a quarter before 6. Seeing a portrait of Mr. Angerstein, He spoke of Him with great respect which Sir Thos. remarked to be a proof of the candour of the Prince Regent, as with all duty and respect to His Royal Highness, Mr. Angerstein always showed great attention to the Princess of Wales up to the time of Her departure from England.—While the Prince Regent was with Sir Thomas, He did not keep Him standing, but desired Him to sit down which of course He did and they continued to converse together'.

On 15th October, Lawrence dined with the Prince Regent at half-past seven. The conversation was 'easy and entertaining' and the wine very fine. Lawrence thought that 'not much less than a Bottle each was drank, but the quality of the wine was such that He felt no inconvenience from it'. The Prince had received from the Pope a number of casts from the Antique which had been completed under the eye of Canova. Lawrence asked that these casts might be sent to the Royal Academy and the Prince consented.

An interesting sidelight on the condition of medical science at this period is thrown by a remark of Colonel McMahon, the Prince's favourite and adviser, who was sitting to Lawrence in October. He was much better in health and ascribed this change 'to his having much reduced the *quantity of Opium* which he had been accustomed to take, which was 60 drops at a time and very frequently. This He had done by the advice of His physicians'. Kemble, we are told, also 'takes *Opium* each night before he appears which stills the Asthmatic disposition He labours under'.

Lawrence, through his intimate knowledge of theatrical celebrities like Sheridan, Mrs. Siddons and the Kembles, possessed a fund of anecdotes about them with which Farington enlivened the pages of his incomparable diary. He himself had as many stories to tell of the whims, vanities, jealousies and animosities of painters, although their value for present-day readers is chiefly to remind them how little human nature has changed.

That Lawrence, in spite of his tendency to melancholy and the rather pompous tone of some of his letters, had an irrepressible sense of humour and delighted in funny stories, which he told with inimitable skill, is established by Miss Croft, who quotes several examples of them. She says that 'when he had heard any comical anecdote I could tell instantly by his countenance and it was droll to see his eagerness to communicate it to me'. One of his favourite stories was about Fuseli, who, when on a visit to some friends in the country, disappeared after dinner for so long a time that a search was made for him. 'It appeared that on leaving the dining-room he had enquired of a footman his way to a certain temple in the garden. The man brought a lantern and also a stout cudgel. "What you bring that great stick for?" ask'd Fuseli in his broken English. "Why, Sir, our house dog is let loose after dark, and as he is rather fierce you had better take the stick." "Oh no, you go wid me and carry the stick yourself!" Fuseli, whose timidity was well known, was ashamed to detain the footman, but had not long been left by him before he heard this awful animal at the door, where he continued to sniff, sniff, sniff at the bottom of it, with an alternate bow, wow, wow, and there poor Fuseli would most unquestionably have pass'd the night had they not arrived to his rescue.'

A theatrical anecdote which was one of Lawrence's favourites concerned a young actor 'who made his "first appearance on any stage" at a Provincial theatre in Ireland, in the character of "Lothario" in the "Fair Penitent". He was habited in complete sables, and was greeted by shouts of applause on his entrance by his friends and supporters; these were speedily followed by a burst of laughter, which was so general as entirely discomfited the poor fellow, who bow'd, and shuffled and stammered, and at last offered to retire, but cries of "No, No" brought him back, and just as he hoped to obtain a hearing, and enquire the cause of the merriment, a kind-hearted countryman and friend got up in the Pit, and in an audible whisper said "Larry, my dear, there's the laste taste in life of your shirt hanging out".'

Miss Croft also records an occasion when Lawrence read a comic dialogue to Canning, who was sitting to him, and they both laughed so immoderately that they were obliged to defer the sitting to another day.

Other qualities, besides his sense of humour, which Miss Croft refers to in her description of her friend's endearing personality, are his love of children and animals, particularly cats. Like all who knew him well, she pays her tribute to his unshakeable loyalty to his friends and relations, his generosity and benevolence, his breadth of mind, his lack of professional jealousy, his tact and good feeling and the freedom from snobbery which enabled him to 'walk with Kings yet keep the common touch'. This digression may be a suitable occasion for mentioning another aspect of Lawrence on which Miss Croft lays stress. The opposing strains in his heredity, as in the case of so many artists and writers, were never completely blended, a fact which makes the study of his complex character all the more fascinating. The long line of squires and squire-parsons from whom he descended on his mother's side no doubt accounted for his prowess in field-sports and love of country pursuits, his good looks, his innate modesty and his ease of manner in society. His paternal grandfather, the dissenting Minister, comes out strongly in his urge to express, on all serious occasions, the loftiest sentiments, in his very genuine regard for virtue and honour, both in men and women, and in a kind of prudishness which we are apt to think of as peculiarly Victorian. Miss Croft relates that one night he returned to her house, after a visit to Covent Garden, in a very ill humour. When she enquired the reason of his displeasure, he asked her for a pencil and 'in a few minutes he produced a likeness of a lady's bare back and broad shoulders, which were exposed quite down to her girdle; and he said she was an Englishwoman, or he would not have been so incensed at her. No one had such utter abhorrence of any indecent display in dress as himself, and he said in one of his letters to me from Vienna that "if it must exist it ought to be confined to ugliness and vice" '. So far as is known, Lawrence never drew or painted from the female nude.

Towards the end of 1816 Lawrence was asked to supervise the cataloguing and valuing of the Prince Regent's pictures for Insurance and to help him in this important task he enlisted the services of a well-known writer on art and publisher of prints, William Young Ottley (1771–1836). In a letter headed 'Secret', he tells Ottley that 'a matter of some difficulty and delicacy is confided to me, in which your knowledge of art would greatly assist me, and those feelings and principles of honour proper to gentlemanly station will give additional value to that assistance'. He asks Ottley to meet him at the York Coffee House, St. James's Street, and says 'the business and occasion are very pressing'. It was from Ottley, who became one of his closest friends, that Lawrence bought a number of his Old Master drawings.

Other events of this summer in which Lawrence was concerned were the Fiftieth Anniversary of the foundation of the Royal Academy, the retirement from the stage of John Philip Kemble, who chose the parts of Brutus and Coriolanus for his farewell performances, and the ceremonial opening of Waterloo Bridge. Lawrence remarked to Farington that Kemble had been very unwell for a fortnight, because he had abstained from drinking wine for three years past but 'drank *Champaigne* at a public dinner in greater quantity than he intended', with the result that it brought on a bowel complaint. Lawrence thought the scene at Waterloo Bridge 'very striking, but that the Prince Regent had judged *ill in not riding on Horseback* from the Bridge to Carlton House, as the People were very well disposed towards him.'

On 20th June Farington notes that Lawrence had begun a portrait of the Duke of Wellington on horseback, the horse being his famous charger, Copenhagen, which 'he rode at the Battle of Waterloo and before, and on which He sat 16 hours on the day of that Battle'.

A month later Lawrence received a command to go to Claremont for the purpose of painting the portrait of the Princess Charlotte who was expecting a child within three months. She had previously promised to come to Russell Square to be painted but was unable to keep to this arrangement, no doubt because of her advanced state of pregnancy. Although it was extremely inconvenient for Lawrence to leave London, he thought it his duty to go and Farington strongly advised him to do so. His visit to Claremont lasted nine days, and immediately after his return he wrote a long account to Mrs. Wolff of his impressions of the Princess, on whose successful accouchement the hopes of the direct succession depended, and of her husband, Prince Leopold. This letter, and the one which he wrote shortly after receiving the news of the Princess's tragic death, constitute the best first-hand descriptions of this event, which was destined, by bringing Queen Victoria to the throne twenty years later, to have such momentous consequences, which are available to the historian. Lawrence formed a high opinion of the young couple, was impressed by the harmony in which they lived and convinced of their deep affection for each other.

'The Princess is, as you know, wanting in elegance of deportment,' he writes, 'but has nothing of the hoyden or of that boisterous hilarity which has been ascribed to her: her manner is exceedingly frank and simple, but not rudely abrupt nor coarse; and I have, in this little residence of nine days, witnessed undeniable evidence of an honest, just, English nature, that reminded me, from its immediate decision between the right and the wrong of a subject, and the downrightness of her feeling that governed it, of the good King, her grandfather. If she does nothing gracefully, she does everything kindly'. After describing the simple mode of life of the Prince and Princess, he tells an amusing story which illustrates the good manners and tact which made George IV describe him as 'the most finished gentleman in my dominions'. After dinner, when coffee had been served, 'the card-table was brought, and they sat down to whist, the young couple being always partners, the others changing. You know my *superiority* at whist, and the unfairness of my sitting down with unskilled players; I therefore did not obey the command, and from ignorance of the delicacy of my motives, am recommended to study Hoyle before my second visit there next week, which indeed must be a very short one'.

The long letter he wrote to Mrs. Wolff after the Princess's death shows Lawrence at his best as a correspondent. It is direct, unaffected, sincere and deeply moving and is without a trace of the involved, highfalutin style in which he too frequently indulged.

. . . 'Certain I am', he says, 'that she would have been a true monarch, have loved her people,—charity and justice, high integrity (as I have stated), frankness and humanity, were essentials and fixed in her character: her mind seemed to have nothing of subtlety or littleness in it, and she had all the courage of her station. She once said, "I am a great coward, but I bluster it out like the best of them till the danger's over". I was told by one of the members of the council awaiting her delivery, that Dr. Baillie came in, and said in answer to some inquiries, "She's doing very well; she'll not die of fear: she puts a good Brunswick face upon the matter". . . . I was stunned by her death: it was an event in the great drama of life. The return from Elba! Waterloo! St. Helena! Princess Charlotte dead!—I did not grieve, I have not grieved half enough for her: yet I never think of her, speak of her, write of her, without tears, and have often, when alone, addressed her in her bliss, as though she now saw me, heard me: and it is because I respect her for her singleness of worth, and am grateful for her past and meditated kindness.

Her manner of addressing Prince Leopold was always as affectionate as it was simple: "My love"; and his always "Charlotte". I told you that when we went in from dinner they were generally sitting at the pianoforte, often on the same chair. I never heard her play, but the music they had been playing was always of the finest kind.

I was at Claremont on a call of inquiry the Saturday before her death. Her last command to me was, that I should bring down the picture to give to Prince Leopold upon his birthday, the 16th of the next month.'

Then follows a long and affecting account of his interview with Prince Leopold after the Princess's death, which shows the Prince, who subsequently became the first King of the Belgians, in a most amiable light.

On 4th November Lawrence showed Farington his portrait of the Duke of Wellington, and also his portrait of Princess Charlotte, then nearly finished, and 'a Portrait of Prince Leopold of Saxe Coburg finely drawn with chalk, but not painted upon. Some days after the Princess had died after giving birth to a still-born male child, Lawrence took his portrait of her to Carlton House to show her father, but the Prince Regent was so much affected that he could not look at it.' Sir Richard Croft, Bt., the *accoucheur*, the brother of Miss Croft, was strongly criticised for his unsatisfactory conduct of the confinement. Farington notes that he was said to be a man of rough manners and had lately 'been very unfortunate in losing several ladies in child-bed'. He was publicly accused of negligence and was so stricken with grief that he shot himself in February of the following year.

On 15th December, the day before Leopold's birthday, Lawrence took the picture of the Princess in a coach to Claremont and had the interview with the Prince which he described in great detail to Mrs. Wolff.

An interesting sidelight on the addition to Lawrence's income brought him by the sale of the prints of his pictures is afforded by the fact, which Farington notes, that Colnaghi paid him seven hundred guineas for the right to publish a print of the Princess's portrait.

In 1818, the year of his departure for Aix-la-Chapelle, Lawrence exhibited eight portraits at the Royal Academy, including those of 'Lady Acland and Children', made familiar through the en-graving by Samuel Cousins, H.R.H. the Prince Regent, and the Duke of Wellington in the dress he wore and on the horse he rode at the Battle of Waterloo, which was engraved by W. Bromley. For this picture, which was painted for Earl Bathurst, Lawrence received eight hundred guineas.

At the exhibition Farington says the Prince took his hat off 'and seeing Lawrence standing in the ante-room, he walked up to him, took off his glove and shook hands with him. Sir Thos. L. observed that He never saw Him in better spirits'.

The Duke of Wellington gave Lawrence another sitting at the beginning of May and told him, in the course of conversation, that the greatest hostility existed in France (among the people) towards England and spoke of France as 'a country totally demoralised'.

In June Farington had a conversation about Lawrence with Samuel Rogers. Rogers spoke of Lawrence as being a very reserved character and said that Mrs. Siddons had made the same remark. He asked: 'What Lawrence does with Himself—He [is] seen but little in company, and when He does appear He is always the first to go away? I replied,' says Farington, 'that He is incessantly occupied in His profession, and so much engrossed by it as to have but little time for any other pursuit. I added that I believed He read a good deal—He mentioned that it had been reported that he *gamed*,—and that he might have *connexions* that occupied Him. I negatived both these suppositions, the first from His having assured me He never lost £5 by gaming in his life; for the latter I had reason to believe he had no such connexions. I added that his professional occupation left Him no time for such purposes—He must be very rich, sd Rogers.—I said that at His outset in life He was very unfortunately circumstanced and that money had never been an object to Him.—As an artist I sd he always endeavoured to do his best, whatever subject He might be employed upon,—and that His integrity is perfect in all matters of serious consideration, but He had been much blamed for making light excuses to His *sitters*—for disappointing them'. This summing-up, by Lawrence's most intimate male friend, may be regarded as conclusive. The conjectures, rumours and calumnies circulated about Lawrence suggest that, in an age when gossip was universal, the excessive reserve which was habitual to him was fraught with danger. Indeed, it suggests that the safest method by which a man can keep his private affairs to himself and prevent people from prying into them is to tell everybody *almost* everything.

Two family bereavements, which occurred in 1818, caused Lawrence great distress. On 22nd February his second brother, Major William Read Lawrence, died of apoplexy at the house of his eldest brother, the Rev. Andrew Lawrence, at Haslar Hospital.

MASTER LAMBTON. 'THE RED BOY'

This painting was exhibited at the Royal Academy, 1825, as 'The son of J. G. Lambton, Esq.' Engraved in 1829 by S. Cousins, R.A. In the Durham Collection.

RT. HON. SIR WILLIAM GRANT
Exhibited at the Royal Academy, 1820. In the National Portrait Gallery.

In writing to his sister, Mrs. Bloxam, about this loss, he said: 'The modesty of William's heart, the absence of self and of vain self-applause, in the meekness of his benevolence, were qualities that gained him our fixed esteem, and will make him beloved by us, and revered and mourned, while his remembrance and our reason last.' In November, while he was abroad, his niece Susan Bloxam died at the age of sixteen. Lawrence was much attached to this beautiful girl and had made a charming drawing of her which was engraved by F. C. Lewis. When the news of her death reached him, he wrote to tell Miss Croft of the sad event. 'I have lost,' he said, 'a sweet, good, modest little being, in my niece Susan; but who can, for the innocent, lament the death of the innocent? It is a severe affliction to her parents, sisters, friends. I feel thankful that this one talent, which God has given me, has, in this case, afforded consolation to my good sister and her family; by perpetuating the form, and expressing the nature of this lovely, lamented being, my dear Susan.'

XIV

THE GRAND TOUR

IN 1818 'the allied sovereigns, with the principal military and diplomatic characters of the age, were to assemble at Aix-la-chapelle, to dispose of kingdoms, and settle the *arrondissement* of Europe, upon principles of convenience and utility, which, in conjunction with a Holy Alliance, would render the earth a millennium, and prevent the recurrence of war for ever.

These immense projects did not so entirely absorb the attention of princes and statesmen, but that the congress was deemed an excellent, and, probably, the only opportunity for a great artist to take the likenesses of the persons assembled at it.'

In these sentences, in which a sub-acid note may be detected, Williams describes the event which brought, for Lawrence, the most important commission of his career. It had been understood for some years that Lawrence should attend the Congress when it assembled, as the Prince Regent's portrait painter, so that the Prince's command must have been anticipated. While Lawrence was naturally flattered by the signal honour conferred upon him, the state of his finances, combined with the doubt whether his loss of time would be adequately remunerated, caused him much anxiety. He had been required by the Prince to 'name his own terms', always an embarrassing request and in this case particularly perplexing. Miss Croft, in whom he confided his difficulty, tells us that he was 'so fearful of being exorbitant in his demands, that I walk'd with him on Waterloo Bridge one evening for almost three hours before he could at all make up his mind on the subject. I was ignorant then of what has been so painfully proved since his death, that the embarrassment of his affairs made his leaving England at all a matter of risk and alarm to him, and could not comprehend the thousand difficulties he conjured up. He insisted on my naming the sum it appeared to me reasonable he should demand for two months' absence, and when I mention'd £1,000 he was almost in a passion with what he called my "absurd rapacity"; not being at all disposed to come to my proposed terms, he left me at the door in Hart Street in no amiable temper. I could not sleep in the fear of misleading him, and rose early to persuade him to mount his horse (which I had ventured to order to his door as I pass'd the livery stables) and go direct to the Duke of Wellington for advice. To be sure, I did feel very exultingly triumphant when he called on his way back to confess that the Duke had, without a moment's hesitation, proposed the same sum. His stay was prolonged to twenty months instead of two, and so great a part of the time, both at Rome and Vienna, for his own gratification that his agreement (which was complied with unhesitatingly) went for nothing, and I believe he was only paid for the whole lengths 500 guineas, and for the three-quarters 300, for all the portraits of the Waterloo Gallery [at Windsor Castle].'

The details of the arrangement are more precisely stated in a letter which Lawrence wrote from Vienna to Angerstein. 'The terms on which I undertook this mission,' he says, 'were, to be paid my usual prices for the portraits, and £1,000 for travelling expenses and loss of time. My journey to Rome will be on the same. These appear to be liberal terms, and I am sure are meant as such by the Prince. The first was of my own proposing, when the question was asked me; but I must still look to the honour I have received, and the good fortune of having been thus distinguished in my profession, as the chief good resulting from it, for many unavoidable circumstances make it of less pecuniary advantage.'

The Government evidently attached great importance to Lawrence's mission. Fearing that there might not be a suitable painting room at Aix, they ordered a temporary building in wooden frame-work, containing three rooms, to be constructed at a cost of £1,200. Lord Castlereagh, our Ambassador at Aix, made arrangements for the portable rooms to be erected in the grounds of his house, which was centrally situated. Lawrence left London on 29th September. The portable house and all his painting materials, large canvases, etc., was shipped at the Custom House of London on 3rd. October. Through mismanagement, the whole consignment got hung up at Antwerp, to which port it had been sent, and when Lawrence reached Aix nothing was known about it. This mishap might have had serious consequences had not the magistrates of the city come to the rescue by offering Lawrence the use of part of the large gallery of the Hotel de Ville which, he says, in a letter to Farington, 'was immediately fitted up as my painting-room, *and it is certainly the best I ever had*. The building itself is of vast size, and the length and height of the gallery, and the portions of it reserved for me, are in proportion to it. It has three large windows, one north, and though it is of great depth, from an excellent German stove, it is of the most temperate heat throughout'.

The only disadvantage was that the gallery was at the top of seventy stairs, which somewhat fatigued and annoyed the sovereigns. The portraits of the Emperors of Russia and Austria which Lawrence painted aroused the admiration of their entourage and, as Lawrence put it, 'my exertions have been repaid by complete success'. In a letter to his niece, Ann Bloxam, he wrote:

'On Tuesday last I had the honour of receiving, in the entrance hall of the Maison de Ville, the Empress dowager of Russia, and of accompanying her up to my painting room, where I had the happiness of witnessing her delight on seeing the portrait of the Emperor, and of receiving from her the fullest and frequently repeated testimonies of her approbation, in sentiments that I will not trust to paper, even to you, my dear Ann. I think that, relatively to my professional life, it was the happiest and proudest day I have ever known, the Emperor who had returned but the night before from Brussels, having visited me in the morning just as he was setting off again, and honoured me (being entirely alone) with the most gracious and flattering conversation—at the close of it, firmly holding and pressing my hand for many minutes.

The Emperor has commanded me to paint a copy of it for the

Empress dowager—(you should have witnessed her apprehensions, frequently uttered, lest it should not be as identically her son as the original picture)—a copy of the Emperor Francis, of the King of Prussia, of the Prince Regent and, in the garter robes, of the Duke of Wellington.

The King of Prussia has commanded a copy of his own portrait for Berlin, and of the two Emperors, and of the Prince Regent in military dress. The ministers, in whose portraits I have equally succeeded, all request copies of them—Prince Hardenberg, Prince Metternich, Count Nesselrode and the Duc de Richelieu.'

He goes on to tell his niece that the Emperor of Russia has presented him with a superb diamond ring and that, when dining with Prince Hardenberg, 'his highness presented me with another from the King of Prussia'. The amount of labour involved in making all these copies must have been prodigious while the mere task of replying in suitably courtier-like terms to the gifts and 'gracious messages' which were showered upon him by august personages must have occupied many hours. The question of how the difficulties of language were overcome by Lawrence during his 'Grand Tour', remains, for the writer, an unexplained mystery. He mentions being honoured with the most gracious and flattering conversation, when entirely alone with the Emperor of Russia, which suggests that, among his numerous accomplishments, Lawrence had by this time acquired a knowledge of colloquial French. Never once, in the course of his travels, does he seem to have had the slightest difficulty either in making himself understood or in understanding what was said to him, so that as French, not English, German or Italian, was then the international language of Courts and diplomatic circles, it must be assumed that Lawrence's French was adequate to the demands made on it. The letter to Ann Bloxam continues: 'My professional intercourse with the Emperor Francis is not terminated. I have again to paint him, and am just setting off to Vienna for that purpose, and (to complete the general plan of the Prince Regent) to paint the portrait of Prince Schwartzenburgh who, as you know, was generalissimo of the armies in the last campaign against France.

The Emperor Francis has promised a copy of his portrait to the Town House of Aix la-Chapelle. Providence has enabled me to give the fullest exertions of my faculties to this arduous business, and a coincidence of rare circumstances has given a professional distinction to it that has never yet occurred.' He goes on to tell her that the Emperor Francis of Austria sat to him seven times at Aix, the Emperor of Russia seven times, and the King of Prussia six times, the average length of each sitting being two hours, and adds that his exertions were accompanied and crowned with the most complete success. He mentions that his health continues good, although he has had colds, and that both his servants are well, and asks that her reply should be directed to him at his 'Excellency's, Lt-General Lord Stewart etc, etc, Vienna.'

Lawrence proceeded by carriage to Vienna, stopping a night en route at Heidelberg, which he greatly admired. He reached Vienna in December 1818 and remained there until the beginning of May in the following year, as the guest of his 'kind friend Lord Stewart', the British Ambassador. In a letter to Smirke, dated 21st December 1818, he says:

'Lord Stewart's friendship is equally zealous and active in securing facilities for my professional mission, and in making my stay as agreeable as possible at moments when I am not employed upon it. Comfortable Dinners and the Theatre—Splendid Dinners and High Society—Reviews and Court Fetes form part of the History of my present residence with Him.

I have been presented to the Emperor and to the Empress, and was last night at the most superb Assembly at the Palace that I ever yet beheld; the most beautifully splendid in Decoration, the most gorgeous in the magnificence of Dress in the Individuals.

I am greatly indebted likewise to Prince Metternich, whom you may remember I painted in England. . . .'

In addition to that of the Emperor Francis, he painted portraits of the Archduke and Archduchess Charles, Prince Schwartzenburg, Baron Friedrich von Gentz, Lady Selina Meade, Napoleon's son, the boy King of Rome, afterwards Duc of Reichstadt, and several other notabilities, besides greatly altering, improving and nearly ompleting his portrait of Prince Metternich. In this series the portrait of Gentz, now in Vienna, and the beautiful unfinished oval portrait of the Duke of Reichstadt, which was engraved by Bromley in 1830, were outstanding. In addition to these major activities he found time to make numerous drawings of leading personalities, male and female, in Viennese society, including a beautiful drawing of Metternich's younger daughter, the Princess Clementine. 'You will, I am sure, give me credit,' he says to Farington, 'for as full and intense occupation of my time during my stay at Vienna, as during any period of the same limitation in London.'

Viennese society was the most exclusive in Europe as regards the number of quarterings of nobility considered necessary to secure admission to its highest circles. Out of respect for the Prince Regent and in view of the example set by the Emperor the rigid laws were waived in Lawrence's favour and it was in 'the first circle only' that he passed his hours of relaxation, 'unless when tempted by such invitations as could not be resisted without offence to my own nature and my sense of right'. He certainly did not avoid the society of his brother artists, for his influence upon portrait painting in Vienna survived long after his visit there. Two of the leading Viennese society portrait painters of the nineteenth century, Friedrich von Amerling (1803–87) and Moritz Daffinger (1796–1849), took him as their model. The latter altered his style to comply with that of Lawrence's 'grand manner' and imitated his formal backgrounds, while the former, when he came to London in 1827, frequently visited Lawrence's studio, made copies of his paintings and was for some months his pupil.

In Vienna, as previously at Aix-la-Chapelle, and subsequently at Rome, the dignity of Lawrence's appearance and the perfection of his manners caused him everywhere to be regarded as a fine example of the 'English Gentleman'.

The Prince Regent had asked him to visit Rome to paint the Pope and Cardinal Gonsalvi, but for various reasons, among them, as usual, financial anxieties, he was not as eager to take advantage of this commission as might have been expected. In a letter to Angerstein, he says: 'To visit Rome has been one of those day-dreams that I have frequently indulged in; and the circumstances under which I may now gratify that wish are, perhaps, the most favourable that could have been imagined, unless I had procured an ample fortune, and proceeded thither at my entire leisure. Yet I will own that, either from my unfitness for much enterprize in travelling, or from the proposition not forming part of the original plan, and therefore being unprovided for, in my professional arrangements at home, in which indeed this journey to Vienna was not in my contemplation—from these and many home feelings, I have certainly had less pleasure in the anticipation of this extended close of my mission, than perhaps it is grateful in me to feel.' Lawrence would have liked to put off his visit to Italy till another year, but Lord Stewart was afraid lest even a hint of this might offend the Prince Regent, so he resigned himself to making further efforts. Lawrence was now a man of fifty. He was very nearly bald and what remained of his hair was quite grey. As he admits to Farington, 'other indications of increasing age are not wanting, and amongst them decreasing strength; so that I am now not equal to that whole Day's occupation of my mind and employment of my Faculties which I could at one time command'.

Lawrence left Vienna on 3rd May and travelled to Rome with all possible rapidity. He slept every night in his carriage, en route, except one, when he reached Bologna at two in the morning and put up at an hotel. He was up again at seven and before continuing his journey inspected the pictures at the Academy, paying special attention to those of the Caracci, Domenichino and Guido Reni. After this brief pause, he tells Farington that he started off again and 'came to Rome by the Farlo-Monte road, through magnificent scenery and (with one day's exception) fine weather —catching my first view of St. Peter's on an exceedingly fine morning, between six and seven o'clock. Mr. Thomson and Mr. Howard can well imagine the pleasure of that moment—a pleasure increasing every fifty yards, till I entered the Porto del Popolo, when (what will they say of me?) I found Rome small. If, however, they are indignant at this, tell them the injustice has been amply punished; for I am at this moment overpowered with its immensity and grandeur'. Lawrence's fame had preceded him from Vienna and he was received by the Pope and by Cardinal Gonsalvi, by Canova, by Italian society and by the English colony in Rome, headed by his friend the Duchess of Devonshire, with a warmth of welcome and a lavishness of hospitality which proved the respect with which he was regarded. Characteristically, on the evening of his arrival, he took his servant Holman with him in an open carriage round the walls of Rome, 'to point out some of its scenery, and at every two minutes, he was affectionately dropping his head on my shoulder in a most glad sleep. . . . But he has been a most admirable servant to me the whole time of my absence'. A day or two later Lawrence was received by Cardinal Gonsalvi and honoured with an audience of the aged Pope Pius VIIth at the Quirinal Palace. On leaving the Pope he found the Cardinal's *maître d'hotel* waiting to conduct him to apartments in the palace which had been prepared for his occupation. 'They consist,' he says, in the long letter to Farington, part of which has been quoted above, 'of four sitting-rooms, newly and handsomely furnished, bedrooms, rooms for my servants, kitchen with its attendants, another servant; and, in addition to these comforts, a carriage is ready for me at all hours.' In the course of the nine months he spent in Rome Lawrence wrote constantly to his friends in England, to Miss Croft, Mrs. Wolff, Mrs. Boucherette, Farington, Smirke and Lysons. His letters fill many pages of 'Sir Thomas Lawrence's Letter-Bag' and of his official biography by Williams. The most interesting of them, for the light it sheds on Lawrence's emotional life, is a long letter to Mrs. Wolff which, according to Layard, seems to have been mutilated with the intention of putting any inquisitive person off the track of its recipient. The reference to 'the little pew at Charing', the village in Kent where Mrs. Wolff frequently stayed with her sister, Mrs. Marshall, clearly indicates to whom it was addressed. At the end of a long description of an evening spent with Prince Metternich, his elder daughter, Marie Esterhazy, and Prince Kaunitz, the Austrian Ambassador, he says:

'I had the last Look from him [Prince Metternich] at his driving off, and had pass'd a sweet evening in his company with him, having gone with him, his Daughter and Prince Kaunitz to look once more at St. Peter's and drive afterwards to Monte Mario, a villa near Rome, from whence it was to be seen in its greatest Beauty. When in St. Peter's, and as we were leaving it, we suddenly miss'd his "Marie". Neither Prince Kaunitz nor I could tell him where she was. At length I saw the back of a little kneeling Figure at a distant Altar that we had left. I pointed it out to Pr. Metternich, and he immediately with a grave and significant look to me put his Finger on his Lips and we waited till we saw her returning. Not a word was said, and we left St. Peter's in silence.

I thought instantly of you and the little Pew at Charing and long'd for your society, as I always do whenever Beauty or Virtue present themselves before me.

Do we connect Words with Ideas of Persons or Things when we think of or address them in absence? I think I seldom *name* you—my Feeling generally has this form, "that you were here now!" "that you could see this!" or, "that she were here now". "How delighted SHE would be."

My Bed Room Window is so small that only one Person can conveniently look out of it, but it looks over the Pope's garden and St. Peter's, Monte Mario, etc. and as sweet Even'g closes I often squeeze you into it tho' it *does* hurt you a little by holding your arm so *closely* within mine. . . .'

On the slender basis of the passages which close this letter conjectures have been made about the nature of Lawrence's relations with Mrs. Wolff, but they remain only conjectures. To the writer they do not seem inconsistent with the view that these relations were platonic, at least in a Stendhalian sense.

In July Lawrence spent twelve days in Naples, during which he had a dangerous and exciting adventure in climbing Vesuvius while it was erupting, visited Pompei, enjoyed, as usual, 'good society', and looked at fine pictures, statues and bronzes. In a letter to his brother Andrew, he writes: 'I cannot be too grateful to the Prince not only for having so distinguish'd me by this Mission (which fortunately has been successfully executed), but for having at this period of my Life given me so much of rational

Enjoyment. It is pleasant on the Continent to be greeted by one's Countrymen, who all seem'd to consider my presence, or rather my Works, as general advantage to the Character of England, in what relates to the progress of the Arts.' As an unofficial Ambassador at large, charged with the mission of putting his country on the cultural map of Europe, no one was so well fitted for his task as Lawrence or could have carried it out so brilliantly. His portraits of the Pope and Cardinal Gonsalvi are masterpieces of 'court painting', while the smaller head of Canova, which he altered and completed while he was in Rome, shows qualities of a still higher order. Among the Englishmen in Italy during Lawrence's stay, apart from numerous members of the aristocracy, were Chantrey, Jackson, the portrait-painter, and Thomas Moore, who was on a visit to Byron. They were joined, before he left for home, by Turner, whom Lawrence had constantly encouraged to visit Italy. How strongly he felt that a sojourn in Italy was essential to the full development of Turner's genius, of which he had a profound appreciation, appears in his correspondence with Farington. After describing a visit to Tivoli where, he says, 'I have passed a day of such enjoyment to a painter, as I think only those who have been in the finest weather, and pleasantest society at that interesting place, can have known', he remarks that 'the only person who, comparatively, could do it justice, would be Turner'. He tells Farington that it is the true impression on his eye and on his mind that Turner 'approaches, in the *highest* BEAUTIES of his noble works, nearer to the fine lines of composition, to the effects, and exquisite combinations of colour, in the country through which I have passed, and that is now before me, than even Claude himself . . . in Mr. Turner, it is injustice to his fame and to his country, to let the finest period of his genius pass away, (when, as Lord Orford happily expresses it, "it is in flower") without visiting those scenes which, if possible, would suggest still nobler images of grandeur and of beauty than his pencil has yet given us, and excite him to still greater efforts than those which have already proved him the foremost genius of his time'. To those who have been accustomed to think of Lawrence as no more than a fashionable portrait painter, his disinterested passion for the art he practised and his quickness to recognise the genius of men as dissimilar from himself as Turner and Blake may come as a surprise. Like Hokusai, he was 'mad about painting' and, though fully conscious of his own exceptional talents, was never satisfied with the way in which circumstances forced him to employ them. In a later letter to Farington, written on 2nd July 1819 from the Palazzo Quirinale, he repeats that 'Turner should come to Rome. His genius would here be supplied with materials, and entirely congenial with it. It is one proof of its influence on my mind, that, enchanted as I constantly am, whenever I go out, with the beauty of the hues, and forms of the buildings—with the grandeur of some, and variety of the picturesque in the masses of the ordinary buildings of this City—I am perpetually reminded of his pencil, and feel the sincerest regret that his powers should not be excited to their utmost force. He has an elegance, and often a greatness of invention, that wants a scene like this, for its free expansion; whilst the subtle harmony of this atmosphere, that wraps everything in its own milky sweetness—for it is colourless compared with the skies of France and England, and more like the small Claude of Mr. Angerstein's and Lord Egremont's, though the latter has a slight tendency—has it not?—to heaviness—this blending, I say, of earth and heaven—can only be rendered according to my belief, by the beauty of his tones. I must already have written the substance of this to you, as I have to Lysons; but my dwelling on the subject arises from no affectation or assumed feeling. It is a fact, that the country and scenes around me, *do* thus impress themselves upon me; and that Turner is always associated with them; Claude, though frequently, not so often; and Gaspar Poussin still less'. After expressing his regret that he cannot have Farington and Benjamin West with him in Rome, he continues: 'The person next to you two and Mr. Turner whose mind and eye would be most in unison with mine, in the contemplation of these effects and scenes, would be a lady—would be Mrs. Wolff, to whose friendship, with that of Miss Croft, I am indebted to that arrangement of my pictures which you mention in your letter. To you three I am under more obligation, for just and nice criticism of my works, and (I hope) for consequent improvement of them, than to any other friends. Be not offended, grave and experienced artist, that I place a female with you. There is sometimes a nice taste and quickness of perception in woman, that supplies the place of labour and study; and where it is accompanied by a sound and clear understanding, may be resorted to to great advantage.'

Lawrence found it difficult to tear himself away from Rome, where, as the writer of a letter which was printed in the *Collector* after his departure, expresses it, he had made a 'sensation beyond description' and was 'regarded as a superior being, and a wonder, as indeed he was here. His elegant manners made him so many friends, and these and his talents procured him so many distinctions, that he could scarcely prevail on himself to quit the place'.

He left it at last on 22nd December 1819 and reached Florence, in company with Lord Elgin, who overtook him on the road, on Christmas Eve. Writing from Cremona to Farington, on 19th February 1820, he says: 'On my arrival at Florence, I fixed ten days to be the limit of my stay. On the second day Holman again fell so dangerously ill, as to make the attendance of two physicians necessary; nor did he rise from his bed till within four days of my departure; my residence having been about five weeks. It is true, that I had the alternative of leaving him to the chance of recovery, and of constant careful attention; but he was himself so alarmed and anxious, and it was impossible for me, on recollection of his long services, to resort to so painful a measure.' He set off for Bologna, in dreadful weather, with Holman still unwell by his side, and got there in the middle of the night. After another visit to the Academy he went on to Parma, where he made a short stay, and proceeded to Cremona, Mantua and Venice. His letters express his grief for the death of his friend Samuel Lysons, which had occurred in the preceding year, his anxiety about the health of Benjamin West and his reflections on the Prince Regent's accession to the throne. 'My generous patron,' he wrote, 'will, I think, now suffer less from the outrages of insult and calumny, for the people of England love the Monarch of England, and the title of King has its high authority.' The journey was continued in uncomfortable conditions, he complains of 'incessant rain and snow', but he seems to have stood the strain of travel better than his servants, both of whom were unwell. He arrived in England on 30th March 1820, bringing with him eight whole-length portraits for the King, who, Lord Stewart had lately written to tell him, had talked 'in wild rapture of all the delight he expected from your treasures on your return'. Benjamin West had died on 10th March, and Lawrence, whose crossing had been delayed by contrary winds, arrived just too late to attend his funeral. The day after it he was elected President of the Royal Academy, with only two dissentient votes, the dissentients being Flaxman and Jackson.

Writing to his brother Andrew on Good Friday, 1820, he said: 'I am arrived in perfect safety, with all my packages uninjured. I came yesterday morning. I knew not that there was to be an election of President of the Royal Academy in the evening, till a few hours before it. I did not go to it, but with the exception of two votes, I was unanimously elected. It is very cheering to me to receive this unsolicited mark of the confidence of my brother artists on the first day of my return, after an absence of more than a year and a half.'

XV

PRESIDENT OF THE ROYAL ACADEMY

GEORGE IV's gratification at the success of Lawrence's mission and his admiration of the portraits he brought back with him were unbounded. In proof of his esteem he presented the 'Principal Painter in Ordinary to His Majesty', as Lawrence was now officially called, with a gold chain and medal bearing his likeness, and inscribed: "FROM HIS MAJESTY KING GEORGE IV TO THE PRESIDENT OF THE ROYAL ACADEMY", which the Presidents have worn as their insignia ever since.

Lawrence was now at the height of his vogue, diplomas from continental Academies rained down on him, clients to whom he had already given sittings humbly besought him to finish their portraits, and new clients besieged him with their applications. The blaze of glory by which he was surrounded had, however, no effect on his 'invincible modesty' and he scarcely needed Faringon's advice to him to apply himself steadily and without interruption to completing his pictures for the Spring Exhibition. Faringon wrote on April 3rd:

'My Dear Friend,—Though I have so lately parted with you, I cannot refrain from further expressing my sentiments.

There is a tide in the affairs of men, which taken at the full, leads to fortune. You have now a *spring tide*, a command of every thing that can be had in this world. That you may avail yrself of the glorious opportunity afforded you is my warmest wish.

Again accept my advice.

Do not gratify any curiosity, but take full leisure for consideration. You have the strongest plea for reserve. I shall not be quite easy till I know that yr pictures are *safely lodged upstairs*, to be brought down to your *painting room singly*, for you to work upon them *privately and undisturbed*.

I cannot express how much I am gratified with what you have done. Your situation in the Art is decided for future ages. Truly yrs.

JOS: FARINGTON.'

To the exhibition of 1820 Lawrence sent five portraits including one of Lady Selina Meade which he had painted in Vienna. In spite of his desire to get on quietly with his work, he felt it his duty, as President of the Royal Academy, not to refuse the flattering invitations which were now showered upon him. In a revealing letter to his brother Andrew, dated 20th July 1820, he says that his time 'is more perpetually and fatiguingly occupied than it ever yet was at any period of my life, and from the propriety and necessity of supporting the credit of the Royal Academy, who have behav'd so handsomely to me, I cannot decline the too numerous Dinner Engagements and Parties to which Persons of high Rank invite me; so that the Evening hours which us'd to bring tranquillity and repose to me and some little of leisure, have been as completely fill'd as the mornings of occupation. But my Nephews saw how I am circumstanc'd. I have no independent Fortune to maintain the Dignity of the Royal Academy with, and if I do it by Station in Society (never seeking the distinction, but only receiving it) it is in reality incumbent upon me and particularly in this first year of my Election and return to England. In the next I shall gradually retire from it, devoting myself to my numerous Works and to necessary but quiet employment of the Evn'gs'.

His brother, with whom Mrs. Bloxam was staying, was suffering from a 'painful Complaint', from which he died in the following year and Lawrence grieves to learn that it threatens to stop the performance of his 'sacred Duties'. He records the death of his horse Azor, which had been given him by Lord Stewart, and mentions that he was buried in Mrs. Marshall's grounds at Charing.

Queen Caroline had entered London, amidst popular rejoicings, some weeks before this letter was written. She had rejected the offer of a settlement on condition that she lived abroad and did not claim the title of Queen. A Bill of Divorcement was promoted in the House of Lords and subsequently abandoned for

MISS CAROLINE FRY

One of Lawrence's last female portraits. It was exhibited posthumously in the Royal Academy of 1830. In the National Gallery.

JOHN SCOTT, FIRST EARL OF ELDON

This portrait of the Lord Chancellor was exhibited at the Royal Academy in 1825.
In the National Portrait Gallery.

fear of a revolution. Parliament voted her an allowance, but she was forcibly excluded from the coronation at Westminster Abbey and died shortly afterwards of despair and grief. Lawrence had no illusions as to her guilt, but though he wrote with rather surprising bitterness to Farington about her trial and 'the unlimited means of Perjury plac'd at her disposal', at her death he braved the King's possible displeasure by ordering the schools and library of the Royal Academy to be closed until her remains had been removed from Brandenburg House.

On 10th December 1820, the anniversary of the founding of the Academy, Lawrence made his first appearance as President, dressed in a full court suit and wearing the insignia of office which the King had presented. We can be certain that he played his part with the utmost grace and distinction and that his address to the Academy was listened to with flattering attention. Shortly after this event, Lawrence was consulted by Charles Grant, the Irish Secretary, as to the desirability of establishing an Academy of Painting in Ireland and unhesitatingly expressed his approval of the scheme. Williams claims that the Royal Hibernian Academy was established chiefly through his influence, and he evidently spared no effort, in spite of the numerous claims on his time, in helping the Irish artists to secure their charter of incorporation. At the close of a letter to one of them he says: 'Remember, in palliation of my delay, the number of my engagements. That my life has been both a public, and yet an entirely private one— that I have unfortunately no wife and, inconveniently, no secretary; and that long habits of solitude at home leave me in mature life too much without assistance. For exertions of the zealous artist this is all the better; but not for other businesses, that at last become our duties.' The number and length of the letters which Lawrence wrote with his own hand, after long hours of work in his studio, are astonishing. They provide conclusive proof that, in spite of his numerous appearances in Society and his unflagging interest in the theatre, long hours of 'solitude at home' must have been the rule rather than the exception.

In 1821 Lawrence showed eight portraits at the Academy Exhibition, among them being those of H.R.H. the late Princess

Charlotte, Sir Humphrey Davy, Bt., Lady Louisa Lambton and the late Benjamin West, P.R.A. In the opinion of contemporary critics, his work, since his return from abroad, had gained in strength and brilliance of execution and it continued to arouse universal admiration. It is to-day generally conceded that some of his finest pictures were painted during the closing decade of his life.

On 10th March 1821 Lawrence had his last recorded meeting with Mrs. Siddons, although she wrote to him several times before his death. She was living in semi-retirement in her house in Baker Street but still gave parties. On this occasion Lawrence and Haydon were among those invited to hear her give a private reading of *Macbeth*. In his account of the evening, Haydon said that she acted Macbeth better than either Kemble or Kean. 'It is extraordinary,' he continued, 'the awe this wonderful woman inspires. After her first reading the men retired to tea. While we were all eating toast and tingling cups and saucers, she began again. It was like the effect of a mass bell at Madrid. All noise ceased; we slunk to our seats like boors, two or three of the most distinguished men of to-day, with the very toast in their mouths, afraid to bite. It was curious to see Lawrence in this predicament, to hear him bite by degrees, and then stop for fear of making too much crackle, his eyes full of water from the constraint, and at the same time to hear Mrs. Siddons' "Eye of newt and toe of frog!" and then to see Lawrence give a sly bite, and then look awed and pretend to be listening.' Haydon had not the slightest reason for suggesting that Lawrence 'pretended' to be listening and his jeer at Lawrence's good manners merely suggests that he was deficient in such refinements himself. If Lawrence's eyes were 'full of water', it was far more likely to have been due to excess of emotion than to his difficulties with a piece of toast. His loyalty to his friends and his affection for them only increased with their advancing years. The passage affords another example of that lack of insight into the motives and feelings of others which makes Haydon so unreliable a witness.

The coronation of George IV at Westminster Abbey took place on 19th July 1821 and Lawrence was careful to make representations to Sir George Nayler, Clarenceux King of Arms, who had charge of the arrangements, that, as President of the Royal Academy, he had 'strong claims, altho' not by Right or Precedent' to take his place in the procession.' The King accorded this privilege and directed that he should walk with Sir Humphry Davy, the President of the Royal Society. With his usual kindness, Lawrence secured three seats for his nieces, 'in an admirable situation, commanding the whole scene and act of the Coronation'. He also procured for Miss Croft and her relatives six tickets for the Abbey and as many for Westminster Hall. As she remarks, 'few families could boast such an advantage'.

Immediately after the ceremony the King sent for Lawrence and directed him to paint a full-length portrait of him, in his coronation robes, seated in St. Edward's chair, with his regalia, as he appeared at the altar in Westminster Abbey. Although the King's patronage was, and continued to be, of immense value to Lawrence, the prices paid by George IV for his official portraits were not as generous as was generally supposed. Williams notes that 'it will surprise the public to learn, that the numerous full-length portraits of His Majesty in his garter robes, were paid for only at the rate of three hundred guineas each—less than one half of Sir Thomas' regular price'.

Lawrence's elder brother Andrew died on 3rd July after a long illness, and Lawrence hastened to Haslar to attend the funeral which, as the Rev. Andrew Lawrence, in addition to his living at Long Parish, had served as Chaplain to Nelson and other famous naval commanders, and also held the chaplaincy of Haslar Hospital, was accorded naval honours and attended by the principal officers of the Service.

During the remainder of this year Lawrence was much occupied with executing commands for the King, finishing several portraits, the completion of which may have been years overdue, and superintending alterations to his house, and the preparation of his gallery in Pall Mall for his exhibition in the spring. The latter, it is interesting to note, had been built or adapted for him by John Nash. The work at his house was done by Smirke.

In a letter to J. J. Angerstein he says:

'I have long been in want of a large room for pupils and assistants, but the difficulty of finding one near me, and the inconvenience and probable loss attending the progress of their labours at any distance from me have hitherto prevented my attaining this highly necessary object.

From this difficulty I shall now be relieved, by converting the attics of my house into one large room or possibly two; in which I can have one superior disciple, (a phrase in the good old style) and in the largest room, others who may be painting together. All will then be under my own eye, and my progress be thus extended and quickened. Besides this essential advantage, it will give me the use of a second living-room below, which is now rendered useless, by the number of works that I have been obliged to place in it. At present, I have but one sitting-room, in which I breakfast and dine; and am denied, by this privation, from paying necessary attention to my friends.'

One of the best of these friends, Joseph Farington, died on 30th December 1821. He had fallen and fractured his skull, while on a visit to his native Lancashire, and died a fortnight later without recovering consciousness.

Up till the publication of his famous diary, some thirty years ago, Farington was remembered, if at all, for the spiteful references made to him by such men as Northcote and Haydon. The Royal Academy, particularly during the first fifty years of its existence—Farington was elected A.R.A. in 1783 and R.A. two years later—was such a hotbed of intrigue, petty jealousy, hatred, uncharitableness and malicious gossip, that contemporary comments by members on each other have to be carefully checked by the available evidence. That he was a remarkable personality, an excellent friend and a man of great intelligence the diary establishes, and the high opinion of his wisdom and sound judgment, formed by both Lawrence and Constable, must be set against the disparagements of men who knew him less well. He was born in 1747, was the son of a country clergyman and, when a young man, had the advantage of being a pupil of Richard

Wilson. As a painter of uninspired but unpretentious landscapes he was no more than reasonably competent and it is difficult to explain how he managed to defeat Opie by fifteen votes to two, in the contest for the Associateship in 1783, except on the ground that his personal qualities made him seem a desirable member of the Academy circle. The fact that he had adequate private means, without being rich, lent him an amateur status which gave him surprising authority in Academy discussions. As he was a capable man of business and had ample leisure, he was able to devote much time to its financial affairs and charities. He had an undoubted talent for intrigue and diplomacy, but, having no personal axe to grind, he was ready to devote it to the service of his friends. Northcote, who, like Haydon, disliked most Academicians and found them insufferably insolent, particularly those with the least pretensions, in one of his recorded conversations burst out: 'How Farington used to rule the Academy! He was the great man to be looked up to on all occasions—all applicants must gain their point through him. But he was no painter. He cared nothing at all about pictures, his great passion was the love of power.' Haydon, who was constantly quarrelling with the Academy, detested him and, once after complaining that carpers and intriguers always manage to work their way into corporate bodies like the Royal Academy, quoted Farington as an example of this. 'I will give you an instance,' he said, 'of a man I daresay you never knew—Farington, a man never heard of, the worst painter that ever was inflicted upon art. This man by intrigue, by artifice, and knowing how to take men at certain weak moments, contrived to get such an influence that Reynolds, the first man who by his genius, manly integrity and independence raised the character of the profession, was obliged to succumb to him. He opposed Reynolds and Reynolds had to resign.' It is true that Reynolds resigned in 1790 and that Farington was one of those who voted against him in the division about Bonomi's drawings, but there is no other evidence that he was responsible for the resignation. As has been remarked, Haydon can seldom be regarded as a reliable witness.

An obituary notice which appeared in a newspaper after his

death sums up what Lawrence thought about Farington and may possibly have been written by him.

'His private character was marked by a zeal for genius, in whatever sphere of art it might appear, and by a rare union of discretion and liberality. His knowledge of the world, long experience, matured judgment, even temper, and candour, induced all who wanted advice in the important concerns of life to resort to him for advice, which he was always ready to afford.'

A letter written to Eastlake, then in Rome, on 12th February 1822 is worth quoting for its references to Lawrence's youth and his tribute to his departed friend.

'You tell me that you have the gratification of Sir George Beaumont's society. He is not now to wonder at my recommendation of the study of the Sestini Chapel, since in very early days of my London life his account of its impression upon him rekindled my own vague yet *sincere* admiration of it; for when a boy of fourteen or fifteen at Bath, Night after Night, and from Weeks to Months, I copied the Figures and Details of the Prophets and Sybils from the Prints by Mantuanus, when I had read Richardson and not Sir Joshua; and when no one round me could understand my passion nor indeed *I* its *source*, except that I felt an Image of Grandeur in them that I was impress'd with by no other Work; tho' I had previously made a Crayon Copy of a small carefully painted Picture of the Transfiguration.

They produced an effect on me similar to that which Bouchardon experienced on his first reading Homer, for I immediately afterwards drew in Chalks colossal Heads of Satan, Adam and Eve, Raphael and Michael, which, tho' I am certain they were greatly deficient in Drawing and therefore Character, I know had something in characteristic expression and obvious elevation of aim that spoke a mind however fettered, strongly and singularly excited.

Although therefore I may differ with many of my Friends respecting the master Genius of Michael Angelo (yet I think with no injustice to in-imitable Raffaele), you see that it is no passion of recent date—that it has "grown with my growth and strengthen'd with my strength", and that the conviction of manhood and of age had its origin in the happiness of youth.

We have sustain'd here (I personally) a very great loss in the death of Mr. Farington; an early Friend of Sir George Beaumont and a most constant one of me. Rome brings him to my mind with fresh grief. My longest letters from it were to him, and some of the most valued that I received there were from his condescending (in Age it is condescension) affection and regard.'

Lawrence's eight pictures in the Academy of this year included the well-known portrait of the Countess of Blessington, which was engraved by S. W. Reynolds, Samuel Cousins and others and aroused widespread admiration. So popular had Lawrence's work now become that he was able to make a contract with Messrs. Hurst and Robinson by the terms of which they agreed to pay him the sum of £3,000 per annum for two years, with the option of seven years more, for the right of engraving his pictures.

In the following year Lawrence lost his old friend and patron John Julius Angerstein, who died 'in the most placid easy way' at the age of eighty-eight. Shortly afterwards news reached him from Lausanne that John Philip Kemble was dead. In replying to his letter of condolence, Mrs. Kemble said: 'As much pleasure as I am at this moment capable of feeling, I felt on reading your most kind and friendly letter, my dear Sir Thomas, and the greatest happiness I can now know will be to merit the esteem of those he loved. Of that number none stood higher than yourself, nor can any one have had a more true sense of your extraordinary talents, and he felt a pride in having a conviction that by your aid he should be remembered.' Beginning with the first drawing he made of Mrs. Siddons in 1775, when she was twenty and he was six, Lawrence made at least fifty portraits of various members of the Kemble family, most of which were engraved. If his portraits in oils of Mrs. Siddons can hardly be compared with the masterpieces of Reynolds and Gainsborough, it is certainly true that J. P. Kemble, Charles Kemble, Fanny Kemble and Sally and Maria Siddons are now remembered, at least as regards their appearance, very largely by his aid.

The question of what was to become of the magnificent collection of pictures which had been formed by Angerstein with the help of Lawrence's expert advice naturally exercised many minds. For some years past the need for a National Gallery had been urged on the Government by the Press and by various influential people of whom Sir George Beaumont was, with Lawrence, one of the most untiring. The younger John Angerstein consulted Lawrence as to the disposal of the collection, and the Prince of Orange was mentioned as a possible purchaser. In his reply Lawrence wrote: 'I do most sincerely think that you should not ask less than £70,000 from the Prince of Orange; and as sincerely do I pray and implore that *at* that price he may not have them. At least, before they are sold, as just patriotism and duty to our country, they should be offered for a less sum to the Government—to Lord Liverpool. Ever most truly yours, but at this moment with great anxiety and dread.' Angerstein, who had been left a fortune by his father and could well afford to be generous, was not able to resist this appeal and the pictures were accordingly offered to Lord Liverpool who had already mentioned to Elizabeth, Duchess of Devonshire, his wish to acquire them. The King had also been one of the first to suggest their purchase. After the usual protracted negotiations, during which Lawrence, to his annoyance, was not consulted, the pictures were bought for £57,000. As Angerstein's executors were willing to sell the remainder of the lease of the house, 100 Pall Mall, in which the pictures were hanging, the problem of where to find a home for them was easily solved. The necessary preparations were quickly made and the long-desired National Gallery was at last opened to the public on 10th May 1824. Sir Charles Long, afterwards Lord Farnborough, who was one of the leading connoisseurs of the period, and one of the heads of the British Institution, notified Lawrence on 7th April that he was to be appointed a trustee. 'What I said in the House of Commons respecting yourself,' he wrote, 'was simply that the Angerstein Collection having been chiefly collected under your sanction and advice was a full guarantee to the public that they were particularly well chosen; this observation I need hardly add was received with very general assent. The Bill to include you as a Trustee of the Museum is to be brought in on Thursday. I shall be very glad to have you among us.'

Lawrence, by this time, with the aid of his friend W. Y. Ottley and the four brothers Woodburn, was seriously engaged in forming the collection of Old Master drawings which, at his death, had become the most important in Europe. His temperament being such that if he wanted a thing 'he will have it', he spent more freely than even his enormous income could warrant, with the inevitable result that he continued to have recourse to borrowing. With Farington's restraining influence removed, without either a businesslike wife or a competent secretary to manage his finances, his incapacity to keep proper accounts and his general incompetence as regards the handling of money, led to his being constantly in difficulties. In the light of what is known regarding his lavish expenditure on works of art and his open-handed generosity, not only to struggling artists, but to people in distress who had no real claim upon him, no mystery attaches at the present day to his recurrent crises. His reticence about his private affairs was, however, carried to such lengths that many of his contemporaries, including intimate friends who had a high regard for him, could not understand why he should find himself so frequently in ignominious predicaments. Louis J. Jennings, who edited *The Croker Papers*, containing the correspondence and diaries of John Wilson Croker, made some observations on this subject which deserve quotation. He wrote:

'Mr. Croker had always been warmly attached to the great painter, and had rendered him many services, the necessities for which were constantly arising, for Sir Thomas Lawrence was never out of the hands of his creditors. No one could understand how it was that, notwithstanding his large gains, the President of the Royal Academy was invariably without a shilling to call his own. He was always in love and always in debt . . . With regard to his pecuniary affairs, there could be no room for doubt. In 1825 Mr. Croker had a conversation with the King (George IV) on the subject: "He talked," Mr. Croker wrote in his diary, "a good deal of Sir Thomas Lawrence, and praised his portraits as to the countenance, but complained of his slovenly draperies and backgrounds, although he often imitated the last from old masters. 'He is a great deal too spotty and fond of colours in ladies' draperies. Cannot think what keeps him so poor. He ought not to be poor. I have paid him £24,000 and have not got my pictures. The Duke of Wellington is £2,800 in advance to him. All the world is ready to employ him at £1,000 a picture, yet he never has, as I am told, a farthing.' "

'Sir Thomas had painted an excellent portrait of Mr. Croker, and he was still more successful with Miss Croker (Lady Barrow) Of this latter portrait, Allan Cunningham declares that "men stood before it in a half circle, admiring its loveliness in the Exhibition". It was "all airiness and grace." '

The portrait had been voluntarily offered to Croker 'as a just return for important kindness', which included favours shown by Croker to one of his nephews, but Lawrence was compelled to write and say that although he 'would not and will not receive payment for that effort . . . I am unexpectedly in want of that exact sum (150 guineas) to enable me to keep my word with a coarse man, whom I have appointed to-morrow at three o'clock to receive it'. He promises to repay the loan in the next month 'no longer, not to one day'. Jennings adds that 'there are frequent entries in Mr. Croker's books of loans made to the artist; none of any money being returned'. After Lawrence's death Croker wrote to Lord Hertford: 'Poor Lawrence died of an ossification of the heart. I suppose he was kept poor by great generosity to women. I know two or three to whom he was very liberal. I find that he lived a great deal more at home than I believed. He had *at least* two distinct societies, the individuals of each of which never met the other.'

A similar passage occurs in the *Table Talk of Samuel Rogers*, collected by H. Dyce. 'On coming home late one night,' Rogers recalls, 'I found Sir Thomas Lawrence in the street, hovering about my door, and waiting for my return. He immediately began the tale of his distress—telling me that he was in pressing want of a large sum of money, and that he depended on my assistance, being sure that I would not like to see the President of the Royal Academy a bankrupt. Accordingly, I went early to Lord Dudley. "As you", I said, "can command thousands and thousands of pounds, and have a truly feeling heart, I want you to help a friend of mine,—not, however, by a gift, but either by a loan or by purchasing some valuable articles which he has to sell." Dudley, on learning the particulars, accompanied me to Sir Thomas's house, where we looked at several pictures which he wished to dispose of in order to meet the present difficulty. Most of them were early pictures of the Italian school, and, though valuable, not pleasing perhaps to any except artists. Dudley bought one of them (a Raphael, in his first style, as it was called, and probably was) giving, I believe, more than a thousand guineas for it; and he lent Sir Thomas, on a bond, a very considerable sum besides. No doubt, if Lawrence had lived, he would have repaid Lord Dudley by instalments; but he died soon after, and not a penny was ever paid back. This to so very wealthy a man as Dudley was of no consequence; and I dare say he never thought about it at all.—Sir Thomas at the time of his death was a good deal in my debt; nor was I ever repaid.—He used to purchase works of art, especially drawings of old masters, at immense prices; he was careless in keeping accounts; and he was very generous: hence his difficulties, which were every now and then occurring.'

It was by the means of which Rogers gives this characteristic instance that Lawrence, on numerous occasions in the course of his life, managed to stave off bankruptcy. So far as we know, he was never, like Sheridan, actually arrested for debt and carried off to a sponging house, but, as Haydon informs us, he was very well-known to those 'coarse men', the Sheriff's officers. The straits to which Haydon was at times reduced are revealed in his Journals. In an entry made in April 1822 he tells us: 'Just as I was beginning, I was arrested by Smith the colourman in Piccadilly, with whom I had dealt for fifteen years. The Sheriff's officer said: "I am glad, Mr. Haydon, you do not deny yourself; Sir Thomas Lawrence makes a point never to be denied". I arranged the affair as rapidly as I could, for no time was to be lost; and wrote to my landlord for bail. The officer took it, and appointed to meet him in the evening, and then I set to work. For a few minutes my mind, hurt and wounded, struggled to regain its power. At last, in scrawling about the brush, I gave an expression to the eye of Lazarus; I instantly got interested, and before two I had hit it. My pupil Bewicke sat for it, and as he had not sold his exquisite picture of Jacob, looked quite thin and anxious enough for such a head. "I hope you get your food regularly," said I. He did not answer; by degrees his cheeks reddened, and his eyes filled, but he subdued his feelings. This is an illustration of the state of historical painting in England. A master and his pupil—the one without a pound, the other without bread!'

Lawrence's iron self-control and habitual serenity enabled him to survive these distressing experiences without any undue agitation of mind and, when painting in his studio, he seems to have been able to throw off his anxieties and concentrate on his work, over which he always took an infinity of pains. Lord Ronald Gower quotes an interesting impression of his 'studio manner', recorded by Lady Grosvenor some sixty years after he had painted her portrait. 'I do not think,' she wrote, 'he ever beguiled the time by repeating Poetry—it would have been more amusing. His manners were what is called extremely "polished" (not the fault of the present times). He wore a large cravat, and had a tinge about him of the time of George IV, pervading his general demeanour. He was very like Mr. Canning in appearance. I should not say he was amusing, but what struck me most during my two hours' sittings in Russell Square, was the *perfection* of the *drawing* of his portraits before any colour was put on—the drawing itself was so perfectly beautiful that it seemed almost a sin to add any colour. He had a large room full of unfinished portraits, of which the heads alone were completed, as he always began by that, before putting in any accessories. I should suppose many of these were never completed. I have been told that he was very extravagant in materials, and never used the same brush twice.'

It was characteristic of Lawrence that although, when at the height of his fame, he could exact enormous prices from sitters eager to be, as they supposed, immortalised by his 'pencil', many of his finest works were painted either for love or for fees specially reduced because of his personal interest in the subjects. Of the eight portraits which he sent to the Academy exhibition in 1824 the one which aroused most admiration was the small circular picture of the 'Children of Charles B. Calmady, Esqre'. Prints of this rather tiresome little picture enjoyed enormous popularity not only in England but in France and other Continental countries. Lawrence first saw the children in July 1823, when their mother took them to Russell Square. The regular charge for painting the two little girls in one frame would have been two hundred and fifty guineas, but Lawrence was so captivated by their loveliness that he reduced the price to two hundred guineas. 'I suppose' said Mrs. Calmady, in her account of the interview, 'I must still have looked despairingly, for he immediately added, without my saying a word, "Well, we must say one hundred and fifty pounds, for merely the two little heads in a circle, and some sky—and finish it at once"!' As Lawrence had been known, on occasions, to take a dozen or fifteen years to 'finish' a portrait, of which he had drawn in the head, the promise to 'finish it at once' proved with what real pleasure he looked forward to his task. He began work on it the next morning at half-past nine and quickly sketched in the two heads. When Mrs. Calmady expressed her delight at the drawing, he replied 'that he would devote that day to doing a little more to it, and would beg her acceptance of it, as he would begin another'. Williams remarks that 'the public, in one sense, must be glad at this liberality, for a more free, masterly, and exquisitely beautiful sketch was scarcely ever made'. This drawing was engraved by F. C. Lewis, who specialised in reproducing Lawrence's plain and tinted drawings, and Lawrence was so pleased with it that he paid the engraver twenty guineas more than the sixty guineas which was the price agreed upon. Williams thought that the first drawing of the Calmady children gave promise of an even more beautiful picture than the one he afterwards completed, about which he is more critical than most contemporary opinion including that of Lawrence himself. 'The whole piece is too painted and fine,' he writes; 'all positive and no neutral colours—even the shadows of the neck and arms are of purple, as if reflected from jewelry or painted glass; and might almost be taken by an orientalist as the rainbow tints of a Peri. The deep bluish shade in the neck of the youngest child, the red in the righthand corner, and the purple reflection upon the infant's legs, are all proofs of almost a meretricious taste. It is singular that the French who are accused of being gaudy, in publishing prints of this celebrated painting, made the children much more delicate.'

Lawrence was so pleased with his work that he declared to Mrs. Calmady: 'This is my best picture. I have no hesitation in saying so—my best picture of the kind, quite—one of the few I should wish hereafter to be known by.'

The picture was taken to Windsor Castle and shown to the King, who was so delighted with it that he offered to buy it for £2,000, but the parents, very properly, declined to part with it. The picture was exhibited at the French Salon, where it excited even more admiration than it had done at the Academy, and the coloured lithographs made from it, Williams says, 'were very widely circulated throughout the provincial towns, and were to be seen in the farm-houses'.

While Lawrence was staying at Buckingham House, where he was completing a portrait of the Duchess of Gloucester for the Academy, he received news of the death of his old friend, Sophia Lee. In writing to her sister, Harriet, he says: 'You have characterised most beautifully your sister's genius and nature, and that happy usefulness of wisdom—perhaps the most enviable gift, except the youthfulness of her heart, that heaven had sent her. I now ask from you a great favour, and what I shall esteem a particular kindness and regard: I ask a ring, and more than that, a small lock of hair from an aged person, that I shall value more than the highest and the most beautiful.' In the robust, licentious age so vividly described by Lord Glenbervie and Charles Greville it is curious to find Lawrence behaving, in obvious sincerity, like a sentimental Victorian spinster. The whole letter might well have been written from Cranford.

Of Lawrence's personal appearance at this period a description was given by one whom Williams describes as 'a lady of discernment'. After meeting him in company this lady observed: 'I thought I never saw anybody look so pale, to be in health—yet so very handsome. When we could catch him without the animation which lights him when speaking, he looks like a marble statue, with the lips and eyes only tinted. I cannot think but that he applies much too closely for his health, and indeed that he cannot be quite well, whatever he may say. His gaze made me melancholy when sitting opposite to him in the evening: to my idea, there never was so much sweetness, and benignity, and gentleness expressed in any countenance, where also go such genius and brilliant animation, and such forcible and searching inquiry, are depicted.'

In his presidential address to the students of the Royal Academy in the autumn of 1824 Lawrence expressed views on historical painting, from which John Wilson Croker said he 'differed wholly'. He 'very much struck' Lord Liverpool by giving the opinion 'that the Picture by Sir Joshua Reynolds of Mrs. Siddons as the Tragic Muse, is the finest female portrait in the world'. The address, which was printed and distributed by Lawrence to his friends, brought him many compliments from Fuseli, Canning and others and elicited a queer, emotional and rather confused response from Mrs. Siddons, who wrote the following from Arran Lodge, Bognor, on 23rd December, 1824:

'Situated as I am, with respect to the glorious Picture so finely eulogised, and with its illustrious Panegyrist, what can I say, where should I find words for the various and thronging ideas that fill my mind? It will be enough, however, to say (and I will not doubt it will be true to say) that could we change persons, I would not exchange the gratification you have experienced in bestowing this *sublime* tribute of praise, for all the fame it must accumulate on the memory of the Tragick Muse.—Yours most truly,

S. Siddons.'

In Williams's biography there are many passages which show that he was a man of independent mind and an art critic of some discernment. Writing in praise of Lawrence's tinted drawings, he says: 'In the correctness of drawing he was unrivalled, and he gave to these works a fancy, a poetry and a taste beyond conception. He seemed to unbend, and give way to his humour, without the awe of the public, which sometimes restrained or modified his disposition in his oil paintings. Many of these exquisite pencillings have been made public by Mr. Lewis's plates; and almost all the best of them were selected by Sir Thomas Lawrence, for this gentleman's engraving. And he superintended the process, touching and re-touching the proofs with a sort of affectionate anxiety for that branch of art, which in boyhood had raised him to fame, and in which he delighted thoughout his life. Many of the finest of these engravings have been kept strictly private; but a work is about to be published, which will contain facsimiles of some of the best of these beautiful emanations of the mind and heart of Sir Thomas Lawrence. Among these are extraordinary portraits of his father and mother, and of several delightful children of his sister's, as well as a likeness of himself, hitherto unknown. There are also portraits of many beautiful women and public characters'. Even the most carping critics of Lawrence's portraits in oils have been unable to deny that his drawings are masterly.

Lawrence sent in eight remarkably fine portraits to the Academy exhibition of 1825, among them those of Lord Chancellor Eldon, John Wilson Croker, Canning, the 'son of J. G. Lambton, Esqre' (afterwards Lord Durham) and Mrs. Peel. The picture of young Lambton—he was seven years old when the portrait was taken—was described by a contemporary critic as 'one of the most exquisite representations of interesting childhood that we have ever beheld. The simple action and sweet expression of infantile nature which we see in this portrait, were never excelled by Sir Joshua Reynolds, in his happiest moments'. Williams who, condemns Lawrence's 'singular indecision in the choice of his colours' and says that 'the glossy blue handkerchief with yellow spots, is a great blemish; and the moonlight is not well managed', nevertheless concedes that it is 'perhaps one of the most beautiful paintings of a child, ever produced by art; and, in my opinion, decidedly the best portraiture of childhood by Sir Thomas Lawrence'. The engraving of this picture by Samuel Cousins,

SIR WALTER SCOTT

Exhibited at the Royal Academy, 1827. Engraved by J. H. Robinson, R.A., in 1833.
At Windsor Castle and reproduced by gracious permission of His Majesty The King.

ROBERT STEWART, SECOND MARQUESS OF LONDONDERRY
Exhibited at the Royal Academy, 1821. In the National Portrait Gallery.

R.A., which was produced two years later, achieved enormous popularity. Scarcely less popular was the much engraved portrait of Mrs. Peel about which Layard quotes a letter to the painter from Sir Robert Peel, which throws doubt on what has been suggested regarding Lawrence's knowledge of French. Apparently Croker and Sir Robert Peel had been guilty of the gross discourtesy of discussing the portrait in French, in the presence of Lawrence, on the assumption that he was unfamiliar with the language. It seems afterwards to have occurred to Sir Robert that his manners had been at fault, for he wrote at some length what is tantamount to an apology. He said:

'I doubt whether our mysterious conversation in French would not (if faithfully reported) please you much more than our remarks in English, but I feel I must say that our admiration of Mrs. Peel's portrait was unqualified. I thought it, and so did Croker, eminently beautiful. I wish for no alteration in a single fold even of the gown. I wondered how it was possible to blend so much of simplicity and modesty with all that is elegant and refined.

Croker said in French that you attributed your success in expressing perfect identity of character, to skill in drawing, and that you thought this—namely skill in drawing—a less important branch of the art of painting than some others, such as colouring etc. etc. and that he thought it the first qualification of a painter. He said, you always appeared to throw away the first two hours of a sitting, because you made little use of that which you then sketched in—but you were in fact studying the expression and character of the person, and that they were the two most important hours.'

Lawrence had received some French lessons as a boy at Devizes; he had a retentive memory, a quick ear and an alert intelligence. He had spent twenty months on the Continent, during which he must have heard French constantly spoken. It seems, therefore, probable that he was perfectly well able to follow the conversation of Peel and Croker although too polite to embarrass them by indicating the fact.

Honours from abroad continued to flow in upon Lawrence. In November 1823 his friend and former pupil William Etty had written from Paris, on his way home from Italy to say that

'In about three weeks from this time I hope to have the pleasure of seeing you; and presenting you with something that I think will be pleasant to you. I bring (for your already well and justly honoured brows) another wreath of laurel!—laurel, grown in the country of Titian and Canova!

In plain language, I bring you your Diploma, making you an Honorary Member of the Imperial and Royal Academy of Venice . . . It is delightful to hear in every part of Italy the favourable idea of English art your works and name have left. . . . In France too, they seem beginning to think *we can paint* A LITTLE!'

Early in January 1825 Lawrence received a letter from the Vicomte de Rochefoucault announcing that Charles X had appointed him 'Chevalier de l'ordre Royal de la Légion d'Honneur . . . Elle (Sa Majésté, le Roi) a exprimé le désir que cette faveur devint pour vous une preuve éclatante de l'estime particulière qu'Elle vous porte et la justice qu'Elle rend à vos talents'.

By this time he was becoming rather indifferent to the honours lavished upon him, which only served to remind him of the things he had missed. Writing on his fifty-fourth birthday to Mrs. Wolff, he gives expression to his feelings of disillusion.

'I had forgotten the Day. So many years are then past of this Scene of Trial, and I am at length sensible to that change of thought, which I suppose takes place in every Mind but those whom absolute Guilt has impress'd with Terror.

I look to the termination of my existence here (shall I say it?) with almost Hope. You endear it to me, but that sweet comfort endanger'd, not even the limited Fame that success in this pleasing Art holds out is temptation enough to make me wish for longer Life. I know all that it can give.'

George IV was anxious for Lawrence to complete his series of Royal portraits by painting Charles X of France and the Dauphin.

Canning, who was then foreign secretary, sounded the French monarch on the subject and received a letter in answer from Prince Polignac, 'announcing the compliance of the King of France and the Dauphin with His Majesty's desire; and promising to sit for their Portraits to you, so soon as the Fêtes etc. shall be over'. This information he conveyed to Lawrence, warning him to be prepared to set out for Paris as soon as he received His Majesty's commands.

The commands duly came and Lawrence paid his third and last visit to Paris in the middle of August 1825. He was accompanied by Mrs. Wolff's son, Herman, and by his faithful servant, Edward Holman, and was provided with handsome lodgings, commanding 'a delightful view over the Garden of the Tuileries to the golden Dome of the Invalides', by the British Embassy. In his first letter to Mrs. Wolff he mentions that he has seen Lord Granville, the British Ambassador, Mr. and Mrs. Agar Ellis and Mr. Frere, that the Duke of Wellington is in Paris, also David Wilkie who is 'very unwell' and that he and Herman have visited the Louvre. A week later he wrote to tell his 'dearest friend' his first impressions of His Most Christian Majesty, who had given him a sitting of nearly nearly two hours at St. Cloud. The King spoke 'a little English and that very correct and good', and during the greater part of the sitting, the children of the Duc de Berry were with him, accompanied by their Governess, Madame de Gonthot. 'The little things,' he says, 'sprang on his knees, twined round him, rac'd round his Throne, got up on his Chair behind, then on the large Council Table screaming with mad pleasure, and He as delighted as either of them, but every now and then attempting to frown and scold them into order, from gracious apprehension of their interrupting me; which you may be quite sure the sight of so much happiness could never do.' Lawrence adds that 'I am not fram'd (chiefly because I am too old) for the full swing of Parisian Dissipation, so that I have been but once to the Theatre . . . but we have driven out sometimes in the fine Even'gs and enjoy'd nature and what is fine in Art' .

Charles X, who seems, like other monarchs, to have been captivated by Lawrence's polished manners, assigned him a 'magnificent saloon' for his painting room, and another adjoining, equally handsome though smaller, for Holman. 'Mine is the best Painting Room I ever had,' he wrote, 'and I only regret that His Majesty will not be tempted to let it to me for a term of years. He is nobly, nay, feelingly gracious to me, and so equally is the Dauphin.'

Apart from the courtesies shown by members of the French Royal family to England's court painter, among them being the gift of a beautiful service of Sèvres china which, not realising that he was to die insolvent, he bequeathed to the Royal Academy, Lawrence was cordially entertained by the eminent naturalist Baron Cuvier, with whom he dined at the Jardin des Plantes, and by other leading personalities in the French capital, including Baron Gérard. François-Pascal, Baron Gérard (1770–1837), who had painted many of the heroes and beauties of the Napoleonic court when it was at the height of its splendour, was regarded in his day as the only Continental portrait-painter worthy to be considered in any way a rival to Lawrence. At one of Gérard's weekly conversazioni, Lawrence encountered Mrs. Lavinia Forster, a daughter of the sculptor, Thomas Banks, R.A., whom he had met, in his 'frivolous' youth, at the house of Mrs. Siddons, with whose daughters she had been intimate. He asked to be presented to her, 'renewed an acquaintance which had been neglected, for so many years' and afterwards remained on terms of cordial friendship with her and her family until his death. She and her husband, the Rev. Edward Forster, had migrated to Paris in 1815, to enable the latter to evade his creditors, and Mrs. Forster had established a finishing school there. Adelaide Kemble (later, Mrs. Sartoris) was one of her pupils and William Callow was her drawing master. Among the young English artists working in Paris who frequented her house were Thomas Shotter Boys, Ambrose Poynter, an architect who married her daughter Emma, and Richard Parkes Bonington. Julia Forster, her youngest child, married the sculptor Baron Henri de Triqueti. Mrs. Forster, in a letter to Alan Cunningham, remarks that 'when Bonington visited England in 1827, I gave him a letter of introduction to Sir Thomas Lawrence but he returned from

London without having delivered it. On my enquiry why he had not waited on the President, he replied—"I don't think myself worthy of being introduced to him yet, but after another year of hard study I may be more deserving of the honour". The following spring he went to London with his pictures; those which brought him such well-merited fame. He carried a letter from me to Sir Thomas, which he presented, and was received with his friendship; but alas! it was of short duration, for the great success of his works, the almost numberless orders which he received for pictures and drawings, together with unremitting study, brought on a brain fever, from which he recovered only to sink in a rapid decline'.

Bonington died on 28th September 1828, and some months later the bereaved father wrote from Paris to Lawrence to express 'his sincere and heartfelt thanks' for his 'successful exertions in affairs relating to my lamented and never to be forgotten dear departed son' and for his 'active benevolence'.

Writing to Mrs. Forster about Bonington's death, Lawrence said: 'Except in the case of Mr. Harlowe (George Henry Harlow, 1787–1819, Lawrence's most brilliant pupil) I have never known in my own time, the early death of a Talent so promising and so rapidly and obviously improving.'

It may be as well here to make a brief reference to Lawrence's relations with Harlow, of whom he has been supposed, quite wrongly, to have felt jealous, because the story illustrates his generosity and breadth of mind. Lawrence always spoke of Harlow's genius in the most generous terms in spite of the base ingratitude with which that impudent young man had treated him. At fifteen, when he first became Lawrence's pupil, he had displayed a precocious talent for drawing almost equal to that of his master at the same age. Lawrence accepted him as a pupil at the request of Elizabeth, Duchess of Devonshire. In due course Harlow became such an accomplished imitator of his master's style that he was able to circulate a report that he had painted the Newfoundland dog, introduced by Lawrence in his portrait of Mrs. Angerstein. 'He had even,' we are told, 'intruded himself at the house of Mr. Angerstein, Woodlands, Blackheath, and taken credit for the performance, in a manner so confident and positive, that nothing but the repute in which the honour of Lawrence was held, could have prevented the perfect reliance on the assertion. All that Sir Thomas Lawrence did, in a case which would have justified strong resentment, was to say to him, "As the animal you claim is one of the best things I ever painted, of course you have no need of further instruction from me. You must leave my house immediately." Harlow went at once and betook himself to the Queen's Head at Epsom, where he ran up a bill which he was unable to discharge. Like Morland, in a similar predicament, he proposed to the landlord that he should paint a sign-board in liquidation of the score. This was accepted. He painted both sides, the one was in a good imitation of Sir Thomas's style; and the other represented the back view of the queen, as if looking into the signboard, and underneath was printed T. L. Greek, Soho. When Sir Thomas met him, he addressed him with, "I have seen your additional act of perfidy at Epsom, and if you were not a scoundrel, I would kick you from one end of the street to the other." "There's some privilege in being a scoundrel, for the street is very long," replied Harlow, unabashed, but moving out of reach of the threatened resentment.' Some of Harlow's best portraits are, admittedly, worthy of his master and have been successfully passed off as genuine Lawrences. When, shortly after Harlow's death, Lawrence's favourite engraver, F. C. Lewis, brought him a proof of Harlow's best work, his portrait of Northcote, Lawrence resolved to retouch it, observing: 'It never shall be said, that the finest work, from so great a man, went into the world without such assistance as I can give. Harlow had faults; but we must not remember the faults of one who so greatly improved himself in his art.'

'This alone,' says Williams, who tells the story, 'removes the aspersion of Lawrence's jealousy of Harlow, and of his resentment at his unjustifiable conduct.' He adds that Lawrence was 'above all vanity and selfishness'.

During Lawrence's stay in Paris he actively continued his search for Old Master drawings, the collection of which had long been his ruling passion, and kept up a voluminous correspondence with Samuel Woodburn on this subject. Some of Lawrence's extreme politeness to Mrs. Forster may possibly have been prompted by the fact that he was aware that her father had left a valuable collection of drawings and was anxious to secure tracings of some of the most notable of them. In return for some of the tracings he asked for, Lawrence sent her, 'with a little engraving from his picture of Mr. Lock's son, a very small drawing of his, done when he about eight years old, written under it, in a child's hand, "Thomas Lawrence, Devizes", and in his own hand at the time of sending it "Done when three weeks old, I believe".' The Rev. Edward Forster died in 1828, and proposals were made for printing his Sermons by subscription, which prompted Lawrence to a characteristic act of generosity. Writing to Mrs. Forster, he said: 'I will hereafter give you the names of subscribers to it, but as the amount will be at present about Fifty Pounds, may I beg you to inform me in what way I may transmit to you that sum?' Mrs. Forster adds: 'This act of liberality and friendship, so delicately conceived not to wound my feelings, was immediately executed; and when I afterwards applied for the names of the "subscribers" for the publication, he gave me only two or three, stating that he had lost the list, and begging that I would excuse his carelessness.'

In exchange for some drawings by Dürer, an exchange which to-day we may think decidedly in Lawrence's favour, he made, in the last year of his life, a 'most lovely portrait' of Mrs. Forster's eldest daughter. He urges her to come soon to be drawn, 'for I shall too soon be an old man, and the sight of Age (especially in these smaller tasks) may have less power of doing justice to my subject'. Mrs. Forster says of this drawing: 'I have reason to believe that it was nearly, if not the last small drawing that he finished unless that of Miss Fanny Kemble was done subsequently to the date of my daughter's which was (in his own hand) June 1829; for he told me that he should not attempt any more in that style, as it was become too trying for his eyes.'

In 1826, after his return from Paris, Lawrence, says Williams, 'confined himself so much to his professional labours in his Attelier, that his correspondence by letter was little, and his social intercourse with his friends was scarcely more frequent'. From the latter statement we must except Miss Elizabeth Croft who, we may be sure, was constantly by his side in his rare moments of leisure. To the Academy Exhibition of this year Lawrence contributed his usual eight portraits, the most notable being that of the Hon. Mrs. Hope, whom he represented as 'an oriental Fatima, in a turban splendidly embroidered with gold, and a gown of a rich glowing red, ornamented gorgeously with jewels'. Williams describes this picture as 'glowing, rich, and gorgeous, without being meretricious, or in the least overpainted'. It was at this exhibition that Turner, by an act of great unselfishness, showed his sincere regard for Lawrence. A picture of his, a view of Cologne, had been hung between two of Lawrence's portraits which were, in consequence, entirely killed by the glowing richness of its colours. When the exhibition opened, however, Turner's picture was seen to be much toned down. It was so dull and dirty-looking that a friend rushed up to the painter to ask what had happened. 'Oh,' muttered Turner, 'poor Lawrence was so unhappy. It's only lampblack; it'll wash off after the exhibition.'

In the following year Lawrence's eight portraits again showed him at the height of his form, those of his friend Croker's adopted daughter, to which allusion has been made, and of Sir Walter Scott, being the most remarkable. The latter is in the Royal Collection at Windsor Castle. Scott and Jane Austen were Lawrence's favourite novelists and, as Miss Croft records, he used to read aloud from their works during his quiet evenings with her in Hart Street. He took immense pains with his portrait of Scott and the story has often been told of his efforts to get his distinguished sitter to assume a characteristic expression.

In the last two years of his life, even when his health was failing, Lawrence's powers showed little sign of diminution. His portrait of Lady Lyndhurst was harshly criticized, but those of Peel's young daughter, and of the Countess Gower and her child, exhibited in 1828, and those of Mrs. Lock senior, Robert Southey, Lord Durham and Miss Macdonald, exhibited in the following years, well sustained his reputation.

XVI

THE LAST ROMANCE

WHEN A man reaches the fifties it is inevitable that friends and associates of his youth should one by one disappear from the scene. By 1827 Lawrence had lost John Julius Angerstein, Benjamin West, Farington, Elizabeth, Duchess of Devonshire, his two brothers, his sister Lucy, and two artists whom he greatly admired, Fuseli and Flaxman. Cantankerous old Fuseli, who once said of Lawrence 'By Christ, he paints eyes better than Titian', died in 1825 at the ripe age of eight-four. Lawrence had bought many of his pictures and had a high opinion of him both as a man and as an artist. For a long time after his death Fuseli was almost forgotten, but in recent years there has been a tendency to regard him as one of the forerunners of Surrealism and his powers as a draughtsman have been generally recognised. Flaxman, one of the two Academicians who voted against Lawrence's election as President, died in 1826 at the age of seventy-two, and Lawrence paid a warm tribute to his memory in his address to the Academy students, on 11th December of that year. In the Duchess of Devonshire, who had settled in Rome in 1815 and established a salon frequented by her intimate friend, Cardinal Gonsalvi, and by such artists as Canova, Camuccini, Thorwaldsen and Granet, Lawrence lost a friend whom he greatly valued and with whom he was in constant correspondence. Writing of her death to Miss Croft, he says: 'Indeed, dear Elizabeth, I *have* lost a very true and sincerely valued Friend in this amiable Woman, and the many, the daily obligations that I ow'd to her during my stay at Rome, rise perpetually before me.'

Among the more recent friends who, to some extent, filled the gaps left by the older ones, John Wilson Croker, Secretary to the Admiralty, and Peel, later Sir Robert, were outstanding. Williams notes that Lawrence received from Peel 'more commissions than from any other person whatever, his late Majesty excepted: they were most liberally remunerated. The principal portraits he painted for this gentleman were of the Earl of Aberdeen and Mr. Huskisson; whole-lengths of the Duke of Wellington, the Earl of Liverpool, and Mr. Canning; Bishops——half-lengths of Lord Eldon and Lord Stowell, and Dr. Southey; a portrait of the late Sir Robert Peel, and portraits of the present baronet, two portraits of his lady, and one of their daughter. These form by far the most costly, valuable, and excellent collection of the portraits of Sir Thomas Lawrence. Sir Robert Peel is likewise the possessor of Lawrence's portrait of John Kemble in the character of Rolla'.

Lawrence's generosity in helping young artists in whose work he was interested was unfailing. Not only was he a lavish buyer of pictures and drawings from men who had not yet made their names, but he was prodigal of his time and trouble in aiding those who called on him with introductions. His prompt appreciation of Bonington's talent has already been referred to; less familiar is the help he gave to the American naturalist, Audubon, who came to England in 1826 to arrange for the publication of his famous and, to-day, much sought-after book, *Birds of America*.

Audubon, who was at that time quite unknown, presented himself at 65 Russell Square one morning at half-past eight, with a letter from an American artist, Thomas Sully, whose acquaintance Lawrence had made some years earlier. He had been warned by Sully that the President would be working in his studio at that early hour, and this proved to be the case. Lawrence read the letter, expressed his pleasure at meeting any American introduced to him by Sully, invited the visitor into his painting-room and insisted on his staying to breakfast. Audubon subsequently, in his memoirs, gave a detailed account of the interview and its sequel, which illustrates Lawrence's unfailing benevolence. The description he gives of Lawrence at work has sufficient interest to be worth quoting. After expressing his astonishment at finding the room had a southern light, Audubon says that: 'Upon his easel was a canvas (Kitcat) on which was a perfect drawing in black chalk, beautifully finished, of a nobleman; and on a large

easel a full-size portrait of a lady represented in the open air.
On the latter he went to work. I saw that his palette was enormous, and looked as if already prepared by some one else, with the
various tints wanted, and that he had an almost innumerable
number of brushes and pencils of all descriptions. He now glazed
one part of his picture, and then re-touched another part with fine
colours, and in a deliberate way which did not indicate that he
was in any haste to finish it. He next laid down his palette and
turning to the chalk drawing upon the unpainted canvas, asked
how I liked his manner of proceeding . . .'

A servant came in and announced that breakfast was ready. On
their way down to the living-room Audubon remarked on the
very large number of unfinished portraits he saw, to which
Lawrence mildly replied: 'My dear Sir, this is my only misfortune. I cannot tell if I shall ever see the day when they will all
be finished.' When Audubon left the house at ten o'clock three
carriages were waiting at the door. Later, in spite of his press of
work, Lawrence made time to go to Audubon's lodgings and
examine his pictures. He asked the prices of several of them and
then, to the young American's surprise, said 'he would bring a
few purchasers that very day if I would remain at home. This I
promised, and he left me very greatly relieved. In about two
hours', Audubon continues, 'he returned with two gentlemen
to whom he did not introduce me, but who were pleased with
my work. One purchased the *Otter Caught in a Trap*, for which
he gave me twenty pounds sterling, and the other *A Group of
Common Rabbits* for fifteen sovereigns. I took the pictures to the
carriage which stood at the door, and they departed, leaving me
more amazed than I had been by their coming.' Lawrence paid
Audubon a second visit, this time bringing three friends with him
who each bought a picture for £7, £10 and £35 respectively
and, as before, 'the party and pictures left together in a splendid
carriage with liveried footmen'. Although, on this occasion, it
was by an expenditure of his valuable time and exertion of his
far-reaching influence that Lawrence was able to help an unknown
and penniless stranger, on the principle of *qui facit per alios facit
per se*, Audubon's gratitude was well deserved. 'Without the sale

of these pictures,' he writes, 'I was a bankrupt before my work was seriously begun, and in two days more, I should have seen all my hopes of the publication blasted; for Mr. Havell (the engraver) had already called to say that on Saturday I must pay him £60. I was then not only not worth a penny, but had actually borrowed five pounds a few days before, to purchase materials for my pictures. But these pictures which Sir Thomas sold for me enabled me to pay my borrowed money and to appear full-handed when Mr. Havell called.'

In 1827 the health of his deeply loved surviving sister caused Lawrence great anxiety, and although he was 'toiling with distracted attention between sitters and the Exhibition', he yet managed to pay her a hasty visit at Rugby. Later in the year, when she had recovered from her illness, Mrs. Bloxam invited him to stay with herself and her family at Aberystwyth. He was reluctantly compelled to decline this invitation, and in the course of a long letter to Mrs. Boucherette he tells her why he felt bound to join Lord Londonderry's party at Doncaster instead. He writes:

'You will be surprised at the date of my letter. I am sure it demands explanation. Lord Londonderry, as Lord Stewart, I knew above twenty years ago; and from that time to the present hour, he has been my constant and zealous friend. With him, in the year 1815, I lived at Paris—with him, for five months, at Vienna. Through him, very principally, that mission (if not originating with him) was conducted, which led to all subsequent distinctions in my profession. For him I painted my first portrait of His Majesty—for him my first of the Duke of Wellington. For some five years past he has each year invited me to see him at Winyard, and I have been compelled to decline each invitation; but it has this year been so kindly, strongly urged, coupled with the desire that I should meet the Duke of Wellington, (who knows of my invitation), and it has likewise been so seconded by the pain of fearing that I might seem to treat it with ungrateful indifference, when political circumstances have separated him from the government, and the private regard of His Majesty;—all this, I say, has made it impossible for me to decline the pleasure of joining him.

And I have therefore, by agreement, met him, with Lady L., at this place, where for two days more, I am engaged in all the dissipation and important (to many fatally deep) interests of these races, which I see for the first time, and for the fourth in my life of any race. The scene has for me all the novelty that youth could have given it, and almost all the pleasure, in the race itself; whilst the company is only all London, with the slight addition of all Yorkshire and Derbyshire added to it. I was at Almack's the night before last; and dined at Devonshire House yesterday. But you have been lady steward or lady patroness of Lincolnshire, and know what it all is. Lord Fitzwilliam's set-out beats even the Duke's, who is steward. The former, with six horses, four gentlemen following the carriage, and twelve outriders; and Lord Milton's the same—the Duke with twelve outriders. Immense sums were yesterday lost by Lord B—d, by Lord M—n, and his brother (absolute ruin!) and many others to large amount.

How I rejoice to hear of the continued health of all my loved friends, so deeply (and oh, how justly!) valued by me! . . .

Dear Mrs. Lock's [portrait] will be my greatest beauty, and best picture, of my next exhibition.'

If Lawrence forbore to plunge at the Doncaster races, he made up for it by his lavish expenditure on works of art and soon after his return to London he was again in financial difficulties. The following letter, addressed to Peel, speaks for itself.

'MY DEAR SIR,

My servant, I believe, informed you that I could not benefit by your kind invitation for Wednesday. I should speak of the pleasure which your visit gave me; but I am now writing on an unpleasant topic, and with an unquiet mind.

By notice from my banker, late this day, I find myself more inconvenienced in money matters than I had ignorantly expected, and the occasion is urgent. In this exigency, I take the liberty to ask you if your present arrangements admit of your affording me an essential service, by the payment, at this too early period, of the last moiety of the portraits of Mr. Canning and Mr. Southey.

I think I may be sure, without report from others, that you like the latter picture; but it is far from finished;—it may be wholly changed. They will both, however, with your permission, be in the Exhibition.

I write this letter this Saturday evening. Early in the morning I go to Windsor, to carry the successful print of His Majesty to the King. May I hope for your answer, friendly in either case, on my return in the evening?'

Peel's reply was prompt and satisfactory.

The last two years of Lawrence's life were two of the most active and eventful of his term as President. Of his eight portraits in the exhibition of 1829, although that of Southey came in for a certain amount of criticism, two were, in his own estimation, the best he had painted. These were whole-lengths of the Duchess of Richmond and the Marchioness of Salisbury. Like many other artists, Lawrence was a poor judge of his own work.

In a letter to his sister, dated 7th May 1829, he says: 'Many, many thanks for your remembering my birth-day. It is not attended to as it ought to have been; but at least professional fame is mine; and the hope of my youth, and pursuit of my life, comparatively achieved; and the love of my family still continued to me. At this moment I have been called from my letter by a visit from Mr. Prince Hoare, my old Bath friend, who for many years has been our Foreign Secretary [at the Royal Academy] having spent a life of activity and rectitude, which now terminates in ease and wealth. You remember old Mr. Hoare well. Let me hope to know that your health is improving.' In this letter he tells Mrs. Bloxam of the 'severe illness of Mrs. Wolff, who is suffering from cold, and constant fever; though the physician's report is still decided, that the lungs are not affected and that she will recover soon'. The physician's report was, unhappily, fallacious, for she died a few months later. After her separation from her husband, Mrs. Wolff went to live with her sister, Mrs. Marshall, at Charing, in Kent, about fifty miles from London, but no doubt she frequently stayed with Elizabeth Croft in Hart Street. About eight years before her death, however, she retired to Herefordshire, near Monmouth, and Lawrence was only able to pay her two short visits. He kept up a constant correspondence with her, and the letters which have been preserved, some of which contain long passages of literary criticism, show that, apart from their tender feelings for each other, they shared intellectual interests. At her death he accompanied her brother into Herefordshire to attend her funeral and for some time afterwards he was so upset that he felt unable to meet his friends. In a letter to Mrs. Angerstein he says: 'You will naturally look for some adequate cause for this depression, and it is told in a few words. I have lost a deeply valued and revered friend! one who, without injustice, I could almost say, even to you and dear Mrs. Boucherette, was worthy, from genius, right principle, benevolence and piety, to have been known, and been esteemed and loved by you.'

The extraordinary contrast between the sexual morals of the court and aristocracy, with whom Lawrence, for professional reasons, was forced to spend so much of his time, and those of the middle classes was never more clearly revealed than by the expressions of horror in which Mrs. Angerstein and others indulged at the suggestion made by a gossip-writer in the *Literary Gazette* that Mrs. Wolff had been Lawrence's mistress. The Duke of Wellington and Lord Abercorn unblushingly paraded their mistresses before the public gaze, and Lawrence had painted both the ladies in question. Marital infidelity was the rule rather than the exception in the fashionable world, and, in a loose-living and philoprogenitive age, natural children abounded in the households of the great, from the Royal Family downwards. Yet Lawrence and his intimate circle were more Victorian than the Victorians in their respect for female virtue. Mrs. Angerstein wrote to another woman, after Lawrence's death, saying that she 'spurned the calumny with all the indignation it merited', quoting Lawrence as having said of Mrs. Wolff that 'her purity and exalted piety were such that you would have found in her a congenial spirit'. She remarks also, as proof of Mrs. Wolff's 'purity', that Lawrence introduced the lady 'to Mrs. Ottley and her daughters, a family for whom he entertained the warmest friendship and an exalted esteem'. Although, in an age which has outgrown

Victorian hypocrisy and in which a woman who takes a lover is no longer regarded as 'fallen', this sort of talk strikes rather a false note, it should be said at once that there is no reason to suppose that Mrs. Wolff's morals were not as spotless as her friends declared or that Lawrence's relations with her were other than platonic.

After Mrs. Wolff's death, Lawrence's health and energies suffered a decline and the effects of long years of ceaseless labour began seriously to tell on him. 'Outwardly,' says Allan Cunningham, 'he had something of the look of health; his fine frame continued erect, and his finer countenance retained its vivacity; but he began to feel that a little fatigued him; that he could not move without pain; while the utter confusion of his accounts, and the trouble which he had in making his income meet his outlay, pressed sorely on him, and between them occasioned that melancholy drooping of the spirit to which he was latterly liable.' In the speech he made in reply to the toast of his health at the dinner of the Artists' Fund in 1829 he revealed a premonition that his years in harness were drawing to an end. 'I am now advanced in life,' he said, 'and the time of decay is coming; but, come when it will, I hope to have the good sense not to prolong the contest for fame with younger and, perhaps, abler men. No self-love shall prevent me from retiring, and that cheerfully, to privacy; and I consider I shall do but an act of justice to others as well as mercy to myself.'

During the autumn of this year and as the winter advanced, his friends began to notice that he looked pale, walked feebly and was apt to be overtaken with drowsiness in company. 'He complained that his eyes and forehead felt hot in the evenings; and he frequently relieved himself by bathing them in cold water.' It was when he was in this melancholy condition of mind and body that Lawrence suddenly found himself involved in what was to prove his last romance. The stage début of Mrs. Siddons's eighteen-year-old niece, Fanny Kemble, rekindled the embers of his life-long passion, and gave him a new interest in life during the short space that remained to him. Like the hero of Thomas Hardy's *The Well-Beloved*, he was still faithful in his old age to his youthful ideal. Fanny, who was the daughter of Charles Kemble and his

FANNY KEMBLE

From a lithograph by R. J. Lane after the drawing by Lawrence. In the Lawrence Collection, British Museum.

LORD BROUGHAM AND VAUX 1778–1868
In the National Portrait Gallery.

French wife, Marie-Thérèse, bore little resemblance either in character or looks to the sweet, unassuming Sally Siddons with whom Lawrence had been so passionately in love and for whom he had never ceased to wear mourning. She was, however, distinctly a Kemble, had some of the bold good looks of the tall, dark, brown-eyed Maria Siddons and a share at least of the talent, if none of the genius, of her incomparable aunt. The psychological complexities of the relationship between Mrs. Siddons and Lawrence, both when he was in love with her daughters and after their death, are so great that even the most perceptive investigators have not succeeded in unravelling them completely. It has been assumed that Mrs. Siddons realised after Sally's death that, despite the disparity in their ages, she herself had always been in love with Lawrence and therefore subconsciously jealous of her daughters. Whether Lawrence's feeling for her was ever complicated by the appeal of her physical attractions or whether he was only enraptured by her genius is not so clear. Did they ever embrace, in their more emotional moments? We shall never know. Perhaps the truth is that none of the parties concerned could have analysed their feelings or explained, either to themselves or to others, the exact nature of the emotional chains which bound them together.

Although it is improbable that Lawrence met Mrs. Siddons except on very rare occasions during the last ten years of his life, two letters at least have been preserved which show that their affection for each other continued to the end unimpaired. On 29th June 1826 Lawrence wrote a hasty note, marked 'Private', which speaks for itself. He says:

'At a moment of hurry I am obliged to enter too abruptly on the subject of the intended publication of the Life of Dear Mrs. Siddons.

Do you give me your reactions for my lending to Mr. Boaden the Portrait I had the honor and happiness to paint of you for Miss Lee? In entire ignorance of your objections to the Work, I wrote to Miss Harriet to borrow the Picture, being naturally anxious that no representation of you should be given to the World that had not *something* of you.

Miss Lee informed me as her answer, that you disapprov'd of the publication—I can easily imagine many motives for your doing so, but as Mr. B. informs me that he confines himself solely to your public Life, and is so pledg'd to the Booksellers that the Work must go on, may it not be as well that the Portrait should be engraved for it?

Alas! It is not what I expected it would be—I think it inferior to that from which it was painted; which is now either with you or with Mrs. Kemble. I should be very glad to get that, and the time for which it would be wanted would be short.

With a thousand respects and a fixed, the very highest, Esteem, that has never known diminution

Ever

Dear Mrs. Siddons

Oblig'd and Devoted

LAWRENCE.'

The second letter, from Mrs. Siddons to Lawrence, has no formal beginning, is dated 12th June 1828 and contains a request, on behalf of some person well-known to them both, which she has no hesitation in making. It runs:

'Poor Rowsham was with me this morning TO SAY FAREWELL, and to beg that I will inform you, the two situations for which he has solicited your influence, are now vacant; I know it is unnecessary to urge any motive for your performance of a benevolent action, and therefore only take the liberty of recommending him to your recollection; I have no more to say but— Farewel! and God bless you! SARAH SIDDONS.'

The announcement that Fanny Kemble was about to make her début aroused in Lawrence a more than paternal excitement. Owing to his long friendship with her parents, he was able to put at her disposal both his knowledge and experience of the stage, and of the art of acting, and his exceptional social influence. The fact that the President of the Royal Academy, whose studio was besieged by eager clients desirous of having their portraits painted or finished, had begged her to sit for him, afforded her début a publicity-value which no other young actress on the threshold of her career could have hoped to secure. Writing about her to John Angerstein, Lawrence said that she had 'eyes and hair like Mrs. Siddons in her finest time', and a voice 'at once sweet and powerful', and no doubt he wrote to numerous other friends in a similar vein. He told Angerstein that he had for many years given up the theatre, but 'this fine genius has drawn me often to it, and each time to witness improvement and new beauties. . . . Her manner in private is characterised by ease and that modest gravity which, I believe, must belong to high tragic genius, and which, in Mrs. Siddons, was strictly natural to her, though, from being peculiar in the genial gaiety of society, it was often thought assumed'.

The début took place early in October when she played Juliet at Covent Garden, with great success. Old Mrs. Siddons, in a black velvet gown, was ushered into a box just before the curtain rose and was at once recognised and warmly applauded by the audience. Charles Greville, who had not Lawrence's reasons for regarding Fanny with special interest or favour, was not greatly impressed either by the girl or by her performance. 'I saw Miss Fanny Kemble for the first time on Friday,' he wrote, 'and was disappointed. She is short, ill made, with large hands and feet, an expressive countenance, though not handsome, fine eyes, teeth and hair, not devoid of grace, and with great energy and spirit, her voice good, though she has a little of the drawl of her family. She wants the pathos and tenderness of Miss O'Neill, and she excites no emotion; but she is very young, clever, and may become a very good, perhaps a fine actress. Mrs. Siddons was not so good at her age. She fills the house every night.'

Although Lawrence's letters to Fanny have not been preserved, we can gather, from her replies to them, how greatly he exerted himself on her behalf. 'I know not how properly to express my sense of the favour you conferred on my performance,' she says, in one of them, 'by your kind and tasteful criticisms, but I prefer thanking you inadequately to not expressing at all how much I feel obliged to you, for the kind interest you take in my improvement. The promptest method of testifying my gratitude I have however adopted, that of carefully avoiding those defects and embracing those refinements which you pointed out to me.' In another letter she shows that in spite of her appreciation of Lawrence's tasteful criticisms she has a decided will of her own. 'I do not know that you have convinced me about "Shall I Swear"', she writes, 'and tho' I feel the utter impossibility of opposing any judgment of yours, yet unless my own feeling agreed with the alteration, I think you would but find it a change for the worse. I have your letter by me and shall read both that and the part again very carefully before Wednesday—and even then do not be very disappointed if I should be flat and ineffective, for I really hardly can tell myself on what success depends'. Later, after thanking Lawrence for his 'kind and magnificent remembrance of me on my birthday', she says: 'My Mother has communicated to me your criticism on my way of falling . . . if you were there (at the theatre) you will I hope have seen that I endeavoured to improve my last moments, and fell indeed (not without a few cowardly misgivings) in a straight line with the lamps. . . .'

On 1st December Greville notes that he dined in London 'with Byng, [Thomas] Moore, [Washington] Irving, Sir T. Lawrence, and Vesey Fitzgerald; very agreeable'. He makes no record of the conversation, but it is unlikely that Lawrence, who by this time was entirely captivated by Fanny Kemble, refrained from discussing her performances. Three days before his death, on 4th January 1830, he wrote to his friend, Mrs. Hayman, about Fanny's growing success and mentions that she showed greater power in the part of Belvidera, (in Otway's *Venice Preserved*), than she had in Juliet. 'Let me give you Washington Irving's opinion of her to me, the other night at Mr. Peel's,' he continues. 'She is much more beautiful in private than she is on the stage, and the nearer one gets to her Face and to her mind, the more beautiful they both are. Now *I* have never ventured to say half as much, for why my Dear Friend? Why, because be it known to you, I have the shackles of "Sixty" upon me, and therefore these Love-chains would turn into skeletons of Roses, did anyone attempt to throw them round me. But tho' I seldom see her, I have almost a Father's interest for her, and a Father's resentment towards those who will not see the promise of almost all that genius can do, because they have seen the unequall'd Power, the glorious countenance and Figure of Mrs. Siddons or are captivated by the contortions of Mr. Kean . . . To give you [a] notion of the range of power of which Fanny Kemble is capable, her Juliet is the sweetest that I have ever seen, and I should not have the slightest doubt of her success were she to appear tomorrow as Lady Macbeth. In five minutes she would conquer all disadvantage of figure and people would only feel that creatures of the most daring energy were to be found in women of small stature as in Men.'

Fanny Kemble, although, in one sense, Lawrence's last romance, was able to capture his heart, although she was unaware of it, because of his Siddons 'fixation'. Whereas she thought of her Aunt Siddons as an old lady 'tottering on the brink of the tomb', a figure from the past, to Lawrence she remained the most wonderful woman he had ever known. None of the passions of the mind, not even his passion for the genius of Michaelangelo, exceeded his passion for the genius of the Tragick Muse. The keynote of his character was fidelity in every essential human relationship. No man was ever more loyal to his parents and his family, to his friends, to his art and to the women he loved. In the sole recorded instance of his infidelity, his remorse at having let Maria seduce him from his allegiance to Sally nearly drove him out of his mind. Mrs. Kemble, when she was looking at his finished drawing of Fanny, tactlessly remarked: 'She is very like Maria Siddons.' Lawrence in a choked voice replied: 'Oh, she is very like her! She is very like them all!' In her memoirs, written many years after these events, Fanny recalls that when her mother told Lawrence that Mrs. Siddons had said to her husband: 'Charles, when I die, I wish to be carried to my grave by you and Lawrence', he was too upset to go on with work. 'This strange man,' Fanny remarks, 'fell into one of these paroxysms of emotion.'

On Fanny's birthday, the 'magnificent remembrance', for which she thanked him, had taken the form of a proof-plate of an engraving of Reynolds' picture of the Tragick Muse. On this he had inscribed the words: 'This portrait by England's greatest painter, of the noblest subject of his pencil, is presented to her niece and worthy successor, by her most faithful humble friend and servant, Lawrence.' He had the picture elaborately framed and sent it round to Buckingham Gate, where the Charles Kembles were then living, with his compliments. But later on trains of thought, started, perhaps, by Mrs. Kemble's unfortunately timed remarks, made him uneasy. Had he allowed himself to be betrayed into disloyalty? Mrs. Siddons, the incomparable, could have no real 'successor' and, if Fanny did in fact resemble Maria, she could hardly be described as a 'worthy' one. Whatever may have been his secret reflections and motives, he called at Buckingham Gate and recovered the picture on the pretext that he wanted it differently framed. For some days it lay on his table, untouched. Then he told his servant to take out the engraving and with his pen he cancelled the words 'and worthy successor'. When the picture had been put back into its frame, he said to the man 'Cover it up. I cannot bear to look at it'. In the light of what we know about Fanny Kemble in the later stages of her career, it is interesting to speculate as to whether Mrs. Kemble's chance reference to Maria had given Lawrence an inkling of Fanny's real nature. The strain of ruthlessness in the Kemble character, of which Maria had provided so devastating an example, became exaggerated in Fanny when she reached middle age. Mrs. Lynn Linton, who as a young girl had the misfortune to come in contact with her, left among her possessions an account of the effect she made. 'The deep voice and stage-stateliness of her manner,' she wrote, 'the assumption of supremacy and really cruel strength of this lady, crushed me flat. The way in which she levelled her black eyes at me, and calmly put her foot on me, was an experience never to be forgotten. The pitiless brutality of her contradictions, her scathing sarcasm, the contemptuous taunts, knowing that I was unable to answer her, the way in which she used her matured powers to wound and hurt my even then immature nature, gave me a certain shuddering horror for her, such as I fancy a man would feel, for one who had flayed him in the market-place. I am thankful to Fate who never threw us together again.'

Lawrence's unfinished portrait of Maria, which reveals the same 'pitiless brutality', is immediately called to mind by this description of the virago which the girl who so resembled her was to become in later life.

Lawrence intended to paint a full-length portrait of Fanny Kemble in the new year, but his sudden death intervened. He had wanted to spend Christmas at Rugby with his sister, who had again been ill, but was prevented from doing so owing to pressure of work which included the completion of his portrait of Canning for Peel. In a letter written on 26th December he tells Mrs. Bloxam: 'I have unfortunately made engagements that demand my attention till the 5th or 6th. *On the 6th I have sacredly pledged myself to be with you*, and to that ALL circumstances shall bend.' On 6th January, he wrote: 'I meant, my dearest Ann, to be with you by dinner time to-morrow, and have made exertions to do so, but it may not, cannot be! You must be content to see me to a late simple dinner on Friday. Pray pardon a disappointment so painfully given by your faithful and affectionate brother.' This was the last letter he was destined to write, for he died on the following day, 7th January. Miss Croft, who, with his friend and sole executor, Mr. Archibald Keightley, was constantly with him during the last days of his life, gave Williams a detailed description of its closing scenes. She had returned to London on 31st December and found Lawrence apparently as well as usual. On New Year's Day, when she called, he was engaged with a sitter, Lord Seaford, but he returned her visit later in the afternoon and mentioned that Mulready [William Mulready, R.A.] was dining with him and that Mrs. Ottley and her children were coming afterwards to spend the evening. On the following day (Saturday, 2nd January) when she called to ask the loan of his carriage she was struck by his pallid countenance and was distressed to learn that he had been very ill most of the preceding night. He sent for his doctor, Doctor Holland, who considered his illness to be an 'attack of the stomach', but gave him leave to keep an important dinner engagement with Peel, on condition that he was careful as to what he ate and drank. Miss Croft dined with him on the Sunday, met Mr. Keightley and Herman Wolff at his house, and passed 'one of those delightful and never-to-be-forgotten evenings, of which it has been my pride and happiness to partake, in common with other intimate friends, as often as three times a week for the last three months. He complained of feeling weak, and looked extremely pale. . . . In the course of this evening, he gave the finishing touches to a proof engraving from the beautiful drawing which he did for me in 1812, of Mrs. Wolff, with the boy and dog; and expressed great pleasure at the way in which Mr. Bromley had executed it—the eye in particular'. Miss Croft saw him again on the Monday and Tuesday. On Tuesday he went out in his carriage and did some work on a portrait of the King. He was in better spirits and told some amusing stories. On the morning of the 6th he complained of a slight return of his pain, but he 'made an effort to rouse himself to exertion, and painted nearly an hour, on his Majesty's portrait'. Miss Croft asked him if he was not tired of 'painting on those eternal robes of the Bath (Garter)?—He replied, "No, I always find variety in them"— What then do you mean, that the pictures are not all precisely alike?—"In outline precisely, but not in detail; for if you would compare them, I hope you would find the last was still the best". That evening after dinner, he had intended going to the Athenæum and had his great coat hanging before the fire, but apparently Mr. Keightley and Miss Croft, who called at half past nine, managed to dissuade him as he "complained a good deal of distressing sensations, and feared his pain was returning". Mr. Keightley assisted him by lifting a portfolio, containing the engravings of Miss Kemble, which he owned he had been looking wistfully at, and felt too listless to remove'. Miss Croft suggested that a little weak brandy and water might do him good. He seemed pleased at the suggestion, making the revealing comment that the few times in his life he had tried brandy, it had always been with so happy an effect as to make him fear growing fond of it. Finding he had no good brandy in the house, Miss Croft says: 'We came away, taking one of his servants, to fetch him a bottle from Mr. Keightley's chambers.'

During the night he was taken seriously ill and his valet, Jean Duts, had to call in Dr. Holland, who applied leeches and fomentations, and relieved him of sixteen ounces of blood. Miss Croft was appalled by the change of his countenance when she saw him after the doctor had left. In the afternoon Sir Henry Halford called and approved of what had been done and 'merely ordered a more active cathartic'. Two hours later Lawrence, feeling better, sent his servant to fetch Mr. Keightley to read him an article by Campbell on the genius of Flaxman, in the *New Monthly Magazine*, and when the reading started he stretched out a hand to Miss Croft, who was sitting close beside him. 'I did not see it, till he gently touched my knee,' she relates, 'and I then pressed his hand between mine, which friendly grasp he ardently returned—and this was the last mark of his long-tried affection.'

After Mr. Keightley had read for about a quarter of an hour, Lawrence asked him and Miss Croft to leave the room and 'send Jean to him and no one else. In about ten minutes we heard hurried steps in the passage and found that, in moving, his arm had bled again . . . The loss of blood was immaterial, but the effect of the medicine brought on faintness'. Sal volatile was given him, but later he slipped from his chair and expired in the arms of his devoted servant. His last words were: 'Jean, my good fellow, this is dying.'

The news of Lawrence's sudden death caused the greatest grief to his family, his small circle of intimate friends and the great majority of his professional colleagues. The King, who was himself to die before the end of the year, sincerely mourned one who was not only his favourite painter but also a friend for whom he had a sincere regard. Everyone connected with the arts in Britain, from his brother Academicians to connoisseurs and picture dealers and from struggling painters and engravers to actors, art critics, poets and men of letters, felt that the cultural life of the nation had suffered a great loss from his departure. What Fanny Kemble's personal feelings were, we do not know, but at least she had the grace to dash off a note to Mrs. Siddons's youngest daughter, her cousin Cecilia, which shows that she realised what pain the news of Lawrence's death would cause her aunt.

'MY DEAREST CECY,

[First word illegible] never fly fast and the loss of a great man is soon known everywhere', she wrote, 'but in case your Mother should not yet have heard of it, you had better prepare her for the news of Sir Thomas Lawrence's death—if she has not yet been apprised of it you may save her in some degree the shock which I fear the intelligence must give her.

With love from all, ever affectionately yours,

FANNY KEMBLE.'

According to Williams, the ossification of the aorta and vessels of the heart, to which his death was attributed, was too slight to have occasioned it. 'The real cause,' he alleges, 'was probably the depletion of the blood-vessels: or, in other terms, this great and estimable character was bled, or rather had bled, to death.' Archibald Keightley, however, against this passage wrote in the margin of his copy of Williams's biography: 'This is entirely false —A.K.' Layard thought it of interest to submit the report of the post-mortem to a medical friend of wide experience, and the result was inconclusive. If Williams, who had many ideas which in his day would be regarded as progressive, was a convert to the 'Brunonian system' and an opponent of phlebotomy, it can only be said that time has justified him.

The newspapers paid their conventional tributes to the memory of the late President of the Royal Academy, but of more interest to present-day readers is the account of Lawrence which Charles Greville jotted down the day after his death. This gives a fair picture of Lawrence as he appeared to contemporaries who had only a slight personal acquaintance with him and knew him chiefly as a public figure.

'He was *longè primus* of all living Painters,' Greville wrote, 'and has left no one fit to succeed him in the chair of the Royal Academy. Lawrence was about sixty, very like Canning in appearance, remarkably gentlemanlike, with very mild manners, though rather too *douceureux*, agreeable in society, unassuming, and not a great talker; his mind was highly cultivated, he had a taste for every kind of literature, and was enthusiastically devoted to his art and seldom came into a room without carefully examining every picture it contained; he was very industrious and painted an immense number of portraits, but many of his earlier works are still unfinished, and great complaints used to be made of his exacting either the whole or half payment when he began a picture, but that when he had got the money he could never be prevailed on to complete it.' It should be interposed here that to ask payment of half the agreed price, when the first sitting was given, was a recognised practice among portrait-painters at this period. The complaints made against Lawrence, admittedly justified in very many cases, were due to the fact that he often let years elapse before finishing portraits of which the heads alone were drawn in. At the time of his death an enormous number of unfinished portraits were found in his studio. No reliable record seems to have been kept of what eventually happened to them. It is probable that many were completed by other painters and have since been put on the market as genuine Lawrences which, as the drawing of the heads was the essential part of them, in a sense they are.

'Although he is supposed to have earned immense sums by his pictures,' Greville continues, 'he has always been a distressed man, without any visible means of expense, except a magnificent collection of drawings by the ancient Masters, said to be the finest in the world, and procured at great cost. He was, however, a generous patron of young artists of merit and talent. It was always said that he lost money at play, but this assertion seems to have proceeded more from the difficulty of reconciling his pecuniary embarrassments with his enormous profits than from any proof of the fact. This and some other trifling circumstances (quite insufficient to establish a case) have sometimes excited surmises of another mode of spending his money, which would fully account for his poverty. He was a great Courtier, and is said to have been so devoted to the King, that he would not paint anybody who was personally obnoxious to H.M.; but I do not believe this is true. He is an irreparable loss; since Sir Joshua there has been no painter like him; his Portraits as pictures I think are not nearly so fine as Sir Joshua's, but as likenesses many of them are quite perfect. Moore's was the last portrait he painted, and Miss Kemble's his last drawing.'

XVII

THE LAST WILL AND TESTAMENT

WHEN Lawrence died he was as usual in financial difficulties and one of the last letters he received was from
his bankers, acquainting him that they would make 'in
anticipation the advance mentioned'. The terms of his will show
that at the time it was drawn up he had no real appreciation
either of the value of his estate or the extent of his liabilities.
Actually he died insolvent, and had it not been for the generosity
of his creditors in assenting to the greater part of the cost of his
elaborate funeral being paid out of his assets, his executor would
have had to foot the bill. Campbell the poet, who was prevented
from writing Lawrence's life by business considerations, which he
explained convincingly, and at great length, in a letter to Miss
Croft, was well acquainted with his personal affairs and was
convinced that his chronic impecuniosity was due in great part
to his carelessness about money matters and a lack of ordinary
circumspection which made him utterly heedless about keeping
accounts. 'I could not credit the fact,' he says, 'unless I had had it
from the best authority, that he kept his books so imperfectly as
to have omitted a debt of five hundred guineas due to him from
one of the noblest families in the kingdom; and it is probable that
he omitted other sitters who were not so punctilious as that family
in volunteering the payment of the unclaimed debt to his
executor.'

The Royal Academy passed a resolution expressing the strong
wish that the funeral should be a public one, and agreeing to pay
'the expense incurred under their own roof and by the attendance
of their own body'. This amounted only to £152 9s., out of a
total cost of £1,000, the balance being paid out of the estate.
Lawrence's remains were removed the night before the public

ceremony, which took place on 21st January 1830, in a hearse and four and conveyed to Somerset House. The body was received by the officers and council of the Royal Academy and placed in the model-room, which had been previously hung with black cloth, and lighted with large wax tapers and numerous wax candles in silver sconces. Here it lay in state until the procession started to St. Paul's Cathedral on the following morning. It is interesting to note that at the head of the coffin was placed a large hatchment of the armorial bearings of the deceased, and that the pall over it 'bore the escutcheons of his arms wrought in silk'. The arms were, of course, as bogus as the pedigree which Lysons, through misplaced zeal, invented to justify Lawrence's use of them, but the social conventions of the period condoned such laxity. Half the arms in use during the early part of the nineteenth century were neither registered nor authorised by the College of Heralds.

The love of pageantry engrained in the English character found full expression in the arrangements made by the undertaker, Thornton, for the President's burial in St. Paul's. Both the procession and the service at the Cathedral were conducted with masterly stage-management and the effect must have been impressive in the extreme. As an example of what public funerals were like at the close of the Georgian era, it may be excusable to quote the exact order of the procession which followed Lawrence's body to the great West door of St. Paul's.

'Twelve Peace-officers to clear the way.
Four Marshalmen, with hatbands and gloves, two by two.
Two City Marshals, on horseback, with scarves, and hatbands and crape round their left arms.
The Lord Mayor's carriage.
Carriages of the Two Sheriffs.
The Two Under-Sheriffs.
The Undertaker on Horseback (Mr. E. Thornton).
Four Mutes on horseback.
Six Horsemen in cloaks, two by two.
The Lid of Feathers and two Feather Pages.

THE HEARSE.
Drawn by six horses, with five Pages on each side.
Mourning Coaches and pairs, with Feathers and Velvet hangings and two pages to each.

Eight Pall Bearers.

Earl of Aberdeen	Rt. Hon. Sir G. Murray
Earl Gower	Rt. Hon. J. W. Croker
Rt. Hon. Robert Peel	Hart Davis, Esqre, M.P.
Hon. Agar Ellis	Earl Clanwilliam.'

The mourners, who included seven members of the Bloxam family, other relatives and connections, Mr. Keightley, the Executor and 'the confidential attendant of the deceased', presumably Jean Duts, followed the pall-bearers. After them came the officers and members of the council of the Royal Academy, Academicians, Associates, Associate engravers, including W. Bromley and R. J. Lane, and students of the Royal Academy. An impressive concourse of the 'nobility and gentry' came next, headed by Washington Irving, Esqre, American Secretary of Legation, and two Gentlemen in the suite of the Ambassador. An enormous number of carriages, most of which, as Turner bitterly remarked, were empty, followed in the rear of the procession. Lawrence's body was deposited in the grave prepared for it, in the crypt of the Cathedral, adjoining the remains of Benjamin West and close to the graves of Reynolds, Fuseli, Barry, Opie and Sir Christopher Wren. He could hardly have found himself in more congenial company.

The task which faced the Executor, Archibald Keightley, was one of the utmost difficulty, and he performed it, in the ensuing years, in a manner which gained him the approbation and respect of everyone concerned with Lawrence's affairs. That it proved impossible for him to give effect to Lawrence's public-spirited intentions was due to no lack of zeal on his part, but resulted from circumstances which could not have been foreseen by the testator. Not only was the late President's estate heavily encumbered and his accounts in their usual confusion, but it was exceedingly difficult, owing to market fluctuations and other causes, to arrive at any accurate computation of the value of his assets. Conscious that he had spent much more money than he could afford on his drawings by the Old Masters, Lawrence refused to face the facts and made matters more difficult for his Executor by omitting to keep any accurate accounts of his expenditure on them. Shortly before his death, and about two years after his will was drawn up, he happened to meet the picture-dealer Hogarth who, in a published letter, left a record of their conversation. After Hogarth had expressed his hope that a collection which had cost £70,000 would never be dispersed, Lawrence said: 'I have taken care that it never will be. But why do you say it cost so much? You are mistaken.' Hogarth then rapidly calculated the cost of the outstanding drawings alone, and Lawrence was forced to admit that his estimate was correct. Unfortunately, as we shall see, Lawrence's elaborate precautions for preserving his collection as a whole and assuring its retention in England proved abortive.

The provisions of Lawrence's last Will and Testament are so interesting for the light they throw on his character that some extracts from it must be quoted.

'*July 28th* 1828—My collection of genuine drawings, by the old masters, which in number and value, I know to be unequalled in Europe, and which I am fully justified in estimating, as a collection, at twenty thousand pounds, I desire may be first offered to His most gracious Majesty, King George IV at the sum of eighteen thousand pounds; and if His Majesty shall not be pleased to purchase the same at that price, then, that the collection be offered, at the same price to the trustees of the British Museum, and afterwards, successively, to the Right Honourable Robert Peel, and to the Right Honourable the Earl of Dudley; and if none of such offers shall be accepted, then I desire that the Collection may be forthwith advertised in the principal capitals of Europe and elsewhere; and if, within two years, a purchaser shall not be found at the sum of twenty thousand pounds, then I desire that the same may be sold by public auction, or private contract, in London, either altogether or in separate lots, at such price or prices, and in such a manner, as my executor shall think best.

And I desire that like offers may be made to his Majesty (and if he shall not be pleased to make the purchase, then to the trustees of the British Museum) of two volumes of drawings by Fra Bartolomeo, from the collection of the late President of the Royal Academy, Benjamin West, Esqre, at the sum of eight hundred pounds; and that the series of original cartoons of *The Last Supper*, by Leonardo da Vinci, at the sum of one thousand pounds, and my picture by Rembrandt, of *The Wife of Potiphar accusing Joseph*, at the sum of one thousand five hundred pounds, and the two small pictures by Raphael from the Borghese collection, namely one of the *Entombment*, and one of the groups called *The Charity*, at the sum of one thousand pounds, be also offered to his Majesty; and if he shall decline the same, then to the directors of the National Gallery; and if they decline, at the same prices to the Right Honourable Robert Peel; and, if he decline, to the Earl of Dudley. And if a purchaser shall not be found, I leave to my executor's discretion to adopt such measures for disposing of the same as he may think proper. . . .

Having, in the year 1825, been honoured by a mission from his most gracious Majesty, King George IV, to paint the portraits of his most Christian Majesty, Charles the Tenth, and of his Royal Highness the Dauphin of France, I had the honour to receive from that Monarch, as a mark of his distinguished favour, a superb service of Sèvres porcelain. This splendid token of Royal courtesy, I bequeath to the President and Council for the time being, of the Royal Academy of Arts, to be by them used on the birth-day of the King, and at the annual dinner on the opening of the Exhibition, and on other public occasions, in remembrance of the honour conferred by a foreign prince on the President of the Royal Academy of Great Britain.

And as to all other works of art in my possession at the time of my decease, whether pictures, drawings, engravings bound and unbound, casts, marbles, bronzes, models, or of whatsoever other kind, and also as to my books and plate, silver, china and furniture, and all other my estate and effects, I bequeath the same to Archibald Keightley, the younger, of No. 5 Hare Court, Temple, my executor; to sell and dispose of the same, as to him shall seem

QUEEN CHARLOTTE

Lawrence's first royal commission. Exhibited at the Royal Academy, 1790. In the National Gallery.

WILLIAM WILBERFORCE

William Wilberforce (1759–1833), philanthropist, entered Parliament in 1780. His bill for abolition of the slave-trade received royal assent in 1807. In the National Portrait Gallery.

meet; and the monies upon trust, in the first place, to pay off my just debts, funeral expenses etc. etc., and to divide the residue into three equal parts . . .'

The equal parts were to be apportioned among his relatives. The will concludes by recommending 'my highly intelligent friend, William Young Ottley, Esqre, as a person, from his sound knowledge of art, peculiarly competent to the task of arranging my various works of art for sale, if he will kindly undertake the office'.

The refusal of all the parties mentioned in his will to accept the offers made to them may be regarded as the last frustration in the career of this brilliantly successful but nevertheless unlucky man. Frustrated in his desire to marry the girl he loved, and denied the pleasures of paternity, he was also frustrated in his desire to enrich his country by the magnificent collection of works of art which he had impoverished himself to bring together. His legacy to the Royal Academy whose prestige he had, during his term of office as President, done so much to enhance, had to be sacrificed to the demands of his creditors, while his nephews and nieces, whom he was so anxious to benefit, did not receive a penny from his estate, the proceeds of which barely covered the claims made on it.

The Royal Academy to-day possesses but few relics of the most illustrious of its Presidents, after Sir Joshua Reynolds. In the Diploma Gallery, up many flights of stone steps, the gigantic 'Satan' was, in May 1950 when the writer examined it, leaning on its side against a wall, unframed and covered in dirt and yellow varnish. The blazing eyes and distended nostrils of the devil surmount the huge torso and massive thighs of gentleman Jackson. The second figure and the infernal regions at their feet are now more than half obscured by the effects of time and neglect. Except as a curiosity, this vast canvas, no doubt, has little interest. It would, however, be an act of piety on the part of some Academician, skilled in picture restoration, to bring it back to something approaching the condition it was in when the painter showed it so proudly to Lord Mountjoy. It would then be possible for art critics to try to discover what it was which accounted for

Lawrence's aberration and made him regard it, all his life, as his masterpiece. In addition to the Satan, which may in due course be replaced in its original position on the wall of the staircase, the Diploma Gallery possesses a delightful and little-known picture which Lawrence presented in 1794, when he was elected R.A. It is called 'A Gipsy Girl' and portrays a pretty girl in a woodland setting, clutching a white hen to her bosom. Lawrence was always an uncertain colourist, but in this instance he was particularly happy, although the redness of the girl's cheeks might be considered too pronounced. The whole picture, in spite of its defects, is curiously radiant, almost sparkling, and has a lyric charm which few of his later works surpassed.

In one of the private rooms of the Academy there hangs an unfinished self-portrait of Lawrence, purchased in 1867, which shows his mature style at its best.

After the collection of Old Master drawings had been declined as recorded, by all the parties to whom Keightley was directed to offer it, an attempt was made to purchase it for the nation by means of a public subscription. This also failed although the Royal Academy agreed to subscribe £1,000. Keightley, with the help of Sir Charles Eastlake, who was well aware of the unique value of the drawings, now made an effort to persuade the Government to purchase them for the National Gallery. Unfortunately the Chancellor of the Exchequer at the time was Lord Althorp who, as Eastlake bitterly observed, 'sets his face against the arts altogether, and said once that if he had his way he would sell the National Gallery and have nothing of the kind'. Other Ministers were approached including the Lord Chancellor, Lord Brougham, who expressed a wish to see the drawings, if Keightley would entrust them to him. In a published letter, which Whitley quotes, Eastlake says: 'I attended therefore on Good Friday, at two o'clock at the Lord Chancellor's new residence in Great Stanhope Street. Lord Lansdown and his daughter, Prince Talleyrand, Lady Sefton, Lord Moncrieff and several others were present. The best place for seeing the drawings was given to Talleyrand, and the conversation was conducted in French, on his account. I had more, of course, to say than anybody, as I was asked questions about every drawing; and even while talking with the Chancellor the conversation was still in French (and at least I beat him there!) which was amusing enough. After having seen all the collection, Talleyrand said *"Si vous n'achetez pas ces choses là, vous êtes des barbares"*, in which two Cabinet Ministers agreed.' The Government, however, declined to put up the money, and all his efforts to carry out Lawrence's wishes having proved unavailing, Keightley was forced, in 1835, to let Woodburn have the drawings for £15,000. This was the only offer he received. The price seems ridiculous, in view of what Lawrence is known to have paid for them, but it has been stated that at his death he was in debt to the Woodburns to the extent of £20,000. If the debt was taken into account, and the sum of £15,000 paid in addition, the transaction appears less unreasonable. Even so, the Woodburns made a very substantial profit out of the deal.

The failure of the Government, the nation, and the various wealthy private collectors who could, without difficulty, have acquired the drawings, to take any action to prevent the collection from being dispersed abroad, was not due to any omission on the part of Keightley, Eastlake and others to give adequate publicity to the matter. Eastlake supplied William Brockedon, an artist and author well-known at this period though since forgotten, with the material for an article on the Lawrence collection which appeared in the press over the signature 'Veritas'. As this remains the fullest and most authoritative contemporary account of the nature of the collection and the manner in which it came to be formed, the following extracts from it, given by Whitley, are essential to an understanding of the services to the cause of art in England which Lawrence did his best to render.

'The public have little idea of the value—the mere marketable value—of this extraordinary collection. Sir Thomas Lawrence acknowledged to an outlay of £60,000 for what he directed by his will should be offered to the nation for £18,000. Often, in order to possess himself of these precious and exquisite specimens of art, he paid sums which he was reluctant to record, and in one instance within the writer's knowledge, he left a memorandum of what he had paid one-third less than the sum actually given. The character of this collection, the research, care, and cost of its formation, are not sufficiently known; and it is difficult to make it known without incurring the suspicion of interested motives for doing so. I will not, however, be deterred by the fear of being misunderstood (my name is in your possession) from stating what I know of the collection, though I have not seen one of these drawings since Sir Thomas Lawrence's death.

The well-known specimens which were formerly in the Collection of Richardson, Sir Joshua Reynolds, West, Ottley and other celebrated collectors, were gradually brought together in Sir Thomas Lawrence's; but the astonishing number of drawings by Michael Angelo and Raphael could only have been collected by a concurrence of circumstances which can never happen again.

At the time of the invasion of Italy by the French a Commission was appointed to select the best works of art, and one of the Commissioners, the Chevalier Wycart, became possessed of a great number of the finest drawings by Michael Angelo and Raphael. The choice of his collection was purchased by Mr. Woodburn and is now to be found among the Lawrence drawings.

The celebrated cabinet of Monsieur Crozat, called the *Cabinet du Roi*, was chosen from a numerous selection of drawings originally in the possession of the executors of Raphael; the remainder of these drawings, descended to Count Antaldi, of Ancona, from whom Mr. Woodburn purchased them. The catalogue showed what drawings had been purchased in the last century by Monsieur Crozat. Lastly, the Crozat collection itself was almost entirely purchased, and thus the original collection possessed by Raphael's executors has by singular exertions, and good fortune, been united. The Arundel collection of Parmigianos, which passed into the hands of Zenetti of Venice, more than a century ago, has also been added, having been restored to this country greatly augmented. The sale of Monsieur Denon again enriched the portfolio of the late President; and on the death of Mr. Dimsdale, who was his rival collector, the whole of the Raphaels possessed by that gentleman became the property of Sir Thomas Lawrence. The drawings of Leonardo da Vinci, of

Coreggio, of the Carracci and Guercino; of Claude, of Rubens, of Vandyck, and of Rembrandt, in this extraordinary collection have, perhaps, never yet been surpassed in number, certainly not in excellence.

When the French invaded Austria, General Andreossi was enabled to possess himself of the finest Albert Dürers in Vienna, and at the sale of the General's property the whole of them were added to the treasures above-mentioned. The studies of Bellini, Titian, Giorgione and Paul Veronese, for many of their celebrated works are to be found here, together with the whole of the series of Primaticcio's designs for the galleries at Fontainebleau, the Poussins of the Mariette collection; and many admirable specimens of art from Cimabue, Giotto, Mantegna and others, to the time of Fra Bartolomeo.

The National Gallery in Pall Mall might, if tomorrow destroyed, be replaced by works of equal excellence, by the same masters at the same cost; but this collection of drawings, once broken, can never be restored at any price, for the accident can never again be hoped for which brought them together, supposing even unlimited means'.

When it is remembered that, in addition to his enormous outlay on original drawings, Lawrence employed young artists, studying in Italy, to make outlines of works by Michaelangelo and others and paid them generously for their services, the fact that he was constantly short of ready money ceases to be a mystery.

Woodburn held exhibitions, at intervals, of selected drawings, and gradually disposed of the whole collection, the King of Holland being one of the principal purchasers. Many of the best drawings by Michaelangelo and Raphael were later acquired by Oxford University, with the assistance of Lord Eldon, and are now among the principal treasures of the Ashmolean Museum. The British Museum is, however, today the most important repository of drawings from the Lawrence collection. Besides those which it has acquired by the usual processes of gift and purchase, it also contains the Malcolm Collection, which was formed with the expressed intention of repatriating and assembling important drawings from the Lawrence collection which had gone abroad, and has 185 of them. The most notable aggregation from the point of view of quantity is that formed by Sir Thomas Phillips, which is now in the possession of his grandson. At the Lawrence sale at Sotheby's in 1860, Sir Thomas bought 186 lots containing over 1,100 drawings. These were catalogued by Mr. A. E. Popham of the British Museum in 1935.

Of the Lawrence drawings which remain abroad, a number found their way into Léon Bonnat's collection and were bequeathed by him to the museum at Bayonne, and to the Louvre. There are also about thirty in Berlin, half a dozen in the Albertina, and others scattered about Europe in the great public and private art galleries. In America, the Metropolitan Museum has two, the Fogg Museum fifteen, and the Morgan Library fifteen. (For these particulars I am indebted to the courtesy of Mr. Mahonri S. Young, of the Sarah Lawrence College, Bronxville, New York, who has made a special study of the Lawrence collection, and very kindly put the results of his investigations at my disposal.) The whole story is a lamentable one and reflects little credit either on the Government in power at Lawrence's death or on the private patrons on whom he relied to prevent what he justly regarded as an important part of his life's work from being lost to his country. R. J. Lane, A.R.A., who engraved an enormous number of Lawrence's portraits, put it on record that Sir Robert Peel, who bought a few drawings from Woodburn at a high price, always regretted that he had not bought the entire collection when it was offered to him. His heirs must also have regretted it. It is impossible to blame George IV for not having added the drawings to the other art treasures which, during his reign, he amassed at Windsor Castle, for he was already far too ill to exert himself over such matters. He had done enough for art and artists to ensure that his many follies would be excused, and his real character and achievements vindicated, by succeeding generations of his more civilised compatriots. No more could be expected of him.

Lawrence's great 'picture factory' in Russell Square stood empty and desolate for years after his death. Haydon visited it in

1832 and has left, in his Journals, the following account of the state of neglect into which it had fallen.

'I passed Lawrence's house. Nothing could be more melancholy or desolate. I knocked and was shown in. The passages were dusty, the paper torn, the parlours dark; the painting-room, where so much beauty had once glittered, forlorn, and the whole appearance desolate and wretched, the very plate on the door green with mildew.

I went into the parlour which used to be instinct with life! "Poor Sir Thomas, always in trouble", said the woman who had the care of the house. "Always something to worrit him." I saw his bedroom, small; only a little bed; the mark of it was against the wall. Close to his bedroom was an immense room (where was carried on all his manufactory of draperies, etc.), divided, yet open over the partitions. It must have been five or six rooms turned into one large workshop. Here his assistants worked. His painting-room was a large back drawing-room: his showroom a large front one. He occupied a parlour and a bedroom; all the rest of the house was turned to business. Anyone would think that people of fashion would visit from remembrance the house where they had spent so many happy hours. Not they; they shun a disagreeable sensation. They have no feeling, no poetry. It is shocking. It is dirty.'

XVIII

REGENCY PORTRAIT PAINTER

I N ENGLAND, to a far greater degree than in France or the
United States, Lawrence's reputation as an artist has been
subject to violent fluctuations throughout the period which
has elapsed since his death. The enormous popularity which he
enjoyed when he was at the pinnacle of his success was, as he
foresaw, not likely to last. He once remarked, with his habitual
modesty: 'I do not for a moment suppose that my reputation will
ever stand as high after my death as it has been in my lifetime.'
The penalty for an artist of being in the fashion is the partial
eclipse which inevitably follows when the fashions change. In
Lawrence's case, owing to the work of such engravers as Samuel
Cousins, his pictures of mothers and children, of beautiful women
and 'sweetly pretty' little boys and girls, continued for some
time to make a strong appeal to unsophisticated Victorian sentiment, but this fact, in itself, contributed to a gradual hardening of
critical judgment among those who regarded themselves as
connoisseurs.

In the first two decades of Queen Victoria's reign several minor
artists, whose pictures were engraved for drawing-room scrap-
books and books of beauty, achieved a transient popularity by
imitating Lawrence's most obvious faults. 'Household Treasures',
for example, a picture of a young mother with two laughing
children, by E. T. Parris, which was engraved by Thomson for
Fisher's Drawing-Room Scrapbook, issued in 1840, is like a caricature
of Lawrence at his sentimental worst. Partly as a result of these
debased imitations, there came a revulsion of feeling against
Lawrence, and by the 'sixties of the last century his reputation had
suffered a marked decline. The legend which grew up about his
character, based on his supposed heartless treatment of the Siddons

girls, undoubtedly, in a moral age, helped to influence opinion against him. After Thackeray had lambasted George IV and made the Regency period unpopular with the virtuous, it became the fashion for art critics to call attention to Lawrence's 'insincerity' and to repeat the charge that his portraits of women were 'meretricious', and those of men and monarchs flattering to the point of vulgarity. Much of this Victorian denigration has been repeated parrotwise by later historians of British painting. Indeed, the ability to write scathingly of Lawrence's defects, many of which he himself was fully aware of and successfully overcame, seems still to be regarded by some professional art critics as a proof of competence. It is, in reality, rather the reverse, for appreciation requires far higher gifts of insight, technical knowledge and sound judgment than its opposite, which any clever beginner can accomplish, at least to his own satisfaction. As Lawrence remarked in one of his Presidential addresses: 'We are to judge of works by the *presence* of beauties, not by the absence of defects.'

In a book on English painting, published in 1932, the writer repeats all these critical clichés, refers to Lawrence's 'total lack of refinement' and says he 'scarcely ever failed to betray in his painting his essential shallowness, insincerity and vulgarity'. He adds that Lawrence's portraits have nearly always the taint of insincerity and show a cheap desire to make the sitter 'look pleasant', so that the 'mouth is twisted into an unnatural simper, and the true character of the sitter can only be guessed'. He then cites the portrait of William Wilberforce, in the National Portrait Gallery, as 'one of the most exasperating examples' of this habit. The short answer to these charges is that Lawrence carried 'refinement' almost to excess, that, as a man, he was neither shallow, insincere, nor vulgar, and that the suggestion that Wilberforce's sanctimonious simper was artificially induced to make him 'look pleasant' betrays very little knowledge of his character. It is far more probable that this unfinished portrait was one of the most faithful likenesses that Lawrence ever produced, and one of those which most truly reveal the personality of the sitter. In a *Short History of English Painting*, published in the following year, the author states that, with Lawrence, English portraiture shows a marked decadence, and that his gifts were enormously overrated by contemporary society. He once again trots out the usual charges, that most of his work is 'vulgar and insincere', that his 'pleasing effects are superficial and his colour defective', and that his portraits show 'no depth, little effort to depict character, but much to make pictures which shall please the sitters'. It would be easy to multiply instances of such second-hand verdicts, repeated without any sign of fresh consideration of the evidence on which they were based.

The Autobiography and Journals of Benjamin Robert Haydon, published in 1853, contained several references to Lawrence which are as waspish as might be expected from this disappointed man. He said that Lawrence 'perfumed' his sitters, that 'his flesh has certainly no blood' and is 'detestably opaque'. Commenting on the Academy exhibition of 1828, he wrote: 'Lawrence sacrifices all for the head; and what an absence of all purity of tint in comparison with Vandyke and Reynolds! His excellence is expression, but it is conscious expression; whereas the expression of Reynolds, Vandyke, Titian, Tintoretto and Raffaele is unconscious nature. Lawrence is not a great man: indeed posterity will think so. Lady Lyndhurst's hands are really a disgrace in drawing, colour and everything. He affects to be careless in subordinate parts, but it is not the carelessness of conscious power; it is the carelessness of intention.'

As Haydon was, and continues to be, very widely read, his disparagements set the tone of much subsequent criticism. Humphrey Ward, writing forty years later about the acquisition, by the Louvre, of Lawrence's portrait of Mr. and Mrs. Angerstein, was one of the first to note the signs of a change of opinion in his favour. 'French critics and amateurs,' he said, 'have always assigned to Lawrence a relatively higher place in the list of English artists than has been conceded at home during the last fifty years. Taste in England is now setting Lawrence-wards again, perhaps because we have been taught by the French to appreciate his marvellous draughtsmanship and his other fine technical qualities, and to forgive, in consideration of these, his self-consciousness and mannerism. The opinion of the last generation unconsciously echoed the saying of the sour critic who declared that "Lawrence made coxcombs of his sitters, and his sitters made a coxcomb of Lawrence"; and people who, after the manner of their time, thought so much more of meaning than of method, of tendency than of technique, left the great President thus condemned. But even the critics of this date and school made exceptions in favour of the fine Lawrences of the first period—that is, broadly speaking, the pictures painted before the year 1805, while the influence of his master, Sir Joshua, was still strong upon him.'

Roger Fry, writing nearly forty years after Humphrey Ward, goes so far as to describe Lawrence as 'one of our greatest masters', though he qualifies this by adding: 'I use the word master in rather a narrow sense. I do not mean by it quite the same as one of our greatest artists. I mean that he showed a consummate mastery over the means of artistic expression—that he had an unerring eye and hand.'

It will be remembered that Lawrence's first royal commission was to paint a portrait of Queen Charlotte. Of this early work Fry says: 'It is an astonishing performance. In the royal presence this boy had not the least flicker of hesitation—nothing could shake his complete self-confidence. It gives one the impression of having been done at full speed, without the least alteration or correction anywhere, carried through, as it is, with such fluent ease and such consistency of light and colour. No one since Rubens had possessed quite this kind of confidence. And the tone is perfectly held, the accents of light are never uniform or monotonous, the transitions follow one another rhythmically throughout the whole design. Lawrence was not a great colourist, but here he has confined himself within a rather narrow range of bluish-green, whites and greys—a kind of aquamarine tint, which is certainly harmonious.'

In sharp contrast to the opinion of Lawrence expressed by Roger Fry, who was a practising artist of merit as well as a critic, is that of Mr. John Steegmann, whose *Hours in the National Portrait Gallery* was published in 1927, when he was the 'official Lecturer' at that institution, and may thus be regarded as the 'official' view.

'The reputation of Sir Thomas Lawrence,' he wrote, 'has recently been drastically revised; despite sensational sale prices and the aura that popularity has cast around his name, the position that he now holds is far lower than that of even a generation ago. While it would not be quite accurate to call Lawrence a fourth-rate painter, it would yet be nearer the truth than to call him a first-rate one. He had powers of draughtsmanship which he hardly ever chose to exercise, and although he was capable of evolving a good composition or placing his sitter in a striking pose, he could at his worst be so dull that criticism becomes impossible, as in the portraits of Canning (1832) and Lord Liverpool (1804), immense canvases whose one merit is that they are both entirely negative.' There is more in this strain, including the astonishing statement that Lawrence's 'cleverness as a boy *removed any incentive to serious work*'. The italics are mine.

For a more balanced and far better-informed judgment on Lawrence, it is a relief to turn to Sir Walter Armstrong, who was one of the first authoritative art critics to form a new and individual estimate of his portraiture.

'You will scarcely find a picture by Lawrence,' he writes, 'in which, so far as it goes, the first steps to a masterpiece are not to be descried. In this he is comparable to Reynolds and superior to Gainsborough. I might even say that he is superior to both, for there is a spontaneity in the fling of Lawrence, in the way in which he throws the germ of a design upon canvas, which Sir Joshua never equalled. . . . Lawrence . . . saw a picture on his empty canvas. Masses fell into place in his mind without an effort. Form was easy to him, indeed he could not have avoided it had he tried. . . . His facility, vivacity, and real aesthetic gift made their inception easy and the first stage of their execution delightful; whilst his instability, his alternation of hot fits with cold, turned their prosecution into a labour and made him instinctively choose those methods which shortened his task'. Sir Walter admits that Lawrence was deficient in the colour sense and says that in the Old Masters he was attracted chiefly by design, but, as might be expected from so discerning and erudite a critic, he refrains from talking nonsense about his 'vulgarity'.

Men like Farington and Wilkie, who frequently watched Lawrence in his studio, agree as to his artistic integrity and the amount of pains he took with all his portraits in spite of the number of his commissions and a pressure of work which sometimes all but exhausted him. David Wilkie has thus described his methods: 'He would draw the portrait in chalk, the size of life, on paper; this occupied him but one sitting, but that sitting lasted nearly one whole day. He next transferred that outline to the canvas. His picture and his sitter were placed at a distance from the point of view, where, to see both at a time, he had to traverse all across the room, before the conception which the view of his sitter suggested could be proceeded with. In this incessant transit his feet had worn a path through the carpet to the floor, exercising freedom both of body and mind; each traverse allowing time for invention, while it required an effort of memory between the touch on the canvas and the observation from which it grew.'

In America, where many of Lawrence's finest portraits have found a home, some of them having been purchased for enormous sums, and in France, where he is well represented in the Louvre, his prestige appears never to have undergone any diminution, and both his character and his talents seem to have been more justly appreciated than, till recently, they have been in his own country. In 1891 and 1892 the distinguished critic, J. de Wyzewa, contributed four articles to the *Gazette des Beaux Arts* entitled 'Thomas Lawrence et la Société Anglaise de son Temps', which showed more sympathy and understanding than has generally been accorded Lawrence by his compatriots. The following passage, which Layard has quoted, indicates the impression which he formed of Lawrence's character, an impression, be it said, which the evidence given in the preceding chapters of this book fully supports.

'Sous les dehors de l'homme du monde sceptique et sans préjugés, il avait gardé une âme profondément droite, et simple comme l'âme d'un enfant . . . Jamais un artiste n'eut plus de droit à notre indulgence, car jamais un artiste n'a été plus passionné pour son art, plus désireux de bien faire, et plus sincèrement, plus cruellement, et plus injustement, sévère pour lui même . . .

Lawrence paraît avoir toute sa vie désarmé les rancunes par la simplicité, la douceur et la bienveillance de son caractère.'

Prince Metternich, who had the warmest personal regard for Lawrence, and was a good judge of character, described him in one of his letters to Princess Lieven as an excellent man, adding, 'il est, de plus, très intelligent'. This view was generally held by those who knew Lawrence best and whose opinion, for that reason, carries most weight.

Since the revulsion of feeling which set in a century ago against the period of the Regency and the character of George IV, the wheel may be said to have turned a full circle. At the present day few people regard the former as merely vulgar and dissolute or the latter as no better than a congenital liar, a profligate and a cad. On the contrary, few epochs in English history have acquired a greater glamour than that which saw the victories of Nelson and of Wellington and of few monarchs are we more inclined to condone the weaknesses in consideration of his many excellent qualities and accomplishments. The fantastic Pavilion at Brighton, instead of being derided for its eccentricity, is now perhaps over-valued for the charm of its romantic exuberance and the many beauties of its interior decoration.

In Lawrence's portraits we see reflected, as in a looking-glass, a cross-section of English society in the age in which he lived. Campbell said of him: 'This is the merit of Lawrence's painting— he makes one seem to have got into a drawing-room in the mansion of the blest, and to be looking at oneself in the mirrors'. Part at least of his continuing power to charm us lies in this fact: that he interpreted his own time in terms of his own time. It was a time of stupendous historical events, which followed each other in quick succession and, in the aggregate, redounded immeasurably to the honour and glory of Great Britain. Throughout the period of the Napoleonic wars the nation produced men of action of outstanding merit, and the monarchs, statesmen and military leaders of the countries in alliance with her were scarcely less distinguished. It was Lawrence's destiny, with the encouragement of his Royal patron, to employ his unrivalled talents in com-memorating these personalities on canvas, and the Waterloo

Gallery at Windsor Castle reveals how superbly he succeeded and with what consummate skill he accomplished his task. It had been his ambition, ever since the days of his youth, to paint 'sublime History'. He realised it, though not in the manner he may have intended, by his series of portraits of historical personages.

To these he brought not only a technical equipment which no contemporary portrait-painter equalled, but a quality of romantic imagination which no other European artist possessed in anything like the same degree. Lawrence was, in his own way, no less fundamentally romantic than Byron. It was this romantic idealism, rather than 'insincerity' or a mere vulgar desire to please his sitters, which led him to idealise the many beautiful women his 'pencil' commemorated. A quality which perhaps detracts from the value of his female portraits can be attributed to the peculiarity of his temperament. The type known as the 'repressed homosexual' which modern psychologists are fond of analysing and discussing, is one to which many great artists and many men of genius are now recognised as having belonged. In suggesting that Lawrence was psychologically in this category, as his appearance, certain recorded mannerisms and his attitude towards women would seem to indicate, not the slightest reflection is made on his character or morals. Never of robust physique, his energies, mental and physical, were concentrated on the practice of his art, to which he devoted himself with unremitting toil. He was, moreover, in every sense of the word an aesthete, that is to say, a man absorbed in the study of the science of the beautiful. He was of unusually temperate habits as regards eating and drinking—in an age characterised by excess in both—and all his passions were predominantly passions of the mind. If his aesthetic appreciations made him susceptible to feminine beauty, there was an absence of carnality in his appreciation of it which is apparent in his portraits of women, though it should be said that this opinion is totally at variance with that of many of his contemporaries, whose views as to the lack of 'chastity' which they discerned in his female portraits have been repeated ever since without examination. It may be that the handsome painter sometimes aroused in his sitters emotions which he duly recorded, but there is no sign of his having reciprocated them. Lawrence's women friends were, as we have seen, always chosen for their qualities of heart and mind and the fact that, in common with many artists, he had a feminine streak in his nature, no doubt accounts for this. His platonic love for Mrs. Wolff, his long intimacy with Miss Sophia Lee who was twenty years his senior, and his fraternal feelings for Miss Croft and others, provide a clue to his temperament which sexual psychologists are not likely to miss. Many women have found in men of a repressed homosexual type their truest, most under-standing and most sympathetic friends. Speculations about the complexities of Lawrence's nature which, in an age less prejudiced than his own in such matters, can be made without any hint of censure, are only of value because of the light they may throw on his art. There is no doubt that his sense of form and the beauty and precision of his drawing are sometimes combined with a certain lack of creative energy, for which his surface vivacity hardly affords sufficient compensation. This lack can be not unreasonably associated with a parallel lack of animal as opposed to mental passion. Lawrence looked at his fashionable beauties with the detachment from sexual urges which a *couturier* or the impresario of a *corps de ballet* might display. He had none of the frank physical gusto of a Renoir or a Rodin. As a draughtsman, he was the equal of Ingres, but he would have been profoundly shocked by the 'coarseness and sensuality' which, at the age of eighty, enabled Ingres to infuse vitality into 'La Source' and afterwards to seduce his model.

Lawrence's portraits of pretty young women and idealised children, delightful as the best of them are, cannot always be absolved of the charge of shallowness and surface glitter, nor can it be denied that he sometimes evinced more interest in the clothes of his sitters and in the landscape backgrounds he designed to show them off, than in their personalities. As a 'face-painter', apart from the series of historical portraits which are in a special category, he was at his best when painting men and old women. In his early portrait, evidently much influenced by Rembrandt, of the Deal bluestocking, Elizabeth Carter, in his portrait of Queen Charlotte,

PRINCESS LIEVEN

This portrait was transferred from the National Portrait Gallery to the Tate Gallery in 1950.

PHILIP SANSOM

This masterly portrait, formerly in the National Gallery, was transferred to the
Tate Gallery in 1950.

and in the best of his portraits of men there is no sign of the qualities which his detractors labelled 'meretricious' or 'artificial' and
his admirers, perhaps with more justice, partly ascribed to his
overmastering passion for the romantic and the picturesque. His
Mr. Sansom, which has recently been transferred to the Tate
Gallery, is a masterly portrait, perfectly managed, so also are his
portraits of the elder Angerstein and of the aged Warren Hastings.

It is a great loss to British art that the circumstances of Lawrence's life made it impossible for him to develop his marked
gift for landscape painting. His *Homer Reciting his Poems to the
Greeks*, at Downton Castle, the *Gipsy Girl* in the Diploma Gallery,
the landscape backgrounds of many of his portraits, a watercolour
in the British Museum of fields near Sloane Street and one or two
others are unfortunately the only examples of it we have. His
portrait drawings, tinted and plain, and his crayon pictures, which
some have thought his finest achievements, on the other hand,
are almost numberless. His versatility was remarkable and his
competence and natural ability were displayed in everything he
undertook. He once modelled a head of Mr. Lock, when he was
staying with the Princess of Wales at Blackheath, and he knew
almost as much about the art of engraving as those who practised
it.

In addition to the vast number of works he produced, of which
only a comparatively small proportion can be dismissed as
definitely bad, the services to the cause of the arts in England
which Lawrence rendered are sufficient in themselves to make
his name revered. When it is recalled that he was mainly responsible for forming the Angerstein collection which provided
the nucleus of the National Gallery, that he acted as adviser to
George IV when he was filling Windsor Castle with art treasures,
that he made an unrivalled collection of Old Master drawings
with the conscious though frustrated intention of enriching his
country with them, that he acted with triumphant success as
Britain's cultural ambassador in Paris, Rome and Vienna,
encouraged youthful talent wherever he discerned it and was
unfailingly generous in proclaiming the genius of those of his
contemporaries and rivals whose fame is now established, we can

appreciate how much we owe to this painter of princes who can fairly be described as a prince among painters. The passage of time, the mutations of taste and the revaluations which follow them, have acted in Lawrence's favour and have now brought him the reward of his deserts. To have been, par excellence, the Regency Portrait Painter, no longer carries with it any stigma of contempt. On the contrary, when we contemplate the position into which our beloved country has now fallen, we look upon the Regency as a glorious period in our history and on Lawrence as one of its most brilliant and fascinating figures. Like John Nash, the Regent's architect, the name and fame of the Regent's favourite painter are indissolubly associated with those of his Royal master. The work of neither man can be detached from its period-setting without loss; but whereas Nash, though an admirable architectural landscape artist, in sympathetic relationship with the spirit of his age, can hardly be regarded as an architect of the first rank, Lawrence is established to-day as one of the great masters of British painting.

INDEX

INDEX

INDEX

Norbury Park, Surrey, 96, 180, 196, 207, 230, 236
Northcote, James, R.A., 68, 80, 93, 106, 232, 244, 292, 293, 310
Northumberland, Duchess of, 65

O

Ogilvie, Miss, 134
Opie, John, R.A., 67, 228, 229, 293, 334
Ottley, William Young, 268, 297, 337, 340
    Mrs., 319, 327

P

Palmer, Mr., 57
Papendieck, Mrs., 77
Parris, E. T., 344
'Pasquin, Anthony' (John Williams), 105, 106, 110, 111
Peel, Robert (later Sir Robert), 305, 313–314, 324, 327, 334–6, 342
    Mrs. (later, Lady Peel), 304, 305
Pennington, William, 143, 144
    Mrs., 135, 143, 144, 146–71, 176–83, 187, 191, 192, 198
Piozzi, Mrs. (Mrs. Thrale), 41, 42, 117, 118, 135, 143, 150, 162, 178, 264
Pitt, William, 48, 51, 211–13, 228
Place, Dorothy, 129, 132, 178, 180
Platoff, the Hetman, 252, 254
Poggi, Mrs., 61
Poore, Edward, 59
Pope Pius VII, 279, 280, 282, 283
Poynter, Ambrose, 308
Priestley, Lady, vi, 137

Q

Quincey, Thomas de, 222

R

Raimbach, Abraham, 107
Read, Lucy (see Lawrence, Mrs. Lucy)
    Rev. William (father of Mrs. Lucy Lawrence), 18
    Mrs., 21, 33
    Rev. William (brother of Mrs. Lucy Lawrence), 22, 92
Recollections of Sir Thomas Lawrence, P.R.A., by Elizabeth Croft, 33
Records of a Girlhood, by Fanny Kemble, 130, 131
Reni, Guido, 53, 280
Retrospections of the Stage, by John Bernard, 57, 115
Reynolds, Sir Joshua, P.R.A., 39, 42, 58–62, 64, 67, 70, 76, 78, 80, 81, 85, 86, 88, 90–3, 96, 107, 113, 222, 223, 230, 233, 238, 246, 293–5, 303, 304, 325, 330, 334, 337, 340, 347, 348

Rock House, Bath, 52
Rockingham, Marquis of, 51
Rogers, Samuel, 53, 194, 211, 238, 272, 299
Rogers's Lives of Foreign Painters, 38
Romilly, Sir Samuel, 246
Romney, George, 64
Rose, Samuel, 102
Ross, General Alexander, 47
Royal Academy, 15, 52, 63, 66, 69, 72–4, 76, 78, 80, 83–5, 89, 92–4, 102, 107, 110, 185, 198, 201, 202, 205, 207, 212, 228, 232, 239, 240, 255, 257, 261, 262, 265, 268, 282, 313, 330, 333, 334, 336, 337
    Diploma Gallery of, 110, 337, 338, 353
    Schools of, 58, 72
Royde-Smith, Naomi, 110, 121, 125, 127, 130, 162
Russell, John, 99
Russia, Emperor of, 251, 252, 276–8
    Dowager Empress of, 276, 277
Rutland, Duke of, 48, 91
    Duchess of, 68

S

Sandby, Paul, 230
Schwartzenberg, Prince, 277
Scott, Sir Walter, 113, 119, 211, 312
Semple, Mrs., 137, 172
Seward, Anne, 143
Sheridan, Richard Brinsley, 28, 51, 180, 182, 196, 199–201, 211, 238, 265, 299
    Mrs., 146
Sherwin, John Keyse, 44
Siddons, Cecilia, 143, 329
    George, 172
    Maria, vi, 116–68, 194, 295, 321, 325, 326
    Sally, vi, 109, 112, 117–65, 168–95, 197, 198, 203, 207, 208, 213, 295, 321, 325
    Mrs. Sarah, vii, 40, 45, 46, 54–8, 98, 109–12, 117, 119, 120, 122, 123, 127, 130–3, 139, 142–53, 159–66, 168, 174, 176–8, 180–9, 195, 205, 209, 210, 218–234, 240, 265, 272, 290, 295, 303, 308, 320–3, 325, 326, 329
    William, 125–7, 130, 145, 148, 149, 162, 170, 176, 177, 180, 182, 186, 192, 193, 195, 208, 210
Sir Thomas Lawrence's Letter-Bag, by George Somes Layard, vi, 39, 137, 281
Smirke, Robert, R.A. (the elder), 72
    Sir Robert (the younger), 204, 232, 234, 238, 239, 242, 243, 246, 247, 249, 278, 281, 291
Smith, J. R., 46, 150
    Sir Sidney, 49, 217
    T. B., 31, 37, 38
Soane, Sir John, 230
Society of Arts, 53, 58

INDEX